The Essentials of Ibāḍī Islam

Modern Intellectual and Political History of the Middle East
Mehrzad Boroujerdi, *Series Editor*

OTHER TITLES IN MODERN INTELLECTUAL AND POLITICAL HISTORY OF THE MIDDLE EAST

Britain and the Iranian Constitutional Revolution of 1906–1911: Foreign Policy, Imperialism, and Dissent
MANSOUR BONAKDARIAN

Class and Labor in Iran: Did the Revolution Matter?
FARHAD NOMANI and SOHRAB BEHDAD

Democracy and Civil Society in Arab Political Thought: Transcultural Possibilities
MICHAELLE L. BROWERS

The Education of Women and The Vices of Men: Two Qajar Tracts
HASAN JAVADI and WILLEM FLOOR, trans.

A Guerrilla Odyssey: Modernization, Secularism, Democracy, and the Fadai Period of National Liberation in Iran, 1971–1979
PEYMAN VAHABZADEH

The International Politics of the Persian Gulf
MEHRAN KAMRAVA, ed.

The Kurdish Quasi-State: Development and Dependency in Post–Gulf War Iraq
DENISE NATALI

Modernity, Sexuality, and Ideology in Iran: The Life and Legacy of Popular Iranian Female Artists
KAMRAN TALATTOF

Pious Citizens: Reforming Zoroastrianism in India and Iran
MONICA M. RINGER

The Urban Social History of the Middle East, 1750–1950
PETER SLUGLETT, ed.

Valerie J. Hoffman

The Essentials of Ibāḍī Islam

جواهر العقيدة الإباضية

Syracuse University Press

First Edition 2012

12 13 14 15 16 17 6 5 4 3 2 1

∞ The paper used in this publication meets the minimum requirements of the American National Standard for Information Sciences—Permanence of Paper for Printed Library Materials, ANSI Z39.48-1992.

For a listing of books published and distributed by Syracuse University Press, visit our Web site at SyracuseUniversityPress.syr.edu.

ISBN: 978-0-8156-3288-7

Library of Congress Cataloging-in-Publication Data

Hoffman, Valerie J. (Valerie Jon), 1954–
The essentials of Ibadi Islam / Valerie J. Hoffman.
p. cm. — (Modern intellectual and political history of the Middle East)
Includes bibliographical references and index.
ISBN 978-0-8156-3288-7 (cloth : alk. paper) 1. Ibadites—History.
2. Ibadites—Doctrines. I. Title.
BP195.I3H64 2012
297.8'33—dc23 2012002857

Manufactured in the United States of America

CONTENTS

Acknowledgments ❁ *vii*
Abbreviations ❁ *xi*

PART ONE

Introduction ❁ *3*

PART TWO
Al-'Aqida 'l-Wahbiyya
by Nasir b. Salim b. 'Udayyam al-Rawahi

Author's Introduction ❁ *55*

Chapter 1. The Knowledge of God's Unity ❁ *57*

Chapter 2. The Knowledge of God ❁ *74*

Chapter 3. God's Essence and Attributes ❁ *87*

Chapter 4. The Roots of Religion, the Impossibility of Seeing God, and What Is Necessary and Impossible for God ❁ *105*

Chapter 5. Affiliation (*Walaya*) and Dissociation (*Bara'a*) ❁ *156*

Chapter 6. How to Deal with People Who Are Not of Muhammad's *Umma* ❁ *212*

Chapter 7. Knowledge and Action ❁ *231*

PART THREE
'Abd al-'Aziz al-Thamini al-Mus'abi on God's Power and Human Acts, from *Kitab Ma'alim al-Din*

Chapter 3. On the Necessity of the Absolute Oneness of God Most High • 241

Chapter 4. On What Is Possible Concerning the Most High • 246

Glossary • 279
Biographical Dictionary • 291
References • 313
Index • 327

ACKNOWLEDGMENTS

The bulk of this research was conducted in Oman during the 2000–2001 academic year, thanks to a research grant in the Fulbright Middle East, North Africa, and South Asia Regional Research Program run by the Council for International Exchange of Scholars. I did some follow-up on this research when I returned to Oman for a two-month period in February and March 2010 on a scholarship from the Carnegie Corporation. My interest in Ibadism was sparked initially by two summers of research in Zanzibar. In summer 1998, I went to Zanzibar with a travel grant from the University of Illinois' Center for African Studies, and the following summer I went specifically to study Ibadism in Zanzibar with a William and Flora Hewlett award granted by the Office of International Programs and Studies at the University of Illinois. I was granted some relief from teaching in order to concentrate on my research, thanks to an appointment as an associate in the Center for Advanced Study at the University of Illinois in spring 2003. I am very grateful for all the support that has made this book possible.

My research sponsor in Oman was Professor Ibrahim Soghayroun, the infinitely gracious and patient chairman of the Department of History at Sultan Qaboos University. I owe Dr. Soghayroun a very great debt of gratitude for his help, his wise counsel, and his friendship during my time in Oman. His wife and family also offered hospitality to me and my daughter. I am also grateful to Richard Wilbur, the former public affairs officer at the American Embassy in Muscat, and his assistant, Sa'id al-Harthy, who were extremely helpful in introducing me to the people and institutions I would need to know for my research.

The people of Oman are some of the most wonderful people in the world, and I cannot say enough to express my gratitude to the many who went out of their way to help me. Sa'id al-Harthy escorted me to his hometown of Mudhayrib in order to meet the eminent scholar, Shaykh Salim ibn Hamad ibn Sulayman al-Harithi, who, along with his wife, his son ʿAbdallah, and his daughter, extended great courtesy to me and was very helpful in answering my questions. Saʿid al-Harthy also took me to the town of Mintirib, so I could meet the descendants of the great scholar, Nur al-Din ʿAbdallah ibn Humayd al-Salimi, and visit the family's private library. The al-Salimi family was extremely hospitable to me; for an entire week during Ramadan my daughter and I were guests in their home, while Hamza bin Sulayman bin Muhammad bin ʿAbdallah al-Salimi was extremely helpful in acquainting me with the holdings of the family library and answering my questions about scholars and sources. My memories of the week spent with the Salimi family are very warm, and I am grateful to all of them, especially to Hamza and his sister, ʿAzza. Saʿid al-Harthy also arranged for my meeting with the Grand Mufti of Oman, His Eminence Shaykh Ahmad ibn Hamad al-Khalili, who received me with the utmost grace and honesty, and invited me to his home to meet his wife and daughters. I am very grateful to this kindhearted and humble man, who has done so much to foster Islamic unity while knowledgeably and effectively continuing to teach traditional Ibadi theology.

I owe a very special debt of gratitude to His Highness Sayyid Muhammad bin Ahmad Al-Bu Saʿidi, in whose wonderful library I conducted some of my most valuable research. I thank him for granting me special permission to photograph manuscripts of the creed by al-Rawahi, which enabled me to check the accuracy of my transcription of the text even after my return to the United States. I am also very grateful to the library's former caretaker, Mubarak ʿAbd al-Rahman, who was extremely helpful in locating sources of interest to me. I also wish to extend my thanks to the staff of the manuscript division of the Ministry of National Heritage and Culture (now the Ministry of Heritage and Culture), especially its former director, ʿIsa al-Harithi.

I am deeply indebted to Dr. Wilferd Madelung, who offered some very helpful advice after reading an early draft of this book, and did a meticulous reading of a late draft. Dr. John Wilkinson and an anonymous reviewer also made comments and suggestions on an earlier draft of the book. I am grateful to all of these scholars, whose comments enabled me to improve the quality of the book. All errors that remain are entirely my responsibility.

Last but not least, I wish to thank my family, fully cognizant of the sacrifices they made in order for me to be able to do this research: my husband, Dr. Kirk Hauser, my daughter Rachel, and my son Michael, who all remained in the

United States when I went to Oman, and endured an often painful separation; and my daughter Deborah, who accompanied me to Oman and made my stay there so much more enjoyable than it otherwise would have been. I would also like to thank my husband for doing the artwork for the book cover.

To all these people, and to the other friends and colleagues who enriched my time in Oman, I say "thank you."

ABBREVIATIONS

b.	ibn ("son of")
d.	indicates the year of that person's death
n.	footnote or endnote
pl.	plural
ch.	chapter
Q	the Qur'an. References to Qur'anic passages are preceded by this notation unless the context makes it obvious that the quotation is from the Qur'an, for example, if it is preceded by "God's words" or something similar.
AH	after the *Hijra,* dates according to the Islamic calendar.
CE	the "common era," dates according to the Gregorian calendar.
S	Student, the hypothetical student who poses questions in al-Rawahi's *Al-ʿAqida 'l-Wahbiyya.*
T	Teacher, the hypothetical teacher who responds to these questions.
SA	manuscript of *Al-ʿAqīda 'l-Wahbiyya* copied by Salim b. Sulayman, Bu Saʿidi no. 1651 *ʿayn,* 181 pages, dated 8 Jumada al-Ula 1343/5 December 1924.
N	manuscript of *Al-ʿAqida 'l-Wahbiyya* copied by Sayf b. Musallam b. Nujaym, Bu Saʿidi no. 270 *ʿayn,* 111 pages, dated 20 Ramadan 1380/8 March 1961.
R	manuscript of *Al-ʿAqida 'l-Wahbiyya* copied by Abu Muhammad Ahmad b. Sulayman b. Zahran al-Riyami, Ministry of Heritage and Culture no. 2443, 191 pages, dated 5 Dhu al-Ḥijja 1351/1 April 1933.
F	an unpublished copy of *Al-ʿAqida 'l-Wahbiyya,* typed on a word processor. It was edited by Shaykh Sayf b. Muhammad b. Sulayman

al-Farisi, a teacher at the Institute of Shari'a Studies in Muscat, from an annotated copy done by one of his students, Salih b. Sa'id b. Nasir al-Qunubi.

Guide to Abbreviated Titles for Hadīth Collections

Fath al-Bari: Ibn Hajar al-'Asqalani, Ahmad b. 'Ali (773–852/1372–1449). *Fath al-Bari bi-sharh al-Bukhari.*

Al-Jami' al-sahih musnad al-Rabi': Al-Rabi' b. Habib (d. ca. 170/786), *Al-Jami' al-sahih,* following the arrangement of Abu Ya'qub Yusuf b. Ibrahim al-Warglani (d. 570/1174–1175).

Musnad Ahmad b. Hanbal: Ibn Hanbal, Ahmad (164–241/780–855). *Al-Musnad.*

Sahih al-Bukhari: al-Bukhari, Abu 'Abdallah Muhammad b. Isma'il (194–256/810–870). *Al-Jami' al-musnad al-sahih al-mukhtasar min umur rasul Allah.*

Sahih Muslim: Muslim b. Hajjaj al-Qushayri (206–261/821–875). *Al-Jami' al-sahih.*

Sunan Abi Dawud: Abu Dawud al-Sijistani, Sulayman b. al-Ash'ath (202–275/817 or 818–889). *Kitab al-sunan.*

Sunan Ibn Maja: Ibn Maja, Abu 'Abdallah Muhammad b. Yazid (209–273/ 824 or 825–887). *Jam' jawami' al-ahadith wa-'l-asanid wa-maknaz al-sihah wa-'l-sunan wa-al-masanid.*

Sunan al-Nasa'i: al-Nasa'i, Abu 'Abd al-Rahman Ahmad b. 'Ali al-Nasa'i (215–303/830–915), *Kitab al-sunan.*

Sunan al-Tirmidhi: al-Tirmidhi, Abu 'Isa Muhammad b. 'Isa (210–279/825–892). *Al-Jami' al-sahih.*

PART ONE

INTRODUCTION

> This was the first of the schools of Islam (*al-madhahib*) to be founded, and its scholars have written more than those of any other school. They were the first to write a commentary on the Qur'an, the first to write a collection of Hadith, and the first to write a book on Law (*fiqh*). (Al-Harithi 1974, 3)

So writes a modern Ibadi scholar of Oman, in words that express a point of view common among adherents of this sect. Ibadi Islam is a distinct sect of Islam that is neither Sunni nor Shiʿite. Although, as the quote above indicates, Ibadis see their sect as the oldest and most authentic form of Islam, they remain largely a mystery to other Muslims and even to many scholars of Islam, among whom the study of Ibadism has been "the game of the happy few."[1] Both Muslim and non-Muslim scholars of Islam tend to call Ibadis "moderate Khawarij," the only Kharijite sect that survived after the first two tumultuous centuries of Islam. For their part, contemporary Ibadis regard it as an insult to be considered Khawarij, though this was not always the case (Hoffman 2009), although they recognize that their sect originated in the Kharijite secession of 37 AH/657 CE.[2] From their point of view, the Khawarij erred so thoroughly in castigating other Muslims as unbelievers worthy of death that they removed themselves from the pale of Islam. In recent decades, the points of rapprochement between Sunnism and Ibadism have been emphasized. Ibadis read Sunni writings and often quote them with approval, especially the Hadith collections of al-Bukhari, Muslim,

1. Josef van Ess, at the "Ibadhism, Ibadhi Studies, and the Sultanate of Oman" conference at Aristotle University, Thessaloniki, November 9–10, 2009.

2. The "AH" dates refer to the Islamic calendar, which began "after the *hijra*." Islamic dates are given before CE ("common era," i.e., Gregorian) dates, separated by a slash.

and others.[3] Nonetheless, Ibadis maintain a special interest in Kharijism, and even if they are interested in distinguishing themselves from the Khawarij, they feel compelled to defend the Khawarij on a number of points (Al-Harithi 1974, 36–80; Al-Sabi'i 1999).

Ibadi Muslims complain, with some justification, that although they read the works of all other Muslim sects, none of the scholars of the other Muslim sects read Ibadi works, and often choose to reiterate false information rather than study the works written by Ibadis themselves. An Ibadi scholar of modern Libya, 'Ali Yahya Mu'ammar (1919–1980), wrote a two-volume work on the place of Ibadism among the Islamic sects (Mu'ammar 1972). The entire first volume is a study of the faulty information on Ibadism found in both old and new works written by non-Ibadi Muslims, and some by non-Muslim scholars as well.

This book is an attempt to introduce Ibadi Islamic theology to students and scholars of Islam,[4] mainly through annotated translations of two basic Ibadi theological texts, in order to address the general unavailability of Ibadi texts to all but the most specialized scholars of Islam. The focus of this study is Ibadi theology, not law, in which the differences with Sunni Islam are minor, although some subjects that are covered in this book have implications for both theology and jurisprudence, such as the status of sinning Muslims and the rules for spiritual association (*walaya*) and dissociation (*bara'a*).

Such academic studies on Ibadism as do exist, with two exceptions (Cuperly 1991; Ennami n.d.), largely ignore theology and focus mainly on political history

3. *Hadith* is the body of literature that contains narratives about what the Prophet said and did—that is, his *Sunna*. The Hadith collections of Muhammad b. Isma'il al-Bukhari (194–256/810–870) and Muslim b. al-Hajjaj (206–261/821–875), both entitled *Al-Jami' al-sahih* [The Authentic Collection], are considered the most sound and authoritative collections. These collections are often referred to simply as "al-Bukhari" and "Muslim" or *Sahih al-Bukhari* (the *Sahih* of al-Bukhari) or *Sahih Muslim*. Less reliable but frequently used are *Sunan* collections of Abu 'Isa Muhammad b. 'Isa al-Tirmidhi (210–279/825–892), Abu 'Abdallah Muhammad b. Yazid b. Maja (known as Ibn Maja, 209–273/824 or 825–887), Abu 'Abd al-Rahman Ahmad b. 'Ali al-Nasa'i (215–303/830–915), and Abu Dawud Sulayman b. al-Ash'ath al-Sijistani (202–275/817–889). "Hadith" with a capital *H* refers to the literature as a whole, and "hadith" with a lowercase *h* refers to a particular narrative.

4. In order to make this book comprehensible to students of theology who are not specialists in Islam, I provide some information that is unnecessary for scholars of Islam (such as the comments on Hadith in n. 3 and the summary of the events of the great *fitna* that led to the formation of sects in Islam).

and theory.[5] Indeed, much of the interest in Ibadism among Western scholars concerns its role in the development of early Islamic thought. The relative lack of interest in Ibadi theology may be partly because Ibadi literature is often very long, dry, dense, and difficult to understand. That is why I selected Nasir al-Rawahi's theological primer as the centerpiece of this book, although very few people, Ibadi or otherwise, have read it:[6] it is an unusually brief text intended as a primer for Ibadi theology students. It condenses and clarifies concepts that otherwise must be learned through a very arduous process, while allowing us to hear the voice of an Ibadi scholar trained in the classical tradition. The one drawback of this text is that al-Rawahi appears to have died before completing it. For this reason, I have included a translation of 'Abd al-'Aziz al-Thamini's discussion of the relationship between God's power and human acts, a topic of tremendous importance in Islamic theology but omitted from al-Rawahi's primer.

The Origin and Political History of the Ibadiyya

The history of Ibadi Islam, like the history of Sunni and Shi'i Islam, is inextricably linked with the controversies over leadership of the Muslim community that developed during the reign of the third caliph, 'Uthman b. 'Affan (23—35/644–656),[7] and the events following his assassination on 18 Dhu 'l-Hijja 35/17 June

5. Ennami's book, based on his Ph.D. dissertation (Cambridge University, 1971), contains valuable information, but the English is not very good and the book is not readily available. Both Cuperly and Ennami include translations of some brief Ibadi creeds. Besides the works of Cuperly and Ennami, the most important studies on early Ibadism in Western languages include Cook 1981; Madelung 2006; Crone and Zimmerman 2001; Gaiser 2010; Lewicki 1953, 1955, 1962; Savage 1997; van Ess 1992, vol. 2; and Wilkinson 1982, 1985, 1987, 1990, 2010. Many of these are source-critical studies of Ibadi origins, with the exception of Wilkinson 1990, which lists major Ibadi sources but does not explain Ibadi theology. Ersilia Francesca has written a number of articles on Ibadi law. On aspects of modern Ibadism, see Eickelman 1989; Ghazal 2005a, 2005b, 2010; and Hoffman 2004, 2005, 2009. For a complete bibliography of Ibadi publications and secondary literature on Ibadism, see Custers 2006.

6. The grand mufti of Oman, Shaykh Ahmad b. Hamad al-Khalili, and some students at the Institute of Shari'a Sciences have read this text, but I have never found any references to it except for in A. al-Khalili 1993.

7. *Ibn* means "son of"; in keeping with standard usage in Islamic studies, subsequent references to names will use the abbreviation *b.* instead of *ibn* if the given name is also mentioned.

656.[8] Sunni Muslims see the first four caliphs as righteous men, the "rightly guided caliphs" (*al-khulafa' al-rashidun*). Sunni political theory as articulated by al-Mawardi argued that the caliph must belong to the Prophet Muhammad's tribe, Quraysh. All the caliphs up to al-Mawardi's time—the "rightly guided caliphs" (11—40/632–661), the Umayyad caliphs (40—132/661–750), and the 'Abbasid caliphs (132—656/750–1258)—had in fact belonged to this tribe. Shi'i Muslims believe that the leadership of the Muslim community must be more narrowly placed within Muhammad's immediate family. They believe that Muhammad appointed his cousin and son-in-law, 'Ali b. Abi Talib, as his successor, and although 'Ali did become the fourth caliph after 'Uthman's assassination, the Shi'a see the first three caliphs as usurpers of the power that rightly belonged to 'Ali from the time of the Prophet's death in 11/632. Some early Shi'i sects, including the one that played an active role in the 'Abbasid revolution, did not limit leadership to 'Ali and his descendants who were descended from the Prophet, but allowed the imamate (leadership) of other descendants of 'Ali, and even descendants of the Prophet's uncle, al-'Abbas. But when the 'Abbasids came to power in 132/750, they championed Sunni Islam, and afterward the Shi'a limited the imamate to the descendants of 'Ali and Muhammad's daughter, Fatima.[9] Western historians largely reject as fabrications of history Shi'i claims that Muhammad appointed 'Ali as his successor and say there is no evidence that Muhammad appointed anyone as his successor. Madelung (1997) suggests

8. This section lays out this history in a form that adheres to the Ibadi point of view—a viewpoint that has been vigorously debated and challenged by Western scholars, most notably Wilkinson (2010). As important as that project is in contemporary scholarship, it is not the task of this book. The forces driving the conflicts in early Islam were, in reality, multiple and complex and cannot be reduced to theoretical differences over the nature of Islamic leadership; they include struggles over the allocation of Iraq's resources after the last of the great conquests in that region in 639–640 (cf. Hinds 1971).

9. The term *imam* ("leader") has religious connotations and can be used in many different contexts—an imam is someone who leads congregational prayer; in classical Sunni literature, "imam" and "caliph" (*khalifa,* meaning "successor" or "deputy") were interchangeable titles for the supreme ruler of the Islamic empire; and among Sunni Muslims today "imam" may be an honorific title applied to superior scholars—but among the Shi'a, "imam" as a title means the only legitimate leader of the Muslims, chosen by God from among the descendants of 'Ali and Fatima. In Ibadism, the imam is a righteous ruler who is selected by the leading men of the community and rules according to Islamic dictates.

that the succession of Abu Bakr was not as unproblematic as modern historians have supposed, and that 'Ali may indeed have expected to assume leadership on the death of the Prophet.

The Ibadi perspective on the early caliphate differs from that of both Sunnis and Shi'a. From their point of view, the only legitimate way to come to power is not through familial or tribal affiliation or through divine selection, but through selection by the leading men of the Muslim community. The only way to maintain legitimate government is by ruling according to Islamic law. Any infringement of those rules, or any commission of a grave sin or persistence in a minor sin, makes one unfit to be a ruler of the Muslims, and it is the Muslims' duty to remove such a person from power. The Ibadis believe that the first four caliphs, Abu Bakr (ruled 632–634), 'Umar b. al-Khattab (ruled 634–644), 'Uthman b. 'Affan (ruled 644–656), and 'Ali b. Abi Talib (ruled 656–661), were all selected on the basis of religious merit, not on tribal or familial affiliation, so they all came to power in a legitimate fashion. They see Abu Bakr and 'Umar as righteous rulers who committed no grave sins throughout their caliphates. They divide 'Uthman's twelve-year rule into a six-year period of righteous rule and a six-year period of unrighteous rule. As Madelung notes (1997, 85–87), this perspective was very common among 'Uthman's critics, but the policies of nepotism and distribution of lands conquered by the Muslims were already in place in the early years of his caliphate. 'Uthman's tendency to appoint as governors of the provinces his own relatives—who were often capable but unprincipled leaders—and his allocation of the proceeds of the conquests to his kin were controversial among many pious Muslims of the time.[10] Muslim soldiers stationed in Egypt and Iraq converged on 'Uthman's residence in Medina, demanding his repentance and a change in policy. 'Uthman promised to meet their demands and the soldiers dispersed, but soldiers returning to Egypt intercepted a letter allegedly written by 'Uthman to his governor in Egypt ordering him to kill the rebels. The second siege of 'Uthman's home in Medina ended in his assassination (Madelung 1997, 78–140).

10. Today 'Uthman's collection of the Qur'an and destruction of variant versions is often hailed as the crowning achievement of his reign, but at the time it was resented as an unwarranted demonstration of authoritarianism. However, this event does not figure prominently in Ibadi discussions of early Muslim history.

The assassination of 'Uthman immediately exposed conflicting points of view concerning the qualifications of a ruler. Some Muslims, especially members of 'Uthman's own clan, the Banu Umayya, felt that 'Uthman's policies were justifiable interpretations of the Qur'an, and that he was not obligated to implement the policies of his predecessors, Abu Bakr and 'Umar. From this perspective, his killing was an outrageous murder of a righteous Muslim who had been legitimately selected for leadership of the community. On the other hand, other Muslims felt that 'Uthman had failed to rule by Islamic laws, that he had wrongly favored his own kinsmen (who included the former rulers of Mecca who were the Prophet's main antagonists and who embraced Islam very late in Muhammad's career), and persecuted those pious Companions of the Prophet who had criticized his policies and those of his governor in Syria, his kinsman, Mu'awiya b. Abi Sufyan. From their point of view, 'Uthman had committed grave sins, failed to repent, and clung to leadership despite widespread discontent. He had abdicated his responsibility to the people and his right to rule, and his adamant refusal to step down necessitated the drastic action of assassination. For some Muslims, the group that came to be called the Khawarij (singular Khariji/Kharijite), commission of a grave sin and failure to repent nullifies faith; such a person has apostatized from Islam and deserves execution. In short, 'Uthman's killing raised a host of contentious questions concerning the relationship between faith and works, the definition of a Muslim and an unbeliever, and the proper qualifications for a Muslim ruler.

'Ali b. Abi Talib's election as fourth caliph was not a true *shura* (consultation) as mandated by 'Umar b. al-Khattab on his deathbed. It was, as Madelung describes it, "irregular . . . supported by the rebels from the provinces [who had participated in 'Uthman's assassination] and the Ansar [Muslims of Medinese origin] disenfranchised by Abu Bakr," and "left the Community deeply divided into three factions" (Madelung 1997, 146). Many prominent Muslims, including the Prophet's youngest wife, 'A'isha, blamed 'Ali for 'Uthman's death, and the fact that 'Uthman's assassins remained unpunished among 'Ali's supporters strengthened the impression of complicity. After suppressing a revolt in Basra, 'Ali faced his most dangerous opposition, led by Mu'awiya b. Abi Sufyan, 'Uthman's cousin and governor in Syria. 'Ali's main base of support was in Kufa, a military garrison city in Iraq. Their two armies met at Siffin, on the right bank of the Euphrates River in what is today eastern Syria. The armies are said to have stayed there for seventy-seven days, reluctant to shed blood in a conflict that split tribes and families, before battle was joined in Safar 37/July 657. In the course of the battle, as 'Ali's soldiers pressed hard against their opponents, Mu'awiya's troops are said to have tied copies of the Qur'an to the end of their lances as a call to subject to arbitration the question of whether or not 'Uthman was justly killed. Despite his initial reluctance, 'Ali acquiesced to this request, to the outrage of a significant segment of his followers, who promptly abandoned him on the battlefield.[11] These were known as the *Muhakkima,* because of their slogan, "Judgment (*hukm*) belongs to God alone," and as *al-Khawarij,* "those who go out." This last appellation is usually interpreted to mean those who left 'Ali's camp, but is interpreted differently by some Ibadi writers, as we shall see.

From the Kharijite point of view, 'Uthman, by virtue of his grave sins, was an apostate deserving of death, and Mu'awiya and his followers, who claimed the right to avenge that death, were likewise guilty of apostasy. 'Ali's right to rule had been self-evident from his selection by the leading righteous men of the community and by his protection of 'Uthman's assassins. But now that he had agreed to subject the matter to human arbitration and negotiate with "unbelievers," he himself had become an unbeliever. They felt compelled to withdraw from the

11. Hinds (1971, 364–65) says that 'Ali was pressured to acquiesce to the arbitration by the Qur'an reciters (*qurra'*) of Kufa, the very group that later led the secession in protest of this same acquiescence. They initially favored arbitration because they believed that the arbitration would result in peace and acceptance of 'Ali's leadership. However, when 'Ali agreed to omit his caliphal title of "Commander of the Faithful" from the agreement, and also agreed that the arbiters could make their judgment based on custom in addition to the Qur'an, the *qurra'* turned against the arbitration, arguing that "judgment belongs to God alone." Significantly, the matter that was to be decided by the arbiters was not specified. 'Ali may well have understood it to be the rightness of his leadership, a matter on which he might have anticipated a ruling in his favor. Perhaps this is why he allowed the selection of one of his less enthusiastic partisans as arbiter. The question on which they ultimately issued a decision, however, was the rightness of 'Uthman's assassination, and the decision that he was unjustly killed was interpreted by many as a ruling in favor of Mu'awiya's claim to the right of revenge and the demand that 'Ali punish the assassins. As Madelung points out, however, this demand overlooks the fact that some of the main agitators who instigated the assassination (e.g., 'Amr b. al-'As and 'A'isha) were then among the greatest rabble-rousers calling for revenge and rebellion against 'Ali. The number of those who left 'Ali after his return to Kufa was several thousand; some historians place the number as high as 12,000 or 14,000, and their numbers swelled as they were joined by others discontented with 'Ali.

society of "unbelievers" in a new emigration (*hijra*), following the example of the Prophet's emigration from Mecca to Medina, in order to build a just Muslim society. Anyone who did not join them and embrace their cause was considered an apostate deserving of death.

That the Ibadis deeply identify with much of this history is evident by the fact that they recognize as their first imam 'Abdallah b. Wahb al-Rasibi, whom the Khawarij selected as imam after their withdrawal from 'Ali's camp. Ibadis use the term *Wahbi* (from 'Abdallah b. Wahb's name) to refer to what they see as the purest version of Islam; the title of the theological primer translated in this book is *Al-'Aqida 'l-Wahbiyya,* "The *Wahbi* Creed." The author of this primer, Nasir b. Salim b. 'Udayyam al-Rawahi, was also a great poet known as Abu Muslim, who wrote a poem in praise of the courage and faith of the thousands of Kharijite soldiers, including Ibn Wahb, who met their death in battle against 'Ali at Nahrawan on 9 Safar 38/17 July 658 (*Al-Qasida 'l-Nahrawaniyya,* in al-Rawahi 1987, 7–16), a battle that in truth was a massacre that undermined the legitimacy of 'Ali's caliphate (Vecca Vaglieri 1999). Modern Ibadi scholars have defended the Kharijite secession and the Kharijite verdicts on 'Uthman, 'Ali, and Mu'awiya. According to the Algerian Ibadi scholar, Muhammad b. Yusuf Atfayyish (1820–1914), the term *Khawarij* was originally praiseworthy, meaning "those who go out to struggle (*jihad*) in the way of God," but because of the negative connotations the term acquired, "our companions do not call themselves by this name, but call themselves 'the people of straightness,' *ahl al-istiqama,*" a reference to the Qur'anic prayer that God would "guide us to the straight path" (Q 1:5), in contrast to "those who go astray" (Q 1:7), because of the Ibadis' "straightness in practicing their religion." On the other hand, says Atfayyish, the epithet "people of the Sunna" [which came to mean the Sunni Muslims] was originally an insult, referring to Mu'awiya's custom (*sunna*) of cursing 'Ali from the pulpits. "When [the Umayyad Caliph] 'Umar b. 'Abd al-'Aziz [reigned 99–101/717–720] stopped that *sunna,* people began to think that 'people of the *sunna*' referred to the Sunna (practice) of the Prophet. All of this is explained by al-Mas'udi" (cited in al-Harithi 1974, 70–71).[12] Ibadi scholars point out that the Kharijite camp

12. Al-Mas'udi's Shi'i sympathies could account for his preservation of a tradition so unfavorable to the Sunnis.

included many of Muhammad's most pious Companions and veterans of the battle of Badr, the first great Muslim victory during the lifetime of the Prophet on 21 Ramadan 2/17 March 624 (al-Harithi 1974, 45–48).

Although 'Ali defeated the Khawarij at Nahrawan, it was allegedly a Kharijite who assassinated him in 41/661, though some have argued that 'Ali's assassin was not a Kharijite, nor was he motivated by Kharijite ideology (Ma'ruf 1988, 59; al-Sabi'i 1999, 164–65). His assassination left the field open for Mu'awiya to seize power. Mu'awiya's capital was Damascus, and his successors were members of his clan, the Banu Umayya. The Umayyad dynasty ruled from 41/661 until their overthrow by the 'Abbasids, who made Baghdad their capital and ruled the vast but increasingly fragmenting Islamic empire from 132/750 until the Mongol conquest in 656/1258.

Not all those sympathetic with Kharijite ideals about personal piety and righteous leadership believed it imperative to separate from the larger Muslim community or go out to wage war. One of the earliest of these "quietist" (*qa'ada*) Khawarij was Abu Bilal Mirdas b. Udayya al-Tamimi (d. 61/680–681), a Kharijite leader from Basra, in southern Iraq. Brother of one of the instigators of the Kharijite secession and a veteran of the massacre at Nahrawan, he nonetheless disagreed with the more violent tactics of the Khawarij, which included acceptance of the principle of *isti'rad,* religious assassination. Basra became a major center of moderate Kharijism, and Abu Bilal is seen as a precursor of the Ibadiyya.

Kharijite rebellions posed a serious threat during the civil wars that plagued much of the Umayyad period after the death of Yazid I, Mu'awiya's son and successor, in 64/683. The earliest and most violent Khawarij were the Azariqa or Azraqites, followers of Nafi' b. al-Azraq, who conquered Basra in 65/684, opening the doors of the prisons there and assassinating the governor. Outraged Basrans of the Azd tribe, of Omani origin, expelled the Azraqites, and Nafi' was killed in battle the following year. 'Abd al-Malik b. Marwan (65–86/685–705), one of the most capable of the Umayyad caliphs, was nonetheless able to regain control of all provinces of the Islamic empire.

The Ibadi sect is named after 'Abdallah b. Ibad (or Abad), who is said to have broken with the Azariqa after 'Abd al-Malik b. Marwan became caliph. Lewicki suggests that he hoped to come to an understanding with the new caliph, and two letters are said to have been written by Ibn Ibad to 'Abd al-Malik b. Marwan (Lewicki 1953a). However, Cook (1981, 51–64) presents convincing evidence that not only is the second of Ibn Ibad's purported letters spurious, but the first letter was probably written by the man whom Ibadis see as Ibn Ibad's successor at Basra, "Abu 'l-Sha'tha'" Jabir b. Zayd, and that the addressee was probably not 'Abd al-Malik b. Marwan but 'Abd al-Malik b. al-Muhallab. Jabir b. Zayd was an eminent authority and a close associate of the Prophet's cousin, 'Abdallah b. al-'Abbas, one of the most important early authorities on Hadith and Qur'an interpretation.[13] Jabir is generally seen as the true organizer of the Ibadi sect, although Wilkinson (1982, 133–36) argues against this proposition. Jabir hailed originally from Oman, from the small town of Farq near Nizwa, and belonged to the Azd tribe, which had many important representatives among the moderate Khawarij of Basra.[14] For many years Jabir had friendly relations with the powerful Umayyad governor of Iraq, al-Hajjaj b. Yusuf, who apparently saw the moderate Khawarij as a bulwark against the growth of Kharijite extremism.

When 'Abd al-Malik b. Marwan died in 86/705 and was succeeded by the pious 'Umar b. 'Abd al-'Aziz, many moderate Khawarij hoped for the realization of their dreams of a righteous Islamic imamate. They were disappointed, and many of the new *qa'ada* leaders wanted to embrace a more activist stance toward jihad. Jabir himself felt compelled to take action, and instigated the assassination of one of al-Hajjaj's spies (Lewicki 1953a). This led to a complete rupture in the relatively friendly relations the moderate Khawarij had enjoyed with the Umayyad regime. Al-Hajjaj imprisoned many of them, and others were exiled to Oman.

Among those imprisoned in Iraq was a prominent scholar and student of Jabir b. Zayd, Abu 'Ubayda Muslim b. Abi Karima al-Tamimi. Released from prison after the death of al-Hajjaj in 95/714, he is seen by Ibadi tradition as the second Ibadi

13. Jabir is often said to be a Hadith scholar, but the "sciences" of Hadith scholarship had not yet been developed. Wilkinson (1985, 245) comments, "Certainly there is a mass of material concerning Jabir but it is almost entirely concerned with his legal opinions and practices and in this there is little sign of his quoting precedent, let alone hadith for establishing them." Nonetheless, Jabir figures frequently in the *isnad*s of hadiths in Sunni collections.

14. The relationship between tribalism and Ibadi movements in early Islam is elaborated in Savage 1997. Wilkinson (1987) makes similar observations with regard to the imamate in Omani history. It is ironic that although Ibadi theory regarding the imamate is that lineage should not be a factor in the selection of an imam, in reality imams have often been selected in dynastic succession, or at least in particular families.

imam (Lewicki 1953a). Inclined at first to come to terms with the Umayyads, his fear of schism among the moderate Khawarij led him to embrace a different strategy. He established missionary teams called *hamalat al-ʿilm,* "bearers of knowledge," to propagate Ibadi teachings and promote anti-Umayyad insurrections in provinces that were less susceptible to immediate Umayyad control, like Khurasan (in northeast Persia), Oman, Yemen, the Hadramawt region (in the southeast of the contemporary republic of Yemen), and the Maghrib. The moderate Khawarij of Basra embraced a strategy later called *kitman,* living in a state of "concealment"—that is, not openly espousing political rebellion, though they were well connected with the rebellions occurring in the provinces. The man who is recognized as the third Ibadi imam and author of the authoritative compilation of Ibadi Hadith, al-Rabiʿ b. Habib, migrated to Oman.[15] Increasingly, in response to persecution, the Ibadis were pushed to the margins of the Islamic empire.

The first Ibadi state was established in 128/745 in the Hadramawt under the leadership of ʿAbdallah b. Yahya al-Kindi, known by the nickname *Talib al-Haqq* (seeker of truth). He was able to conquer Sanʿaʾ, in northern Yemen, in late 129/746, and from there moved on to capture the holy cities of Mecca and Medina. This imamate ended when Talib al-Haqq was killed in battle at the end of the Umayyad period in 139/748. One of Talib al-Haqq's followers, an Omani named al-Julanda b. Masʿud, fled to Oman, where he was elected imam of a new Ibadi state—a short-lived effort that lasted only two years (132–134/750–752), ending in an ʿAbbasid military expedition in which the imam was killed. The next Omani imamate, however, established in 177/793, lasted a century.

In 140/757, North African Ibadis elected as imam Abu ʾl-Khattab al-Maʿarifi, one of the *hamalat al-ʿilm* sent out by Abu ʿUbayda to the Maghrib. He seized

15. The attribution of *Al-Jamiʿ al-sahih musnad al-Rabiʿ b. Habib* to al-Rabiʿ has also been subject to Wilkinson's deconstructionist examination. Wilkinson (1985, 245–46) points out that "a fundamental characteristic of the propagation of early Ibadism was that *ʿilm* was transmitted verbally and not in writing." He examines the components of what became the Ibadi Hadith collection, and notes that "al-Rabi's name only comes into the picture in connection with Dumam's *riwayat* and even then not he, but a pupil, or even a pupil of a pupil, set the material down. I would suggest that his name has been introduced as a deliberate smoke screen to imply that these *Athar,* whose existence was attested but few had seen, were the actual source for the *Musnad;* an implication taken up by Shammakhi."

Tripoli, in present-day northwestern Libya, and in 141/758 he captured Qayrawan (Kairouan), in present-day Tunisia, the chief city of Islamic Ifriqiya (Africa). He entrusted its government to ʻAbd al-Rahman b. Rustam. Although the ʻAbbasids recaptured Qayrawan in 144/761, Ibn Rustam was able to found an Ibadi state at Tahart, in present-day Algeria. The Rustamid Imamate, as it is known, lasted—though not without schisms and political crises—until it was overthrown by the Shiʻite Fatimids in 296/909. Although Ibadi communities remained in small pockets in the Jabal Nafusa mountain range of northwestern Libya, the island of Jirba (Djerba) off the southeast coast of Tunisia, and the Mzab valley of Algeria, the Ibadi imamate ceased to exist.

In Oman, however, aspirations to establish a righteous imamate became a recurring theme in its tumultuous political history, riven by conflicting religious and tribal aspirations. The imamate of al-Salt b. Malik (237–273/852–879) ended with his deposition, and after this the imamate was contested between rival factions headed by the towns of Nizwa and Rustaq. The imamate of al-Khalil b. Shadhan b. Salt b. Malik (406–425/1016–1034) inaugurated a period of important scholarly reflection and exchanges between the Ibadis of Oman and the Hadramawt, although the rivalry between Oman's two chief cities of Ibadi scholarship continued. In the middle of the twelfth century the imamate collapsed when the Nabhani family came to power in Oman, a period seen by Ibadi historians as riven with tyranny and bloodshed, although "[i]n fact, the Nabahina *muluk* [kings] ruled exactly like most Imams, through manipulating tribal and secular power, but without pretension to religious legitimacy" (Wilkinson 1987, 12). New imamates arose in the early fifteenth century, but Oman was reunited under an Ibadi imamate only with the establishment of the Yaʻrubi dynasty in 1024/1615, which lasted until the founding of the Bu Saʻidi dynasty, some time between 1154/1741 and 1167/1753.[16]

The founder of the Bu Saʻidi dynasty, Ahmad b. Saʻid (ruled until 1198/1783), was the last ruler in the dynastic succession to be recognized as imam, though

16. The founder of the Bu Saʻidi dynasty, Ahmad b. Saʻid, originally served as governor of Suhar on behalf of the Yaʻrubi Imam Sayf b. Sultan II, but was recognized as ruler of Oman after he drove out the Persians. There is some disagreement as to when Ahmad was recognized as Imam. Ibn Ruzayq (1992, 347) wrote that power was transferred to Ahmad b. Saʻid in 1154/1741. A. al-Salimi (2000b, 2:179) records 1167/1753–1754 as the year in which Ahmad was officially recognized as an imam.

his son Sa'id also claimed the title. Subsequent rulers were called by the honorific title "Sayyid" (master),[17] or (largely through British influence, it seems) "Sultan," a title that carries no religious signification. Sayyid Sa'id b. Sultan (ruled 1220–1273/1806–1856) commanded an empire that extended over Oman and the East African coast, and in 1247/1832 he transferred his capital from Muscat to Zanzibar. After his death, his son Thuwayni ruled over Oman, while the rule of East Africa, with its capital at Zanzibar, went to another son, Majid, a division that was formalized in the Canning Award of 1861.[18] The Bu Sa'idi family continued to rule in Zanzibar until the anti-Arab revolution of January 1964; they continue to rule in Oman, where the sultan since 1970 is Qabus (Qaboos) b. Sa'id b. Taymur.

The impulse to establish a righteous Ibadi imamate did not die out, however. In 1285/1868, a successful revolt led in part by the esteemed scholar and mystic, Sa'id b. Khalfan al-Khalili, overthrew Salim b. Thuwayni and installed as imam a member of a rival branch of the Bu Sa'idi family, 'Azzan b. Qays. 'Azzan succeeded in subduing or gaining the support of most of Oman, and even managed to oust the Wahhabis from the Buraimi oasis, which they had conquered sixty years earlier; since then, the government of Oman had been forced to pay a tribute that the government in Riyad called *zakat* (the religious tax that is one of the five pillars of Islam). However, Thuwayni's brother, Turki b. Sa'id, who had been living in exile in Bombay, was allowed by the British to return to Oman in March 1870, and he lost no time in trying to raise a force to overthrow 'Azzan. He was greatly assisted in this endeavor when his brother Majid, ruler of the

17. Among Sunni Muslims, "Sayyid" is a title given to descendants of the Prophet, especially in the Hadramawt, where *sayyid* families exercised religious, political, and economic leadership until the communist revolution of South Yemen in 1967. Among Ibadis, the title "Sayyid" does not imply descent from the Prophet, and is given to members of the ruling Bu Sa'idi family.

18. This division was not without controversy and bitter resentment. Indeed, an abortive coup intended to place Barghash b. Sa'id on the throne of Zanzibar in place of his brother Majid was motivated in part by Majid's acquiescence to the division of the Omani empire in order to retain his throne, as Thuwayni was the stronger of the two. Zanzibar was the wealthier partner at the time, thanks to its role in trade in ivory and slaves, as well as its clove plantations. The Canning Award required Zanzibar to remit an annual subsidy to Oman to compensate for its loss of the Zanzibar territories, as the price for Zanzibar's independence from Oman.

Zanzibar sultanate, sent a large sum of money to him, with promises of further payments if he conquered Sur and forged a successful alliance with the Wahhabi *amir*, ʿAbdallah b. Faysal. By liberally bestowing wealth on tribal leaders who resented the centralization of government under the imamate, Turki was able to induce the defection of many tribes from loyalty to ʿAzzan. The imam was killed in battle on the night of 8 Dhu ʾl-Qaʿda 1287/29 January 1871 (A. al-Salimi 2000b, 2:296).[19] On 13 February, Saʿid al-Khalili surrendered to the British resident for the Persian Gulf, Col. Lewis Pelly, on condition that he be guaranteed safety. Pelly turned him over to Turki, and within a few days al-Khalili and his teenaged son were both dead.[20]

19. In Arab parlance, "the night of 29 January" would correspond to the night of 28 January or the predawn hours of 29 January, but Kelly (1968, 707) gives 30 January as the date of the imam's death. Al-Salimi also informs us that the imam's body remained unburied for three days, without suffering any obvious decomposition—a classic sign of sainthood in Islam.

20. Pelly's communication with British authorities in India indicates that he did not see Britain as providing any guarantee of al-Khalili's safety, but Kelly, who is very critical of Pelly's conduct in Oman, wrote that al-Khalili certainly thought that Pelly was providing him with just such a guarantee (Kelly 1968, 708). Nur al-Din al-Salimi saw Pelly as betraying al-Khalili's trust, and did not know what had happened to al-Khalili after he was turned over to Turki (A. al-Salimi 2000b, 296). Turki told Pelly that al-Khalili and his son had died of diarrhea (Kelly 1968, 699), but according to Nur al-Din al-Salimi's son Muhammad (M. al-Salimi n.d., 82), al-Khalili and his son were buried alive. According to Hamza b. Sulayman al-Salimi, the great-grandson of Nur al-Din al-Salimi, it was the author of the primer translated in this book, "Abu Muslim" Nasir b. Salim al-Bahlani al-Rawahi, who discovered what happened to them (personal conversation with the author, Nov. 2000). Al-Rawahi was hosting a visitor in his home in Zanzibar, a Shiʿite from the Mutrah area of old Muscat, who entertained his host with stories from Oman. He said that one day during the reign of Sultan Turki, the sultan brought out Shaykh Saʿid b. Khalfan and his son and placed them in a hole. The crowd began to mock them and throw stones at them, and al-Rawahi's Shiʿite guest also threw his sandal at Shaykh Saʿid's face. As al-Rawahi heard this story, he began to tremble. He rose and told his guest, with the utmost gravity, "Get out, before I kill you." The Shiʿite knew this was no joke, and fled. Al-Rawahi later lamented the tragedy and the contemptible treatment of a noble scholar and leader with whom he closely identified, in a poem entitled *Watani* ["My Country"] (al-Rawahi 1986, 321). Although Pelly was able to shrug off any sense of responsibility for what happened, it may be that the British political agent in Muscat, Major A. Cotton Way, had a livelier conscience and was conflicted over the role he was forced to play in the debacle, for he committed suicide in May of that year (Kelly 1968, 708).

In 1331/1913 another revolt, led by the prolific and extremely influential scholar, Nur al-Din ʿAbdallah b. Humayd al-Salimi (1286–1332/1869–1914), established the imamate of Salim b. Rashid al-Kharusi in the al-Jabal al-Akhdar ("Green Mountain") region of the interior that had always been the heart of the Ibadi impulse in Oman. But this movement was not able to conquer the coast, and Oman was effectively divided between the sultanate in Muscat and the imamate in the al-Jabal al-Akhdar region. This division was formalized by the British-officiated Treaty of Sib (Seeb) in 1920, and remained in effect until December 1955, when Sultan Saʿid b. Taymur reunited Oman under his rule. An initially successful rebellion against the sultan by leaders of the former imamate in June 1957 was quenched by a combined Omani-British force (Peterson 1978, 180–94; Valeri 2009, 51–58). It has been suggested that some of the "Islamic extremists" recently arrested in Oman, who include university professors and scholars of Ibadi law, are not linked in any way to the terrorist policies of al-Qaʿida (al-Qaeda), but were trying to establish a new Ibadi imamate (BBC News 2005a, 2005b).

The Development of Ibadism as a Distinct Sect of Islam

As Wilkinson points out, in traditional Ibadi historiography the Khawarij are seen as a more or less monolithic block, from which the Ibadis split in 64/683. They say that their imamate, seen as a coherent line of succession beginning with Jabir b. Zayd, existed for decades in a concealed state (*kitman*) (Wilkinson 1982, 125), until the establishment of the first Ibadi political imamate in the Hadramawt in 128/745. Wilkinson deconstructs this perspective by pointing out, among other things, that not all the Khawarij "united under ʿAbdallah b. Wahb's banner at Nahrawan," but rather the Khawarij were split early between militants (*shurat,* those whose lives were "purchased" in the cause of Islam) and quietists (*qaʿada*). The most important proponent of the quietist position is said to have been ʿAbdallah b. Ibad, about whom very little is known. Indeed, Wilkinson ponders the possibility that his leadership was a later projection and that "his name was probably resuscitated at a later stage because it provided a convenient label to contrast with the Azariqa: the eponym of the third 'color' label, the Sufriyya, is probably a complete fabrication." ("Ibadi" suggests a link with *abyad* [white], while "Azraqi" suggests a link with *azraq* [blue] and "Sufri" with *asfar* [yellow].) Wilkinson says that the quietist Khawarij were almost entirely lacking any political organization at this period. Wilkinson also points out that some of the men claimed by the Ibadis as their leading figures are also claimed by other schools, and they include people "whose attitudes and actions are not really reconcilable with Ibadi views, or who can at best only be considered sympathizers" (ibid., 132–33). Wilkinson doubts that Jabir had any formal leadership among the nascent Ibadis, and asserts that he could not have ordered the execution of Khardala, a former Ibadi accused of betraying the movement (ibid., 134). Ennami also doubted that Jabir had any formal leadership: "In my personal opinion he was no more than a religious leader to whom his followers came to learn Islam, and to ask questions concerning religious matters" (Ennami n.d., 57).

As we have seen, the questions that led to the formation of the Kharijite sect were the status of gravely sinning Muslims and the definition of the Muslim community and its leadership. Ibadi doctrine on these pivotal issues was several centuries in the making, during which Ibadis debated many issues among themselves. In the early ʻAbbasid period, disputes concerned questions such as whether Friday prayer was required in the absence of a righteous imamate, how to classify degrees of sin, and how to draw the boundaries of the community, in addition to debates on theological issues that were discussed among scholars of the broader Muslim community: interpreting the anthropomorphic descriptions of God in the Qur'an, the relationship of reason to revelation, the essence and attributes of God, and whether the Qur'an was created or uncreated. A number of Ibadi subsects developed out of these debates, beginning in the first half of the second/eighth century. One of the earliest of these subsects were the al-Harithiyya, who are said to have broken from Abu ʻUbayda by accepting the Muʻtazilite position of free will. Two other early groups, usually mentioned together in discussions of Ibadi history, though their relationship is uncertain, were the ʻUmayriyya, followers of ʻIsa b. ʻUmayr, and the Husayniyya, followers of Ahmad b. al-Husayn of Tripoli, Libya. Ahmad b. al-Husayn wrote one of the earliest Ibadi treatises on theology, *Kitab al-Maqalat,* followed by a work on jurisprudence, *Mukhtasar fi 'l-fiqh.* Among the distinctive doctrines of these sects was that no one who believes in God, even if his beliefs contradict those of Islam, can be called a polytheist. It is said that the Husayniyya were won back to mainstream Ibadism by Abu Yahya Zakariyya b. Ibrahim al-Baruni in the seventh/thirteenth century.

By far the most important split within the Ibadiyya occurred when a group known as the Nukkar ("Deniers," also called the Nakkara or al-Nakkariyya) denied the legitimacy of the second Rustamid imam, ʿAbd al-Wahhab b. ʿAbd al-Rahman (168–208/784–823), demanding that he subject all decisions to the consensus of the leading men of the community and agree to abdicate if a more worthy candidate than he were discovered. However, the theological schism began earlier, during the leadership of Abu ʿUbayda in Basra, with the composition of *Kitab al-rudud,* one of the oldest works on Muslim theology, by ʿAbdallah b. Yazid al-Fazari, one of the early leaders of the Nakkari schism. He and several associates were expelled by Abu ʿUbayda from Ibadi assemblies, but it is said that they repented and were reinstated, but reasserted their views after Abu ʿUbayda's death (Cuperly 1991, 34–35; Ennami n.d., 181). They were also known by other names, most importantly al-Nakitha, al-Nakkatha, and al-Nukkath, meaning "violaters," because they violated their oath to ʿAbd al-Wahhab. The Nukkar are said to have followed ʿAbdallah b. ʿAbd al-Aziz, Abu 'l-Muʿarrij, and Hatim b. Mansur in jurisprudence, and ʿAbdallah b. Yazid al-Fazari in theology (Ennami n.d., 181–82). Ennami provides an extensive list of divergences between the Nukkar and the mainstream Ibadis, including the view that Muslims who hold anthropomorphic views of God are polytheists, that the imamate is not obligatory, and that the names of God are created. This last heresy prompted a rebuttal in the first theological treatise to emerge from mainstream Ibadism: *Kitab al-tawhid al-kabir,* written by an Egyptian scholar, ʿIsa b. ʿAlqama (100–150/718–767) (ibid., 35). The Nukkar became particularly important in the Maghrib after the fall of the Rustamid Imamate to the Fatimids in 296/908–909; in the first half of the fourth/tenth century, one Nakkari uprising nearly defeated the Fatimids (Lewicki 1953b). Mainstream Ibadism came to be called by the adjective "Wahbi," following the putative original teachings of the sect of ʿAbdallah b. Wahb al-Rasibi. Some have suggested that "Wahbi" is derived from the name of the Rustamid Imam ʿAbd al-Wahhab, as the term seems not to have come into use until after the Nakkarite secession. Muhammad b. Yusuf Atfayyish (1820–1914) argued that if "Wahbi" was derived from ʿAbd al-Wahhab, the form would be Wahhabi, not Wahbi (Atfayyish 1924–1925, 10: 325, cited in Ennami n.d., 174).

Aside from ʿAbdallah b. Yazid al-Fazari's *Kitab al-rudud,* early Ibadi writing consisted of letters (called *sira*s). Ibadism remained a mainly oral tradition with the exception of letters written by the authorities in Basra to inquirers in the Maghrib. One of the earliest works dealing with religious teaching is a letter on *zakat* written by Abu ʿUbayda to a scholar in the Maghrib. Although Ibadis claim, as the words of Salim al-Harithi at the beginning of this introduction indicate, that Ibadism is the oldest sect of Islam, Wilkinson places its development as a full-fledged *madhhab* (denomination, or school of theology and jurisprudence) in the period of its political decline, following the demise of the Rustamid Imamate in North Africa and the end of the second imamate in Oman. His study of early Ibadi Hadith points to a lack of *isnads*[21] even as late as the early fourth/tenth century, and that the authoritative collection attributed to al-Rabiʿ b. Habib (d. 170/786), an Ibadi leader of Basra who later relocated to Oman, is a compilation of the work of a number of scholars, with *isnad*s added to fit the criteria of later Hadith scholarship, probably first set down by a Maghribi scholar of the early third/ninth century, Abu Sufra ʿAbd al-Malik b. Sufra, in a document known as *Kitab Abi Sufra*. He suggests that this collection did not reach Oman until the beginning of the nineteenth century (Wilkinson 1985, 255, 258).

Ibadi literature first developed under the Rustamid Imamate of Tahart, including two works written by Rustamid imams: Ibadi sources mention a *tafsir* (commentary on the Qur'an) written by ʿAbd al-Rahman b. Rustam (ruled 161–171/778–788) and theological treatises by Abu 'l-Yaqzan Muhammad b. Aflah (ruled 260–281/874–894) on the question of human capacity to act (*istitaʿa*) and the creation of the Qur'an. A second Ibadi *tafsir* was composed in the Maghrib by Hud b. Muhakkam al-Huwwari of the third/ninth century, whose father was a judge for Imam ʿAbd al-Wahhab b. ʿAbd al-Rahman b. Rustam (ruled 171–208/788–824). Two decades later came the first Ibadi *tafsir* written in Oman, by Abu 'l-Hawari Muhammad b. al-Hawari. During the late Rustamid period, one of the first major works of Ibadi theology was written, *Usul al-daynuna 'l-safiya* by ʿAmrus b. Fath al-Masakini of Nafusa, known as Abu Hafs (d. 283/896). He also wrote a refutation of the doctrines of the Nukkar and the Husayniyya, entitled *Al-Radd ʿala 'l-Nakitha wa-Ahmad b. al-Husayn*.

In the third/ninth century Ibadi scholars began to write collections of jurisprudential opinions. Especially noteworthy is the work of the Omani scholar,

21. By the mid–eighth century CE, Sunni Hadith scholars required that each report have an *isnad*, a chain of transmitters, that would list, preferably in an unbroken fashion, all those who had transmitted the report, beginning with the most recent transmitter and proceeding backwards to the Companion who witnessed the Prophet say or do what is recorded in the report.

Abu Jabir Muhammad b. Ja'far al-Izkawi, known simply as *Jami' Ibn Ja'far* ("The Compendium of Ibn Ja'far") or even simply as *al-Jami'* ("The Compendium").

The collapse of the Rustamid and Omani imamates at the end of the third/ninth century and the consequent lack of an Ibadi political entity led to the development of the doctrines of *taqiyya* (religious dissimulation) and *kitman*, the state of a religious community living in secret dissension from the ruling authorities. In North Africa, *'azzaba* councils developed to replace the imamate; and just as the decline of the power of the 'Abbasid caliphate led to the emergence of Sunni writings on political theory, so during this period of decline did Ibadi scholars delineate the various types of imamate and the circumstances under which an imam could be deposed (to be discussed below). As Wilkinson points out, the threat of the sect's extinction led to the development of literature outlining Ibadi doctrine. In Oman, a treatise on the rules for fighting jihad was composed in the late third/ninth century by Bashir b. Abi 'Abdallah Muhammad b. Abi Sufyan Mahbub b. Rahil.

The fourth/tenth century saw a rapid development in Ibadi jurisprudence. One of the most notable contributors to this literature is a scholar who remains one of the most important legal authorities, especially in Oman: Abu Sa'id Muhammad b. Sa'id b. Muhammad b. Sa'id al-Kudami, author of a number of works, including *Kitab al-Istiqama*, on spiritual affiliation and dissociation, and *Al-Mu'tabar*, a comprehensive work on jurisprudence, including a critique of the compendium of Ibn Ja'far. His compatriot and younger contemporary, Abu Muhammad 'Abdallah b. Muhammad b. Baraka al-Bahlawi, published a compendium that became a standard work of reference and the foundation for other legal works, such as Salama b. Muslim al-'Awtabi al-Suhari's *Al-Diya'* (fifth–sixth/eleventh–twelfth century) and Muhammad b. Ibrahim al-Kindi's (d. 508/1115) *Bayan al-Shar'*.

Beginning in the fourth/tenth century, and far more in the fifth/eleventh century, a number of theological works were written, especially in North Africa, including a refutation of Mu'tazilite doctrine by Abu Nuh Sa'id b. Zanghil of Tunisia and Algeria (early fourth/tenth century); a comprehensive refutation of all theological opponents by Abu Khazar Yaghla b. Zaltaf of Tunisia (d. 380/990); *Kitab al-wad'*, a summary of Ibadi teachings on theology and jurisprudence by Abu Zakariyya' Yahya b. Abi 'l-Khayr al-Jannawuni (fifth/eleventh century); *Kitab al-Tuhaf*, containing the teachings of Abu 'l-Rabi' Sulayman b. Yakhlaf (d. 471/1078–1079); and several works written by his student, Abu 'l-'Abbas Ahmad (d. 504/1111).

The sixth/twelfth century witnessed prodigious compositions in Ibadi theology, including *Kitab al-Su'alat* by Abu 'Amr 'Uthman b. Khalifa al-Sufi al-Marghini,[22] a collection of detailed responses to diverse questions, of which nine form the articles of the Ibadi creed; *Kitab al-Dalil* by Abu Ya'qub Yusuf b. Ibrahim al-Warjilani (d. 570/1175), who also created the arrangement of the Hadith collection attributed to al-Rabi' b. Habib; *Usul al-din* by Tabghurin b. 'Isa al-Malshuti of Jabal Nafusa; and a creed set to verse by Abu Nasr Fath b. Nuh al-Malusha'i, also of Jabal Nafusa, entitled *Al-Qasida 'l-nuniyya fi 'l-tawhid.*

The most eminent of all the Ibadi theologians of the time was Abu 'Ammar 'Abd al-Kafi b. Abi Ya'qub Yusuf b. Isma'il b. Yusuf b. Muhammad al-Tanawuti al-Warjilani (d. before 570/1174), of the Algerian oasis town of Wargla (conventionally Ouargla). After studying in Tunis, he returned to Wargla, where he helped stimulate an Ibadi intellectual florescence, attracting students from throughout the Maghrib, especially Jirba. His most important work is *Kitab al-Mujaz fi tahsil al-su'al wa-takhlis al-maqal fi 'l-radd 'ala ahl al-khilaf,* a theological synthesis in two parts, published under the title *Ara' al-Khawarij al-kalamiyya* (1978). This much-admired book has been compared to the writings of al-Ghazali and al-Baqillani. The first part of the book is a refutation of heretics: those who believe in the eternity of the world, dualists, those who deny the mission of the Prophet (the Jews and Christians), and those who describe God in anthropomorphic terms. The second part examines the principles of speculative reasoning and major theological questions: the creation of human acts and a refutation of the Qadariyya, a discussion of the will of God and divine justice as they pertain to human acts, a refutation of the Prophet's intercession for grave sinners, an affirmation that gravely sinning Ibadis are infidels (*kuffar*) but not polytheists, an exposition of the doctrine of the creation of the Qur'an, proofs for God's existence, an explication of doctrine on the divine names, and the imamate. His other writings include *Kitab Sharh al-Jahalat,* a commentary on a theological work attributed (wrongly, according to Cuperly, 34) to Tabghurin b. 'Isa al-Malshuti.

In the eighth/fourteenth century Abu Tahir Isma'il b. Musa al-Jaytali of Jabal Nafusa (d. 750/1349) wrote a number of important works, including a creed entitled *'Aqidat al-tawhid,* a theological treatise entitled *Qawa'id al-Islam* (on which

22. "Al-Sufi" refers to the valley of Suf (El Oued) in Algeria, not to Sufism (Islamic mysticism).

a number of glosses have been written), several works on jurisprudence, and a three-volume commentary on Abu Nasr Fath b. Nuh's previously mentioned theological poem.

A revival of Ibadi scholarship in Oman went hand-in-hand with the revival of the Omani Imamate: Khamis b. Sa'id al-Shaqsi of Rustaq, author of the influential *Manhaj al-talibin wa-balagh al-raghibin,* a work on Ibadism in general but especially jurisprudence, played a key role in the recognition of the first Ya'rubi Imam, Nasir b. Murshid, in 1024/1615.[23] Nur al-Din al-Salimi tells us that during the reign of Bil'arab b. Sultan b. Sayf b. Malik (1091–1104/1680–1692), an Ibadi shaykh named 'Umar b. Sa'id b. Muhammad b. Zakariyya came to Oman from the island of Jirba in Tunisia. He was delighted to see the revival of righteous Ibadi rule in Oman, but observed few assemblies of learning. So he wrote to the imam advising that he encourage his people to study and build schools. In Jirba, he wrote, although the people are few, weak, and poor, there are more than twenty schools of learning, in which everyone teaches what he knows—grammar, philology, religious obligations, morphology, interpretation, rhetoric, logic, theology, fiqh, mathematics, and poetic meter. Furthermore, the leading scholar of Jirba, Abu Zayd b. Ahmad b. Abi Sitta, gives lessons twice a week. "Despite this," wrote Shaykh 'Umar, "they regret their lack of knowledge, for the true *hanifi,*[24] Rustamid sect increases with an increase in knowledge, and decreases with its decrease." Therefore, he counseled the imam to place a teacher in each fortress to teach the people about the faith, instruct them to be ascetic with regard to this lower, ephemeral world, and instill in them a desire for the precious, eternal life of the hereafter. He warned the imam sternly not to neglect this important matter, "because by God's grace you are his viceregent (*khalifa*) in this world." The imam heeded this advice. He gathered teachers into his new fortress, called

23. This is the date given in A. al-Salimi 2000b, 2:4, but Wilkinson and some other authors place the beginning of his imamate in 1624.

24. *Hanif* is a Qur'anic word of uncertain meaning, but in context it means "the original, pure monotheistic faith." The Qur'an tells Muslims to follow the faith of Abraham as a *hanif* (10:105). The Qur'an also says that Abraham, the model for Islam, was neither a Jew nor a Christian, but was a *hanif* (3:67). Some scholars have speculated concerning the possible existence of a group of non-Jewish, non-Christian monotheists known as *hanif*s in Mecca at the time of Muhammad before his call to prophethood.

Jibrin; it is even said that he himself served them, perfumed them, and offered them foods to strengthen their understanding, and that fifty scholars graduated from this school, all people capable of doing *ijtihad* (independent reasoning in law) and delivering *fatwas* (legal opinions) (A. al-Salimi 2000b, 2:86–91). Nor was scholarship limited to the highlands of the interior: in Qalhat, a town in the Hormuz region of the Persian Gulf, another scholar of the eleventh/seventeenth century, Abu 'Abdallah Muhammad b. Sa'id al-Azdi, wrote *Al-Kashf wa-'l-bayan,* "an exposé of the complete Ibadi theology through rebuttal of other doctrines and, in emulation of the *milal wa-'l-nihal* literature, finishes by expounding it as the only true *firqa*" (Wilkinson 1990, 38).

The late eighteenth century marks the beginning of what Wilkinson calls "the modern Ibadi renaissance," starting in the Mzab valley of Algeria with the social reformism of Abu Zakariya Yahya b. Salih al-Afdali (d. 1202/1787) and his student, 'Abd al-'Aziz b. Ibrahim al-Thamini al-Mus'abi (1130–1223/1718–1808), who was nicknamed *Diya' al-din,* "the Brightness of the Religion." Al-Thamini wrote, among other works, the monumental *Kitab al-Nil wa-shifa' al-'alil* on jurisprudence, which Wilkinson calls "the Mozabite 'bible' of the renaissance" (Wilkinson 1985, 232), as well as *Ma'alim al-din* on theology (a section of which is translated in the current volume), *Al-Taj,* a ten-volume abridgement of Khamis b. Sa'id's *Manhaj al-talibin,* and a 536-page commentary on the theological poem of Abu Nasr Fath b. Nuh al-Malusha'i. One of al-Thamini's most important students was Ibrahim b. Yusuf Atfayyish, who was in turn the teacher of the most outstanding Ibadi scholar of the modern period, his younger brother, Muhammad b. Yusuf Atfayyish (sometimes written Attafayyish, Itfayyish, or Atfiyash), whose contribution to modern Ibadism will be discussed shortly.

In Oman, the most outstanding scholar of the late eighteenth and early nineteenth century was Abu Nabhan Ja'id b. Khamis al-Kharusi, who died at the age of ninety on 3 Dhu 'l-Hijja 1237/20 August 1822. According to al-Salimi, "Abu Nabhan was the most outstanding scholar of his time in knowledge, virtue, and nobility (*sharaf*)"—a reference to the fact that many Ibadi imams had come from his tribe, the Banu Kharus—"and the people took him as an example for guidance in all matters of their religion as well as their worldly affairs. The virtuous people obeyed him, because they knew his knowledge and piety" (A. al-Salimi 2000b, 2:192). Not only was Abu Nabhan a formidable scholar, but he was also credited with mystical and talismanic powers. When the brother of Sa'id b. Ahmad, second ruler of the Bu Sa'idi dynasty, who came to power in 1196/1782, wrote to Abu Nabhan asking him to lead a rebellion against the sultan, Abu Nabhan is said to have used his secret arts (*'ilm al-sirr*) to destroy the sultan's power, and his brother, Sultan b. Ahmad, took over almost the entire kingdom (ibid., 202–3). Abu Nabhan's son, Nasir b. Abi Nabhan (1192–1263/1778–1847), became the major scholar of the next generation in Oman, and accompanied Sayyid Sa'id b. Sultan to Zanzibar when the capital of the Omani empire was moved to East Africa. It was one of Nasir b. Abi Nabhan's pupils, Jumayyil b. Khalfan al-Sa'di, who composed the ninety-volume *Qamus al-shari'a 'l-hawi turuqaha 'l-wasi'a* from 1260/1844 until 1280/1863, the first volume of which was the first publication produced by Sayyid Barghash's printing press in Zanzibar in 1297/1880.[25] Another of Nasir b. Abi Nabhan's pupils, however, became the greatest scholar of his generation: Sa'id b. Khalfan al-Khalili (1226–87/1811–71). Despite his wide erudition, he was an extremely humble man who declined to be seen as an authority in theology or law. He was a mystic, poet, and master of the rules of rhetoric and grammar, who is seen by literary scholars of contemporary Oman as having inaugurated a literary renaissance in that country. But the motive for his poetry was neither literary nor personal; it was deeply spiritual. Through poetry he described the mystical teachings of Islam, his despair over the violence and injustice that reigned in his country, and the need for a righteous imamate to be established in Oman. As we have seen, he became the leading scholar behind the movement that successfully overthrew Salim b. Thuwayni in 1868 and installed 'Azzan b. Qays Al Bu Sa'idi as imam, and he was killed following the overthrow of the imamate in early 1871.

Despite becoming blind from an illness at the age of twelve, Nur al-Din al-Salimi (1286–1332/1869–1914) was active in the fields of history and poetry as well as Qur'an commentary and Shari'a, in addition to leading the imamate rebellion of 1913. Muhammad al-Salimi described his father as beyond a doubt the leader

25. Oman's Ministry of National Heritage and Culture has published only twenty of the ninety volumes of this encyclopedia so far, but there are complete manuscripts of this work in the library of the Ministry of National Heritage and Culture in Muscat as well as in the library of His Highness Sayyid Muhammad b. Ahmad Al Bu Sa'idi in Sib, Oman.

of the Ibadi renaissance par excellence, "the greatest pillar in the return of the Imamate to Oman and its achieving the highest rank, passionately enthusiastic for the Omani nation to rise up and reclaim its glory, which it had lost for so long through factionalism and conflict" (M. al-Salimi n.d., 120).

The long life of the eminent Algerian authority, Muhammad b. Yusuf Atfayyish (1235–1332/1820–1914), overlapped the careers of Nasir b. Abi Nabhan, Sa'id b. Khalfan al-Khalili, and Nur al-Din al-Salimi. Atfayyish was honored by the sultans of Zanzibar, and his works were first published there by the Zanzibar sultanate's printing press (Sadgrove 2004), and later by the Salafiyya Press in Cairo established by the Libyan Ibadi, Sulayman b. 'Abdallah al-Baruni (1870–1940) (Custers 2004). Atfayyish is so highly respected in the world of Ibadi scholarship that he is universally referred to as "the Pole of the Religion" (*qutb al-din*) or "the Pole of the Imams" (*qutb al-a'imma*), or simply "the Pole" (*al-Qutb*). In some respects he was untraditional, ready to reconsider issues that had long been decided in Ibadi tradition. His influence on al-Rawahi is evident in the fact that Atfayyish's *Hamayan al-zad ila dar al-ma'ad* appears to have been used as the basis of parts of the theological primer translated in this volume, and the last three chapters of al-Rawahi's text closely follow portions of Atfayyish's *Al-Dhahab al-khalis al-munawwih bi 'l-'ilm al-qalis.*

Muhammad Atfayyish's international contacts and publication venues are one indication of the impact of globalization on the world of Ibadi scholarship since the late nineteenth century. This is much more dramatically evident in the life of his brother's grandson, Abu Ishaq Ibrahim b. Muhammad Atfayyish (1305–1385/1886–1965), like his great-uncle a native of the Mzab valley in Algeria, but who studied in Muscat, Algiers, and Tunis. After his expulsion from Tunisia by French authorities because of his nationalist agitation there, he settled in Cairo, where he followed the example of earlier Ibadi émigrés to that country by forging liaisons with modernist Sunni reformists (Ghazal 2005b). Throughout the twentieth century Ibadism underwent desectarianization, a process hastened by the policies of the current sultan of Oman, Qabus (Qaboos) b. Sa'id (Eickelman 1989; Valeri 2009).

The Distinctive Teachings of Ibadi Islam

What follows is a brief summary of Ibadism's distinctive teachings.

The Status of Sinning Muslims

The status of sinning Muslims was the earliest issue to be discussed by Muslim scholars, emerging as it did directly from the controversy over the killing of 'Uthman. As we have seen, the radical Khawarij believed that those who committed grave sins had renounced the faith. They were unbelievers (*mushrikun,* literally "polytheists") and apostates deserving death. On the other end of the spectrum, from the vantage point of Muslim heresiographies, was the perspective taken by those the heresiographers call the Murji'a ("postponers"), who said that works do not affect faith, judgment should be postponed until the Day of Judgment when God would decide, and sinning Muslims must be regarded as believers in this world. Although Sunni Muslims regard this group (the membership of which is unclear) as heretics, probably because their viewpoint could easily lead one to think that works are unimportant, their position is actually quite close to what came to be regarded as the Sunni point of view, and Abu Hanifa (d. 150/767), eponym of the Hanafi legal school of Sunni Islam, was said to be a Murji'i. The most common Sunni point of view is that anyone who professes faith in Islam is a Muslim, even if he commits grave sins and neglects his religious obligations. It is for this reason that radical modern Muslims who practice *takfir* (accusing other Muslims of *kufr,* or unbelief) are not in keeping with traditional Sunnism, and are often castigated as Khawarij by moderate *Sunnis.* From the typical Sunni perspective, what makes someone a Muslim is the acknowledgment of the truth of Islamic teachings and the obligation of Muslim duties, regardless of whether or not one observes these in practice. So someone who acknowledges, for example, that prayer is obligatory, yet fails to pray, is a negligent Muslim, but remains a Muslim deserving all the privileges that status confers in this world. As is stated in the *Fiqh Akbar I,* a creed derived from statements of Abu Hanifa: "We do not hold anyone to be an infidel (*kafir*) on account of sin, and we do not deny their faith. . . . We do not disavow any of the Companions of the Messenger of God, and we do not adhere to one rather than another. We leave the question of 'Uthman and 'Ali to God, who knows things secret and hidden" (Wensinck 1932, 103, 104). This creed clearly links one's attitude toward the relationship between faith and works with one's position on the schisms that rent the Muslim community after 'Uthman's assassination. In fact, many Sunni hadiths indicate that Muslims who commit grave sins—"even theft and adultery"—will obtain entrance into paradise in the afterlife (al-Bukhari n.d., nos. 3222, 5827), and that even some who are at first condemned to hellfire will enter paradise by virtue of the Prophet's intercession (ibid., nos. 7509, 7510; Abu Dawud 2000, no. 4115). The Mu'tazila, on the other hand, a theological school that emerged in the early second/eighth century and reached the apex of its influence in the early third/ninth century, said that an unrepentant sinning Muslim is neither a believer (*mu'min*) nor an unbeliever (*kafir*), but occupies a status between the two (*manzila bayn al-manzilatayn*).

The Ibadi position on this question differs from all of the above. They utterly reject the Sunni position that faith is unaffected by works, and do not believe, as the Mu'tazila did, that there is an intermediary status between faith (*iman*) and infidelity (*kufr*), though neither do they castigate grave sinners as unbelievers or "polytheists" (*mushrikun*) deserving death, as did the radical Khawarij. Rather, they distinguish between different levels of *kufr*. Unbelief, or polytheism, is *kufr shirk*, the infidelity of polytheism, but a sinning Muslim is not to be called such. Rather, a sinning Muslim is guilty of *kufr nifaq*, the infidelity of hypocrisy, or *kufr ni'ma*, ingratitude for or denial of God's blessing. The root meaning of *kufr*, which is often translated as unbelief or denial, is ingratitude; believers are described in the Qur'an as characterized by *shukr* (gratitude), while those who reject the message of the prophets are characterized by *kufr* (ingratitude, e.g., 14:7). For this reason, in my translation of these terms, I render *kufr* as "infidelity" and reserve "unbelief" of any sort for translations of *shirk*, for though *shirk* literally means "associating" other beings with God as objects of worship, in Ibadi parlance the term is used for any type of wrong belief, not only polytheism.

From the Ibadi perspective, the only people worthy of being called "Muslims" are righteous Ibadis. The terms "Muslims" and "people of straightness" (*ahl al-istiqama*) are references to Ibadis, and "our companions" (*ashabuna*) means Ibadi scholars. Non-Ibadi Muslims are referred to as *ahl al-khilaf*, "the people of opposition," who are nonetheless included among the "monotheists" (*ahl al-tawhid* or *muwahhidun*), the "people of the *qibla*" who face the Ka'ba in prayer, and the *umma*, the religious community of Muhammad.

*Religious Affiliation or Association (*Walaya*) and Dissociation (*Bara'a*)*

Although all Muslims are familiar with these concepts, which are derived from the Qur'an, Ibadis are distinct in their insistence on their priority. One of the most helpful aspects of al-Rawahi's primer is its very clear presentation of this complicated and sometimes rather murky issue. Religious association or "friendship" (*walaya*) is reserved for "Muslims," who are righteous Ibadis living in obedience to God. Sinning Ibadis and non-Ibadi Muslims are *kuffar* and are therefore subject to "dissociation" (*bara'a*). Although this term has sometimes implied communal ostracism radical enough to be translated as excommunication[26]—although no Ibadi institution carries a Vatican-like authority so as to issue an official declaration of such—from al-Rawahi's perspective *bara'a* need not mean a severance of all contact or cordiality with such people; he appears to interpret *bara'a* as an inner awareness of separation that does not imply social avoidance or discourtesy, and need not even preclude genuine affection. "Dissociation," therefore, may be more cognitive than actual. This interpretation may be a product of the cosmopolitan environment in which al-Rawahi lived, compared to the relative isolation of Ibadi communities in the regions of al-Jabal al-Akhdar in Oman, the Mzab valley in Algeria, and Jabal Nafusa in Libya, where these concepts were hammered out by scholars in the premodern period.

On this topic, in modern Ibadism, there is a definite inconsistency between Ibadi theory and actual practice. One would expect that those who believe that faith can be found only within a small group, and that one must dissociate from all others, would be extremely intolerant of those outside their group, but one British observer of Ibadis in Oman and Zanzibar came to the conclusion that Ibadis are the most tolerant of people, living in harmony with all religious and ethnic groups (Ingrams 1931, 191). Ibadis teach that all "monotheists" (non-Ibadi Muslims) are to be treated as "Muslims" under the law, people with whom there can be intermarriage, mutual inheritance of one from the other, and other privileges, all of which are discussed at length in chapter 5 of al-Rawahi's primer. But though one is tempted to think that al-Rawahi's social milieu impacted his views on dissociation, the same cannot be said regarding his discussion of relations with non-Muslims: although Zanzibar was ruled by

26. For example, Wilkinson (1987, 11) writes that scholars of the Rustaq school "excommunicated" the more moderate members of the Nizwa school, and Savage (1997, 20–21) says *bara'a* means "foreswearing all contact." Savage wrongly interprets *wala'* (a variant of *walaya*) as being associated with the unity of God (*tawhid*). This is incorrect, because non-Ibadi Muslims are recognized as monotheists, but are nonetheless subject to dissociation.

the British Colonial Office, al-Rawahi uses the traditional discourse of Muslim rule and non-Muslim subjugation.

Unlike the Khawarij, Ibadis do not endorse the execution of ordinary sinners (as opposed to perpetrators of crimes like murder or adultery) or of Muslims who neglect their religious obligations, although they (like many Sunni Muslims) believe it is the duty of a righteous Muslim ruler to call such a person to repentance and to punish him in order to induce such repentance. Violence is reserved for tyrannical rulers and those who actively oppose Islam and the Muslims.

Reward and Punishment in the Afterlife

Although one must treat non-Ibadi Muslims with the courtesy that all monotheists deserve, according to classic Ibadi doctrine, neither they nor sinning Ibadis will be allowed into paradise; they are doomed to hellfire. Ibadis also deny that the Prophet will intercede for grave sinners. Although the Qur'an implies that punishment in hellfire is eternal (2:217 and elsewhere) and that there is a barrier between paradise and hellfire that makes it impossible for one to pass from one to the other (7:46), these passages are far from straightforward, and are subject to various interpretations. Sunni Muslims believe that there are different levels of punishment in hellfire, and that those in the upper levels are sinning Muslims who may enter paradise after paying the penalty for their sins. Furthermore, as we have seen, there are hadiths that say that sinning Muslims will enter paradise by virtue of their profession of faith, and that the Prophet Muhammad will rescue people out of hellfire and bring them into paradise. All of this is denied by the Ibadis, who traditionally insisted that punishment in hellfire is categorical and eternal, and paradise is reserved for righteous believers in their own creed.

Free Will versus Predestination

In Islamic theology, the question of free will versus predestination[27] is called *al-qada' wa-'l-qadar*, "the (divine) decree and determination," and it focuses not on the question of will or choice, but of power: do humans have the capacity or power to

27. My discussion of this topic is greatly indebted to Watt 1948.

do what they are commanded to do as well as its opposite? The Qur'an speaks of *qadar,* the measure or determination of things, usually in a verbal form, *qaddara,* to refer to God's determination of the phases of the moon (10:5), the sustenance of mountains (41:10) and of people (89:16), death (74:19, 56:60), and the prior determination that the wife of Lot would not be saved (15:60). Q 65:3 says, "He gave everything its measure (*qadr*)." The word *qada',* "decree," occurs only in the verbal form of *qada* in the Qur'an, for example, "It is He who created you from clay, then decreed a term (of life) for you" (6:2). It is most often used in connection with God's decree that something exist. Four times the Qur'an says, "If He decrees something, He merely says 'Be!' and it is" (2:117, 3:47, 19:35, 40:68). It is also used in the sense of command, without any implication that God causes obedience: "Your Lord decreed that you not worship anything but Him, and that you be kind to parents" (17:23).

There are also numerous references to God guiding people and leading them astray, for example, "If God wishes to guide someone, He enlarges his breast to accept Islam; but if He wishes to lead him astray, He makes his breast narrow and constricted, as if he were evaporating into the sky; thus does God lay abomination on those who do not believe" (6:125). Some Qur'an passages indicate that God's guidance and leading astray follow upon human acts of belief and righteousness or unbelief and wickedness; that God's guidance is only effective when people are willing to receive it, whereas being led astray by God is a sort of punishment for unbelief: "He has guided some of you, and some have justly incurred the penalty of going astray" (7:30). Although there are Qur'anic passages that indicate that whoever wishes may believe and whoever wishes may disbelieve (18:28–30), there are others that indicate that human will is nonetheless subject to God's: "You will not will unless God wills" (76:29–30); "It is not for anyone to believe except by God's permission" (10:99–100).

Much more explicitly deterministic is a large body of Hadith, of which the following is a very small sample: the first thing God created was the Pen, which He commanded to write the destinies of all things until the Day of Judgment (Abu Dawud 2000, no. 4702); an angel visits each unborn child after 120 days in the womb and writes its sex, sustenance, term of life (i.e., time of death), its deeds, and whether it will be happy or miserable in the afterlife (Muslim 2000, *bab* 98, no. 1; Muslim 1977, nos. 6390, 6392, 6393).

This obviously raises a host of moral problems. First at stake is the question of God's justice: if a person's fate is sealed before birth, that person is not responsible for his or her actions, and God is unjust for punishing people for what they were predestined to do. God must be unjust if He commands people to do one thing and determines that they do the opposite. On the question of sustenance, it was asked whether God predetermined the sustenance of those who gain it by immoral means, such as theft. If so, then God participates in an immoral act. Similarly, on the question of one's life term, it was asked whether God wills for people to commit murder. If so, God is again implicated in an evil act.

The opposite claim, that people act and choose by their own power, was seen by many as limiting the power and dominion of God. If God does not provide the sustenance of a thief, the thief steals provision God had intended for someone else, which implies that His power over human sustenance is limited. If God does not will murder, then its victims die before God's appointed time, and His power over life and death is limited.

By the second/eighth century the idea that God predetermines all things, including human acts, had gained popularity, as reflected in the growing body of Hadith with this point of view. The opposite point of view, that people have been given power and responsibility over their own actions, was taken by an early group known as the Qadariyya, who were most concerned with avoiding "fixing evil upon God." If what is recorded of their teachings in Sunni heresiographies is accurate, the Qadariyya resorted to religiously unacceptable doctrines in order to avoid "fixing evil upon God": for example, they denied that God provides sustenance to someone who steals for a living or that He creates a child who is born of adultery, and they said that a murderer precludes his victim from reaching the life term set by God. Such statements appear to contradict the Qur'an's affirmation that God provides sustenance to all creatures and sets the life term for everyone. Another problematic issue was God's knowledge of the future, which many believed causes and determines events. Although most Qadaris denied a linkage between God's knowledge of the future and the determination of human acts, one Qadari subgroup called the Shabibiyya was allegedly driven to deny that God knows what people will do until they do it (Watt 1973, 94). This clearly goes against the reiterated Qur'anic affirmation of God's omniscience.

The free-will position was then taken up by the Mu'tazila, the first systematic theologians of Islam. The Mu'tazila's self-designation was "the people of unity and justice." "Unity" refers to their doctrine that God is internally one ("simple," in the language of the philosophers), requiring a negation of the reality of His attributes—a doctrine the Ibadis also embrace. The second part of this appellation indicates their belief that God's justice requires that humans must have power over their own acts. All power belongs to God, they argued, but He has delegated power to human beings in such a way that they have power in themselves at all times either to do something or not to do it or to do its opposite. On the tricky questions of God's knowledge, provision of sustenance, and setting of life terms, they suggested solutions that took into account both God's power and His justice: God does know what people will do before they do it, but that knowledge is merely descriptive and does not determine what they will do; God provides sustenance to all creatures, and a thief steals the sustenance God provided to someone else; God does not will murder, but the life term He sets is fixed, so when a person is murdered, he dies at the time already determined by God, and would have died some other way if he had not been murdered. But some aspects of Mu'tazili teaching involved them in intricate dilemmas, especially their notion that God's absolute justice means that He must do what is best for His creatures. If God is all-powerful and He must do what is best, how do we explain suffering that is not the result of human sin? Some of their suggested solutions to problems of this type are imaginative, but not necessarily satisfying. For example, it is obviously unjust for innocent children to suffer and die, yet they do. Some Mu'tazili thinkers suggested that this happens as a warning to adults, and that the children are compensated in paradise. But since paradise is meant as a reward for good deeds, is it really just to give such a reward to children who do not reach the age of accountability before they die? And although the suffering of unbelievers and evil-doers in hellfire does meet the strict standards of justice, how can one argue that this is actually the best for them? Some Mu'tazila suggested that while suffering in hellfire, they were at least prevented from unbelief. But none of these solutions really satisfies.

The two sides on this issue in the third/ninth century were the Mu'tazili theologians, who argued for free will, and the "people of Hadith," represented by such people as Ahmad b. Hanbal (d. 241/855), founder of the Hanbali school of law in Sunni Islam, who upheld predestination and disapproved of theological reasoning altogether. Hadiths even warned that entire peoples had perished by discussing God's decree and determination (al-Tirmidhi 2000, *kitab* 28, *bab* 1). It was only in the early fourth/tenth century that Sunni thinkers adapted the methods of the Mu'tazila to explain and defend the teachings of the people of

Hadith, which by then had come to be identified as Sunni Islam. The most influential of these early Sunni theologians was Abu 'l-Hasan al-Ash'ari (d. 324/935), originally a Mu'tazili, who is said to have left the Mu'tazila in 300/912 when his teacher, al-Jubba'i, one of the most eminent Mu'tazili scholars of the time, could not explain how it could be just for some children to die and go to paradise, while others live to adulthood and suffer damnation. Al-Ash'ari said that God, as creator of the law, is above the law and cannot be judged by human concepts of justice. He argued that all human acts are created by God, and humans merely "acquire" these acts. The power God gives for an act is for that act only, not for an act "or its opposite," as the Mu'tazila had said. Human beings have no latent power; the power God gives for an act immediately produces the intended act once it is acquired. The distinction between an act that we perceive as voluntary and one that we perceive as involuntary, like shivering, lies in the fact that God gives humans the power to choose between an act or its opposite (which can mean either not doing the act or, in the case of faith, choosing unbelief). Human choice does not grant a person the power to act, but God is in the habit of creating acts that accord with human choice. In this way, al-Ash'ari upheld both God's absolute power over human acts and people's responsibility for what they do.

The Saljuq Turks who conquered Baghdad in the mid–eleventh century actively embraced the Ash'arite school, and a number of theological colleges were established to teach Ash'arite theology as a bulwark against Isma'ili Shi'ite propaganda. Although there have always been Sunni Muslims who distrust theology altogether, especially in the Hanbali school, there is a rough correspondence between the geographical areas where the Shafi'i and Maliki schools of law predominate and the teaching of Ash'arite theology. The Hanafi school of law, which predominates in central and south Asia, tends to be associated with another Sunni theological school, that of al-Maturidi (d. 333/944).

Ibadis embraced the Ash'arite solution to the question of free will versus predestination. Some Ibadi exposés deal with this question at length—al-Sa'di (1983, 5:5–227), for example, devotes more than 200 pages to this topic—and Nasir b. Abi Nabhan (1848, 20) considered this doctrine to be of such importance that he said that the Mu'tazila had deviated more seriously from the straight path than the Sunnis, despite large areas of theological agreement between the Ibadis and the Mu'tazila, because, from his point of view, by claiming to have power over something over which they say God has no power, they deny that God is all-knowing and all-powerful, in defiance of the express words of the Qur'an. Nonetheless, Nasir al-Rawahi, author of the primer translated in this book, barely touches on this topic. The reason for this might have to do with the fact that he was writing in a largely Sunni/Shafi'i/Ash'ari environment, and this is the one area in which the Ibadis do not disagree with the Sunnis—or it may be that al-Rawahi died before he could address this issue in a separate chapter. Therefore, in order to provide a fairly complete presentation of Ibadi theology, I also translate the relevant portions of 'Abd al-'Aziz al-Thamini's *Ma'alim al-din.*

Anthropomorphic Descriptions of God

The Qur'an sometimes describes God in anthropomorphic terms: he is described as has having hands (38:75, 39:67), eyes (54:14), a face (28:88), and being seated on a throne borne by angels above the heavens (20:5, 40:7). He is also described as "the Light of the heavens and the earth" (24:35). Nonetheless, the Qur'an also describes God as different from all other things (42:11), too exalted to be compared with created beings. Q 75:22–23 says that on the Day of Resurrection and Judgment, "faces will be radiant, looking at their Lord." This would appear to imply that God is in a particular place and can be seen. On the other hand, 6:103 says, "Vision does not comprehend him, but He comprehends all vision," which implies that God cannot be seen, and 2:115, "wherever you turn, there is the face of God," implies that God is not in a particular place, but is beyond all places and yet in them at the same time. These contradictory passages posed problems for Muslim theologians.

Hadith reflects a simple folk piety with little or no accommodation to the demands of human reason. Compiled in the eighth and ninth centuries, it presents a "picturesque" depiction of God, as Macdonald put it, with details on His relationship to the angels and demons (Wensinck 1932, 63). It also says that the greatest gift that God will give the believers in paradise is the vision of Himself, a vision so complete that they will see nothing but Him (Muslim 2000, *bab* 80, no. 297; Muslim 1977, no. 347; Bukhari n.d., no. 4851; Wensinck 1932, 63).

Muslims agree that *tashbih,* "likening" God to human beings, is sinful, and that all Muslims must practice *tanzih,* the "exaltation" of God above all other things. Some early Muslims who were accused of anthropomorphism said that by saying God is a body they meant only that He exists, for nothing exists except bodies.

But bodies imply finitude (having finite dimensions) and perceptibility (the ability to be seen). Can God be seen? Since He is the creator of places, can He be in a place? The Muʿtazila denied that God has a body or can be seen, and interpreted anthropomorphic descriptions of God in the Qur'an as metaphors. For example, they interpreted His sitting on a throne as a metaphor for His dominion over all creation; His hand means His power; and gazing (*nazira*) at God means expecting (*muntazira,* from the same root as *nazira*) His reward. But many pious Muslims refrained from such discussions by saying the Qur'anic descriptions of God must be believed "without saying how" (*bi-la kayf*), that is, without explanation or rationalization, and this became the official Sunni position.[28] The Ibadis agree with the Muʿtazila that the anthropomorphic descriptions of God in the Qur'an must be interpreted as metaphors, that God is not perceptible and does not occupy space. They also agree with them in seeing as mere metaphors such eschatological symbols as the scale in which deeds will be weighed on the Day of Judgment, because deeds are accidents, not bodies, and cannot literally be weighed.

Reason and Revelation

The Muʿtazila argued that the truths of Islam can be discerned by the intellect without the need for prophetic revelation. Prophets are really a grace from God, sent to remind people of what they already know, or to force upon them the evidence of the truth they could perceive with their senses and their intellect. Prophets are needed only to reveal specific laws. It is entirely impermissible to adopt religious belief through *taqlid,* blindly following the opinions of others. Rather, reason must be employed. The revelation of the prophets is entirely compatible with reason; if a verse's literal interpretation is incompatible with reason, it must be subjected to an alternative interpretation, such as interpreting God's

28. Frank (1992, 25) argues that the denial of *kayfiyya* in God is not a renunciation of reason but an affirmation of God's transcendence and lack of comparability to created things. For an excellent summary of early Muslim interpretations of the possibility of seeing God in the afterlife, see the tenth-century exegete al-Tabari's discussion of 6:104 in Gätje (1971, 156–62). This is directly followed by Zamakhshari's Muʿtazili interpretation of 75:22–23. Tabari, a Sunni, favors the position that although God cannot be seen in this life, believers (but not unbelievers) will be somehow made to see Him in the afterlife.

throne as only a symbol of His dominance, or interpreting the scale in which deeds are weighed as mere metaphor. Sunni theologians, while also promoting the use of reason, nonetheless feel that one must accept the literal meaning of the Qur'an and Hadith without rationalization. On this issue, the Ibadis agree with the Mu'tazila. They believe that human knowledge of God is innate from childhood, whereas Sunni Muslims believe knowledge of God comes through education and occurs at the age of legal accountability.

The Unity of God, His Essence, and Attributes

Early Muslim theological discussions revolved around the question of whether or not God's attributes are real things distinct from His essence. For every one of the ninety-nine beautiful names of God given in the Qur'an, such as "the all-Merciful," "the Living," "the all-Powerful," "the all-Knowing," "the Creator," there exists a corresponding attribute, which for the above-mentioned names would be mercy, life, power, knowledge, and creation. As Wolfson (1976, 112) says, "As early as the first part of the eighth century, . . . there arose in Islam the belief that certain terms which are attributed to God in the Koran stand for real incorporeal beings which exist in God from eternity." Like the Mu'tazila, Ibadis believe that the unity of God is compromised if one posits the existence of the attributes as real things distinct from God's essence; God's unity implies that He cannot be composed of parts (essence and attributes), but must, in Aristotelian terms, be "simple," not composite.[29] They said that God's attributes have no real existence, but are merely descriptions of His essence. Those who affirmed the ontological reality of God's attributes as distinct from His essence (whom Wolfson calls the "Attributists") pointed out that if God's power is the same as His essence, and His knowledge is the same as His essence, then His power must be the same

29. The Aristotelian argument is that the combination of matter and form in the phenomenal world requires four causes, and that these causes are themselves caused by other things, but at the origin of the entire series of causes must be an uncaused cause, a First Cause, who is not composed of parts, because any such composition would require another being to cause them to come together. An infinitely regressing series of causes is rationally intolerable, so the First Cause must be absolutely "simple" and internally one. With the translation of Greek philosophical and scientific works into Arabic in the 830s, theological discussion was directly impacted by Aristotelian logic.

as His knowledge, which is logically absurd. They also said that by denying the existence of God's attributes, the Mu'tazila were guilty of *ta'til,* "stripping" God of all meaning. The Mu'tazila, favored briefly by the ruling 'Abbasids in the ninth century, became discredited, and the Attributist position was adopted by Sunni Islam; Mu'tazili theology continues to be upheld by the Zaydi Shi'a. The Ibadi position on God's attributes is similar to that of the Mu'tazila, although they use formulas that avoid some of the quandaries caused by Mu'tazili semantics.

The Creation of the Qur'an

The question of whether the Qur'an is created or eternal was the topic of heated discussions in the ninth century. It is connected with the controversy over God's attributes as well as the belief in the existence of the Qur'an before its revelation, even before the creation of the world: the Qur'an speaks of the Qur'an being on a tablet preserved in heaven (85:22).[30] Sunni Muslims believe the Qur'an is uncreated or eternal, because it is associated with God's attributes of word, speech, and knowledge, which are eternal. The Mu'tazila, on the other hand, denied the reality of God's eternal attributes, and said that belief in the eternity of the Qur'an was tantamount to polytheism. They were supported in this view by the 'Abbasid caliph al-Ma'mun (ruled 218–227/813–833), who in the *Mihna* ("Inquisition") persecuted religious scholars like Ahmad b. Hanbal who insisted that the Qur'an was uncreated. Ahmad b. Hanbal held that the Qur'an is knowledge from God, and since God's knowledge is uncreated, the Qur'an must be

30. This is the typical interpretation of this verse. Hadith also says that the first thing God created was the Pen, which He commanded to write on the Preserved Tablet all that would happen until the Day of Resurrection. Muhammad Ali translates *lawh mahfuz* as "guarded tablet" rather than a heavenly "preserved tablet," and comments: "The *lauh,* or tablet, occurring here, is the same as the *alwah* (singular, *lauh*), or tablets, occurring regarding the book given to Moses (7:145, 150, 154). The Qur'an is here spoken of as being in a guarded tablet. The significance of these words is simply this, that the Holy Qur'an is guarded against corruption and against the attacks of its opponents; compare 15:9: 'Surely We revealed the Reminder and surely We shall guard it.' There is no mention here or anywhere else in the Qur'an of the *lauh mahfuz* on which the decrees of God are written . . ." (M. Ali 1991, 1162–63, n. 2706).

uncreated. Furthermore, if the Qur'an is merely a created thing, then it is no different from any other speech, because God is the creator of all things, including human speech; in that case, it does not necessarily express who God is, and one could not be certain of receiving any communication that really came from God. For Ibn Hanbal and other "people of Hadith," God creates both good and evil, including the evil acts of human beings, so God's creation might exhibit qualities like weakness or ignorance that do not express God Himself. But the Mu'tazila believed that God creates only good, so they did not have the same dilemma on this issue. Despite—or perhaps because of—the Mihna, the doctrine of the eternity of the Qur'an came to be embraced by the majority of Muslims.

The revelation of the Qur'an in history and its preservation in writing and memory raise other questions concerning the eternity and temporality of the Qur'an, questions which in some sense are analogous to those raised by the incarnation of Christ: just as, in Christian belief, the eternal Christ (the Logos, or Word) became flesh and revealed God in history, so in Islamic belief did the eternal Qur'an (the Word of God) become "embooked" in Muhammad's revelation—what Wolfson (1976, 235–44) calls "inlibration." Just as the question was raised whether Christ had two natures (divine and human), so was the question raised whether the Qur'an had two natures (eternal and created). One early Attributist theologian, 'Abdallah b. Sa'id b. Kullab (d. ca. 241/855), held that the written or spoken Qur'an is only an expression or imitation of the Word of God; the real Word of God is an idea subsistent in God. Ibn Kullab denied that God's eternal speech can be characterized by commands, prohibitions, and announcements—which is what the Qur'an contains—so he denied that the Qur'an is eternal; it is a temporally produced or originated (*hadith*) expression of God's eternal speech. The creed entitled *Wasiyat Abi Hanifa* ("The Testimony of Abu Hanifa," though scholars believe it actually represents the views of Ahmad b. Hanbal) held that what people hear and recite is the uncreated Word of God, but it implies that the material component of the Qur'an is created, while the essential Qur'an transcends this. The *Fiqh Akbar II,* possibly composed by al-Ash'ari, says, "Our utterance, writing and recitation of the Qur'an are created, but the Qur'an itself is not created" (Wensinck 1932, 189). According to the Ash'arite scholar al-Juwayni (419–478/1028–1085), the divine speech that is eternal is the speech that subsists in His essence (*al-qa'im bi-'l-nafs*) (al-Juwayni

1950, 117).[31] Unlike Ibn Kullab, al-Juwayni insisted that God's eternal speech is characterized as commands, prohibitions, and announcements. "Eternal speech existed in anticipation of the moment for the communication to Moses and, when he came into existence, it was a communication to him in actuality. The newly existing thing was, however, Moses, not the speech." Nonetheless, he describes as foolish the idea that God's speech consists of letters and sounds. "The recitation, according to the orthodox (*ahl al-haqq*), consists of the sounds of the readers and their intonation, which are acquisitions of theirs. . . . The Word of God Most High is written in copies of the Qur'an and preserved in breasts, but it does not inhere (*hall*) in a copy, nor does it subsist in a heart" (al-Juwayni 1950, 120, 127, 130, 132; al-Juwayni 2000, 67, 71, 72, 73). A creed of the Maturidite school of Sunni Islam says that the Qur'an, as the Word of God, is an eternal attribute subsisting in God's essence, though not in the Arabic language or in the form of letters and sounds. "Rather, His creatures express that one attribute with varying expressions. . . . The Ash'arites have said that what is in the text is not the Word of God, but is only an expression of the Word of God, which is an attribute, and the attribute is not to be separated from that to which it is attributed. We say, it is the Word of God, but the letters and sounds are created, for we do not say that the Word of God inheres in the text so that there can be any talk of separation" (al-Maturidi 1953, cited in Williams 1994, 147).

Ibadis distinguish between God's essential speech (*al-kalam al-nafsi*), which is an attribute of God's eternal essence, and the Qur'an and other revealed scriptures, which are created indicators (*madlulat*) of His knowledge and consist of letters and words. God's knowledge of the revealed scriptures as letters, sounds, and words is eternal, as all His knowledge is eternal and unchanging, including His knowledge of all His creatures, but that does not mean that the objects of His knowledge are eternal or unchanging. Nasir b. Abi Nabhan compared God's essential speech with the unspoken commands issued by the human intellect to the limbs of the body, and said that the divine command "Be!" that brings all things into being (Qur'an

31. Paul Walker (al-Juwayni 2000, 65) translates this as "the speech that arises in the soul," but one does not speak of God having a soul, and *al-kalam al-nafsi* is usually translated as God's "essential speech." Al-Juwayni's authority was such that he was nicknamed "Imam al-Haramayn" (leading scholar of the two holy cities).

16:40) is of this type, a command without words (al-Sa'di 1983, 3:239).[32] Most Ibadis affirm that God has an eternal attribute of speech (although none of God's attributes are real things subsisting in God's essence, as the Sunnis would say) in order to deny that He is mute, although some Ibadis feel it is unnecessary to affirm specifically the attribute of speech as an eternal characteristic of His essence, as this is subsumed under the affirmation of omnipotence as an eternal characteristic of God's essence. The affirmation of an attribute is only necessary to deny its opposite, but the opposite of speech is silence, not muteness. The affirmation of God's eternal omnipotence is enough to guarantee that He is eternally capable of speech; it is not necessary to affirm that He is eternally speaking.

In a book defending the distinctive doctrines of Ibadism, Shaykh Ahmad b. Hamad al-Khalili, the current grand mufti of the Sultanate of Oman, writes, "When we speak of the creation of the Qur'an, we are only speaking of this Qur'an that is recited by tongues and written on pages. We are not speaking of God's essential speech, because there is no proof from the Book or from the Sunna that the essential speech should be called the Qur'an, although the Ash'arites have called it such" (A. al-Khalili 2001, 103).

Jurisprudence

The principles of jurisprudence[33] are the same in Ibadism as in Sunni and Shi'i Islam, but unlike the Sunnis, Ibadis do not accept the principle of *taqlid* (the obligation to follow the opinions of earlier scholars) and never closed the gate of

32. To those who are unfamiliar with these theological discussions, this may not seem very different from the doctrine of the Ash'arites, who hold that *al-kalam al-nafsi* does not mean that letters, sounds, sentences, or words subsist in His essence. However, as we have seen, the Ash'arites do believe that the commands, prohibitions, and information in the Qur'an are eternal, although the letters and sounds attached to its Arabic expression are temporally produced. Ash'arites would recoil with horror at calling the Qur'an "created."

33. This section on jurisprudence closely follows Ennami (n.d., 117–30). When Ennami wrote his dissertation in 1970, he stated that very little modern scholarship had been done on Ibadi jurisprudence, and that remains the case, with the exception of the work of the Italian scholar, Ersilia Francesca. The study of Islamic jurisprudence requires a mastery and degree of specialization that is beyond the scope of this volume, with the exception of the topics covered in al-Rawahi's primer.

ijtihad (individual reasoning); it is the duty of those who attain the required standard of knowledge to use their individual judgment. They also do not accept the idea that every *mujtahid* (scholar who does *ijtihad*) is correct; only one opinion can be correct, but Muslims are allowed to adopt other opinions if they believe them to be correct even if they are not, as long as they have exerted themselves in the effort to discern the correct opinion. The Naffathiyya and Husayniyya, two extinct Ibadi sects discussed in the section on Ibadism's historical development, disagreed with this principle and said that those who followed incorrect opinions were *kuffar.* Mainstream Ibadi scholars argued that even the Companions of the Prophet disagreed on derivative legal questions (*furu*ʿ) and considered it lawful for everyone to hold his own opinion. Al-Rabiʿ b. Habib and his cohorts opposed analogical reasoning[34] and felt that one must strictly follow the precedents directly provided by the Prophet and His Companions, but analogical reasoning was later recognized by all Ibadis and was largely exercised (Ennami n.d., 117–18).

Differences between Ibadis and other Muslims in jurisprudence include:

(1) Ibadis developed an elaborate categorization of different types of imamate: the hidden imamate (*imamat al-kitman*), in a situation of political oppression and weakness; the activist imamate (*imamat al-shira*ʾ) that is possible when at least forty men pledge to die in order to establish a righteous imamate; the imamate of defense (*imamat al-difa*ʿ), an emergency appointment of someone as an imam in order to repel an invading enemy; the declared imamate (*imamat al-zuhur*), which is established after enemies have been defeated and there is stability (Al-Rawas 2000, 95–103).

(2) Ibadis regarded the stage of *kitman* as mirroring the corresponding stage of the Prophet's life and the Muslim community in Mecca. Therefore, they suspend

34. Analogical reasoning involves making an analogy between a new situation and one for which there is an explicit verdict provided in the Qur'an or Hadith. The analogy is based on a common factor between the two situations. For example, medieval legal scholars decided that it is lawful to use herbs to prevent conception, although there is nothing on the use of herbs for this purpose in either the Qur'an or Hadith, because there is a hadith in which the Prophet explicitly permits coitus interruptus to prevent conception. As the motive of coitus interruptus is to prevent conception, by analogy all methods of birth control are permissible. On the topic of birth control in medieval jurisprudence, see Musallam (1983). Analogy (*qiyas*) is the operative method for doing *ijtihad*.

all *hudud* punishments during *kitman* and confine their execution to the authority of the declared imamate, except for cases of apostasy, defamation of Ibadi views, blood offenses, and rejecting the authority of the Shari'a (Ennami n.d., 119).

(3) Ibadis believe that Friday prayer should be held only in major cities in which justice prevails—meaning that for centuries Ibadis did not observe congregational prayer because of the lack of a just imam—and they reject the blessing of tyrannical rulers in the *khutba*. There have always been some Ibadis who have disagreed with this teaching, including Nur al-Din al-Salimi, who wrote (A. al-Salimi 1996) in defense of congregational prayer, even in the absence of a just imam.

(4) The duties of association (*walaya*) and dissociation (*bara'a*) are suspended during the period of *kitman* (Ennami n.d., 120).

(5) Unlike Sunnis, Ibadis do not consider it permissible to wipe the shoes or slippers instead of washing the feet for ablutions before prayer (ibid., 121–22).

(6) Ibadis hold that during the noon and afternoon prayers, no portion of the Qur'an is recited but the *Fatiha*. The rationale for this is that in all the silent parts of other prayers, such as the third *rak'a* (cycle of "bowing") of the sunset prayer and the second two *rak'as* of the evening prayers, only the *Fatiha* is recited, and likewise only the *Fatiha* is recited in every prayer or part of a prayer that is silent, whether by night or by day, whereas other portions of the Qur'an are recited in the congregational prayers for Friday or for the feast days, during which the recital is aloud. As both the afternoon and noon prayers are silent, they should be subject to the same rule, namely that in all silent prayer, only the *Fatiha* is recited.

(7) Ibadis, like the Shi'a and some Malikis, keep with their arms down at their sides when they are in the standing position during prayer.

(8) Unlike Sunnis and Shi'a, Ibadis do not say *Amin* after the *Fatiha*, and they do not say the *qunut* invocation in the predawn prayer. Ennami (n.d., 124) translates the *qunut* as "the imprecation against political enemies during the ritual prayer," but the standard formula for *qunut* is a request for blessing and does not involve cursing.

(9) Some Sunnis say it is recommended to shorten prayer during journeys, while the Hanafis make it obligatory for a journey of less than fifteen days. Ibadis say that a traveler must shorten his prayers even if he stays permanently in the place to which he has journeyed, unless he adopts it as a homeland, whereas the Malikis and Shafi'is hold that the traveler should say the full prayer if he stays for four or more days (Ennami n.d., 124–25).

(10) Ibadis require major ritual purity for fasting, just as it is required for praying, in contrast with other Islamic legal schools that say it is not necessary to bathe before morning. Ibadis also say that grave sins cause the breaking of the fast.

(11) Whereas other legal schools permit a person to make up missed days of Ramadan fasting at any time, Ibadis require the days to be consecutive.

(12) In *zakat* (the alms tax), Ibadis calculate the *nisab* (minimum amount of wealth one must own before one owes *zakat*) on cattle in the same way as for camels, unlike the Sunnis.

(13) The person to whom *zakat* is given must be in a state of *walaya*.

(14) Ibadis and Shi'a hold that unlawful intercourse constitutes a permanent impediment to marriage between the two guilty parties, but most Sunnis allow them to marry each other.

(15) Almost all Ibadi scholars held that the property of a *mawla*—a non-Arab taken as client of an Arab tribe—should be inherited by his own people, not by his patron. If he has no relatives, it goes to members of his ethnic group who live in the area. However, this point is moot today, because the system of clientage applied only to the Umayyad period; during the 'Abbasid period, non-Arab Muslims no longer needed to attach themselves to an Arab tribe.

(16) Unlike other Islamic legal schools, the Ibadis impose fixed measures according to which compensation must be paid for inflicting bodily injuries less grave than homicide, rather than leaving it up to the discretion of the judge or the victim.

(17) Like the Twelver Shi'a but unlike the Sunnis, Ibadis allow a man to be killed in retaliation for the death of a woman, provided that the woman's guardian pays the family of the man half the blood money that would have been required if the man had been murdered.

(18) Like the Sunnis but unlike the Twelver Shi'a, Ibadis regard temporary marriage (*mut'a*) as unlawful.

Finally, one might also note that whereas theology, *fiqh* (jurisprudence), and mysticism are generally separate domains in Sunni Islam (though one may well be competent in all three), there is not such a neat separation among them in Ibadi literature. A title like *Qamus al-Shari'a* (al-Sa'di 1983–89), for example, would lead one to think that it deals entirely with law, but in fact it is a compendium of all types of religious knowledge—theological, legal, ethical, and mystical. Likewise, Nasir b. Abi Nabhan's discussion of the ways to know God merges law, theology, philosophy, and mysticism (1848, 48–53), and al-Rawahi in his text often crosses boundaries into matters of philosophy, law, and rhetoric.

Nasir al-Rawahi, Author of *Al-ʿAqida ʾl-Wahbiyya*

Our writer, Nasir b. Salim b ʿUdayyam al-Rawahi, is better known in Oman as Abu Muslim al-Bahlani, Oman's masterful poet. "Al-Rawahi" refers to his belonging to the large tribe of Banu Rawaha, while "Bahlani" refers not to the city of Bahla but to a subgroup of the Banu Rawaha. "Abu Muslim," "the father of Muslim," was an appellation that did not refer to his son's name, but was favored by our author as a symbolic representation of his attachment to Islam. Nasir al-Rawahi was probably born in 1277/1860,[35] son of Shaykh Salim b. ʿUdayyam al-Bahlani al-Rawahi, who became governor and judge of the crucial city of Nizwa during the short-lived imamate of ʿAzzan b. Qays, which stands out in the minds of some Ibadis, including Nasir al-Rawahi, as a great triumph of Muslim ideals against the evils of tyranny, obliterated only with the assistance of infidels who want nothing more than to destroy Islam. As we have seen, the drama was repeated in the early twentieth century with the movement to establish a new imamate under Salim b. Rashid al-Kharusi, a movement that al-Rawahi enthusiastically supported with his poetry, likening his role vis-à-vis that movement to the poet Hassan b. Thabit's role vis-à-vis the Prophet during Muhammad's lifetime.

The late nineteenth century was a period of political unrest and economic hardship in Oman, leading many wealthy Omanis to emigrate to East Africa, where Zanzibar had become a wealthy town and center of Islamic learning. Among the émigrés was Nasir al-Rawahi's father, who became a judge in Zanzibar when Nasir was a young man. Nasir joined his father there in 1295/1878, and although he returned to Oman for a five-year period in 1882, he returned to Zanzibar and remained there until his death on 2 Safar 1339/14 October 1920.

35. There are three different reports on the date of his birth: 1273 /1856, 1277/1860, and 1284/1867, but the middle date appears to be most likely, both because that is the date given by his grandson, according to Ahmad b. Saʿud al-Siyabi's introduction to al-Rawahi (2001, 1:7 in footnote), and because he was circumcised in Nizwa during the brief imamate of ʿAzzan b. Qays, 1868–1871, according to al-Mahruqi (1999–2000, 65).

Some have speculated that Oman seemed too isolated or rigid an environment to someone used to the cosmopolitan intellectual atmosphere of Zanzibar.

Al-Rawahi became a poet and judge of great renown. With Nasir b. Sulayman al-Lamki, he founded and edited the first Arabic newspaper in Zanzibar, *Al-Najah,* in which he expressed his opinions on many of the issues confronting Muslims around the world in his day. His support of Egyptian conferences on pan-Islamism and the *salafi* ideas of Muhammad ʿAbduh needs to be considered as a counterbalance to the ideas expressed in this *ʿAqida,* which appear to rigidly exclude non-Ibadis from the community of true Muslims, although they remain among the *ahl al-qibla.* Al-Rawahi was known as the best scholar in the Arabic language in Zanzibar, and was sought out by Sunni as well as Ibadi students (Farsy 1989, 170, 180).

Al-Rawahi is also considered a great mystic—al-Siyabi (introduction to al-Rawahi 2001, 1:7) described him as "one of the people of secrets and the doyen of poetry as well as a great scholar of jurisprudence"—and indeed many of his poems express his mystical inclinations. He is said to have foretold events that would happen in the future and to have performed other miracles. Yet at the same time he appears to have been a modest, generous, and unassuming man.

Although al-Rawahi authored two major works of prose in addition to his many poems, his prose works until recently remained unpublished, whereas his *Diwan* has been published on three separate occasions, in various forms (al-Mahruqi 1999–2000, 46–63). It is an interesting fact that both his major prose works, *Nithar "al-Jawhar,"* a commentary on Nur al-Din al-Salimi's poetic summary of Ibadi jurisprudence, *Jawhar al-nizam fi ʿilmayy al-adyan wa-'l-ahkam,* and the current work, *Al-ʿAqida 'l-Wahbiyya,* were never completed. According to al-Siyabi (introduction to al-Rawahi 2001, 1:19), al-Rawahi intended *Jawhar al-nizam* to be twenty-two volumes long, but he completed only three, though the manuscript has been published in five volumes. The lack of completion of *Al-ʿAqida 'l-Wahbiyya* may be inferred from the abruptness of its ending, appearing to be at the beginning of a new subject, and lacking the usual author's notes on the date of completion. The manuscript copiers recognized the incompleteness of the work by noting, "This is all I found," and they all stop at the same point. It appears that al-Rawahi did not succeed in being as brief as he had intended, for in his introduction to the text he states that he intends this primer as the briefest of introductions for beginning students of theology.

Al-ʿAqida ʾl-Wahbiyya: Structure and Topics

This primer in Ibadi doctrine, published here in English for the first time, was written in a largely Shafiʿi-Sunni environment. It might have been intended as an Ibadi counterpart to a Sunni text with a similar purpose, written by the fifteenth-century North African scholar, Muhammad b. Yusuf al-Sanusi, who synthesized and popularized doctrines that had been taught through "long treatises containing endless digressions on metaphysical concepts and logical points which few could read" (Kenny 1970; Bencheneb 1999). Sanusi's short creed was the main theological text that Sunni students memorized in Africa and in the Hadramawt, the desert valley of southeast Yemen that historically had the most direct impact on religious life on the East African coast and is credited with the Islamization of East Africa and southeast Asia, where the dominant school of Islam is Shafiʿi, and many of the important religious scholars were of Hadrami origin. Until the twentieth century, Ibadi students faced a quandary similar to that of Sunni students in the fifteenth century: Ibadi doctrine needed to be learned through books that were long, complicated, and difficult to read. In response to the aversion many students had toward Abu Saʿid al-Kudami's classic work, *Kitab al-Istiqama,* because of its length and repetitiveness, the chief Ibadi judge of Zanzibar, ʿAli b. Muhammad al-Mundhiri, composed *Nahj al-haqaʾiq* (1896). It is likely that similar factors led al-Rawahi to compose *Al-ʿAqida ʾl-Wahbiyya.*

Al-Rawahi's primer is impressive for its coverage of many different schools of Islamic theology—Sunni, Shiʿi, Muʿtazili, and Khariji—as well as differences between the Ibadis of North Africa from those of "the east"—Oman and Zanzibar. Clearly, the main adversaries with whom Ibadis have to contend in the modern world are the Sunnis. On the Swahili coast in the second half of the nineteenth century, many Ibadis converted to Sunni Islam, making the exposition and defense of Ibadi doctrines imperative (Hoffman 2005a). It is al-Rawahi's coverage of divergent Muslim interpretations, in addition to the relative neglect of Ibadi doctrine in modern scholarship, that makes *Al-ʿAqida ʾl-Wahbiyya* such an important and interesting text. In this relatively brief introduction to Ibadi doctrine, al-Rawahi on the one hand simplifies and elucidates doctrines that must otherwise be gleaned from massive, dense, and often difficult texts; on the other hand, he provides a thorough and fascinating discussion of the doctrines of many other Muslim groups, past and present, on the points at hand, including the differences between the two major schools of Sunni theology, the Ash'arites and the Maturidites. Because Ibadis must defend doctrines that set them apart from other Muslims, they retain an interest in such questions as the relationship between God's essence and attributes, the distinction between the name and what is named, and the creation or eternity of the Qur'an—questions that have long ceased to interest Sunni Muslims. The resemblance of some of their doctrines to those of the Mu'tazila, whose works have rarely survived destruction at the hands of the defenders of Sunni orthodoxy, adds to the interest scholars should have in Ibadi theological works, although, as already noted, Ibadism diverges from Mu'tazilism on a number of important points, and agrees with Ash'arism on the important question of predestination.

Another theological primer with which al-Rawahi's work might be compared is Nur al-Din al-Salimi's *Mashariq anwar al-'uqul* (A. al-Salimi 1995b).[36] Al-Salimi was the leading Ibadi scholar of Oman during most of al-Rawahi's lifetime, preceding al-Rawahi in death by only six years. *Mashariq anwar al-'uqul* is actually a commentary on a theological poem al-Salimi had written earlier, entitled *Anwar al-'uqul*. It was very common in much of classical Islamic culture to write textbooks in the form of poetry for mnemonic purposes, and then to write commentaries on one's own poem. Many of the scholars of Zanzibar, both Sunni and Ibadi, even wrote letters to one another in the form of poetry, and one Sunni scholar, 'Abd al-'Aziz al-Amawi, wrote extensive diaries of his travels in the African mainland on behalf of Sayyid Barghash in the form of poetry, with a prose commentary written underneath (Hoffman 2006). Some of this poetry can be seen as a kind of conceit; there is no need to render personal letters or diaries in poetic form, except to demonstrate one's skill. Al-Rawahi himself was a superb poet—Muhammad b. Yusuf Atfayyish called him "the poet of the Arabs," and as

36. This celebrated Ibadi text was first published in Cairo in 1314/1896–1897 at the expense of the sultan of Zanzibar, Sayyid Humud b. Muhammad b. Sa'id, but this copy is now very rare and, oddly enough, it fails to note that al-Salimi is the author! Harvard University has a copy, but lists Sayyid Humud as the author, and the University of Minnesota has a copy, but lists Ahmad b. Sumayt, a prominent Shafi'i scholar in Zanzibar, as the author, a confusion apparently caused by the book's inclusion of a laudatory biography of Sayyid Humud written by Ahmad b. Sumayt and placed at the beginning of the book. However, a comparison of the Damascus edition of al-Salimi's *Mashariq* with the Cairo edition makes it clear that this is the same book.

such he is often referred in Oman today—but most of his pedagogical writing has been done in prose. Al-Rawahi's primer is written in the form of a student's questions and a teacher's answers, a technique that is not very common in Muslim textbooks. A number of important early Muslim texts, like al-Shafi'i's *Risala* in jurisprudence and al-Ash'ari's *Kitab al-luma' fi 'l-radd 'ala ahl al-zaygh wa-'l-bida'*, used the technique of a dialogue with an imagined opponent. There are also many books on Islamic theology and other topics in the form of a student's questions and the teacher's answers, but in these cases these are renditions of actual interviews a student had with his famous teacher and are written by the student (e.g., S. al-Khalili 1987). Al-Rawahi's text, however, takes a form somewhat like a Catholic catechism and is not a recording of any actual dialogue. Furthermore, it is not the student who is writing the book, but the teacher.

In terms of topic coverage, al-Rawahi's primer is similar in many ways to al-Salimi's *Mashariq anwar al-'uqul.* Both of them talk about the types of knowledge, the ways to know, and what one must know to be a good Muslim. They both analyze the *jumla,* the basic statement of faith that adds to the *shahada*—the statement that "there is no god but Allah and Muhammad is the messenger of Allah"—the statement that "what Muhammad brought [the Qur'an] is true." They speak of God's incomparability, His attributes, and so forth, in very similar terms. They treat the topics of faith and infidelity, association and dissociation, at length. Both books treat the opinions of varied Muslim groups, including such Muslim philosophers as Abu Nasr Muhammad al-Farabi (d. 339/950) and Abu 'Ali al-Husayn b. 'Abdallah b. Sina (known as Ibn Sina or Avicenna, 370–428/980–1037). But there are differences, too: al-Rawahi analyzes at length the relationship between a name and what is named, and he discusses non-Muslim religions and how Muslims should interact with non-Muslims of different religions. Al-Salimi's coverage of the topic of free will versus predestination is not very long, but it is highlighted more than in al-Rawahi's text. On the other hand, as already noted, al-Rawahi's text is incomplete, probably because the author died before he could complete it.

Al-Rawahi says he composed this work for beginning students, but considering the obtuseness of the questions it entertains, one may surmise that it is a text intended for students who today would be in secondary school or in their first year of seminary. The clarity with which he explains essential theological and philosophical concepts makes this text valuable for pedagogical purposes even today, when few students would have the competence to plunge into more complex works of theology. His reasoning on basic issues like the proofs for the existence of God as the Necessary Being, the First Cause, and the only eternal are standard Aristotelianism, no different from those of Ash'arite Muslim theologians since the twelfth century CE.

One of the striking features of this work, and of other Islamic texts written in the classical style, is its apparent divorce from contemporary realities: keeping to a traditional genre and mode of argumentation, it reflects the situation at the time of the emergence of the sect. Al-Rawahi discusses the ideas of such long-extinct schools of thought as the Karramiyya and the Mu'tazila as if they were still important; he discusses the way in which Muslims should treat Christians as if Christians were a subjugated population wearing the dress they wore in the Middle Ages, utterly ignoring the fact that he was writing in a land administered through the British Colonial Office. Indeed, the pressing issues of the day for Muslims in Zanzibar had nothing to do with how to deal with subject Christian populations, but how to deal with the influence of a foreign power whose styles and way of life were increasingly appealing to Muslims. This is not altogether surprising, as works of jurisprudence preserve an ideal that was formulated in the early days of Muslim ascendancy. Although the present work is more concerned with theology than with jurisprudence, the definitions of the categories of belief and unbelief and the concepts of association (*walaya*) and dissociation (*bara'a*), far more fundamental to Ibadism than to other schools of Islamic thought, need practical description that runs into the realm of jurisprudence.

Translation of al-Rawahi's Creed

When I read al-Rawahi's creed in 2000–2001, no scholars with whom I spoke were aware of any publication of the Arabic text. I have since learned that a lithograph was first produced by al-Matba'a 'l-Baruniyya in Cairo (no date provided), and it was again published in Beirut by Dar al-Fath (1974) and by the Ministry of National Heritage and Culture (1992, 1999), although these editions are no longer in print. Since then, the work was edited in a very cursory fashion by Sultan b. Mubarak al-Shaybani and published by Maktabat Musqat (2003), and again by the same publisher with an extensive commentary by Salih b. Sa'id al-Qunubi and ʿAbdallah b. Saʿid al-Qunubi (2004). I also edited the Arabic text, comparing the four manuscripts described at the end of this introduction, but my edition has not been published.

I have relied on three handwritten manuscripts of *Al-ʿAqida ʾl-Wahbiyya,* two from the library of His Highness, Sayyid Muhammad b. Ahmad b. Saʿid Al Bu Saʿidi, in Sib, Oman, and one at the Ministry of National Heritage and Culture (now the Ministry of Heritage and Culture, *Wizarat al-Turath wa-ʾl-Thaqafa*) in Muscat. There are no significant variations between these manuscripts.

The oldest and most consistently reliable of the manuscripts (Al Bu Saʿidi no. 1651 *ʿayn,* 181 pages, dated 8 Jumada ʾl-Ula 1343/5 December 1924) was copied by Salim b. Sulayman, who states that he checked his manuscript against the author's own copy. In this book, this manuscript will be referred to as SA.

The second manuscript (Al Bu Saʿidi no. 270 *ʿayn,* 111 pages, dated 20 Ramadan 1380/8 March 1961) was copied in a notebook by Sayf b. Musallam b. Nujaym, who claims that no one had previously copied it, though this is obviously an error. This copy will be referred to as N.

The third manuscript (Ministry of Heritage and Culture no. 2443, 191 pages, dated 5 Dhu ʾl-Hijja 1351/1 April 1933) was copied by Abu Muhammad Ahmad b. Sulayman b. Zahran al-Riyami, and will be referred to as R.

Finally, in 2001, the manager of the Al Bu Saʿidi Library also showed me an unnumbered, edited copy, typed on a word processor and printed, although it was never published. It was edited by Shaykh Sayf b. Muhammad b. Sulayman al-Farisi, a teacher at the Institute of Shariʿa Studies in Muscat, from an annotated copy done by one of his students, Salih b. Saʿid b. Nasir al-Qunubi. This copy is extremely flawed, having numerous errors and omissions in the text. Nonetheless, it was useful for the footnotes providing references to Qur'anic verses, hadiths, and the works of Muhammad b. Yusuf Atfayyish and other Ibadi authors. It also provided titles to the chapters, which are untitled in the original, and I have used these titles in my translation. This copy will be referred to as F. The 2004 edition of *Al-ʿAqida ʾl-Wahbiyya,* published by Salih and ʿAbdallah al-Qunubi, also used these titles, so presumably Salih al-Qunubi devised them in the first place. Most of the errors that appear in F are not found in the Qunubi publication.

As the text is in the form of a student's questions and a teacher's responses, for the sake of brevity the student is indicated by S, and the teacher by T.

ʻAbd al-ʻAziz al-Thamini, Author of *Kitab Maʻalim al-din*

As indicated earlier, the omission of significant discussion of the doctrine of predestination in al-Rawahi's text led me, for purposes of completeness, to translate the passages on this subject that are found in *Kitab Maʻalim al-din* by "Diya' al-Din" ʻAbd al-ʻAziz b. al-Hajj b. Ibrahim b. ʻAbdallah b. ʻAbd al-ʻAziz al-Thamini al-Musʻabi (1130–1223/1718–1808), one of the first scholars of the modern Ibadi renaissance. Raised in the town of Bani Yazqin (Beni Isguen) in the Mzab valley,[37] he moved to Wargla (Ouargla), about 170 km (106 miles) away, to take charge of his father's property there. There he studied with Abu Zakariya Yahya b. Salih al-Afdali (d. 1202/1787), alongside whom he devoted himself to "the battle of reforming society, for which he suffered greatly, for that was the beginning of the movement for social reform in the Mzab valley, which continued afterward until the time of Shaykh Bayyud Ibrahim" [b. ʻUmar, 1313–1401/1899–1981] (Ba Ba ʻAmmi et al. 1999, 2:255–56 [no. 555]). In 1201/1786 he became head of the leadership council (*ʻazzaba*), but later resigned from this position in order to devote himself to teaching, writing, and issuing *fatwas*. It is said that he did not leave his home for a period of fifteen years unless it was necessary. Among his chief works of scholarship are *Al-Taj al-manzum min durar "al-Manhaj" al-maʻlum*, a poetic commentary on *Manhaj* [or *Minhaj*] *al-talibin wa-balagh al-raghibin* by Khamis b. Saʻid al-Shaqsi, and *Kitab al-Nil wa-shifa' al-ʻalil*, described as "the pillar of the school in jurisprudence" (ibid.). The greatest of the Ibadi reformers, Muhammad b. Yusuf Atfayyish, wrote a lengthy commentary on *Kitab al-Nil* (Atfayyish 1924–25), and Ibadi scholars have written some thirty summaries or abbreviated versions of it.

Because the published version of *Kitab Maʻalim al-din* is somewhat readily available (al-Thamini 1986), I have inserted the page numbers from the published edition in brackets, so that Arabists who wish to compare this translation with the original may do so. There are, however, many problems with the published text: the insertion of punctuation and paragraphs bears little relation to meaning, and

37. According to Rouvillois-Brigol and Mercier (1999), the Mzab valley is about 500 km (311 miles) from Algiers as the crow flies, about 600 km (373 miles) by road. "Al-Musʻabi," added as an identifier to al-Thamini's name, simply means that he hailed from the Mzab.

there are a number of obvious typographical errors. Another problem with this publication is that it contains a "conclusion" that is clearly written by an Ash'arite rather than an Ibadi: it describes the sects of Islam that are damned (including the Ibadis) and the one that is saved, identified as the Sunnis (*ahl al-sunna wa-'l-jama'a*). Obviously, al-Thamini is not the author of this conclusion!

In order to clarify the use of Ibadi terminology, or my translation of common theological terms, the Arabic words are often placed in transliteration in parentheses after their English translations. If English explanation is added that is not part of the original text and is not put in a footnote, these additions have been placed in brackets.

PART TWO

Al-'Aqida 'l-Wahbiyya

Nasir b. Salim b. 'Udayyam al-Rawahi

Author's Introduction

In the Name of God, the Compassionate, the Merciful

Praise be to God, the One whose existence is necessary by virtue of His essence, the Holy One who is exalted beyond all comparison in His essence, His names, and His acts. May God bless our master Muhammad, His Messenger and the seal of His messengers, the most perfect of His creations, and grant peace to him, his family, his Companions, his children, and his wives.

This is the doctrine (*'aqida*) of the people of straightness (*ahl al-istiqama*). I have abbreviated it for the sake of beginning students, and I have made it in the form of a student's questions and a teacher's answers, examining the most important doctrines that must be believed, while taking care to keep it extremely brief. God is the One who gives aid and insight.

Chapter 1

THE KNOWLEDGE OF GOD'S UNITY

Lesson 1: The Science of Theology (*'ilm al-tawhid*): Its Nobility and of What It Consists

S: Dear teacher, I have come to rely on your guidance. You are a father to my intellect, training me to become a true human being and servant of God, as He desires. You wish to place me before God in the ranks of the righteous. There is no doubt that the useful sciences include those pursued for the sake of things other than themselves (*fi 'l-'ulum al-nafi'a ma huwa maqsud li-ghayrihi*) as well as that which is pursued for its own sake. Undoubtedly something that is pursued for its own sake is nobler than something that is pursued for the sake of something else. Isn't it true that the latter is but a means to the former?

T: Yes, my son, you have hit upon the heart of the matter (*al-fass wa-'l-nass*). "I only wish to reform you as much as I can, and I can have no success unless it is given by God" (Q 11:88). God has enabled you to see the nobility and importance of the science that is pursued for its own sake, so do not go without it, but bind your ambition to it and throw off all impediments, for it is the science of the highest rank and virtue, the most beneficial, useful, and worthy of persistent study.

S: How thirsty I am (*ma a'tash kibdi*) for this science! What is it, then, so I may turn my efforts and time to it?

T: It is the science of theology (*'ilm al-tawhid*), also called (*al-mu'abbar 'anhu bi*) the science of discourse (*'ilm al-kalam*).[1]

1. The term *'ilm al-kalam* (literally, "the science of discourse/speech/debate"), traditionally used to mean speculative theology in Islam, appears to derive from the fact that theology emerged out of and in the form of debates on matters of faith. Ibadis prefer to use the term *'ilm al-tawhid*.

S: Of what does this noble science consist?

T: This science consists of the affirmation of the existence of the eternal Maker (*ithbat al-sani' al-qadim*), His unique divinity (*tawhiduhu fi 'l-uluhiyya*), His transcendence beyond all likeness to originated things (*tanzihuhu 'an mushabahat al-hawadith*), His description with the attributes of majesty (*ittisafuhu bi-sifat al-jalal*) and generosity (*ikram*), which are the attributes of greatness (*'uzma*) and beneficence(*ihsan*). [It also consists of] the affirmation of prophethood, which is the foundation (*asas*) of Islam. The laws (*al-shara'i'*) and regulations (*al-ahkam*) [of the Shari'a] are built upon this science, for were it not for the immutability (*thubut*) of the Maker with His attributes, the sciences of exegesis, Hadith, jurisprudence and its roots would not have been formed. By this science one progresses (*yataraqqa*) in faith in the Last Day from the rank of merely imitating the beliefs of others (*min darajat al-taqlid*) to the rank of verification (*iqan*), which is the only cause (*huwa 'l-sabab al-wahid*) of guidance and success (*najah*) in this world, and victory (*al-fawz*) and prosperity (*al-falah*) in the next. It is the science by which you can prove (*ithbat*) religious doctrines (*al-'aqa'id al-diniyya*) to others and compel them to recognize the truth (*wa-ilzamuhu iyyahu*) by bringing forth proofs (*bi-irad al-hujaj*) and countering specious arguments (*daf' al-shubah*).

Lesson 2: The Definition of *Tawhid*

S: What is the literal meaning of *tawhid* (*ma huwa 'l-tawhid lughatan*)?

T: It is a second-form verbal noun (*taf'il*) referring to one who makes a thing one or declares it to be one or unique. *Tawhid* means declaring uniqueness (*tafrid*), which can also be called *ifrad*.[2]

S: What does *tawhid* mean according to Islamic law (*al-shar'*)?

T: It means believing in God's uniqueness (*ifrad Allah*) in His essence (*dhatihi*), attributes (*sifatihi*), words (*aqwalihi*), acts (*af'alihi*), worship (*'ibadatihi*),

2. The difficulty in translation here is that *tawhid*, which we typically translate as God's oneness or monotheism, is a verbal noun carrying a form of causation, literally meaning "making one," but in this case "declaring one." It therefore refers to the believer who holds God to be one, whereas English correlates do not always carry the same reference. The words *tafrid* (also a second-form verbal noun) and *ifrad* (a fourth-form verbal noun, also implying causation) likewise mean to "make unique."

and the rest of His perfections—that is, belief that He is unique in all these aspects (*fi dhalika kullihi*), with nothing else whatsoever sharing in any of His aspects (*bi-ayyi wajhin kana*). It also means affirming (*iqrar*) that and believing that Muhammad is the trustworthy servant of God and His clear (*al-mubin*) Messenger to all human beings and jinn,[3] and that he is the seal of the prophets, and that what he brought is truth from the Lord of all being, and that he delivered the message with which he was sent to people and then was taken to the abode of peace (*qabadahu ila dar al-salam*), where he was received with honor, on whom be the best blessing and peace. One must profess all these things. These are the three matters that are essential to belief and profession of faith when one first reaches puberty.

S: If a person believes this and professes it, what is the judgment [of the law] concerning him (*kayf yakun hina'idhin hukmuhu*)?

T: Then he is a monotheist (*muwahhid*) in the eyes of God and His creation (*'inda 'llah wa-'l-khalq*), and the regulations pertaining to monotheists apply to him (*tajri 'alayhi ahkam al-muwahhidin*), such as giving the greeting of peace and its response,[4] inheriting from close relatives like his father, washing him if he dies, praying over him, burying him with the Muslims, inheriting his wealth, and the prohibition against killing him, plundering his wealth (*ghunm malihi*), and enslaving his children (*sabyi dhurriyatihi*).

S: If he is ignorant of any of the aspects of monotheism or denies it or has doubts about it, what is his condition (*kayfa yakunu haluhu*)?

T: He is an unbeliever in God (*mushrik bi-'llah*), and the regulations applying to him are those that pertain to unbelievers.

3. Prophets are sent to both people and jinn, according to the Qur'an. Human beings and jinn are the two species that are accountable (*mukallaf*) under the law to believe in God and obey Him—one could say they are burdened with the freedom to choose to obey, whereas all other things in creation are naturally submissive to God, although both Sunni and Ibadi Muslims hold to the doctrine of predestination. In the Qur'an the jinn are said to have been created from a flame of fire before Adam's creation from clay (15:27). They are mainly described in very negative terms, but a group of jinn heard a recitation of the Qur'an and became believers (72:1).

4. The greeting of peace, *salam 'alaykum* ("Peace be upon you"), is reserved for Muslims, and one should respond to such a greeting, according to the Qur'an, with an even better greeting (4:86). By convention, the response is *Wa-'alaykum as-salam wa-rahmat Allah wa-barakatuhu*—"And on you be peace and God's mercy and blessing."

S: What must a person profess, believe, and know as soon as he comes of age?

T: He must know that God has a company (*jumla*) of noble angels, on whom be the purest peace. Among them he must single out Gabriel, on whom be peace, and know him by name and affiliate to him (*yatawallahu*) and know that he is God's messenger to Muhammad, on whom be blessings and peace, [bringing him] the religion, the Qur'an and Islam. And he must affiliate to the whole company of angels by seeking mercy for them (*bi-'l-tarahhum*), but not asking for forgiveness of their sins (*duna 'l-istighfar*), because asking forgiveness implies that they have sinned (*li-iham al-istighfar sabqa dhanb*), which is impossible for them. One must act toward them in a manner appropriate to their natures (*yajib la-hum ma yuwafiq taba'i'ahum*).

He must know that God has a company of prophets and messengers and that they are all sons of Adam. Then he must single out (*yaqsid ila*) Adam, the father of humanity, on whom be blessing and peace, and know that he is the first of the messengers. Then he must single out our prophet, Muhammad, peace and blessings upon him, and affiliate to him and know that he is the last of the messengers.

He must know that God has a collection of books (*jumlat al-kutub*), and among these he must single out the Qur'an and draw near to it.

He must know of the existence of death, resurrection (*al-ba'th*), judgment (*al-hisab*), punishment (*al-'iqab*), paradise (*al-janna*), and hellfire (*al-nar*), each by its proper name. And he must know and believe that God has commanded him to obey Him and has prohibited disobedience, and that God has a reward (*thawab*) unlike any other and a punishment unlike any other, and that they never end (*la yanqati'an*) or change (*la yataghayyaran*).

[He must know] that monotheism (*tawhid*) means declaring [God to be] unique (*ifrad*), and that unbelief (*shirk*) means believing He has partners who are equal to Him (*al-musawat*). He must know the difference between sins leading to unbelief (*kaba'ir al-shirk*) and sins leading to hypocrisy (*kaba'ir al-nifaq*), and the prohibition against [shedding] the blood of Muslims, plundering their wealth and enslaving their children, because of their monotheism. He must know about Islam, the Muslims, unfaithfulness (*kufr*), the unfaithful, the necessity of affiliation [with co-religionists] (*walaya*) and dissociation [from others] (*bara'a*), the six non-Islamic religions (*al-milal al-sitt*) and the regulations concerning them, and the unfaithfulness (*kufr*) of the person who is ignorant of any of these things.

[And he must know] that God has required him to know them, and has appointed a reward for knowing them and a punishment for being ignorant of them.

S: If he knows all these things you have mentioned, in addition to the first three [you mentioned], and believes them and professes them and does all that is required of him and abandons all that is prohibited, what is his condition?

T: His faith is complete (*huwa kamil al-iman*) in the eyes of God and of His creatures. And if he is ignorant of it or of any part of it (*shay'an minha*), or denies it or any part of it, or has doubts about it, he is an unbeliever (*mushrik*).

S: If he neglects to do one of the requirements, like performing ritual prayer (*salat*) or paying the alms-tax (*zakat*), because he is disinclined to do them (*tashahhiyan*), not because he believes it to be allowable to neglect them (*la istihlalan*), what is the status of that neglect (*ma manzilat hadha 'l-tark*)?

T: It is a status of hypocrisy. The one who wantonly neglects his obligation (*al-tarik muntakihan*) is a hypocrite, just as if he had committed a prohibited act like adultery, wine consumption, or murder.

S: If he considers permissible something that a text explicitly requires or prohibits, how is he to be judged (*kayfa hukmuhu*)?

T: He is an unbeliever (*mushrik*), because he goes against the explicit meaning of a text by rejecting it.

Lesson 3: The First Obligations a Person Who Is Subject to the Shari'a (*al-mukallaf*) Must Know

S: Obligations must be prioritized, so what is the most important religious obligation?

T: There is disagreement (*ikhtilaf qa'im*) among the community of Muhammad (*al-umma*) concerning the first obligation, but the truth (*al-haqq*) is that the first obligation is knowledge of God Most High and of His oneness (*wahdatihi*), His creation of the world (*sani'iyyatihi li-'l-'alam*), His attributes, and the rest of the things that pertain to His divinity (*sa'ir ahkam uluhiyyatihi*).

S: Is this knowledge received by intellectual reflection (*tu'khadh bi-'l-nazar*) and seeking proofs (*al-istidlal*), or by imitating the beliefs of others (*bi-'l-taqlid*)?

T: Not at all (*kalla*), our scholars agree that it is not permissible to imitate the beliefs of others (*la yajuz al-taqlid fiha 'indana ittifaqan*). The faith of the imitator is of no consequence (*la 'ibrata bi-iman al-muqallid*), for knowledge emerges from proof (*nashi'a 'an al-dalil*), because religion is taken by compelling proof (*taqyidan*), not by imitation (*taqlidan*). But although the faith of the imitator is weak and unworthy of consideration, it is strengthened by learning through the teaching of someone who makes him aware (*munabbih*) that God is eternal (*qadim*) and uniquely one (*munfarid bi-'l-wahdaniyya*) in His essence, His attributes, His acts, and the worship (*al-ma'budiyya*) [that is due to Him]. You know that to affirm this is monotheism (*tawhid*) and to deny it is unbelief (*shirk*), and that the one who knows these or other attributes and abandons [this teaching] is an unbeliever, though not if he is confused, and that the Majestic One (*jalla sha'nuhu*) is unique in divinity and lordship (*munfarid fi 'l-uluhiyya wa-'l-rububiyya*), indivisible (*ghayr qabil li-'l-tajazzu'*), not described by the word "all" (*kull*), and that the Most High (*ta'ala*) is unique in being named with the word of majesty (*lafz al-jalala*) [Allah].

S: What is the way (*al-sabil*) to know the Creator?

T: The way to know the Creator is by knowing existing things and distinguishing between objects of knowledge by knowing that things are of two types (*darban*), either eternal (*qadim*) or originated (*muhdath*). The eternal is God the Majestic (*subhanahu*), who is unique in His oneness, divinity, and lordship. The originated is of two types: body (*jism*) and accident (*'arad*). If you understand (*in adrakta*) by the proofs of dependency (*bi-dalil al-haja*), incapacity (*al-'ajz*), and composition (*al-tarkib*) that everything except God is originated (*hadith*), then you will know (*'ulima*) that the Creator is unlike all other things in that there is nothing He cannot do (*la ya'jiz*) and He needs nothing (*la yahtaj*). If He were like them, He would also need a creator, which would result in an infinitely regressing series [of causes] (*fa-yatasalsalu*) or circular reasoning (*yadur*), both of which are impossible.[5]

5. The proof of dependency is a proof built on the idea that the existence of all originated things depends on the existence of God, who is the cause of their existence. The proof of incapacity is based on the idea that all originated things are sustained by God's power and are unable to sustain their own existence. The proof of composition is based on the idea that all beings except God are composed of parts (e.g., matter and form) and require a cause to bring those parts together. The cause of the existence and composition of all things must itself be simple and uncomposed, because if it were composed of parts it would require another being to cause the combination of its parts. Aristotle had argued that at

S: What is an accident (*'arad*)?

T: An accident is what cannot exist on its own, like light, darkness, color, life, death, stillness, standing, sitting, and other movements.

S: Is an accident visible (*mushahad*)?

T: It is said that it is not visible to us with the eye.

S: What is meant by saying (*ma 'l-murad*) it is not visible to the eye?

T: What is meant is that it cannot be seen independently (*bi-'l-istiqlal*), but can only be seen by means of a body (*bi-wasitat jism*), like light, darkness, and color. Darkness takes shape (*tartasim*) in the air because air is a body, or on a wall or on the ground, for example. This indicates that air is a divisible body and that the human being or the bird in its speed grabs hold of it and is pushed forward. Against those who say that air does not exist and that the darkness in it is nonexistent (*'adam*), neither accident nor body, it is said that it is subject to extinction (*mulazim li-'l-fana'*), in that it does not remain for more than one state (*hal*), for light and darkness vary in each state from what they are in a different state. No state passes over it that does not change (*la tamdi 'alayhi hal illa taghayyar*), although it is not visible to us because of its subtlety (*li-diqqatihi*).

S: What is movement (*al-haraka*)?

T: It is two locations (*kawnan*) at two different times (*fi anayn mukhtalifayn*) in two different places (*fi makanayn*). It can be explained (*bayanuhu*) as transference (*tahawwul*) from one place to another. Both time and place necessarily change, and this change is either acquired (*kasbiyya*) or involuntary (*daruriyya*).[6]

S: What is rest (*sukun*)?

---

the origin of the chain of causation there must be an uncaused cause, or an unmoved mover. Were this not the case, the chain of causation would regress to infinity, which is rationally intolerable. Although Ibadis, like Sunnis, believe God is the direct cause of all things and therefore do not believe in a chain of causation, they employ the argumentation against an infinite regression in the series of causes to argue for the necessity of the existence of a first cause, Who is God.

6. In *kalam* theology, *kawn* is a technical term meaning "location." *Motion* is defined as "a minimum of two consecutive locations," whereas *rest* is "a single location." Human actions are seen as movements created by God in human beings. All acts, whether or not we perceive them as our voluntary acts, are in fact the acts of God, although there is a distinction between acts "acquired" as a result of our choice and "necessary" or involuntary acts, such as shivering.

T: Rest is a single location (*kawn wahid*) at a single time (*fi an wahid*), or if you like, you may say in a single place. Each part of rest is rest (*kull juz' min al-sukun sukun*), so that no one knows its time but God. Likewise, each part of movement is movement, so that no one knows its time but God. Rest is likewise either acquired, which is the rest of someone who is capable of movement, or involuntary, like the rest of inanimate objects (*al-jamad*) or the rest of someone who is incapable of movement because of illness, sleep, or intoxication.

S: What is a body?

T: A body is something that occupies space (*mutahayyiz*). Occupation of space (*al-hayyiz*) concerns direction (*al-janib*) and place (*al-makan*). Something that occupies space (*al-mutahayyiz*) and whose essence has taken a place (*akhadhat dhathuh makanan*) is called a substance (*al-jawhar*), which is different from an accident. Our [theological] opponents (*mukhalifuna*) say that a substance is what cannot occupy space or be divided into parts, like a tiny dot (*al-nuqta 'l-daqiqa*). We reject this definition, because anything that is tiny must have dimensions (*lahu jihat*), and anything that has dimensions occupies space and is also composed of parts (*'iyan fi 'l-tajazzu'*). It can also be divided (*qabil li-'l-qisma*)—that is, it can be seen, although a body may be invisible, like air, if we say that air is a body, though it is the most subtle (*altaf*) of bodies, like the wind. A body might be visible and lifeless, but with a condition resembling life, like soil into which a grain or seed is thrown for planting; or it might be lifeless and without this condition, like rocks and iron; or it could be visible and alive (*hayawan*), crawling and walking but irrational, like the beasts (*al-baha'im*) and all other things that have spirit (*dhawat al-arwah*); or it can be rational and accountable, like the angels, jinn, and human beings (*al-bashar*). There is no doubt that the prophets see the angels and jinn, as can any of God's servants whom He wishes.

S: Look what you are saying, dear teacher! Don't you know (*alaysa amamaka*) the words of the Most High, that "he [Satan] and his tribe watch you from a position where you cannot see them" (Q 7:27)?

T: Do you think I can fall into a trap from which I cannot escape (*ahsunu 'l-sadr minhu*)? The meaning of the verse is that you cannot see them whenever you wish or whenever they are present, but you can see them through your imagination or in reality some of the time, as proved by incidents of this kind—not as al-Shafi'i says, that they are never really seen (*la yuhaqqaqun qat'an*).

S: Do the angels and jinn see each other?

T: Indeed (*ajal*), the angels see each other and the jinn see each other.

S: Why do you describe the angels as crawling and moving, though they are not flesh and blood?

T: The attribution of crawling and moving does not depend on flesh and blood. No doubt or problem is caused by describing the angels in this way, for they have been described as walking and flying.

S: I see you have placed the angels in the category of animals (*hayawan*).[7]

T: Yes, they are unquestionably *hayawan* in the comprehensive meaning of the word: any creature in whom life inheres (*man hallat fihi al-hayat*) is a living creature (*hayawan*), not dead or inanimate—not in the sense that they are animals who are nourished by material substances and whose natures are full of desires.

S: Why are humans and jinn called "the two heavy burdens" (*al-thaqalayn*) (Q 55:31)?

T: The meaning is that they are burdened with subjection to the law (*al-taklif*), which because of its difficulty is likened to a heavy thing with which they are burdened. Or it might mean that they have burdened the earth with their sins and deeds and the things they have made. It is also said to be because of the weightiness of their opinion.

S: If the meaning of the appellation (*wajhu 'l-tasmiya*) is that they bear the burden of accountability, which because of its difficulty is likened to a heavy thing with which they are burdened, are not the angels also accountable? What is the meaning of accountability other than taking the burden of something for which one is accountable? So how are they excluded from this appellation?

T: The angels are accountable in the sense that they are ordered and prohibited, but in their case that order and prohibition do not weigh them down and are not difficult for them, regardless of its form, extent, or manner; for them, fulfilling God's commands is comparable to (*fi darajati*) what it would be like for us, the two burdened groups, to fulfill our pleasures and desires. Their accountability means that they are commanded and prohibited, but it does not mean that it is heavy or difficult for them. So understand (*fa-'fham*).

7. The teacher had said that angels, jinn, and human beings belong to the category of *hayawan*, a word that can mean "living" or "animal."

S: Is it possible to imagine that the angels and rational, mature animals (*al-hayawan al-'aqil al-baligh*) could be unaware of their accountability?

T: Certainly not (*kalla*)! Divine wisdom (*al-hikma 'l-ilahiyya*) does not allow a rational, mature being to be heedless of the responsibility to worship its Lord according to its capacity and ability (*kama fi was'ihi wa-taqatihi*), just as the divine wisdom does not entail obligating any person or thing that is not rational (*man la ya'qil wa-ma la ya'qil*).

S: Where does immunity from error reside (*ayna mahall al-'isma*) among those who are accountable?

T: It resides in the prophets and the angels.

S: Can an act of disobedience be attributed to one who is immune from error (*hal tudaf ila 'l-ma'sum ma'siya*)?

T: Not like the acts of disobedience committed by those who do not have immunity, though God has described (*wasafa*) some of them as disobeying (*bi-ma'siya*), such as Adam, on whom be peace. It is said that some of the angels were described as disobeying, but they are immune from death without faithfulness (*ma'sumun 'an al-mawt bi-la wafa'*). There are also others who sinned (*adhnaba ghayruhum*) who have been specifically identified (*man nussa 'ala annahu*) as belonging to the people of affiliation (*walaya*), but they are immune from dying without faithfulness. Some reject this opinion (*rudda hadha 'l-qawl*) because God said, "They [the angels] do not disobey God in what He has commanded them," and so forth (Q 66:6). This objection has been rebutted (*ujiba*) by pointing out that what is meant (*al-murad*) by the disobedience that God excluded from them (*nafaha 'anhum*) is not the same as the disobedience that has been referred to. What is possible for them is something that is appropriate for them to disagree with [like when they objected to God's announced intention to create human beings as viceroys on earth], saying, "Will you place there one who will do corruption in it and shed blood?" (Q 2:30), because it has been reported (*warada*) that one angel fell from his original rank (*ba'dan minhum saqata 'an darajatihi*), and the plumage of another was removed from him (*ba'dan suliba rishuhu*), and one of the prophets interceded on his behalf (*shafa'a fihi*).

Lesson 4: The Three Statements of Faith

S: What text indicates (*ma 'l-dall*) the first three teachings?

T: They are mentioned in the statement by which the Messenger of God, may God bless him and grant him peace, calls people to faith (*hiya 'l-jumla 'llati yad'u ilayha*): the testimony that there is no god but Allah alone, without partner (*wahdahu la sharika la-hu*), that Muhammad is His servant and His messenger, and that what he brought is truth from God (*haqq min 'inda 'llah*).

S: Explain the statement to me (*awsi'ni bayanan 'an al-jumla*).

T: The two testimonies and the statement are obligatory (*fard*) on everyone who is accountable. Each of them is monotheism, and their exegesis is monotheism (*kulluha tawhid wa-tafsiruha tawhid*)—that is, each is one of its characteristics because (*bi-ma'na annahu*) monotheism exists only with it, because it is a condition of its existence, or a part of it. To use the term "monotheism" for a characteristic of it is a metaphorical allusion (*majaz mursal*) related to (*'alaqatuhu*) its necessity (*al-luzum*) or its completeness (*al-kulliyya*) and incompleteness (*al-juz'iyya*), together or separately, like naming a conditional thing after the condition that makes it necessary, or like applying the name of the whole to the part. Monotheism is conditional, and this characteristic and others like it (*wa-nahwaha*) are a condition of it. Or [one could say that] monotheism is a whole and the characteristics are parts of it, as stated earlier (*kama marra*). You may draw an analogous conclusion (*qis 'ala hadha*) with everything you come across (*jami'u ma yaridu 'alayka*) that is said to be monotheism (*tawhid*).

S: This is fixed in my mind (*laqad taqarrar hadha min dhihni*). Is it necessary for an accountable person to know that "there is no god but Allah" is monotheism?

T: Indeed (*haqqan*), he must know that it is monotheism.

S: Must he know that the testimony that Muhammad is the messenger of God and that what he brought is truth from God is [an essential part of] monotheism?

T: The predominant answer (*al-rajih*) is that he does not need to know this [as an essential part of] monotheism, though some say it is necessary to know it as [essential to] monotheism.

S: I have learned from the third lesson that an accountable person is either a believer without immunity from sin or a believer with immunity from sin. Inevitably there must be unfaithfulness (*kufr*) corresponding (*yuqabilu*) to this faith. What are the levels (*maratib*) of unfaithfulness?

T: Unfaithfulness is of two types (*kufran*): the first is the unfaithfulness of hypocrisy (*kufr nifaq*), which is ingratitude for God's blessing (*kufr al-ni'ma*), and the second is the unfaithfulness of unbelief (*kufr shirk*). Unbelief (*shirk*) may be polytheism [*shirk musawat,* literally "unbelief of equality"], which is to ascribe to God, whose majesty is great, partnership with another who is equal in worship, or who is equal to Him in one of His attributes, like eternity (*al-qidam*), or in one of the descriptions of the majesty (*nu'ut jalalihi*) of the Most High. Polytheism (*shirk musawat*) includes rejecting (*inkar*) one of the prophets of God or one of His angels or rejecting a single letter of God's speech (*harf min kalam Allah*). Such rejection is included in polytheism because the denier (*al-jahid*) has equated (*qad sawa*) God with something else in His not sending that prophet or revealing that letter or creating that angel, and polytheism means equating God with something else in worship or equating Him with something else in some other matter. Some say that this rejection is to be included in the unbelief of denial (*shirk al-juhud*). Unbelief of denial is to reject God or a prophet or an angel or a letter of God's Book. Some say that rejection of less than a word (*ma duna 'l-kalima*) from God's speech does not constitute unbelief. Others say that rejection of less than a verse (*ma duna 'l-aya*) of it does not constitute unbelief. The correct interpretation (*al-sahih*) is the first [that rejection of a single letter of God's revelation constitutes unbelief]. Likewise, anyone who rejects a single vowel (*haraka*) or a single place without a vowel (*sukun*) of [God's speech] is an unbeliever,[8] though some reports (*athar*) indicate otherwise, because the vowel and its omission are undoubtedly revealed (*tanzil*), though indeed a person is not to be considered an unbeliever concerning the verses on which there are divergent reports, such as the vowel over the letter *waw* [which also means "and"] before the letter *sin* in the saying of the Most High, "And hasten (*sari'u*) to forgiveness from your Lord" (Q 3:133).

S: What is hypocrisy?

T: Hypocrisy is of two types (*al-nifaq naw'an*). The first is the hypocrite (*sahibuhu*) who affirms the statement of faith and believes in it but commits grave sins (*al-kaba'ir*). This person is an immoral hypocrite (*munafiq fasiq*), deviant (*dall*), sinful (*'asin*), unfaithful (*kafir*) because of ingratitude to God for His blessings (*kufr ni'ma*). If he dies without repenting of his deed and persists in it

8. Since the Arabic alphabet consists entirely of consonants, vowels or their absence are indicated in the text of the Qur'an by marks above or below the letters, but are not themselves considered letters. A *sukun* is a mark above a letter, indicating that it has no vowel.

(*musirran*), he will abide in hellfire forever. The second type is the person who gives the appearance of affirmation with his tongue (*muqirr bi-zahiri lisanihi*) without believing in the statement of faith in his heart (*bi-jananihi*). Such a person is an unbeliever (*mushrik*) concerning what is between him and God, although the rules of Islam apply to him [in the way he is treated in this life], because he appears to be a believer (*bi-hasab al-zahir*). He is promised punishment in the lowest reaches of hellfire (*fi 'l-dark al-asfal min al-nar*) (Q 4:145). Many people in our sect say that this threat applies to all hypocrites, but that is not the case. The Qutb, may God have mercy on him, has a treatise proving that the threat of the lowest reaches of hellfire is reserved for the hypocrite who hides his rejection of the faith or who gives the appearance of observing Islam. The scholars of Egypt requested this treatise of him, and he wrote it for them.

Lesson 5: The Intellect Leads to (*muwassil ila*) [Knowledge of] God's Oneness

S: I know that everything besides the Eternal One (*al-qadim*) is originated (*muhdath*), but what is the indication that the Eternal One is the maker (*sani'*) of the originated (*al-hadith*)?

T: You know this by the judgment of your intellect (*min hukm 'aqlika*). If you realize (*tahaqqaqta*) that everything besides the Eternal is originated, you will also realize by the judgment of your intellect that something that is originated must have an originator (*muhdith*) that originated it (*ahdathahu*), because one of the necessary rules of reason (*min ahkam al-'uqul bi-'l-darura*) is that nothing is made without a maker (*la san'a bi-duna sani'*), and there is no effect (*athar*) without a cause (*mu'aththir*), and that cause and maker which bring the originated thing into existence (*al-mujid al-muhdith li 'l-hadith*) cannot be of the same genus (*jins*) as what is made, or else the result is circuitous reasoning (*illa lazima 'l-dawr*) and a [logically intolerable] endless chain of causes (*al-tasalsul*). This thing that is made (*dhalika 'l-masnu'*) cannot be the maker of itself (*ghayr sani' li-nafsihi*) or it would have to exist before itself and after itself, because the maker must exist before the thing that it makes. So the fact that God is creator (*kawn Allah khaliqan*) entails (*yaqtadi*) His existence prior to what is created (*al-taqaddum 'ala makhluqihi*), and the fact that the creature is created entails its coming into existence later than its creator (*ta'akhkhurahu 'an khaliqihi*). The opposite of this is impossible (*'aksu hadha muhal*), because a nonexistent (*al-'adam*) cannot produce an existent (*la yujid mawjudan*). If we say it is not impossible, we violate our intellects (*kabarna 'uqulana*) and necessitate the conjoining of contradictory propositions (*lazimna ijtima' bayna mutanafiyyayn*). The two contradictions here are equality (*al-istiwa'*) and superiority (*al-rajhan*) without either being superior (*bi-la murajjih*), because the existence of anything other than God is equal to its nonexistence, the time in which it comes into being is equal to all other times, the particular place in which it comes into being is equal to all other places, and its particular attributes are equal to other attributes.[9] So consider this rational judgment (*fa-'nzur hadha 'l-hukm al-'aqli*) and rely on this rational proof (*i'tamid hadhihi 'l-hujja 'l-'aqliyya*).

S: Is this the entire argument [for the existence] of God (*ahadhihi kullu hujjat Allah*)?

T: Not at all (*kalla*), it is not the whole argument [for the existence] of God; it is just a rational argument that proves (*taqum dalilan*) the existence of the eternal Maker, the True Reality (*al-haqq*), who is holy and exalted (*taqaddasa wa-ta'ala*). Our [sect's] argument for God is based on scriptures and messengers; we do not obtain the knowledge of God by reflection (*bi-'l-tafkir*) or out of rational necessity (*al-idtirar*), but rather it is acquired by asking questions and learning.

S: Doesn't it seem (*a-la yazharu*) that reason offers enough proof of God's oneness without the need of someone to call attention to it (*munabbih*)?

T: Indeed (*bala*), it does seem that reason offers enough proof of God's oneness without the need of someone to call attention to it, as the Qur'an explicitly states (*kama nassa 'alayhi al-Qur'an*) by making creatures and creation proof of the [existence of the] Maker. Scriptures and messengers are also proof of that and [also] offer the details of the law (*tafasil al-shar'*).

S: How would the law judge an accountable person who is alone on an island?

T: We say (*'indana*) he has no excuse for unbelief or for being ignorant of what is required of him (*al-fara'id*) even if he has never heard anyone (*wa-law*

9. In other words, without positing the existence of a cause for an originated thing, there is nothing to make the moment or place of origination any different from any other moment or place and thereby create the conditions that would bring the originated object into existence. Therefore, it is necessary to posit a cause/creator for every originated thing. Anything that has no cause or creator must, by definition, have existed from eternity.

lam yasma' min ahad) [teaching him the religion], because the proof of God's existence is evident to all those who are accountable, and the laws have spread by means of God's books and messengers since the time of Adam, on whom be peace, until our own time.

S: If a person [alone] on an island (*sahib al-jazira*) follows one of the old Islamic laws that had been abrogated, is he not excused, since he has not heard of its abrogation?[10]

T: Indeed, he would be excused, and he would remain excused until the proof of the abrogation of that law that he follows reaches him, or proof that something has been added to it.

S: What are the means of knowledge (*ma hiya turuq al-'ilm*)?

T: The means of knowledge are the senses (*al-hawass*), for they comprehend the realities of perceptible things (*fa-tudriku haqa'iq al-mahsusat*) by means of the intellect (*bi-wasitat al-'aql*).

S: What is the intellect?

T: Scholars have a number of definitions for the intellect. The best of these is that it is a spiritual light (*nur ruhani*) by which the soul enables you (*qaddaraka bi-hi*) [to acquire] necessary and theoretical knowledge (*al-'ulum al-daruriyya wa-'l-nazariyya*). Its relationship to the soul (*nisbatuhu ila 'l-nafs*) is like the relationship something has to something else that resembles it. What may be learned from this definition (*ustufid min hadha 'l-ta'rif*) is that it is the soul that comprehends (*al-mudriku huwa 'l-nafs*), and the intellect is only a tool for comprehension (*ala fi 'l-idrak*), as is the case (*wa-mithlahu*) with the rest of the faculties (*baqiyyat al-quwa*). For this reason one scholar said that those who have attained realization (*al-muhaqqiqun*) agree that what comprehends the universals and particulars is the rational soul (*al-nafs al-natiqa*), and that the relationship of comprehension to its faculties is like the relationship of the act of cutting (*al-qat'*) to a knife. It is said that it is a body (*qila huwa jism*), as indicated by its ability to distinguish things (*tamayyuzihi 'l-ashya'*) from each other and remember them (*hifzihi la-hu*), and

10. The text appears to be referring to earlier Islamic laws which were abrogated by a later revelation, such as the allowance of the consumption of alcohol (Q 4:43, 2:219, 5:90) or the prohibition of sexual intercourse even in nighttime during the month of Ramadan (Q 2:187), although the earlier context makes reference to pre-Islamic prophets, whose revelations Muslims also believe are superseded by that of Muhammad.

no created thing can act except a body (*la yakun fa'il min al-khalq illa jisman*), because accidents cannot act (*li-anna 'l-a'rada tastahilu minha 'l-af'al*).

S: What is the locus (*mahall*) of the intellect in the rational human being?

T: It is said that it is lodged in the heart (*mutamakkin fi 'l-qalb*), alternately at rest and in motion. Its movement is its distinguishing between things and its rest is its abandoning the act of distinguishing. It is also said that it is an accident and that it is the acts themselves of distinguishing and knowing (*innahu nafsu 'l-tamyizat wa-'l-'ilm*). According to most scholars of our sect (*'inda jumhuri ashabina*), it is a faculty in the heart, and its rank in relation to it (*manzilatuhu minhu*) is the same as the rank of sight (*al-basar*) in relation to the eye, of hearing (*al-sam'*) in relation to the ear, of smelling in relation to the nose, of tasting in relation to the tongue, and of touching in relation to the body. This opinion is also attributed to al-Shafi'i, and it does not contradict what has been reported of him, that it is a tool that God created for His servants by which they distinguish between things and their opposites, composed (*rakkabaha*) by God in them so they can use it to derive proofs (*li-yastadillu bi-ha*) concerning unseen matters (*'ala 'l-umur al-gha'iba*) by signs (*bi-'l-'alamat*) which God has set up for them (*nasabaha*) as a gift and grace from Him (*mannan minhu wa-ni'ma*), for this tool is the aforementioned faculty. One of the North African shaykhs of our sect said it is a conceptual entity (*ma'nan*) in the heart whose ruler (*sultan*) is in the head (*fi 'l-dimagh*), because most of the senses are located in the head and therefore can be lost by a blow to the head. In this case it is an accident, not a body, because it is called a conceptual entity (*ma'nan*).[11] Malik said it is in the head, as indicated by its loss (*dhahabihi*) when the head is beaten. 'Isa b. Yusuf[12] said that God might assemble it in any human limb except the soles of the feet, though one could argue that if by "might" is meant the lack of impossibility, He is also able to put it in the soles of the feet. One can only say that it is more worthy of being placed

11. *Ma'na* (plural *ma'ani*) is a word with distinct technical meanings in the various branches of the Islamic sciences, and has also been used differently by varied thinkers. Its translation is inherently difficult. Muslim scholars also debated whether a *ma'na* is a body or an accident. See Versteegh et al. 1999.

12. A North African scholar of the sixth/twelfth century who recorded the theological teachings of Marsuksun al-Ṣawini; he does not seem to be independently important (Ba Ba 'Ammi et al. 1999, 2:413, no. 875).

higher (*annahu ahaqq bi-'l-'uluww*), and it seems that 'Isa was refusing to commit himself concerning the location of the intellect, so he said that.

S: Is what may be called the intellect divisible (*hal yanqasimu ma sadaqa 'alayhi musamma 'l-'aql*)?

T: Indeed, it is divisible into [first] what is instinctive (*gharzi*),[13] which is the natural instinct (*al-fitri al-maghruz*) in the human being, which is not acquired (*ghayr al-muktasab*). Accountability hinges on this natural instinct. [Second is] what is acquired, which is specifically for those who have virtue (*khass bi-uli 'l-fadl*), and it is the composite intellect (*al-'aql al-murakkab*), an expression (*'ibara*) for knowledge (*'ulum*) obtained (*tustafad*) from the experiences of going through different situations (*min al-tajarib bi-majari 'l-ahwal*), whether pertaining to this world (*al-dunyawiyya*) or the hereafter (*al-ukhrawiyya*), although it is at a very low state for those whose intellect is limited to the instinctive, which is known as the simple [intellect] (*al-basit*), because it acquires only worldly knowledge (*qasara kasbuhu 'ala 'l-dunyawi*).

S: Does the composite [intellect] become separated from (*yanfakku 'an*) the simple?

T: No, the composite, acquired intellect does not separate from the simple, natural, instinctive intellect, because it is its fruit (*thamratuhu*) and its product (*natijatuhu*), unlike the simple, which does separate from the composite in the sense that if a person has not acquired religious and moral virtues and perfections (*al-fada'il wa-'l-kamalat al-diniyya wa-'l-adabiyya*) by means of his instinctive intellect and remains in his natural naïveté (*sadhajatihi 'l-fitriyya*), he remains devoid of both virtues and base qualities (*baqiya masluba 'l-fada'il maslub al-radha'il*), like an ignorant or stupid person (*ka-'l-jahil wa-'l-ahmaq*). The natural and acquired [intellects] both increase and decrease (*yazidani wa-yanqusani*). It is called "intellect" (*'aql*) because it prevents the soul from going after its desires, like the rope (*'iqal*) that ties the feet of a camel.

S: Into how many categories are the perceptions (*madarik*) of the intellect divided?

T: What the intellect perceives is divided into three categories: [what is] necessary (*wajib*), impossible (*mustahil*), and possible (*ja'iz*).

13. *Gharizi* would be more correct, but the manuscripts clearly use *gharzi*.

Chapter 2

THE KNOWLEDGE OF GOD

Lesson 1: The Roots of Knowledge of God's Oneness (*fi usul ma'rifat al-tawhid*)

S: What is the rationally necessary (*ma huwa 'l-wajib al-'aqli*)?

T: It is what the intellect cannot imagine to be nonexistent.

S: Can you give me some examples of it (*ma mithaluhu*)?

T: Some examples are: the knowledge that for a confirmed act (*li-'l-fi'li 'l-thabit*) there must be an actor, and the knowledge that the one who did that act must have power at the time of the act, which is the totality of all the things on which the act depends—that is, the necessary conditions (*wujud al-shara'it*) and the negation of obstacles (*intifa' al-mawani'*). We do not mean power in the sense of negating frailty (*al-zamana*) and incapacity (*al-'ajz*) before the act, but nonetheless [power] must exist for the act [to occur]. Another example of what is rationally necessary is the knowledge that the one who has this power must also have knowledge; and that the one who has power and knowledge must also have life; and that the one who has life must also have existence. So the act requires power, power requires knowledge, knowledge requires life, and life requires existence.

S: What is the impossible (*ma 'l-mustahil*)?

T: It is what the intellect cannot conceive (*huwa ma la yutasawwar fi 'l-'aql wujuduhu*).

S: What are some examples of it?

T: Some examples of it are the conjunction of two opposites (*ijtima' al-diddayni*), or the existence of a single thing in two places at the same time, or the movement of a body in two directions at the same time, which is implied in the previous examples.

S: What is the possible (*ma 'l-ja'iz*)?

T: It is what the intellect can imagine as either existent or nonexistent (*ma yasihhu fi 'l-'aqli wujuduhu wa-'adamuhu*).

S: What are some examples of it?

T: Some examples of it are creation, death (*al-imata*), and resurrection (*al-ba'th*), insofar as these are possible events (*fi haddi dhatiha*). With regard to their actual occurrence (*amma bi-'l-nazar ila 'l-wuqu'*), they become necessary because of something else, not by any rational necessity.

S: Have scholars [*al-'uqala'*, literally, "rational beings"] classified the types of knowledge people may obtain (*al-'ulum al-wasila ila 'l-'ibad*)?

T: Yes, they have classified them into three categories that they have defined as the ways to obtain knowledge.

S: Tell me what they are (*afidni iyyaha*).

T: I am happy to do so (*abshiru bi-'l-ifada*). The first two, which have already been mentioned, are through impressions made on the senses (*hiss matbu'*) and through the intellect, which gathers information (*'aql majmu'*). The third way is by hearing revelation (*al-shar' al-masmu'*).

S: What is the revelation that is heard?

T: It is what is affirmed by the Book, the Sunna, consensus (*al-ijma'*), and analogical reasoning (*al-qiyas*).[1] The Book is the source of [the authority of] the Sunna (*al-kitab aslu 'l-sunna*), because the Most High said, "He [the Prophet] does not speak from his own desires" (Q 53:3), and because He said, "Take what the Messenger has brought to you" (Q 59:7). The Sunna is the source of [the authority of] consensus, because he, may God's blessings and peace be upon him, said, "My community will never agree on an error (*la tajtami' ummati 'ala dalala*)" (Ibn Maja 2000, no. 4085; al-Rabi' b. Habib n.d., 1:13, no. 39). Consensus is the source of [the authority of] analogical reasoning, because it can only

1. These are the four "roots of jurisprudence" (*usul al-fiqh*) in Islam, and as al-Rawahi explains, the ordering of these roots is very important, as each successive root builds on the one before. The Qur'an ("the Book") is God's word and carries paramount authority, but it has many gaps and ambiguities that must be filled in and explained by what the Prophet Muhammad said and did ("the Sunna"). As there are many and various narrative traditions (hadiths) purporting to be the Sunna, only those that scholars agree are genuine may be used; this is consensus (*ijma'*). Answers to questions for which there is no explicit Qur'anic verse or hadith may be obtained through analogy with a ruling given in the Qur'an or Hadith.

be confirmed by consensus. If a hadith is reported by only a single source, it is reported that he, may God bless him and grant him peace, told Mu'adh, "Draw an analogy between what you do not find in the Sunna and the Qur'an with what is in them (*qis ma lam tajid fi 'l-sunna wa-'l-qur'an 'ala ma fi-hima*)" (cf. Abu Dawud 2000, kitab 23, bab 11, no. 3592). Likewise, [the authority of] consensus is derived from the Book and the Sunna, although not everyone knows the exact place in these two from which it is derived (*mawdi' istinbatihi minhuma*). It is not nullified by a person who denies that it is from those sources. The people of our sect (*qawmuna*) say that what is derived from analogy should not be called revelation (*al-shar'*); the rule (*al-asl*) is that [revelation] is the Book, the Sunna and consensus.

S: Can it—I mean this root—be divided into different rational categories (*hal la-hu—a'ni hadha 'l-asl—ma'qul munqasim*)?

T: Indeed, it is divided into three rational categories.

S: What are these three?

T: The first is the express wording of the discourse (*ma'na al-khitab*), which is what is indicated by the expression (*ma dalla 'alayhi 'l-lafzu*), whether it is literally true (*haqiqa*) or a metaphor (*majaz*), such as your saying, "A lion has come to pray (*ja'a asad yusalli*)," in which the lion is a metaphor for a brave man. This category is called the express wording (*mantuq*).

S: What is the second category?

T: It is the signification (*al-mafhum*) of the express wording of the discourse and is in agreement with it (*al-muwafiq la-hu*). If it is judged to be more appropriate than the express wording of the discourse, it is called the import of the discourse (*fahwa 'l-khitab*). The import is what is understood by way of certainty (*'ala sabili 'l-qat'*), as when the Most High said, "Do not say '*uff*' to them" (Q 17:23).[2] The literal meaning is that it is forbidden to say "*uff*" to them, but it is understood that the prohibition extends to what is worse than that, like beating or cursing or other such things, which are even more prohibited than saying "*uff*."

2. *Uff* is a sound of contempt, and the "them" here is dual, meaning one's parents. The full text of the verse is "Your Lord has decreed that you worship none but Him, and that you be kind to your parents. If either or both of them reaches old age with you, do not say '*uff*' to them and do not rebuke them, but speak to them with honorable speech" (Q 17:23).

The fact that they are even more prohibited leads one to judge that it is best to avoid them because of the severity of their prohibition, a judgment derived from the rule that is more easily expressed (*akhdhan min al-hukm al-ashal al-mantuq bi'-hi*). If what is understood from the express wording of the discourse is equal to it in judgment, it is the sense of the discourse (*lahin al-khitab*), and the meaning of "sense" is that the words allude to something else, as when the Most High says, "Do not eat their wealth" (Q 4:2). What is expressly prohibited is eating, but the passage alludes to all wasteful consumption (*itlaf*), and the prohibition of eating and the prohibition of wasteful consumption are the same. We could say that "eating" is used in the sense of wasteful consumption (*fi mutlaq al-itlaf*), and that it is a metaphor derived (*majaz mursal*) from the use of a phrase with a particular meaning to indicate a broader meaning. This has been expanded upon in works on the roots of jurisprudence, so consult them.

S: What is the third category?

T: It is the indication of the discourse (*dalil al-khitab*)—that is, what is indicated by the words, what judgment the words indicate. This is something that is inferred from the discourse but is not found in the explicit wording. There are eight agreed-upon categories of this type.

S: I feel a great thirst and desire to know these eight categories.

T: The first is restriction (*mafhum al-hasr*), as in "No one stood up but Zayd." The second is description (*mafhum al-sifa*), as in "The man honored the scholar." The third is condition (*mafhum al-shart*), as in "If you come to me, I will honor you." The fourth is limit (*mafhum al-ghaya*), as in "He used your servant until nightfall." The fifth is time (*mafhum al-zaman*), as in "He honored Zayd on Friday." The sixth is place (*mafhum al-makan*), as in "He honored Zayd in the mosque." The seventh is number (*mafhum al-'adad*), as in "Give Zayd ten dirhams." The eighth is name (*mafhum al-laqab*), such as "Honor Zayd."

S: Are all these things that are understood from the text proofs (*a-kull hadhihi 'l-mafahim hujja*)?

T: They are all proofs except for the category of "name." Refer to the detailed elaboration of this subject in volumes on the roots of jurisprudence; this is not its place.

S: I have certainly come to realize the necessity of a cause for an effect and a maker for a thing that is made and that the whole matter depends through rational necessity on a Maker whose existence must be eternal. But explain to me the proof for the necessary eternity of the Necessary Being (*burhan al-qidami 'l-wajib li-'l-wajib al-wujud*), Whose majesty is glorious.

T: The Necessary Being, the sublime God (*jalla sha'nuhu*), must be eternal because of a proof that your intellect will furnish for you (*bi-hujja taqumu 'alayka fi 'aqlika*), and that is that all existents must be either eternal or originated; whenever one of these is excluded, the other is affirmed (*fa-mahma 'ntafa ahaduhuma ta'ayyana 'l-akharu*). Origination (*al-huduth*) is impossible with respect to (*fi haqqi*) the Most High because origination requires an originator, and you know that a thing cannot originate itself, because if the originator is itself originated, it would require an originator. Likewise, if the number [of causes] is finite we have circular reasoning (*lazima 'l-dawr*), which is the dependence of the existence of one thing [A] on the existence of something else [B] that likewise depends on it [A] for its existence, on one level or on several levels (*bi-martaba aw maratib*). The impossibility of such circular reasoning is evident (*istihalat al-dawr zahir*) because it would be necessary for each of the two originating things to precede the other as well as to come into being after the other, which is the conjunction of two mutually contradictory propositions. Indeed, it would be necessary for the existence of each to precede and come after its own existence and for the existence of a thing to depend on itself. All that is impossible, and what leads to an impossibility is impossible. If the number is not finite and each originated thing is preceded by another originated thing, this would necessitate a series of infinitely regressing causes, and that is impossible because it leads to the termination of what has no end, which is unintelligible.

Since by definition (*li-dhatihi*) it is impossible for the Necessary Being to come into being or be originated, the necessity and eternity of His existence are inevitable (*ta'ayyana la-hu wujub al-wujud wa-'l-qidam*). And if it is established (*idha thabata*) that eternity belongs to God alone, then it is established that He is the creator (*badi'*) of the heavens and the earth and all that is in them, and that there is no creator or originator beside Him. The Glorious One (*subhanahu*) said, "Is there a creator other than God, Who provides for you out of the sky and the earth?" (Q 35:4). And the Most High said, "Don't creation and command belong to Him? Blessed be God, Lord of all being!" (Q 7:54).

This leads directly to (*yatafarra'u 'ala*) the affirmation of the uniqueness (*wahdaniyya*) of Him whose majesty is glorious, from both rational proof and hearing revelation. But what establishes definitive proof (*al-hujja*) that forces people to believe and makes it inexcusable for them to disbelieve is revelation, according to the dominant opinion (*'ala 'l-rajih*), as the texts themselves indicate (*kama dallat 'alayhi 'l-nusus*). You know (*wa-qad 'alimta*) that there is no obligation unless there is confirmation in revelation (*la fard illa bi-thubut al-shar'*). Indeed, the existence and uniqueness of the Maker Whose praise is glorious are established from rational necessities (*min daruriyyat al-'aql*), as is evident, but were it not confirmed by revelation, no proof would be brought against us and there would be no reward or punishment.

Lesson 2: The Attributes of the Creator (*al-Bari'*) in *Surat al-ikhlas*

S: What are the types of unbelief (*shirk*) that are negated by the Chapter of Sincere Devotion (Sura 112)?

T: The first is multiplicity (*awwaluha 'l-kathra*), which the Glorious One excludes by saying, "Say: He, God, is One" (Q 112:1). The second are change (*al-taqallub*) and defect (*al-naqa'is*), which the Glorious One denies by saying, "God the Eternal/ Solid" (Q 112:2).[3] The third is that His perfection is too holy to have a cause (*'illa*) or to be caused (*ma'lul*), which God denies by saying, "He does not beget, nor is He begotten" (Q 112:3). The fourth is that He can have no opposites (*al-addad*) or resemblance (*al-ashkal*), which God denies by saying, "And nothing is His equal" (Q 112:4).

S: What is the meaning of "One" (*ahad*)?

T: It means He is unique in His attributes (*al-munfarid fi 'l-sifat*), such as necessity (*al-wujub*) and deserving worship (*istihqaq al-'ibada*). It can also mean that there is no composition (*tarkib*) in Him at all.

S: What is the meaning of "the One" (*al-Wahid*)?[4]

3. *Allahu 'l-Samad* is notoriously difficult to translate. *Samad* is usually translated as "eternal," but it also implies something that is solid as a rock and unchangeable. Yusuf 'Ali (1989) opted to translate this verse as "Allah, the Eternal, Absolute."

4. The distinction between the oneness implied in *ahad* and the oneness implied in *wahid* is so subtle that most Arabs would be at pains to explain it. *Ahad* is sometimes thought to imply not only a denial of others that would share the status of divinity, but also to imply an internal unity in the godhead—a concept sometimes denoted in English by translating *ahadiyya* as "unicity," whereas the meaning of *wahid* implies uniqueness—that Allah is the only God.

T: The only true One is Allah, whose majesty is glorified. Don't you see that any one of us, for example, is composed of two things, body and soul, and is from two things, male and female, and exists by two things, food and drink, and is in two things, night and day, and between two things, earth and sky, and with two things, movement and rest. Therefore, each of us is composed of a number of parts, but our Lord, the True Reality (*al-Haqq*), transcends (*munazzah*) all that.

S: What is the meaning of *al-Samad* [translated earlier as Eternal/Solid]?

T: *Al-Samad* is a name that no one really deserves except our Most High Lord. Its root meaning is "the absolute master (*al-sayyid al-muntaha fi 'l-su'dad*)," and no one besides the Most High is really like that. It is also said that *al-Samad* is the source of appeal in need (*al-maqsud fi talab al-hawa'ij*), referring to the meaning we mentioned earlier, for the master is the source of appeal in need. There are other things that are also said about it.

S: What is the philological root of *ism* ("name")?

T: *Ism* is derived from *sumuw*,[5] which means "loftiness." That is the derivation given by the people of Basra.[6] God the Mighty and Exalted is named (*musamman*) and described (*mawsuf*) for all eternity, before the existence of created things (*qabla wujud al-makhluqat*), after they come into existence (*ba'da wujudiha*) and after they pass away (*ba'da fana'iha*). His act of creating has no impact on His names and attributes. That is the belief of our sect, the people of straightness, and the Ash'arites agree with us on this point.

S: What doctrine opposes this (*madha yuqabilu hadha 'l-qawl*)?

T: The doctrine of the Kufans opposes this; they say that "name" is derived from "sign" (*sima*), meaning a distinguishing characteristic (*al-'alama*). That is the teaching of the Nukkar and the Mu'tazila. They said, "God exists from all eternity without name or attribute, and when He created the creation He came to be described by names and attributes, and when He causes them to pass away He will remain without attribute or name." This is a monstrous error (*khata' fahish*).

5. Most Arabic words are based on a tripartite root, but *ism,* which can mean either "name" or "noun," is based on an older root of only two consonants; hence the disagreement concerning its derivation (Fleisch 1999). Most dictionaries today place *ism* under the tripartite *sim mim alif maqṣura,* associated with the verb *samma,* "to name."

6. Basra, Kufa, and Medina were important centers of learning for the emerging Islamic sciences in the seventh, eighth, and ninth centuries CE.

S: What is meant by "name" (*ma 'l-murad bi-'l-ism*)?

T: If what is meant is the word (*lafz*) itself, then it is other than the thing that is named. If what is meant is the meaning, then it is the same as the thing that is named. This is the explanation: If you say, "I have written 'Muhammad,'" you mean the word (*lafza*) that signifies the person named Muhammad. If you say, "I came to Muhammad," you mean the person indicated by the word "Muhammad." If you say, for example, "Muhammad is standing," "Muhammad" is the subject (*mubtada'*) and "standing" is its predicate (*khabar*). Or if you say, for example, "I saw Muhammad" or "I passed by Muhammad," the grammatical declensions are only carried out on the word "Muhammad," although the states, actions, and meanings all refer to the person Muhammad indicated by the word "Muhammad" upon which the grammatical declensions act. Understand that if you say, for example, "I worship God," then you direct your worship toward the essence of God, not the name signifying the true object of worship. Otherwise you would be worshipping a letter (*harf*), so consider (*fa-tabassar*)!

Lesson 3: The Origin of the Word of the Name of Majesty (Allah)

S: What is the origin of the word of the name of majesty (*ma asl lafz ism al-jalala*)?

T: "Allah" is a name signifying (*'alam 'ala*) the essence of the Necessary Being, because it deserves all perfections.[7] As for its derivation, the scholars have disagreed among themselves. Some say it is derived from the verb *aliha* (to be bewildered), following the vowel pattern of *'alima,*[8] because all creatures are bewildered (*li-tahayyur al-khalq*) concerning His knowledge (*fi ma'rifatihi*) and

7. Allah is seen as the comprehensive name of God, containing within it all the other divine names. This section somewhat follows Atfayyish (1980, 1:55–70, especially 65ff).

8. There are ten different verbal forms that can generally be used to derive verbs from their roots (there are some rare roots that take up to fifteen forms). In addition, Form I verbs (of which both *aliha* and *'alima* are examples) can take different patterns, depending on their vowels. The important thing to note here is that the form or pattern of a word depends on its vowel pattern, not on its root consonants. *Aliha* is derived from the consonantal root *alif lam ha'* ('-L-H), and *'alima* is derived from the consonantal root *'ayn lam mim* ('-L-M), and they have entirely different meanings, but they both use the same vowel structure of *fatha* (a)- *kasra* (i)- *fatha* (a) following their respective consonants. Therefore *aliha* follows the vowel pattern of *'alima*.

greatness. Others say again that it is derived from *aliha,* following the pattern of *'alima,* when a person worships, in an active construction, meaning seeking to worship (*bi-'l-bina' li-'l-fa'il ay talab al-'ibada*). Others say it is a proper name that is not derived from any other word, and that was the opinion of al-Khalil b. Ahmad. It is said that he was seen [after his death] by someone in his sleep and was asked, "What did God do with you?" He replied, "He forgave me for saying that the name of the Most High has no philological derivation."[9] Someone else said something to the effect that (*hasiluhu*) when mention is made of the derivation of the name of the Most High, what is meant is the meaning understood by that name; otherwise, a condition of the derivation of a word would be that it be preceded by something else from which it is derived, but the names of God are not preceded by anything, since they are eternal. The author of *Al-Jawhara*[10] said: "We say that His great names (*wa-'indana asma'uhu 'l-'azima*) and likewise the attributes of His essence are eternal (*kadha sifat dhatihi qadima*)." That is, the majestic names of God that signify His pure essence (*al-dalla 'ala mujarrad dhatihi*), like "Allah," or that describe an attribute (*aw bi-'tibar al-sifa*), like the Knower and the Powerful, are eternal with respect to His being named by them, because He is the one who named His exalted essence by them from all eternity. His essential attributes (*sifatuhu 'l-dhatiyya*) are also eternal and not preceded by nonexistence, although the aforementioned disagreement refers only to the word *ilah,* not to the word of majesty (*lafz al-jalala,* i.e., the name Allah). Al-Qushayri said:

> People may be named and described by all the names of the Most High God with the characteristics they signify—as a person might be described as having power, knowledge or mercy, for example, although there is a huge difference between the eternal attribute and the originated attribute—except this name [Allah, which applies only to God], because it is inherently attached to Him

9. Atfayyish (1980, 1:67) adds a similar story concerning the second/eighth-century grammarian Sibawayhi, that he was seen in a dream after his death and said, "He forgave me for saying that His name, be He exalted, is the most well-known of all things."

10. *Al-Jawhara 'l-farida,* attributed to Abu 'Ali Salim b. Sa'id b. 'Ali al-Sayighi al-Manhi, is a poetic commentary on chapters of the Qur'an. It has never been published, but Oman's Ministry of National Heritage and Culture has a copy written in the author's own hand, dated 1210/1795–1796.

> (*li-'l-ta'alluq duna 'l-takhalluq*); it is suitable as a means of worship (*salih li-'l-tawassul bi-hi ila 'l-'ibada*), but not to be described by what it signifies, since it is divinity, and no one can be named with it except Him. The Most High said, "Do you know anyone worthy of His name?"(Q 19:65). So no one but the Most High may be named Allah, for the negative form of the question [in the verse] implies negation (*fa-'l-istifham inkari*).

Some say that the origin of "Allah" is *ilah* (a god), and that its *hamza* was omitted and elided into the definite article *al-*.[11] The Most High Creator is unique in having this designation; as the Most High said, "Do you know anyone worthy of His name?"(Q 19:65). They made *ilah* a term for any of their objects of worship, and likewise *al-dhat* [the essence]. They called the sun a goddess because they took it as an object of worship. *Alaha* (in the past tense), *ya'lihu* (in the present tense) means to worship; some also say this is true of the fifth form, *ta'allaha*. Therefore, *al-ilah* is the worshipped one. Some say it is from *aliha,* which means to be bewildered, and that He is named by this as an allusion to what 'Ali b. Abi Talib said, "All that is beneath His attributes is bewilderment of attributes, and there the alternating expressions of language go astray." That is, if you think of the attributes of God, you are bewildered by them. That is why it is narrated [from the Prophet]: "Think about the commands of God; do not think about God" (al-Suyuti 1981, no. 3348).Some say it is derived from *wallah* and that the *waw* was replaced by a *hamza,* and that is because every creature is bewildered (*walih*) before Him, either by subjugation (*taskhir*) alone, as is the case with inanimate things and animals, or by subjection and will (*al-irada*) together, as is the case with some people. One of the philosophers said in this regard, "God is the beloved of all things, as indicated by God's words, 'There is nothing that does not celebrate His praise, but you do not understand their praise'" (17:44).

Others say it is derived from *laha* (it was veiled), *yaluhu* (it is veiled), *liyah* (veiling), and that is an allusion to what the Most High said: "Vision cannot grasp Him, but He grasps all vision" (6:103), to which His name *al-Batin* (the Hidden) alludes in the words of the Most High, "The Evident and the Hidden" (57:3).

11. That is, the initial consonant of *ilah* (a god) is *hamza,* which is the glottal stop that occurs at the beginning of any word we spell in English with an initial vowel. It is commonly supposed that in saying "the God," this *hamza* was dropped, so rather than saying *al-ilah,* one says *Allah.*

Furthermore, the word *ilah* should not really be used in the plural, because there is no true object of worship beside Him, although the Arabs in their time of ignorance and polytheism believed that there were other objects of worship, and based on that false claim they gave it a plural, *al-aliha*. The Most High said, "Do they have gods (*aliha*) that can defend them against Us?" (21:43) and "that he [Moses] might abandon you and your gods (*wa-alihataka*)" (7:127). It is also read as "and your worship" (*wa-ilahataka*)—that is, worship of you.[12] Some people say "*lah anta*," meaning "You belong to God," with one of the two *lams* [one of the two *Ls*] removed.

The expression *Allahumma* ("oh God!") is said to be the same as *ya Allah* ("oh God!"),[13] and the letter *ya'* at the beginning was replaced by two *mims* at the end. It is used exclusively in calling on God. It is said that it is tantamount to saying, "Oh God, protector!"; in other words, it is a composite expression.

Abu Sahl, one of the scholars of the faith in the Maghrib, said:

> Jabir b. Zayd said, "The greatest name of God is Allah. Don't you see that he begins everything with it?" And Ibn 'Abbas said concerning the use of the phrase "In the name of God."[14] "That is, he seeks protection in it from everything and every source of fear, and it is his refuge." It is said that "Allah" is the greatest name of God because no one shares it with Him. The Exalted One said, "Do you know anyone worthy of His name?"—that is, resembling him in name and deed. And in the *Mujaz* [of Abu 'Ammar 'Abd al-Kafi] he says, "Allah is the name of the only one worthy of being worshipped." It is said that all the

12. The Qur'anic verse is a quote from Pharaoh's chiefs, who ask him, "Will you leave Moses and his people to spread mischief in the land, and to abandon you and your gods?" Al-Rawahi indicates here that there is an alternative reading of this verse which would change the meaning to indicate that Pharaoh's chiefs asked if he was going to let Moses get away with not worshipping him, Pharaoh. On the question of alternate readings of the Qur'an, see Madigan (2001, 13–52).

13. *Allahumma* is an expression that is frequently used in prayers of supplication and represents a form used uniquely with God, whereas *ya* is used to precede the name of anyone else to whom one is calling.

14. The Qur'an tells Muslims to mention the name of God frequently, and indeed it is customary in Muslim societies to say "in the name of Allah" (*bi-'sm Allah*) before embarking on a journey, beginning to eat, beginning a speech, or indeed before doing anything.

> attributes are built on this name, and all the names revolve around it. Some people say it is taken from the attribute of height or exaltation, as when one says, "The sun is exalted (*lahat*)," when it rises. The scholars disagree whether it is a name that refers to the essence or whether it is derived from an attribute. Some have said it is a name that refers to the essence, for it is inevitable that the essence have a name that would signify it, and upon which all the names of the attributes and characteristics would be based. Some say it is derived from *walah* (bewilderment), because people are bewildered by Him. The Qur'anic verse, "Let him leave you and your gods" (7:127), is also read, "Let him leave you and your worship." From this is derived the expression *yata'allah,* meaning "he worships." It is said that it is from His deserving worship. Al-Rummani said, "The root of your saying 'Allah' is *alih.* The letter *hamza* has been removed and the letters *alif* and *lam* have been put in its place, so the name has become like this as a way of signifying Him. This is the teaching of [the eighth-century grammarian] Sibawayhi and the most proficient grammarians."

That is the end of Abu Sahl's words. In *Sharh* [*al-talwih 'ala*] *al-tawdih* [by Sa'd al-Din al-Taftazani] it is written, "'Allah' signifies the essence that is worshipped in truth. It is said that it is a descriptive word derived from *al-ilaha* (divinity). It is also said (by others) that its root is *laha,* from the Syriac, and the final *alif* was removed in its Arabization, and then *alif* and *lam* were put at the beginning."

Someone else said:

> Know that since rational minds are lost in the essence and attributes of God because they are veiled by the great lights and veils of omnipotence, likewise they are bewildered concerning the word "Allah" which signifies this holy essence, because something of the rays of these lights touches it, so minds are bewildered when they try to comprehend it, just as they are dazed when they try to understand what is named by the word "Allah," and they disagree with each other. As the Sayyid [al-Jurjani] said, "Whether it is Syriac or Arabic, a name or an attribute, a signifier or not, derived or not, and from what it is derived and what is its origin, the sayings have been many, and for each saying there is an argument, more than there is room for here."

Scholars have disagreed whether or not the elimination of the *hamza* from *al-ilah* [to form the word "Allah"] follows normal patterns of Arabic morphology (*harf*). The correct answer is that it does not. [Normally,] a vocalized consonant is eliminated in certain cases where it is required due to opposition (*ta'arrud*) and contraction (*iddigham*). If normal patterns of morphology had been followed, it would not have been required in this case, because what is eliminated would normally remain invariable. Abu 'l-Baqa' disagrees, and says that it follows the pattern of reducing emphasis (*takhfif*) [in pronunciation]. That is, the stress in pronunciation is reduced by eliminating the preceding vowel. From the first point of view, the elimination is exceptional because the vocalized *hamza* is ignored and the word is contracted, in conformity to the pattern that when two similar letters are next to each other, the first one drops the vowel. From the second point of view, the elimination of the *hamza* follows the normal morphological pattern because the *hamza* has no vowel, and the contraction is exceptional because the first of the two similar letters is vocalized.

Chapter 3

GOD'S ESSENCE AND ATTRIBUTES

Lesson 1: God's Attributes of Essence and of Acts

S: I have learned what scholars say about the word of majesty (*lafz al-jalala*), that it is the greatest name of God's essence (*al-ism al-dhati al-aʿzam*), around which revolve all the attributes and names. Explain to me the correct teaching adhered to by the people of truth and straightness (*ahl al-haqq wa-'l-istiqama*) concerning the attributes of our high and glorious Lord.

T: Oh seeker after guidance who are so thirsty for the clarification of the truth, may God grant us and you success to do what is right (*li-'l-ʿamal al-haqq*) and to come to God with the truth and in the truth!

Know that our Ashʿarite opponents have a doctrine concerning God's attributes that is different from ours. They say that the meanings (*maʿani*) by which God is described and which are articulated by such words as *knowledge, power, life, will, speech, hearing,* and *sight* are real things (*maʿani*) that are distinct from (*za'ida ila*) His essence, subsisting (*qa'ima*) and inhering (*halla*) in His essence. They thus affirm [the existence of] multiple eternals and have made these eternals inherent and subsisting in His essence, and have made His essence a locus (*mahall*) for things (*li-'l-ashya'*). They have even gone so far as to say that if the veil was lifted from our sight, we would see them! They say that He is living by a life that is other than He, knowing by a knowledge that is other than He, powerful by a power that is other than He, willing by a will that is other than He, speaking by a speech that is other than He, hearing by a faculty of hearing that is other than He, seeing by an attribute of vision that is other than He.

They have thus contradicted their principle that there is only one eternal, the Necessary Being, Whose majesty is splendid, by believing that the attributes are eternal and distinct (*mughayira*) from the essence of God in which they subsist.[1] They must therefore believe in a multiplicity of eternals, and since these eternals inhere in God's essence, they have made His essence a locus for eternal things that are other than He, and have made His Glory in need of (*muftaqir ila*) these eternals—for without the life inhering in Him and distinct from His essence, He would not be living, and without the knowledge inhering in Him and distinct from His essence, He would not be knowing, and likewise for power, will, and the rest of the attributes of essence. This is deviance and error.

The truth embraced by others concerning God's attributes—and this is the teaching of our sect, on which the Mu'tazila agree—is that the meanings contained in the expressions that describe our Lord, the Truth, Allah, Whose stature is exalted, such as life, knowledge, power, and so on, are distinct from the meanings (*al-ma'ani 'l-haqiqa*) that describe created things, which are real and subsist in their essences, and that the attributes of our Lord, Whose majesty is glorious, are not distinct from the essence of the Glorious One, nor do they subsist in it in the way that our attributes subsist in us. Indeed, we are less than God, Whose majesty is glorious, because the attributes of the Most High are His very essence (*'aynu dhatihi*), in the sense that the fruits that result from these attributes, according to the Ash'arites, can be brought into existence, according to us, by His holy essence alone, without any need for additional things in order to produce these fruits. The existence of the essence of the Most High is sufficient to reveal all objects of knowledge to Him, without any need for an eternal attribute called knowledge subsisting in it to reveal these objects of knowledge to Him, as the Ash'arites say; [the existence of His essence] is sufficient to exert power over all things without any need for a distinct eternal attribute called power subsisting in the essence of the Most High in order to produce every possible thing and cause its annihilation in accordance with His will, as they say; it is sufficient for the specification (*takhsis*) for all potential beings (*jami' al-ka'inat al-mumkina*) of such qualities as are possible for them, without any need to posit (*da'wa*) a real attribute subsisting in His essence and distinct from it, the function of which is to specify the characteristics of every possible being, as they claim; it is sufficient to perceive all

1. The Ash'arite scholar al-Juwayni, however, explicitly states that God's attributes are *not* distinct from His essence (*'adam mughayirat al-sifāt li-'l-dhat*) (al-Juwayni 1950, 137; al-Juwayni 2000, 75).

things that can be heard, without any need for an eternal attribute subsisting in the exalted essence attaching to things that are heard (*al-muta'allaqa bi-'l-masmu'at*), according to one opinion, or attached to all things that exist, according to another opinion. His essence has complete perception, not by means of imagination (*la 'ala sabil al-takhayyul*) or visualization (*al-tawahhum*) or as a result of the effect of a sense, or air called "hearing" to reach Him (*wusul hawa' musammat bi-'l-sam'*), as they allege. [Its existence] is sufficient to perceive all visible objects without any need to posit an eternal attribute distinct from the holy essence, subsisting in it and attaching to visible objects [as some say], or attaching to all existent things, as others say. His essence has complete perception, without use of imagination or visualizing, not through the effect of any sense and without rays (*shu'a'*) called vision reaching Him, as they allege. It is sufficient for the firmness and soundness of knowledge (*fi thubut al-'ilm wa-sihhatihi*), without any need to posit an eternal attribute called knowledge subsisting in His exalted essence and distinct from it. It is sufficient for Him to have life by the necessity of His existence, without any need to posit an eternal attribute called life subsisting in His essence, by which He would be living. It is sufficient for Him to command, prohibit, inform, and ask without any need to posit an eternal attribute called speech subsisting in it in order to dispel stillness or impairment, which He can indicate by expressions, writing, or allusion in order to command, prohibit, inform, and ask, as they allege, except in the sense of affirming [these characteristics] and making them His very essence (*ja'liha 'ayna al-dhat*), because of its obvious impossibility—no rational person would say this! We, the Mu'tazila and the philosophers all hold that the attributes of the divine essence are merely verbal attributions (*sifat i'tibariyya*) that have no existence outside our minds (*la wujud la-ha kharijan 'an al-adhhan*), like discernment in knowledge, mastery in power, and specification in His will; they have no reality distinct from His essence—He is far exalted above any such thing! They do not subsist in it or inhere in it in order to necessitate (*mujiba*) these fruits, as the Ash'arites say. Their teaching necessitates the indwelling of something in God (*hulul*), even if they try to evade this conclusion and have an aversion to admitting it, for whatever inheres in something unavoidably subsists in it, and whatever subsists in something unavoidably inheres in it.

S: How many categories are there of God's attributes?

T: Two: those pertaining to His essence (*dhatiyya*) and those pertaining to His acts (*fi'liyya*).

S: What is the difference between the two categories?

T: The difference is that the attributes of act are conjoined with their opposite in relation to the different objects upon which an action occurs, whereas the attributes of God's essence do not have any opposite, although the locus may be different (*wa-law ikhtalafa 'l-mahall*).

S: What do you mean by saying they are conjoined with their opposite?

T: It means that our Lord, Whose name is holy (*taqaddasa dhikruhu*), may give wealth or knowledge or absolute inducement to Zayd and not do any of that for 'Amr.[2] Both of these are His act, so two opposites meet in His act. This is impossible with the attributes of God's essence, which can never have an opposite. God can never know something and not know another, or have power over something and have no power over another, or will something and not will something else [that occurs], and so on.

S: What is the cause of the disagreement between the Maturidites and the Ash'arites on this point?

T: The reason is that the Maturidites and the Ash'arites agree on the subsistence of eternal entities (*ma'anin qadima*) in the essence of the glorious Creator and that they are other than He, and these are the attributes of essence: life, knowledge, power, will, hearing, vision, and speech.[3] The Maturidites added to these an eighth attribute, that of bringing into existence (*takwin*), and have made it an attribute that exists in the same manner as the rest of the hypostatic attributes (*sifat al-ma'ani*).[4] They say, "If the veil were lifted from our eyes we would

2. Zayd and 'Amr are the classic names used in theological and grammatical texts to illustrate points. They simply mean "person A" and "person B."

3. According to Gilliot (2007, 180), al-Ash'ari listed eight attributes of essence, the eighth being permanence (*baqa'*), but the influential Ash'arite theologian al-Baqillani (d. 403/1013) rejected this last.

4. I translate *sifat al-ma'ani* as "hypostatic attributes" to indicate the belief that the attributes are real "things" that exist in God (if they are attributes of essence) or are produced in Him (if they are attributes of act). As Gilliot (2007, 180) says, "To al-Ash'ari and to the Ash'arites, *sifa* (attribute) and *wasf* (attribution/ qualification) are distinct [unlike the Mu'tazila and the Ibadis, for whom they are identical]. What is a 'word' (*qawl*) is the qualification (*wasf*), but the attribute (*sifa*) is a real existent residing in God." Concerning the question at hand, Gilliot writes (ibid.), "The Eastern Hanafites [from among whom al-Maturidi and his school emerged] rejected the distinction between eternal attributes of essence and temporal attributes of act. For them, the attributes of act, which they usually combined into a single notion of 'bringing into existence' (*takwin*), were equally eternal

see it, just as we would see the other hypostatic attributes if the veil were lifted from our eyes." On this foundation they built their doctrine of the eternity of the attributes of act. They said, "Creation (*al-khalq*), provision (*al-rizq*), giving life (*al-ihya'*), and other things that are connected to the will of the Glorious One are not distinct from the attribute of bringing into existence but are the very same thing (*hiya huwa 'aynuhu*), and they are eternal." This is the root of the Maturidite teaching of the eternity of the attributes of act.

S: I know that the teaching of our sect concerning the attributes of essence is that our glorious Lord is described by them from all eternity (*fi 'l-qidam*). What is the teaching of our sect regarding the attributes of act?

T: Our sect has two schools of thought (*madhhaban*) on this. The scholars of North Africa, may God have mercy on them,[5] hold that the attributes of act are eternal, in agreement with the Maturidites. The eastern Ibadi scholars hold that the attributes of act are temporally produced (*haditha*), in agreement with the Ash'arites. You understand the reason for the disagreement between the Maturidites and the Ash'arites and that the root of the Maturidite doctrine on the eternity of the attributes of act is the attribute of bringing into existence, which according to them is eternal; they subsume all the acts within the attribute of bringing into existence.

S: Do any of the scholars add to the eight attributes of essence a ninth eternal attribute subsisting in the essence, as they claim, though our majestic Lord is too exalted for that?

T: Indeed, some of the Maturidites add a ninth attribute, that of perception (*idrak*).

S: How do the Ash'arites argue for the origination of the attributes of God's acts?

T: Their argument is based on God's power. They say, "How is the attribute of bringing into existence different from the attribute of power?" in denying the

---

and subsisted in the essence of God; but His attribute of 'bringing into existence' was distinct from what was 'brought forth' (*mukawwan*)." This became a well-known point of controversy between the Ash'arites and Maturidites.

5. This is a standard expression used after referring to any dead Muslim, and in no way implies that the Ibadi scholars of North Africa were wrong.

teaching of the Maturidites that God brings things into existence and nonexistence by virtue of an attribute of bringing into existence. That is, [the Maturidites] say that the Most High brings things into existence and nonexistence by virtue of His power, and His power, according to them, prepares things that have merely potential existence for actual existence after they had not been possible, and that the attribute of bringing into existence afterwards brings them into actual existence. The Ash'arites respond that things that have potential existence are receptive to existence without anything being added to them.

S: Why do our companions in the east say that the attributes of God's acts are temporally produced?

T: They argue that the Most High God never ceases to bring originated things into existence and to do acts according to His will at the time they occur (*fi awqatiha*), like creating, causing death, giving wealth, giving poverty, exalting some people, humbling others, and so on concerning all His acts which He brings into existence at the time they occur. He cannot be described as doing these acts from all eternity (*fi 'l-azal*), but only as doing an act at the time it occurs. So this attribute is originated (*haditha*) with the origination of the act. It is not eternal, but originated.

S: Why do the scholars of North Africa say that the attributes of God's acts are eternal?

T: They say that God is Creator from all eternity in the sense that He will create, and that He is Provider from all eternity in the sense that He will provide [for His creatures], and that He is pleased from all eternity in the sense that He will be pleased with the people of obedience, and angry from all eternity in the sense that He will be angry with those who disobey Him.

S: In their opinion, what is the difference between the attributes of essence and the attributes of act?

T: The difference, according to them, is that the attributes of essence are necessary for His essence (*wajiba li-dhatihi*), and He has never ceased to be described by them; they were not produced by an act that He does, nor are they based on act. [On the other hand,] the attributes of act are contingent upon (*tawaffaqat 'ala*) acts attributed to Him from all eternity (*fi-ma la yazal*). They consider them eternal, although they are linked with temporal acts, in the sense that (*'ala ma'na annahu*) He will bring them into being, so it is correct to attribute the act to Him before it is produced. Don't you see that you say, for example, "I am praying (*inni musallin*) two *rak'as* tomorrow," or "fasting (*sa'im*) on such-and-such day," or "giving an answer to your legal question (*muftin*) tomorrow," or "sending Zayd to you tomorrow."[6] You describe yourself as praying, fasting, answering a question, and sending before you actually pray, fast, answer, and send—and God's example is best of all. He is Creator, Provider, Giver of life, and Giver of death from this perspective from all eternity, although the acts from which these names derive were, in pre-eternity, yet to occur from the Glorious One.

S: Is this the only aspect (*wajh*) from which they describe the attributes of act as eternal, or is there another aspect?

T: They do have a second aspect, and a third, but you objected to the argument only from this first perspective.

S: I only objected that the reference to what they say goes back to origination. So then, what are the other two aspects?

T: Your eagerness to acquire knowledge and useful sciences is great, so I will tell you that this question was introduced by the North African scholar, Shaykh Abu 'l-Qasim Yunus b. Abi Zakariya, may God have mercy upon him. He took this question to Shaykh Abu Mas'ud Sabir b. 'Isa, may God have mercy on him. [Abu Mas'ud] said:

> Concerning His attributes of act, it is impossible for Him to have had them from all eternity, because that would entail affirming the eternity of creation. It is impossible for Him to have been worshipped from all eternity, or praised from all eternity, or remembered from all eternity, or that His help was sought from all eternity, because that entails affirming the eternity of someone who remembered Him and worshipped Him and praised Him and sought His help. But it is permissible for you to say that from all eternity He is creator, provider, originator, bringing back to life, producing, giving generously, blessing, and other such similar expressions, of which there are many, provided there exists one of three stipulations: (1) that you complete your words by saying "He is

6. These grammatical constructions work better in Arabic than in English. In Arabic the primary distinction between tenses is not between the past, present, and future, but between an act that is completed and one that is incomplete or continuous, including something that will happen in the future. Precisely the same grammatical construct can mean "I am praying" or "I will pray." Al-Rawahi's third example would almost certainly have to be rendered in English as "I will answer your question tomorrow."

> creator from all eternity of a creature that will be, and provider to something that will be, and originator and bringer back to life of something that will be originated and brought back to life"; this is one way; (2) that you mean by these words that He is able to produce a creature, something that will be provided for, a thing that will be originated, and a thing that will be brought back to life, because He is able from all eternity to do this; this is the second way; or (3) that by these words you mean the active participle (*ism al-fa'il*) if it is indefinite, because it is suitable to receive action and condition, as when God said, "He called you Muslims before" (Q 22:78)—and this occurs frequently in Arabic. Whoever says that God cannot be creator or provider from all eternity is an unfaithful hypocrite (*kafir nafiq*), and whoever says He is not creator or provider from all eternity is an unbeliever (*mushrik*).

These are the words of the scholar Abu 'l-Qasim of North Africa. Understand, and do not indiscriminately follow the sayings (*ta'dhukh athar*) of the Muslims.

S: Is it possible for Him to be Lord from all eternity if He wishes?

T: It is possible for Him to be Lord from all eternity over something that He will bring into existence, and its coming into existence is contingent on His will, and what is meant (*wa-'l-murad*) is that if He wishes He will bring creatures into being whose Lord He will be—that is, their master (*sayyiduhum*) or ruler (*malikuhum*) or benefactor (*muslihuhum*), according to one of the meanings by which His name "Lord" is interpreted. The meaning of the linkage (*ta'liq*) of His lordship with His will is from this perspective (*min hadhihi 'l-jiha*). Were there no stipulation of will here, that would suggest (*la-waqa'a iham*) something over whom He is Lord that is with Him from all eternity, which is impossible. As for calling Him "Lord" without any other considerations (*bi-duna tadayuf*) by ascribing lordship to Him (*bi-ja'l al-rububiyya la-hu*) in the sense that He alone deserves lordship, without anything sharing this honor (*la sharika la-hu*), and considering lordship to mean dominion, subjugation (*al-qahr*), exaltedness (*al-'uluww*), vanquishing (*al-ghalaba*), majesty (*al-'azama*), and conquest (*al-isti'la'*), He is deserving of these attributes by virtue of His essence from all eternity, without regard to any other considerations. From this perspective, it impossible to link an eternal attribute of His essence to His will, because none of the qualities of His majesty and none of the attributes of His perfection depends on His will. Only created things that depend on divine power are contingent on His will. Eagerly retain what I am teaching you here, for it is precious (*'ilq madinna*)!

S: You have taught me two categories into which the attributes of God are divided: the attributes of essence and the attributes of act. Is there a third category into which they are divided?

T: The attributes of God are not confined to these two categories. They are indeed divided into three categories from a third perspective, as some of our scholars in the east have done: attributes of essence, attributes of act, and an attribute that can be seen from one perspective as pertaining to the essence, and from another perspective as pertaining to the act. Those pertaining to the essence include any attribute whose opposite is excluded from God. The Glorious One is described by these from all eternity, and they are the seven attributes: life, knowledge, power, will, speech, hearing, and sight. The second category includes any attribute indicating the exclusion of its opposite from the Most High, and He is not described as doing them from all eternity, like creation, giving life, giving death, love, hate, constricting (*al-qabd*), expanding (*al-bast*), friendship (*al-walaya*), and dissociation (*al-bara'a*). The third category is any attribute that can be understood in two different senses, like His name "the Wise": in the sense that it excludes folly (*al-'abath*) from the Most High, it is one of the names of the attributes of essence; in the sense that He places things in their appropriate places, it is an attribute of act. Likewise, His name "Truthful": in the sense that it denies that the Most High can tell a lie, truthfulness is an attribute of essence; in the sense that He informs truthfully, truthfulness here is an attribute of act. Likewise, the Most High's name "Hearing," in the sense that it excludes deafness from Him, it is an attribute of essence; in the sense that He receives prayers, it is an attribute of act. Likewise, the Most High's name "the Subtle" (*al-Latif*):[7] in the sense that He knows [all nuances], the Most High's subtlety is an attribute of essence, but when it expresses His mercy, it is an attribute of act. And so on.

Lesson 2: God's Difference from Originated Things

S: What is the meaning of "He is a thing unlike other things" (*shay' la ka-'l-ashya'*)?

7. *Al-Latif* has sometimes been translated "the Kind," and *latif* in its most common usage means "kind." But it has many other meanings and implications. In the plural, *lata'if,* a term common to Islamic mysticism, means "subtle truths or realities." The context in which al-Rawahi uses the term here requires translating *al-Latif* as "the Subtle."

T: According to our school, the reality of a thing is however it is described (*ma yukhbar ʿanhu*). If you like, you could say that a thing is what has come into existence and remained, as well as what has come into existence and passed away, as well as what will come into existence. According to the Ashʿarites, it is something that exists, and according to them the nonexistent (*al-maʿdum*) is not a thing, whereas according to our school it is a nonexistent thing. Nonexistence (*al-ʿadam*), according to us, is not a thing, so the Glorious One is a thing, because He exists, remains, and true things are spoken of Him, but He does not resemble any other thing, and nothing else resembles Him. He must be one (*la-hu al-wahda*) in His essence, attributes, acts, speech, and worship, and the Most High has no second [thing] (*fa-la thani la-hu*) in His essence. His essence is not composed of parts (*la dhatuhu murakkaba min ajza'*) and His attributes are not multiple but of a single kind (*mutaʿaddada min jins wahid*), and the Most High does not have a partner in any of His attributes or a partner who helps Him in any of His acts. His speech does not resemble the speech of creatures, and no other object of worship rightfully deserves to be worshipped alongside Him.

S: How do we know the unity of His essence (*wahdat dhatihi*)?

T: The unity of His essence in the sense of not being composed of parts is known from His difference from originated things.

S: What is the attribute of essence that is necessary (*al-sifa 'l-nafsiyya 'l-wajiba*)[8] to God Most High?

T: It is His necessary, essential existence that can never admit nonexistence, either in the eternal past or in the eternal future. The one who is accountable need only know that the Most High exists necessarily; he need not know that His existence is the same as His essence or that it is different from His essence, because that is one of the obscure matters of theology.

S: What are the negative attributes that are necessary for the Most High (*ma hiya 'l-sifat al-salbiyya 'l-wajiba la-hu taʿala*)?

T: Nonexistence [must be denied], meaning the exclusion of a beginning to His exalted existence. Second, perpetuity (*al-baqa'*) [must be affirmed], in the sense that there can never be an end to the existence of the Most High. The

8. *Sifa nafsiyya* is an alternative to *sifa dhatiyya*. Paul Walker (al-Juwayni 2000, 19) calls these "attributes of self," in contrast to *al-sifat al-maʿnawiyya*, "the qualifying attributes."

difference of the Glorious One from all His creatures means the exclusion of all similarity between the Most High and originated things; His essence, attributes, and acts are not like the essence, attributes, or acts of originated things. The Most High said, "There is not a thing that does not glorify Him with praise" (Q 17:44).

The meaning of things glorifying Him with praise is that whenever God brings a thing out of nonexistence, it is as if He says with the tongue of that thing, "I am exalted beyond all resemblance to this thing." It is said that when God nullified the words of those who called the angels daughters of God (Q 17:40), He declared that His essence transcended (*nazzaha dhatahu ʿamma*) what they attributed to Him by saying immediately afterward, "The seven heavens and the earth and those in them declare His glory" (Q 17:44), as an indication that all beings indicate and witness to this transcendence, but the unbelievers do not understand their praise. The purpose of this is to rebuke them and chide them for saying that God has partners, although everything else exalts Him beyond all deficiency. It is said that they praise God with the words "glory and praise be to God," but only the perfect ones hear their praise, like the Prophet in whose hand stones and food praised God, and those Companions who were with him heard it (al-Bukhari n.d., no. 3579), and most of the pious ancestors agree that it is literally true, that all things, whether animal or inanimate, praise God in words that can be heard. Some disagree and say that the glorification of rational animals is in words and the glorification of other animals and inanimate objects is in the language of their own condition, so that these creatures give evidence of a Maker, and of His power, kindness, and wisdom, as if they are speaking of that, and it attains the status of glorification.

The negative attributes of the Most High include His self-subsistence (*qiyamuhu bi-nafsihi*), meaning that the Most High has no need of anything for His essence and has no need of a cause besides Himself. It means that the Most High does not need an essence in which to subsist or an originator to bring Him into being, but the Most High is the one who brings all things into being, meaning all generated things (*al-muwalladat*). This requires that the Glorious One be an essence, not an attribute. These five negative attributes are only an attribution of negativity—that is, exclusion—because the reality of each one of them is the exclusion of a corresponding deficiency that is impossible for the Most High. The negative attributes are unlimited, because the deficiencies are infinite, and they are all impossible and excluded from the Most High; these five are their roots.

S: What is the meaning of "There is no beginning to His being first and no end to His being last"?

T: God is first and last with respect to the existence of creatures and their passing away. That is, He existed before them and will remain after them. His existing before them has no beginning, and His remaining after them has no end.

S: What is the meaning of existence (*ma haqiqat al-wujud*)?

T: It is something attributed to a being either now or in the future.

S: What is the meaning of "existent"?

T: It is something that exists in the present.

S: What is the meaning of "the Eternal" (*al-Qadim*)?

T: It means that He exists, not after nonexistence, and that He will never become nonexistent after existence. As long as His eternity is affirmed, His nonexistence is impossible.

S: What is the meaning of eternity?

T: Eternity is the attribute of the eternal.

S: What is the meaning of a name?

T: It is that by which a particular thing (*'ayn*) or a concept is known.

S: What is the meaning of an attribute?

T: It is what distinguishes a thing (*'ayn*) or an entity (*ma'nan*).

S: What is the meaning of naming (*al-tasmiya*)?

T: It is to mention a name, and it is the act of the namer (*al-musammi*).

S: What is the meaning of description (*al-wasf*)?

T: It is the mention of an attribute (*al-sifa*).

S: What is the meaning of a thing that is named?

T: It is what makes the name necessary (*al-mustawjib li-'l-ism*).

S: What is the meaning of something that is described (*al-mawsuf*)?

T: It is what deserves the attribute (*al-mustahiqq li-'l-sifa*).

S: What is the meaning of affirmation (*al-ithbat*)?

T: It means to give information (*ikhbar*) about a particular thing or a concept.

S: What is eternity from before all time (*al-azal*)?

T: It is the absolute nonexistence of creatures, or what is before their origination.

S: Does this mean they are all nonexistent, as is indicated by God's words, "Everything perishes except His face" (28:88), or can one call eternal from before all time (*azali*) what has no beginning, or when God exists with nothing else?

T: No, it is not called eternal from before all time.

S: What is the meaning of everlasting (*al-abad*)?

T: It is what has no end and what will never cease to be.

S: What is the meaning of our Lord mounting (*istiwa' 'ala*) the Throne?

T: It means that He is over it and over all His creatures, in the sense that He has dominion over it and brings it into being and has mastery over all things.

S: What is the meaning of His manifestation (*zuhuruhu*)?[9]

T: He is manifest by indicators [of His existence] (*al-dala'il*).

S: What is the meaning of His hiddenness (*butunuhu*)?

T: He is absolutely hidden from the senses.

S: Is it impossible for God that the attributes of His essence be real things (*ma'ani*) distinct from His essence?

T: Indeed, by God, it is impossible for God that His attributes be real things distinct from His essence. His attributes are only verbalized concepts (*mafhumat i'tibariyya*), as I explained to you earlier: we believe that God's power is an eternal, essential attribute, the verbalized conception of which is linked to bringing into existence and into nonexistence every potential thing when [His] power is linked to it according to [His] will. Will is an essential attribute in the same sense, the concern of which is specification (*al-takhsis*)—He specifies for every potential thing some of what is possible for it when it is linked to it. Knowledge is an essential attribute in the same sense, discerning (*tankashifu*) objects of knowledge (*al-ma'lumat*) from all eternity and to all eternity when they are attached to it. Life is an essential attribute in the same sense, entailing the soundness of knowledge and the issuance of act. Hearing is an essential attribute in the same sense, attaching either to objects of hearing or to all things that exist, as has earlier been mentioned. Vision is an essential attribute in the same sense, attaching to objects of vision, according to one opinion, or to all things that exist, according to another; it attains total comprehension, as was explained earlier. Speech is an essential attribute indicating the exclusion of muteness and the opposite of silence and impediment, for He is beyond such things; by what we call the attribute of speech the Glorious One commands, prohibits, informs, and so on. The attribute is indicated by verbal expression, writing, and symbol. If it is expressed

9. The Qur'an describes God as "the Manifest and the Hidden" (57:3).

in Arabic, it is the Qur'an; if in Syriac, it is the Psalms; if in Hebrew, it is the Torah; and if in Greek, it is the Gospel. What is named is one, even if the expression varies.

S: I know that they are verbalized attributes in the sense that they have no objective reality (*la wujud la-ha fi 'l-kharij*). Does this imply nullifying (*ta'til*) the attributes and excluding them, or not?

T: The existence of eternal (*qadima*) attributes subsisting in His essence must be denied of God the Mighty and Majestic. We describe (*wasafna*) the Most High by eternal (*azaliyya*) attributes as verbalized concepts by which our glorified Lord has described (*ittasafa*) His essence from all eternity (*min al-azal*). This is not a nullification or exclusion of the descriptions that our Lord has given to His essence. The Ash'arites only leveled this accusation at those who rejected their teaching on the divine attributes out of stubbornness and pride. If we say that God is living by virtue of His essence, knowledgeable by virtue of His essence, powerful by virtue of His essence, and so forth, where is the nullification, when we have affirmed that He has life, knowledge, and power? But they are only convinced if we say that they are eternal and other than Him, inhering (*halla*) in His essence. This aspect of the teaching of that school is a great insult to the essence and attributes of God, from which we seek refuge in God.

S: Does anyone say something other than what you said about God's speech?

T: Indeed. Some say that God's speech (*kalam Allah*) and His speaking (*takallumahu*) are His creation of speech wherever He wishes. For example, He could create it in the air or in a tree, as it is related that God created speech in the entire body of Moses, and neither his garment nor Gabriel heard him. God's speech may be given by the tongue of a creature, and all that is His act—but speech in this meaning is one of the attributes of act.

S: Does the knowledge of the Most High attach to what is nonexistent?

T: Indeed, the knowledge of the Most High attaches to all possible things, whether existent or nonexistent, because of His eternal knowledge, which encompasses all things before they are—how they will be, if they will be—and what has already come into existence: how it came into existence, and how it will be after existing. God's knowledge attaches to the existent and the nonexistent and to what He will bring into existence and what He will bring back into existence [after its annihilation] (*sayu'iduhu*). It attaches to what is potential concerning its potentiality, and to the impossible concerning its impossibility.[10] His knowledge of intelligible universals and their particulars has no beginning and no end. Nothing in His knowledge is originated, for He knows the unseen and the seen from all eternity and forever.[11]

S: It appears that the attribute of hearing and the attribute of sight are related to the attribute of knowledge.

T: Yes, indeed, these two attributes are related to the attribute of knowledge. Don't you see that His hearing is His knowledge of sounds and the words that are contained in them, and His sight is His knowledge of acts, attributes, bodies, and

10. Nasir b. Abi Nabhan felt that whatever God knows must necessarily exist, either in the past, present, or future, so one cannot speak of God's knowledge of contingencies—that is, knowing what would happen *if* something else happened, if indeed it does *not* happen. Nasir apparently thought he was unusually wise in his understanding of this question, and insulted his pupil, Sa'id b. Khalfan al-Khalili (later to become even more famous than his teacher), who tried to challenge him on this topic; Nasir said it was a mystery entirely beyond Sa'id's ability to understand. Later, when Sa'id was asked by a student about this, he did not hesitate to denounce this unusual teaching (S. al-Khalili 1986, 1:135–36). Indeed, Nasir appears to contradict the Qur'an, in its story of the "servant of God" whom Moses followed in Sura 18 (*al-Kahf*), who performed a number of seemingly meaningless or immoral acts in order to prevent a worse occurrence that God knew would otherwise happen.

11. One of the important areas of contention between the Muslim philosophers al-Farabi (875–950) and Ibn Sina (980–1037) and theologians like Abu Hamid Muhammad b. Muhammad al-Ghazali (1058–1111) concerned the knowledge of God. The Qur'an clearly states many times that God knows all things, even the grain in the ground, the fetus in the womb, and our own thoughts. Al-Farabi, faithful to Greek philosophical notions of knowledge that saw the objects of knowledge as making an impression on the intellect, said God could only know universals, not particulars, because if God knew particulars His mind would be subject to change. Ibn Sina tried to reconcile philosophical notions with the necessity of God's knowledge of all things by saying that God does indeed know all particulars, but His knowledge of them is the same from all eternity and to all eternity. Using the example of a solar eclipse, he said that God knows from all eternity that a solar eclipse will occur at a particular time, but His knowledge of the eclipse at the time of its occurrence is no different from His knowledge of it before it occurs or after it occurs. In his critique of the philosophers, *Tahafut al-falasifa* [The Incoherence of the Philosophers], al-Ghazali objected that if God's knowledge remains the same, He could not hear the prayers of the faithful or respond to them. Al-Rawahi's wording on this matter makes it seem that his ideas are similar to those of Ibn Sina, although al-Rawahi is much more a mystic and theologian than a philosopher.

accidents? These two attributes are verbalized concepts (*mafhuman i'tibariyān*) by which the Glorified One has described His essence. He does not have hearing or sight in the manner of creatures; rather, He has a comprehensive knowledge of all that is linked with hearing and sight, and God has only expressed them in this way in order to distinguish them from undifferentiated knowledge, because He has said that He is hearing and seeing.

S: Does anyone believe that God's knowledge does not attach to what is nonexistent?

T: Yes, a misguided (*dalla*), cursed (*mal'una*), unbelieving (*mushrika*) sect (*firqa*) holds this belief.

S: Does anyone believe that God can change His mind?

T: Yes, a misguided, cursed sect believes that God can decide to do something and then decide not to do it, or that He can decide to abandon an act and then decide to do it, and so forth. This is the act of someone who is ignorant, lacking knowledge and wisdom, hesitant in His affairs, and God is far exalted beyond what they say.[12] If He knows beforehand that He will bring something into being, and that His will will specify its characteristics, it is impossible for God to contradict His knowledge; it is inevitable that the thing that has been specified will come into existence at the time that He knew it would, whenever His will specifies it to come into existence, and this rule applies to what He knew would not be. Whoever says that His knowledge can change (*al-qa'il bi-tabdil 'ilmihi*) is an unbeliever (*mushrik*).

S: Does anyone believe that God has a body?

T: Indeed, a misguided, cursed sect believes this. They say that God has limbs like their own. One of them even said, "Forgive me for mentioning the genitalia and the beard!" God is far exalted above what they say! The Glorified One cannot be described by any of the attributes of originated things at all![13]

12. The Hebrew Bible does seem to give instances in which God regrets what He has done (e.g., Genesis 6:6) or changes His mind in response to intercession (e.g., Exodus 32:9–14). The Qur'an does not contain any such passages. Jewish, Christian, and Muslim theologians all adopted notions of God's perfection and immutability that precluded His ever changing His mind, notions derived from Greek philosophy. Many of the early Shi'a believed that God can change His mind (*bada'*).

13. There are no Muslim groups today that speak of God in such grossly anthropomorphic terms, although some literalists of the Hanbali school do believe that one must say not that God is everywhere,

S: What does it mean for the Glorified One to be with His creation (*ma haqiqat ma'iyyatihi subhanahu*)?[14]

T: The Glorified One is with His creation through His knowledge [of them], preservation [of them], and power [over them]. His being with His creation does not depend on circumstances (*zuruf*) and is not a togetherness of mixing or coming down in the manner of bodies; rather, as we said, He is with a person by His knowledge and preservation [of that person], in a way that is different from anything that might occur to your mind, as is the case with all His perfections. Were it not for His preservation and maintenance of things, they would all revert to nonexistence, and the order of all things would be corrupted. Were He not with His creation through knowledge, He would be ignorant of any new things that happen in it, and God is too glorified and exalted for that; the Majestic One is with us and with everything by preserving it and knowing it, so understand.

S: To what does the power of our Most High Lord attach?

T: The power of the Glorified One attaches to all possible things. It is not said that it attaches to impossible things, not because of any deficiency in His power, but because His power does not attach to [an impossible thing] because of its impossibility.

---

but that God is sitting on a throne above the heavens, because the Qur'an says so. Their denial that God is everywhere, however, appears to contradict the Qur'anic verse, "Wherever you turn, there is the face of God" (Q 2:115). Heresiographers like al-Shahrastani label as anthropomorphists some of the "extremist Shi'a," those among the "People of Hadith" who are "*hashwiyya*"—a contemptuous term that literally means those who are "stuffed," but is used of those who deny the use of reason and take religious texts literally—and the followers of Hisham b. al-Hakam (al-Shahrastani 1923, 76–77). Madelung (1999a) argues that Hisham's use of the word "body" did not imply crude anthropomorphism, but was based on the notion that only bodies have existence. In fact, he argues that he represented an antianthropomorphic theological perspective among the Shi'a, and that he could only have been accused of anthropomorphism from the vantage point of the Mu'tazila. Some scholars took care to avoid anthropomorphism by saying that God has "a body unlike other bodies."

14. The idea that God is "with" His faithful servant, sitting with the one who remembers Him, and so on, is present in the Qur'an and even more in *hadith qudsi,* the divine sayings given not in the Qur'an but in Hadith. Sufis cherish such notions, and al-Rawahi was very much a Sufi in his personal spiritual orientation. Sufis are often at pains to explain that the notion of "union with God" in no way implies a mingling of the eternal essence with the temporal—indeed, some have demystified the concept altogether by saying that it means that God's servant unites his will with the will of God.

S: Does His will attach itself to something He knows will not be?

T: No, His will does not attach to it, because it is already abandoned (*bi-matrukiha 'l-sabiq*), since He already knows that it will not be.

S: Does anyone believe that potential existents are influenced by God (*anna 'l-mumkinat tanfa'il li-'llah*) without His choice (*la bi-'khtiyarihi*)?

T: Indeed, a misguided, cursed, unbelieving sect believes this. They say that existents are affected through causation, not by God's choice, as when fire burns something and cold freezes something. They say concerning the Most High that He is the first cause (*al-'illa 'l-ula*), and that He is the cause of all causes.[15] This is unbelief, and we seek refuge in God—both reason and religion reject this. No, nothing exists except by His will and choice, just as the Glorified One wills it; no nonexistent thing is delayed from coming into existence unless He does not will to bring it into existence. The Glorified One prevails, chooses, and specifies.

15. Muslim philosophers like al-Farabi and Ibn Sina embraced Aristotelian notions of causation and a Neoplatonic cosmology, in which God is the First Cause whose self-contemplation results in a series of causes that brings all things into being. Such a notion appears to remove all dimensions of will from the creation process. Ash'arites, on the other hand, reject the notion of secondary causation altogether, and see God as the immediate cause of everything that occurs: the creation of fire is the act of God and the burning of a log that is in the fire is a separate act of God. The fire does not cause the burning of the wood, but God's habit of causing the burning of objects after the creation of fire leads people to suppose there is causation. Al-Ghazali's critique of the philosophy of al-Farabi and Ibn Sina is based mainly on a critique of philosophical notions of causation. The response by Ibn Rushd/Averroës (1126–1198) to al-Ghazali's critique, *Tahafut al-tahafut* [The Incoherence of "The Incoherence"], has been translated (Ibn Rushd 1954).

Chapter 4

THE ROOTS OF RELIGION, THE IMPOSSIBILITY OF SEEING GOD, AND WHAT IS NECESSARY AND IMPOSSIBLE FOR GOD

Lesson 1: Religion (*Din*) and Its Principles

S: I congratulate myself on the blessing of success in these precious essentials that my master the teacher has taught me. I think I understand what is necessary for the Necessary Being, my True God (*ilahi al-haqq*), concerning His attributes and how to know them, and that He has a religion according to which all His accountable servants worship Him. Explain to me what this religion (*din*) is, both in terms of its meaning and what it entails according to the law.

T: It is said that *din* ("religion") means obedience and reward, and is used metaphorically to mean the law (*al-Shari'a*). Religion also means a particular religious community (*milla*), but it is said that this is just an expression to mean obedience and being led by the law. The Most High said, "Religion with God is submission (*islam*)" (3:125),[1] and "Who is better in religion than the one who submits his face to God while doing good?" (4:125), that is, in obedience, and "who are sincere in their religion with God" (4:146), that is, in their obedience. The Most High also said, "People of the Book, do not go to extremes in your religion" (4:171), which is an exhortation to follow the religion of the Prophet, may

1. Some scholars have interpreted *islam* in this verse, as well as in 3:85, quoted below, not to mean the particular form of religious devotion brought by Muhammad, but submission to God in a broader sense (Esack 1997, 126–34).

God's blessings and peace be upon him, which is the most moderate of religions, as the Most High said: "Likewise We have made you a median nation" (2:143) and "There is no compulsion in religion" (2:256). It is said that this means obedience, which can only be real if it is sincere, and sincerity is not produced from compulsion. It is said that this applies only to the People of the Book, who are charged with paying *jizya*.[2] He also said, "Do they seek a religion other than the religion of God?" (3:83). That means Islam, because He says, "Whoever seeks a religion other than Islam, it will not be accepted of him" (3:85). On this the Most High also said, "It is He who sent His Messenger with guidance and the religion of truth" (9:33) and "They do not follow the true religion" (9:29), and "Who is better in religion than the one who submits his face to God while doing good?" (4:125) and "Why, then, if you are not obligated (*madinin*)" (56:86), that is, if you are not to be subject to reward or punishment. The one who is obligated is the individual (*al-'abd*) and the community. Abu Zayd said, "It is from 'he obligated' [someone to do something] (*dayyana*), and a person is obligated (*yudan*) if he is forced to do something displeasing to him (*humila 'ala makruh*)." It is also said that it is from "I obligated him" (*dintuhu*), meaning I reward him for his obedience, and some have interpreted *al-madina* in this way. The upshot of all this is that the religion of God by which His servants worship Him is Islam.

S: What are the roots of this religion?

T: The roots of religion are three: faith (*iman*), submission (*islam*), and the Prophet's example (*al-sunna*).

S: What is the literal meaning of faith (*iman*)?

T: It means believing, as indicated by God's word, "You have no faith in us" (12:17), that is, "You do not believe us."

S: What does faith mean, according to the law?

2. Modern-day Muslims generally embrace verse 2:256 as an indication of the tolerance of Islam, but, according to the twelfth-century exegete, al-Zamakhshari, "Some people say that this (verse) is abrogated through God's words: 'O Prophet, struggle with the unbelievers and hypocrites (*munafiqun*), and be harsh with them. Their refuge is *Jahannam* [hellfire], an evil home-coming!'" (9:73, 66:9). Others say that [the prohibition against compulsion] refers especially to the People of the Book [the Jews and Christians], since they have been immunized themselves (from compulsion) through the payment of tribute (*jizya*)" (cited in Gätje 1976, 215–16).

T: It means believing in the heart, affirming with the tongue, and doing the pillars (*tasdiq bi-'l-jinan, wa-iqrar bi-'l-lisan, wa-'amal bi-'l-arkan*).

S: What is the literal meaning of submission (*islam*)?

T: It is like when you say, "I submitted something to someone" when you give it to him. From this also is derived the notion of handing over something (*al-salam*) in a sale.

S: What is submission, according to the law?

T: It is of two types. The first is without faith, and it is verbal acknowledgment, by which a person's life is spared and his possessions may not be plundered without due cause, whether or not he really believes. The second type is higher than faith; it is acknowledgment with the tongue, belief in the heart, faithfulness in deed, and yielding to God in all that He has decreed and determined. As it is said of God's friend Abraham, peace be upon him, "When his Lord told him, 'Submit,' he said, 'I submit to God, Lord of all being" (Q 2:131). And as God Most High said, "Religion with God is submission" (3:19).

S: From what is the word *iman* (faith) derived?

T: It is from the verb *amana,* which is used in two ways. The first is transitive; for example, *amantuhu* means "I have granted him safety," and it is in this manner that God has the name *mu'min* (faithful, guarantor of security). The second way is intransitive, as when one says so-and-so *amana,* meaning he has become safe. *Iman* is derived from *al-amn* (safety); that is, whoever believes in God and His Messenger and believes the message to which he calls is safe from God's punishment and his soul is tranquil because of what he has believed and to which he has been led.

S: In how many meanings is the word "faith" used?

T: It is sometimes used as a name for the law brought by Muhammad, may God bless him and grant him peace, as in God's word, "The faithful and the Jews and the Sabaeans" (Q 5:69). Everyone who enters into His law and affirms God and His messenger Muhammad is described by this faith. It is sometimes used by way of praise, and means the soul's submission to the truth by way of belief. This is from the combination of three things: realization in the heart, affirmation with the tongue, and acting according to it with the limbs. This is illustrated by God's words, "Those who believe in God and His messengers, they are the truthful" (*al-siddiqun*) (57:19).

S: Can each of these three things by itself also be described as faith?

T: Yes, each of these—belief, the true word, and the righteous deed—is called faith. God Most High said, "God would never make your faith fruitless" (2:143), meaning your prayer. And he has placed modesty and removing harm among the branches of faith.

S: Does our dear teacher have a textual support for that?

T: Indeed, a textual support and an authentic root (*asl asil*)! It is related that [Muhammad], may God bless him and grant him peace, said, "Faith has seventy-odd (*bid' wa-sab'un*) branches (*shu'ba*), the best of which is to say 'There is no god but God, and Muhammad is the messenger of God.' The least of them is to remove harm; and modesty is a branch of faith" (al-Suyuti 1981, no. 3096). He also said, "The best faith is that you know that God is with you wherever you are" (ibid., no. 1243). He also said, "The best faith is patience and forbearance" (ibid., no. 1244). He also said, "The best faith is that you love for the sake of God and hate for the sake of God and move your tongue in remembrance of God the Mighty and Majestic, and that you love for people what you love for yourself, and hate for them what you hate for yourself, and that you say something good or be silent" (ibid., no. 1245). He also said, "If your good deed pleases you and your bad deed displeases you, you are a believer" (ibid., no. 677). He also said, "One of the signs that a servant's faith is complete is that he makes everything he says conditional upon God's will" (ibid., no. 2486).[3] He also said, "Faith is two parts: half is patience, and the other is gratitude" (ibid., no. 3106).

S: I have learned that each of the characteristics of faith is faith, but what is the sum of complete faith that is useful both in this world and the next?

T: It is related in a number of hadiths, the most famous and comprehensive of which are the following two. The first is the Prophet's words, "Whoever says 'There is no god but God,' sincerely believing it in his heart, enters paradise." He was asked, "How is it made sincere (*ma ikhlasuha*)?" He said, "Keep it from what God has prohibited" (al-Haythami 2001, 1:31, no. 18). The second is this: 'Ali [al-Rida] b. Musa entered Nishapur. The learned men clung to the reins of his camel and said, "By the right of your pure ancestors, tell us a hadith you

3. Literally, "He makes an exception in everything he says," that is, he uses the formula *in sha' Allah*, "if God wills."

heard from your fathers." He said, "My father Musa related on the authority of his father Ja'far, who related on the authority of his father al-Baqir, who related on the authority of his father, Zayn al-'Abidin, who related on the authority of his father al-Husayn, who related on the authority of his father 'Ali b. Abi Talib, who said, 'I heard the Prophet, may God's blessing and peace be upon him, say, "Faith is knowledge in the heart, affirmation with the tongue, and doing with the limbs."'" Ahmad b. Hanbal said, "If I recited such an *isnad* to a madman, he would be cured!"[4] It is said that it was recited to an epileptic and he was cured.

S: The Messenger of God, may God bless him and grant him peace, spoke truly when he said that faith is knowledge in the heart, words by the tongue, and knowledge of the pillars, but how can this hadith be reconciled with the one that says "Whoever says 'There is no god but God' enters paradise" (al-Bukhari n.d., no. 5827)?

T: That was said at the beginning of Islam, before the revelation of religious duties and command and prohibition. Otherwise, it depends on the stipulation of repentance. When the duties were revealed, they encompassed command and prohibition and the Qur'an's promise [of reward] and threat [of punishment], and God required repentance from sins. At that point, "There is no god but God" no longer sufficed by itself, especially since he explained this hadith which we mentioned earlier, which is the Prophet's words, "Whoever says 'There is no god but God' in sincerity from the heart enters paradise." He was asked, "How is it made

4. 'Ali b. Musa is 'Ali al-Rida (d. 203/818), the eighth imam of the Twelver Shi'a, and therefore a descendant of the Prophet. Although the Shi'a especially venerate members of the Prophet's family, and particularly the authorities in this *isnad,* who are the first seven imams of the Twelver Shi'a, nearly all Muslims give them special reverence, as indicated by the quote from Ahmad b. Hanbal, perhaps the premiere representative of the group that first came to be identified as Sunni (*ahl al-sunna wa-'l-jama'a*). Although certain aspects of Sunni doctrine are clearly offensive to Ibadis, Ibadi authors freely quote from Sunni authorities, especially the Hadith collections of al-Bukhari and Muslim, to support their own teachings.

The story of the people of Nishapur begging 'Ali b. Musa to relate a hadith is connected to a different hadith in al-Munawi (1994, 2:15, no. 6047). This particular hadith is told by 'Ali b. Musa, however (with the slight difference of "doing the pillars" instead of "doing with the limbs"), in Ibn Maja (2000, Introduction, *bab* 9, no. 68), where it is not Ibn Hanbal but Salih Abu 'l-Salt al-Harawi who says that if this *isnad* were recited to a madman he would be cured. The hadith is considered weak because of Abu 'l-Salt's unreliability.

sincere?" and he replied, "That you keep it from what God has prohibited." This is a comprehensive overview of the subject (*mujmal*), whereas the other requires detailed explanation (*mufassar*), and a comprehensive overview carries more weight than [something requiring] a detailed explanation. Likewise he said—may God bless him and grant him peace—"'There is no god but Allah' is the key to paradise" (Al-Bukhari n.d., *Kitab al-jana'iz* [23], bab 1). Concerning this, al-Bukhari said when he was asked about it, "Indeed, but there is no key without teeth; if you have a key with teeth it will open for you, but without teeth, it will not."[5] Likewise, Abu Dharr said this concerning the hadith that says "even if he commits adultery and theft." Therefore, the meaning of faith according to our principles is: faith in God the Mighty and Majestic, with the tongue by affirmation, in the heart by belief, and in the limbs by good works. The outcome is that the true believer is the one who fulfills all conditions of religion and the rules to be followed in this world, and affirms his faith. It has already been stated that the one who affirms without belief in his heart is an unbeliever in the eyes of God and in the eyes of those who become aware of his belief, and the one who affirms the faith and believes in Islam and persists in committing sins is a hypocrite. May the All-Compassionate and All-Merciful God protect us from that!

S: What is the Sunna, the third of the three roots of religion?

T: It is the way of the Messenger of God, may God bless him and grant him peace, which he pursued in speech, deed, and affirmation.

Lesson 2: The Vision of God and the Proofs That Negate and Affirm It

S: What sects that disagree with us believe that God can be seen, exalted be His majesty?

T: All the Ash'arites.[6]

5. Al-Bukhari records this (n.d., *Kitab al-jana'iz* [23], *bab* 1), but the words concerning the teeth of the key are attributed to Wahb b. Munabbih (34–101 or 102/654 or 655–719 or 720).

6. All Sunni Muslims believe that believers will see God in the afterlife, not only the Ash'arites. Al-Rawahi's later apparent inclusion of al-Maturidi among them indicates that he means "all Sunni Muslims," not "all the Ash'arites." Cf. al-Juwayni's defense of the doctrine that God will be seen by believers in the afterlife (al-Juwayni 2000, 93–102).

S: This is a grave matter! To accept such a belief and profess it is appalling! Surely they must have some proof on which they rely and with which they argue against their opponents! What is it?

T: They have two types of evidence, one that is rational and another that is textual (*naqli*). Neither provides them with real proof.

S: They even have evidence from reason?! Can human intellects extend (*tatakhatta*) into the glory of divinity and the majesty of God so as to be able to comprehend the essence of the True Reality (*al-haqq*) that is like nothing else? They make a grave allegation! So what is their illusory rational proof (*hujjatuhum al-'aqliyya 'l-mawhuma*)?

T: How shrewd you are, my son, how penetrating your intellect, and what a sharp mind! You have described their rational proof as illusory, and this is no exaggeration! These people are bound by illusion, and they cannot escape it! For this reason they have adopted as rational proof something inspired by their imagination, so that even one of their own clever theologians understood this and found their proof deficient and refuted it and said clinging to this so-called proof is anthropomorphism.[7] His argument suffices, so let us confine ourselves to their argument from revelation and respond to it.

S: What led them, God forbid, to think it rationally permissible to say that one can see the exalted, glorious Lord?

T: They say that God exists and that everything that exists can be seen, so God can be seen. Their minor premise [that God exists] is evident. Concerning their major premise [that everything that exists can be seen], they say that we see that all things share the property of visibility, and the cause of their shared visibility is that they exist, since existence is the common characteristic all existents share. Thus have they nullified all possibilities other than existence as the cause of the visibility of things, without [seeing this as] hypocrisy or caprice! This is the height of corrupt and feeble thinking!

The proper response to them is this: "You have made existence the common cause [of visibility], and made the eternal Necessary Being come down to the

7. F (31, n. 4) identifies the scholar as 'Abd al-Rahman b. Ahmad b. 'Abd al-Ghaffar, known as Abu 'l-Fadl and nicknamed 'Adud al-Din al-Arihi. Perhaps he means 'Adud al-Din 'Abd al-Rahman b. Rukn al-Din b. 'Abd al-Ghaffar al-Iji, a Shafi'i jurist and Ash'arite theologian who died in 756/1355.

level of potential, originated things by saying that He shares visibility with them because they share existence. What do you say to this: are not substance and accident created, and is not createdness an attribute shared by both? Judgment must be made from a cause they have in common, and this must be either origination or existence. The common cause cannot be origination, because of what you said before, so it must be existence. By such an argument, God must be created, though He is glorified and exalted far above that! If this is false, then so is your proof based on your allegation of existence as the common cause [of visibility]. Furthermore, the sense of touch is shared by all the different things that can be perceived by touch, though their qualities may differ, such as height, shortness, heat, and cold, so perceptibility by touch is something they have in common among them. This argumentation can be carried to its logical conclusion that the Glorified One is perceptible by touch, which obviously must be rejected.

"By whatever path you pursue rational argument to affirm the vision of the True Reality, you will be unsuccessful. If you pursued the matter with true insight and open-mindedness, you would realize that the concept of absolute divinity shared by the divine characteristics is a semantic expression, like the concepts of essentiality and reality, so vision cannot grasp it at all. His characteristics can only be remotely and dimly comprehended, but total and detailed comprehension cannot be mastered. Degrees of totality vary in strength and weakness, and not every totality is a means to detailed knowledge of the elements of the thing that is comprehended and the conditions attached to it."

Their promotion of this imaginary argument comes to naught and ends up in smoke. This is why their theologians, like Abu Mansur al-Maturidi, confine themselves to textual proof, because they are incapable of producing rational proof; and al-Ghazali said that the major premise of their syllogistic reasoning is false. So it remains for me to teach you their textual argument, after which will follow the proof of the people of straightness to uncover the speciousness of the argument on which they rely, and may God grant success.

We say: The people (*al-qawm*) employed textual proofs (*dala'il sam'iyya*) for this teaching of theirs, such as the words of the Most High, "On that day faces will be radiant (*wujuh yawma'idhin nadira*), looking at/to their Lord (*ila rabbiha nazira*)" (75:22–23). They have no proof in this verse, as you will know. Know that the words of the Most High, "to their Lord" (*ila rabbiha*) are [an adverbial clause] describing His word "looking" (*nazira*); in this case, the adverbial clause (*al-muta'allaq*) is placed first in order to attract attention [to it] and keep it from disjunction (*al-fasila*) [from the action it describes]. This mutual connection informs us that the meaning is not that their eyes are looking at the essence of the Most High, because the one who claims that God will be seen in the afterlife does not say that he will look only at His essence for all time.

If someone argues that the preceding phrase is not a restriction on what follows, it remains that looking at the essence, even for less than a moment, requires that God have volume—and He is far exalted beyond that! "Looking" is a second predicate and its meaning is "expecting" or "waiting" (*muntazira*). An example of the use of *nazar* in the meaning of "expecting" or "waiting" (*intizar*) is in the saying, "Look to God and then to you"[8]—that is, "Await the bounty of God, then your own bounty." As the poet said:

Faces were looking (*nazirat*) on the day of Badr
To the All-Merciful to bring success

And elsewhere:

All creatures look to (*yanzuruna*) the Glorified One
As the pilgrims look to (*nazara 'l-hajij ila*) the rising (*tulu'*) of the new moon.[9]

8. This is from al-Rabi' b. Habib (n.d., 3:27, no. 855: "A woman who was a client of 'Utba b. 'Umayr said, 'I only look to God and to you.' He said to her, 'Don't say that, but say, 'I only look to God, and then to you.'"

9. F (32, n. 4) identifies the composer of these lines of poetry as Hassan b. Thabit al-Ansari, who was known as the Prophet's own poet. The Ash'arite theologian al-Baqillani (1987, 1:312) also attributes the first line of poetry to Hassan, but these lines are not found in Arafat 1974, and one should note that al-Jumahi (1974, 1:215) states that not all of the poetry attributed to him was actually his, a point repeated by 'Arafat (1974, introduction). (My thanks to Prof. Suzanne Stetkevych of Indiana University for pointing this out to me.) Concerning the second line, Stetkevych points out (personal communication, June 2009) that the second hemistich of this is nearly identical to a line by the famous Umayyad poet, Jarir b. 'Atiya: "Each one so white (i.e., noble) that people seek light from his face, as pilgrims look for the rising (*khuruj*) of a new moon." Concerning the first line, the battle of Badr, in 2/624, was the first major battle between the Muslims of Medina and the polytheists of Mecca, and the Muslims won a resounding victory, despite being outnumbered three to one. Concerning the second line, pilgrims await the rising of the moon while they stand from noon to

The words of the Most High are also an example of this: "[If the debtor is in difficulty,] let there be a look toward ease [i.e., postponement of repayment]" (2:280). He said "looking toward Me" in the sense of waiting to see when their Lord would allow them to enter paradise. It is possible that what one of our opponents[10] said is true, that *ila* here is the singular of *ala'*, meaning blessings (*al-ni'am*)—that is, it is not a preposition indicating a purpose, but a noun meaning "blessing" which is the direct object of "looking."[11] Although this perspective was mentioned by the Qutb in *Taysir al-tafsir* (Atfayyish 1981), in *Mufradat al-Qur'an* al-Raghib said this is an inaccurate usage from the standpoint of rhetoric (*ta'assuf min hayth al-balagha*), and that it is better to consider it a genitive construction—that is, it means "looking to the blessings of their Lord" or "[to] the mercy of their Lord" or that the eye looks at Him. It is possible that it originally meant "looking to the kindness (*in'am*) of their Lord," and that "looking" means "expecting," for they do not hope for mercy from any but God, just as they do not worship any but Him.

In our opinion, the best exegetical method (*al-'imad al-a'zam*) is that any deletion or metaphorical interpretation, even if it contradicts the original text, is better than the alternative, if the alternative leads to anthropomorphism or to anything else that contradicts the perfection of God and the qualities of His majesty.[12] This preference and interpretation are appropriate because of the Most

---

sunset on the plain of 'Arafat seeking God's forgiveness. This is a time of great trial, and is relieved by the rising of the new moon.

10. F (33, n. 6): "He is Abu Nasr al-Qushayri"—that is, 'Abd al-Rahim b. 'Abd al-Karim b. Hawazin al-Qushayri, an Ash'arite theologian who died in 514/1120 in his eighties. He is the son of Abu 'l-Qasim al-Qushayri.

11. The verb *nazara* (to look) can take a direct object, although it more commonly takes an indirect object using the preposition *ila* ("toward").

12. Al-Rabi' b. Habib (n.d., 3:39–42) discusses exegetical principles in a similar fashion, saying that expressions used in the texts are meant to be understandable, and if they are illogical or violate fundamental principles of the faith (such as God's perfection and difference from all created things), a metaphorical interpretation is required. It also vitiates against excessively literal interpretations by means of a hadith in which the Prophet said, "Every word has two meanings [literally "aspects," *wajhan*], so interpret speech according to its best meaning." The text goes on to say that every word has an inner and outer aspect. This text consistently attributes anthropomorphic interpretations to the Jews, who are described (3:40) as God's enemies.

High's words, "There is nothing like Him" (42:11), on which all scholars agree, because the Glorified One does not have volume (*la yatahayyaz*) and does not have a body (*la yatajassam*), as all Muslims agree, and because He transcends (*mutanazzih ʿan*) originated things, and originated things do not comprehend Him (*la tudrikuhu 'l-hawadith*), as all Muslims agree, and because the Glorified One transcends all inherence (*hulul*) [in a place], as all Muslims agree, and because He transcends time, as all Muslims agree. All of this [is true by virtue of His] essence, and what is of the essence does not change over time, and because He transcends color, height, shortness, thickness (*ghilza*), and thinness (*riqqa*). His being seen contradicts all these principles and implies His absence from other places and His divisibility, and requires that God be perceptible to His creation.

These are a people (*qawm*) whose error concerning some principles is evident, as when they say that Moses heard the essential, eternal speech of God (*kalam Allah al-nafsi al-qadim*); they have said that it was speech and that it was heard, although God's essential speech is without sound. One of their more intelligent scholars said this is wrong, and reviled al-Ghazali and al-Ashʿari for saying that eternal speech (*al-kalam al-azali*) can be heard. He said, "They agreed that only sound can be heard, yet they come back and say that the meaning of hearing the eternal speech (*al-kalam al-azali*) is that it is known by our hearing. It is evident from revelation that the essential speech is unchanging." We also do not concede (*nusallim*) the unchangeability of the essential speech. No rational being abandons (*yatruk*) the affirmation of God's oneness to embrace something that contradicts it.

They forged (*wadaʿu*) hadiths, including one that says that He will look at them and they will look at Him, and they will not cease to look at Him until He is veiled from them (al-Muttaqi 2001, no. 3032); and another that says that the one who is most generous to God is the one who will look at Him morning and evening (Ibn Hanbal 1998, 420, no. 5317).

Those who claim that God will be seen do not neglect to say that it will be an unusual vision (*laysat ʿala 'l-muʿtad*), because it is an unveiling (*hasilaha 'l-inkishaf*),[13]

13. According to the Sunni exegete al-Tabari (d. 310/923), some say that God will create a sixth sense for people, so that they will be able to see God on the day of resurrection, while others say that only believers will be able to see God, whereas unbelievers will remain veiled from seeing Him (Gätje 1971, 156–62).

but He is too exalted for that. They say that they will not be harmed by gazing [at God],[14] because the vigor (*nadra*) they will have is a great blessing that eliminates distress from gazing—indeed, God will make this gazing another blessing.

They cannot say that if "looking" meant "expecting" it would not be linked to the face because expectation is not in the face, because our answer is that what is meant by "faces" here [in the words "faces will be radiant, looking to their Lord"] is their entire being (*al-dhawat bi-jumlatiha*), because the expectation encompasses the whole person, not just the face; looking is linked to faces [in the Qur'anic verse] to express the entire person, just as "neck" is applied to a whole person [in other Qur'anic verses]. This is frequent in the Qur'an, and is very clear, as in, for example, "then the freeing of a neck [meaning freeing a slave]" (4:92). It is not unclear or obscure, as some have claimed.

If they say that what is in the line of poetry [that was quoted earlier, "Faces were looking to the all-Merciful on the day of Badr to bring success"] is in the sense of a request (*bi-ma'na 'l-su'al*), we say yes, and that is proof enough against you, for the expectation of mercy is a request for it. It is also used in the Qur'anic verse in the sense of a request, and the use of "to" gives the verb an object because it is included in the meaning of communication (*al-inha'*)—that is, "We communicate our hopes to you and have brought them to you."

In response to those who say that if "look" was used in the poetic verse (*bayt*) in the sense of waiting, he would not have said, "You increase my blessings"—and by the poetic verse they mean:

> When I look to you as [my] king (*wa-idha nazartu ilayka min malikin*),
> And the sea is less than you [in bounty] (*wa-'l-bahru dunaka*),
> You increase my blessings (*zidtani ni'ama*)[15]

14. In Q 7:143 Moses asked God to let him see Him. God replied, "You will never see Me, but look at the mountain; if it remains in its place, then you will see Me." But when the Lord manifested His glory to the mountain, He made it crumble, and Moses fell into a swoon. Various hadiths say that God is surrounded by tens of thousands of veils of bright light (e.g., al-Muttaqi 2001, no. 142). In the story of Muhammad's ascension before the throne of God, God protects the Prophet by shielding his eyes while giving him a vision from his heart, so he would not be harmed (al-Baghawi 1900, 2:169–72; Jeffrey 1958, 35–39).

15. According to Prof. Muhsin al-Musawi of Columbia University (personal communication, June 2009), this is by the Umayyad poet Jamil b. 'Abdallah b. Ma'mar (d. 82/701) (cf. al-Jumahi

—because the waiting was not in expectation of receiving a gift, [we say] this interpretation is inadmissible, because the poem's intent is exaggerated praise, to the point that waiting for the one who is praised is like making a request of him.

Furthermore, this is metaphorical speech (*al-kalam 'ala 'l-majaz*), and if the Qur'anic verse (*aya*) referred to seeing, it would not have been limited to the Lord—God forbid!—because at the time of gathering [of all creatures on the Day of Resurrection], is there anything the seeing person will not see (*a-huwa illa yabsuruha 'l-basir*)?[16] To this one cannot say, "This does not apply to all conditions (*hadha laysa fi kulli 'l-ahwal*), so it can exclude looking at other things," because we reply that "on that day" (Q 75:22) indicates that this applies to all conditions.[17] This is obvious, and no one may avoid that conclusion without evidence to the contrary. Likewise, if you say, "I tarried a day," "tarry" applies to the whole day unless the context indicates otherwise.

When one of [our theological opponents] looked at places in the Qur'an (*al-tanzil*) and other texts in which "looking" (*al-nazar*) in the sense of "waiting" takes a direct object without the addition of *ila* ("at" or "to"), he claimed that it never takes a direct object by itself, and that whoever says that it also takes an object by means of the preposition *ila* is mistaken, although in fact he is the one who is mistaken. Their specious argument (*shubha*) that has filled them with certainty concerning the vision [of God in the afterlife] is their report (*riwaya*) from the Prophet, peace and blessings be upon him, "You will see your Lord on the Day of Resurrection with your own eyes, and you will not join (*la tadammuna*) your vision of Him with vision of anything else, just as you do not see anything but the moon on the night of the full moon, or anything but the sun when there are no clouds to hide it" (al-Bukhari n.d., 1054, no. 4851). *Tadammuna* has an *a*

1974, 2:669–75). It is quoted by the Mu'tazilite scholar al-Zamakhshari (1966–1968, 1:1321), and is consequently also quoted by subsequent Sunni exegetes like al-Baydawi and al-Razi in order to rebut his interpretation.

16. Cf. Q 50:22, "You were heedless of this, but now We have removed the veil from you, so your sight today [on the Day of Resurrection] is keen (*basaruka 'l-yawm hadid*)."

17. It seems that the objection means to imply that the restriction of vision to God alone need not apply to the entire Day of Resurrection. As al-Rawahi clarifies shortly, the discussion over the restriction of vision to God alone is based on a Sunni hadith to this effect. To this al-Rawahi replies that without evidence to the contrary, "on that day" must apply to the entire day.

after the *t*, although it is possible to have a *u*, and there are two *m*s. *Tadammuna* (join together) means "to crowd" something. Or, if the *t* is followed by a *u* and there is only a single *m*, it would be derived from the root *d-y-m* and it would mean "No injustice will overtake you," meaning that some would see Him, while others would not. It has also been transmitted as *la tadarruna* (you will not be harmed), which has the same meaning. As for the sayings they narrate from the Prophet, on whom be blessings and peace—"The one who is most generous with God is he who looks at His face morning and evening" (Ibn Hanbal 1998, 420, no. 5317) and "He will lift the veil, and they will not be given anything dearer to them than the privilege of looking at their Lord" (Muslim 2000, no. 297; Muslim 1977 no. 347)—all that is a lie on the part of the person who transmitted this saying, and a lie against the Prophet, on whom be blessings and peace, because it contradicts the words of the Most High, "Vision does not comprehend Him, but He comprehends [all] vision" (6:103).[18] The Prophet also said, "If you hear any saying that claims to be from me but contradicts the Book of God, it is not from me" (al-Rabi' b. Habib n.d., 1:13, no. 40). What they relate on the authority of al-Hasan [al-Basri] and Ibn 'Abbas is a lie against them; or, if it is true, "looking" simply means knowledge of His existence. And their saying "with your own eyes"[19] is an addition they made to the hadith, if indeed the hadith is valid. Al-Sa'd collected this hadith from twenty-one Companions of the Prophet, and none of them said "with your own eyes." Or, if the phrase is authentic, "with your own eyes" (*'iyanan*) means true knowledge, like the knowledge of a thing by thorough investigation (*mu'ayana*).

Bashir reported on the authority of al-Dahhak, who heard from Ibn 'Abbas that one day he went out and there was a man calling on God, raising his eyes to heaven and raising his hands above his head. Ibn 'Abbas said to him, "Call on your Lord with your right hand, and let your left hand fall to your side. And lower your eyes, for your hand is enough. You will never see Him or reach Him." The man asked, "Even in the afterlife?" He replied, "Even in the afterlife." The man said, "Then what do the words of God Most High mean, 'On that day faces will

18. On the various possible interpretations of this verse, see Gätje (1971, 156–62).

19. Al-Bukhari (n.d., no. 7435) has this hadith, but it is narrated on the authority of Jarir b. 'Abdallah, not al-Hasan al-Basri and Ibn 'Abbas.

be radiant, looking at their Lord' (75:22–23)?" Ibn 'Abbas replied, "Haven't you read 'Vision comprehends Him not, but He comprehends [all] vision' (6:103)?" Ibn 'Abbas said, "The faces of God's friends will be radiant on the Day of Resurrection, and this radiance is illumination. Then they will look to their Lord to see when He will permit them to enter paradise after He has finished with judgment. It is like in His words, 'Faces on that day will be gloomy, [knowing that a great disaster will befall them]' (75:24–25), meaning that they are darkened as they await punishment" (al-Rabi' n.d., 3:25–26, no. 853).

Likewise, Aflah b. Muhammad reported on the authority of Abu Mu'ammar al-Sa'di, who heard from 'Ali b. Abi Talib and from Mukannaf al-Madani, who heard from Abu Hazim, that Muhammad b. al-Munkadir said, "I never saw any rational man say that any creature would ever see God. 'Vision does not comprehend Him, but He comprehends all vision' (6:103). 'Those who do not hope to meet God say, "Why have no angels been sent to us? Why do we not see our Lord?" How arrogant they are, and how gross is their iniquity!' (Q 25:21)" (ibid., 3:26, no. 854).

Mukannaf also said, "I sat with Malik b. Anas and someone asked him, 'Can any of God's creatures see Him?' He replied, 'Vision does not comprehend Him' and 'Those who do not hope to meet God say . . . '" (ibid.).

Abu Nu'aym reported on the authority of Abu Ishaq al-Sha'bi, who heard from Sa'id b. Jubayr, who heard from Nafi' b. al-Azraq: "Ibn 'Abbas was asked about the words of the Most High, 'Looking to their Lord.' He said, 'They look to His mercy and His reward. "Vision does not comprehend Him."'" Mujahid, Ibrahim [al-Nakha'i], Makhul [al-Dimashqi], [Ibn Shihab] al-Zuhri, Sa'id b. al-Musayyib, 'Ata' [b. Yasar], Sa'id b. Jubayr, al-Dahhak [b. Muzahim], Abu Salih, author of the Qur'anic exegesis, 'Ikrima, Muhammad b. Ka'b, and 'A'isha all reported the same thing. Al-Hasan said it means "looking to the dominion, power and rule of their Lord" (ibid., 3:27, no. 855). The preceding was also reported from Mujahid, al-Fudayl b. 'Iyad, Jalil[20] b. 'Abd al-Majid al-Ta'i, and 'Ammar, the nephew of Sufyan al-Thawri. Mansur b. al-Mu'tamir b. Sulayman heard from his father, who heard from Waki' b. al-Jarrah and Asbat b. Muhhammad, who heard

20. Some manuscripts of al-Rabi' b. Habib's Hadith collection say "Khalil" instead of "Jalil." The Cairo edition prefers Khalil, though it notes the variant in a footnote.

from Yahya b. Abi Zakariya, who heard from Ziyad, who heard from Isra'il, who heard from Yunus and 'Isa b. Yunus,[21] who heard from al-Layth, and he is the transmitter from Mujahid, that the Messenger of God, may God bless him and grant him peace, was asked whether he saw his Lord. He exclaimed, "Glory be to God! And where would I see Him?"—that is, how could I see Him? So he denied that God can be seen.

If it is said that he was denying that God can be seen in this world [but not in the next], we say that what makes God transcendent (*ma yajib tanzih Allah*) in this world also necessarily makes Him so in the next. That is why the Messenger of God preceded his statement with an exclamation of God's glory, as a sign that it is impossible for God to be seen, and that He is too exalted for that. If he was merely denying that God can be seen in this world, he would have replied that God's vision is postponed for a time of His grace (*li-waqt karamatihi*), but instead he immediately opened his response to the questioner with a glorification of God, to cut off all [such] aspirations, and [to indicate] that this is something no angel who is near to God or prophet sent by God would attempt, and nor would he, may God bless him and grant him peace, despite the greatness of his particularity (*'azamat khususiyyatihi*), either in this world or the next.

They say that the verse not only proves that God can be seen, but that God must be seen, because He promised this to His friends. We say that the indication of necessity or permissibility is utterly repudiated, for there can be no permissibility, let alone necessity, because the vision of His reality means that the pupil of the eye is turned toward the object of vision, which requires direction, and that is impossible for the Glorified One.

You [Sunnis] continue to cling to the idea that what is intended by "looking" is actual sight, although the verse denying that vision comprehends Him contradicts you; vision unavoidably means comprehension and the fruit of sense perception, which requires a perceptible object on which it can fall. The Most High's words, "Vision does not comprehend Him," block your path, so turn back!

21. Al-Rabi' b. Habib (n.d., 3:28, no. 857) says, "Yahya b. Abi Zakariya b. Ziyad, from Isra'il b. Yunus and 'Isa b. Abi Yunus, from al-Layth." This source also attaches this *isnad* to a saying of Mujahid rather than to this hadith; this hadith is attributed to Muhammad b. al-Shaybani, who reports it directly from the Prophet (ibid., no. 856).

It does you no good to divert the intention [of the verse] toward this world, for the glory, qualities of majesty, and particularities of divinity that apply to God in this world remain in the next, from all eternity without beginning and to all eternity without end.

So leave alone these ridiculous Ash'ab-like sayings and empty aspirations[22] and these Jahm [b. Safwan]-like doctrines that impugn the essence and attributes of God. This verse, "Vision does not comprehend Him," testifies against you that you are blind and ignorant of the way to exalt your Lord, as there is no evidence of restriction on the absolute and comprehensive applicability of the text. No one will see Him at any time, whether in a vision of the senses or of the heart.

You have no proof that comprehension of a thing is predicated on seeing it, or that seeing it yields knowledge of it from every aspect, or that comprehension is not linked to vision alone; or, if it is limited to a particular thing, it would not yield knowledge of it from every aspect—the Most High has excluded it from Himself. As for it being linked to vision alone, comprehension is not linked to it, for comprehension by itself is not what the verse is denying; rather, what is denied is comprehension linked to knowledge, because we say that the definite participle in the word "vision"[23] indicates real vision (*li-'l-haqiqa*). So comprehension—that is, vision—is absolutely negated in any real sense (*'an haqiqat al-basar*); anything that can be called true vision (*al-basar al-haqiqi*) cannot see God.

Alternatively, by definition vision means true vision in the sense of all vision, and the negation is in that case comprehensive (*kulliyya*) but not applicable to all vision, meaning that it is generally withheld, although the denial is postponed [until the end of the verse]. This rhetorical style is frequent in the Qur'an, as when the Most High says, "Do not obey everyone who swears" (68:10) and "God does not love every arrogant person" (57:23), and so on.

The reason for this is that the claim that it is possible to see God indicates some deficiency in Him, because what can be seen has color and a body and inhabits a place (*hall fi makan*) and has width, because every body has width, composition,

22. Ash'ab al-Tamma' b. Jubayr was a comedian of Medina who told jokes and parodies of hadiths (Rosenthal 1999). Al-Rawahi here also makes a pun on Ash'ab's name, because "aspirations" (*al-atma'*) sounds similar to the name al-Tamma'.

23. What we translate here as "vision," in English an indefinite singular, in Arabic is a definite plural, *al-absar*.

six directions, and needs, and is subject to the passage of time (*jarayan zaman 'alayhi*), and must be originated and must be powerless over what is far from it, and must be veiled from whoever is not present with it. Because vision is necessarily accompanied by deficiencies, the interpretation of the hadith, "You will see your Lord on the Day of Resurrection just as you see the full moon," must be that you will ascertain (*satuhaqqiquna*) the reality of His existence, His promise [of salvation], and His threat [of punishment], and you will increase in certainty, as if you were unveiling the full moon.

As you know, these are things the existence and description of which you definitely know, though you have not seen them or perceived them. If you saw them, you would necessarily have to describe them as being in a place and a direction and having a shape (*takayyufiha*). So what they say is nullified, because we know that He has no place, finite dimensions (*hadd*), or shape. You cannot say, "We will see Him without dimensions or place or shape," because vision requires shape, finite dimensions, and place. Likewise, it is necessary to interpret "looking to their Lord" in the meaning I mentioned here, for seeing God—as is evident to anyone who is fair-minded and does not disdain his intellect—implies deficiency in the Exalted and Most High, Who is necessarily absolutely perfect. So the Glorified One's exclusion of it concerning Himself is an exclusion of deficiency, just as the Most High has excluded all other deficiencies from Himself.

The impossibility (*imtina'*) of describing a thing does not necessarily mean that it is impossible to mention its exclusion. For example, it is impossible for God to have a partner, and God the Majestic and Exalted and has excluded such a possibility. Just as His glory excludes His having a partner, so does His glory exclude His being seen; it cannot be said that He is not necessarily glorified if an impediment prevents His being seen.

If comprehension were linked only to vision, why is it expressly circumscribed (*li-ma khassahu bi-'l-ihata*) in the verse, although the hadith on this subject, the hadith of vision, must be given a nonliteral interpretation (*yajibu ta'wiluhu*), because otherwise it leads to an impossible conclusion? The Ash'arites know this, and have tried to cover the deficiencies of their argument with a spider's web, by saying He will be seen "without how" [or "without form"] (*bi-la kayf*). But God the Majestic and Exalted said, "Vision does not comprehend Him" to indicate that it is impossible to see Him—something that is so remote and illusory, it is like something that has passed away, so if someone wanted to catch it and strove hard to do that, he would not succeed. There is no proof that the exclusion of the possibility of seeing God applies only to this world, except for that hadith and that Qur'anic verse (75:22–23), and you know the necessity of giving them a nonliteral interpretation.

There is no harm in interpreting "He comprehends" in the passage "and He comprehends all vision" to mean that He knows all vision, because the Most High is exalted beyond having limbs.[24] We say that the impossibility of the Most High having limbs indicates that this comprehension that is affirmed of Him means the knowledge that accompanies sight in general, not the comprehension that is excluded from the Most High, which is that others see Him. It is unsound to take these two types of comprehension together in the sense of knowledge, because vision does not know anything, let alone . . . [25] Vision will not know Him, just as it cannot be said that the one who comprehends (*al-ha'it*) does not know you, unless one has recourse to [the Prophet's] words, "The knower is the heart, and the heart knows God." The most obvious meaning of "Vision does not comprehend Him" is that you cannot see Him. Granted, no one knows Him, which means that scholars do not know Him in a comprehensive manner (*'ilm al-ihata*). There is no harm in that, for the denial of seeing Him remains, derived from the exclusion of attributes of deficiency from the Most High, as mentioned earlier. As al-Suddi said, "Vision can mean the vision of the eye or the vision of knowledge."

The mention of vision (*al-absar*) in His words "He comprehends all vision" is to emphasize the denial that the Most High can be seen, in that He comprehends all seeing vision, but it does not comprehend Him. Its denial is further emphasized by His adding [at the end of the verse] "and He is the Subtle, the Aware" (*al-Latif al-Khabir*). Subtlety (*al-lutf*) means fineness (*al-diqqa*) and hiddenness (*al-khafa'*), meaning that He is beyond being seen by any vision (*basarin ma*) at any time (*fi zamanin ma*) and of any type (*ru'yatin ma*), whereas He has

24. Al-Rawahi had previously argued that "vision does not comprehend Him" in Q 6:103 means that creatures cannot see God. Now he wishes to clarify that "He comprehends all vision" in that same verse does not mean that God has eyesight, because God's difference from created things and His freedom from the limitations of bodies mean that His comprehension of all vision can best be understood as His knowledge of all vision.

25. SA says that there is a lacuna in the text at this point, and indeed the words that follow do not follow semantically.

precise knowledge (*'ilm daqiq*) of all vision (*bi-kulli basar*), as well as of everything else. Awareness (*al-khibra*) is precise knowledge of things; so He comprehends (*yudriku*) what the vision of others does not, and He knows what others do not. He cannot be seen, just as anything that has no density (*al-kathafa*) cannot be seen; just as you cannot see the wind, you cannot see the Most High, who is exalted far beyond all deficiency and beyond being compared to wind or to anything else, and beyond being described as having density or real fineness (*litafa*). His calling Himself "the Subtle" (*al-Latif*) refers to His saying "Vision does not comprehend Him," because it is in the nature of a fine thing that is hidden from bodies not to be seen by vision, but God is exalted beyond all bodily subtlety. His calling Himself "the Aware" (*al-Khabir*) refers to His words "and He comprehends all vision." Indeed, how could One Who knows the subtleties of all things not comprehend them? It is said that the meaning of "the Subtle" is that He knows obscure matters and precise meanings and truths and that His awareness is most complete.

Vision (*al-absar*) belongs to the pupil of the eye or the whole eye. It is also possible that what is meant by "vision" is the light by which the eye sees, but which cannot be seen or ascertained by anyone, whereas God has complete knowledge of it in every aspect. *Al-Latif* is interpreted this way because of the context, which is the denial that the Glorified One can be seen and the affirmation that He comprehends all others, in contrast with another possible meaning of *al-Latif*—that is, the One who is gracious to His creatures and removes harm from them so that they do not even know that they are receiving these gracious favors or that harm has been removed from them—indeed, they might imagine the opposite. This interpretation also differs from the meaning of *al-Latif* as the One who does good to you in compassion, or who makes His servants forget their sins lest they feel ashamed, or in the sense of the One who does not tax them with more than they can bear, or who commends them when they are obedient and does not cut off His goodness to them when they sin. These interpretations do not accord in any obvious way with the denial that God the mighty and majestic can be seen.

Furthermore, the Most High's words, "Vision does not comprehend Him," must be taken comprehensively. He could have first given the denial and then made it apply generally, but it is in a comprehensive negative form, meaning that no type of vision can ever see Him. Alternatively, He could have expressed the generality first and then introduced the negation, in which case it would be a partial negation, meaning that only some people's vision would not see Him, such as the vision of unbelievers. The first alternative is the only possible one, because of the deficiency that seeing Him would entail.

If we attach a definite article to a reality, we mean the reality, insofar as it can be considered a single entity. This single entity that is a reality of God Most High suffices for us to exclude the possibility of seeing Him, for whatever can be called "sight" cannot be said to see Him; what forces this interpretation is what is required for vision. This being the case, do not couch your argument in the form of an allegation that some will have the ability [to see Him in the afterlife, to the exclusion of others], for no Qur'anic passage indicates such ability, whether total or partial. Whatever constitutes a deficiency in a thing does not change with the passage of time. If God could be seen, this would be a deficiency both in this world and in the next, whether only the believers saw Him, as they allege, or whether the unbelievers also saw Him, although nobody claims that.

Our school (*madhhabuna*), the people of truth (*ahl al-haqq*) among the Ibadis, as well as the rest of the Ibadi sects (*sa'ir firaq al-Ibadiyya*), the Shi'a, the Mu'tazila, and some of the Murji'a, all deny that God can be seen. If you wish to be healed of all doubt on this matter, read *Ma'alim al-din fi 'ilm al-kalam* [The Teachings of Religion in the Knowledge of Theological Disputation] by Shaykh 'Abd al-'Aziz [al-Thamini] al-Mus'abi, may God have mercy on him and be pleased with him.

In the year 1314 [1896–1897], God granted me the composition of a poem that I called *Tams al-absar 'an ru'yat al-malik al-jabbar* [Obliterating the Possibility of Seeing the Overwhelming King]. There is no harm in quoting it here in order to complete the subject and spread useful knowledge, and to store up a divine reward. So here it is in its entirety, and may God benefit us by it.[26]

Exalt your Lord (*nazzih ilahak*) beyond vision, that you might know Him; do
    you think you can know Him and witness (*tuthbit*) His attribute?
Know that your position (*maqamaka*) is too lowly to attempt it;
    what you attempt is doomed to failure.
You wear yourself out in convoluted fantasies (*zunun*);
    the truth is that the fantasies of your imagination (*wahmika*) are incorrect

26. This poem is published in al-Rawahi 1980, 282–90.

How amazing that you affirm His oneness, yet assign Him the accidents of the natural world!

You flee from asserting that He has a body, yet you affirm that He can be the object of sight, hiding behind "without how"

You say that "how," "what," "where," and such questions are impossible, and that you worship an essence hidden behind a veil.

This contradiction in your doctrine is evident; your faith must be arrogance.

If you have understanding, you know that what you see is limited to finite substance;

Otherwise, you do not understand and are confused, lacking comprehension, so where is knowledge?

If you say He is known, you claim to comprehend His essence, and mistake your inability for ability.

Or do you say He is unknown, stripping Him of all meaning, worshipping something unknown and divesting Him of all attributes?

You affirm that His essence has perceptible accidents if you can see Him with your eye for all eternity.

Woe to you—perception requires something perceptible, finite, occupying space (*mutahayyiz*), having shape;

You deny that He has volume or inheres in a place, yet you affirm what requires the very thing you negate—what is this folly?

If you say it is something beyond our understanding and bring us a proof requiring this doctrine,

Then go ahead, if you dare, explain it rationally; you will find yourself going astray, pursuing a fantasy!

If you can perceive Him without intermediary, the deed does not belong to the doer—we will never know Him.

First, what intermediary do you deem suitable, so you might see His essence with your own eyes?

What you say requires that you see Him with your eye; no other sense can perceive Him,

Following upon (*ridfan li*) God's word "gazing," and there is nothing in your two proofs to support your claim of knowledge.

Suppose for the sake of argument that I agree with your understanding of these two proofs; where is this attribute established?

Do these proofs affirm vision only of the eye, following the folly (*buhtan*) of the people of sophistry (*al-safsafa*)?

They whimsically abandon metaphorical interpretation here, and blindly follow the opinions of others on weighty matters.

Do you see the metaphorical image of His limbs as literally true, if you stubbornly hold this position?

You deny the true meaning of His essence's sitting (*istiwa'*), though its literal meaning would require His composition.

You require that He be seen, so require that He be heard, and on that basis let Him have the same attributes as you!

If you say the one to whom He spoke (*al-Kalim*) heard His speech,[27] do you think this means a voice issuing from lips?

No! Rather, God created for his ear a sound, so He could teach him what He taught.

If you draw an analogy between His vision and His speaking, something must be originated to be seen by the eye.

In that case it would be created, and you would claim a Creator Whom you perceive with your sense and Whose place you can see.

Have you divested Him of any of His other qualities, or are the others identical with His essence—or what is the attribute?

This is an innovation (*tajdid*), assigning Him finite dimensions (*tahdid*), making Him divisible (*taqsim*) and multiple (*ta'did*), what deviance!

If you make Moses' request[28] a proof and spuriously eliminate the laws of logic,

27. Muslims call Moses *al-Kalim* (the one to whom God spoke), because the Qur'an singles him out as one to whom God spoke directly. Q 42:51 says, "It is not for any person that God should speak to him except by revelation, or from behind a veil, or through a messenger sent and authorized by Him to make His will known," but 4:164 says, "We spoke directly to Moses (*kallama Allahu Musa takliman*)." This corresponds to the Bible's insistence that Moses was unique among the prophets in that God spoke to him face to face, as a man talks to his friend (Numbers 12:6–8; Deuteronomy 34:10).

28. In Q 7:143 Moses asks God to show Himself to him so he might look upon Him (cf. Exodus 33:18–23). God replies, "You shall not see Me. But look upon the mountain; only if it remains firm upon its base shall you see Me." But when God revealed Himself to the mountain it crumbled, and Moses fell into a swoon. Moses then asks for God's forgiveness for having made this request. Al-Rawahi interprets Moses' request to see God as a lesson for the Israelites, who, according to the Qur'an, refused to believe in him unless they could see God with their own eyes (2:55, 4:153). In al-Rabi' (n.d., 3:34), Moses' request is also described as made so that God might show his people the futility of hoping to see God.

Tell me, did Moses know its impossibility before he fell trembling into the swoon of denial,

So you might charge him with deficiency in his monotheism, and you might be more perfect in proof and knowledge?

Or did he know it was impossible, yet made the request, transgressing, so you might attribute deviance to prophethood?

Or did he know it was impossible in this life, and his Lord hastened to honor him?

Any of these three implies deficiency in him, in that he asked this of Him; if you don't admit this, you are biased.

Indeed, he knew it was impossible in this life and the next, and the question was for the sake of the foolish,

Who would not believe him unless they saw God with their own eyes, and he denied them this with a frightful rebuke.[29]

Because of his earnest desire that they believe, he wished to convince them that God could not have such an attribute.

Do you think that *al-Kalim* made this request for himself, desiring such a thing, though he had rebuked the Jews for making such a request?

By God, he was not ignorant of his position, nor did he forget the glory of the Majestic One, nor did he overstep his bounds!

But because of their obstinacy and their arrogance he made this request, though his heart knew the truth.

Did he not plainly tell them they were foolish, seduced by God's forgiveness of what was past

And His forgiveness of its issuance from his tongue without permission, or of a terrifying thunderbolt (*sa'iqa*)?

Are you ignorant that "will never" (*lan*)[30] is an everlasting negation, that you might nullify the meaning of its intensity?

29. In Q 2:55–56 the Israelites say to Moses, "We will not believe in you until we see God with our own eyes," upon which they were struck by lightning or were simply stricken into a stupor (*sa'iqa*), but God then raised them from the dead (*min ba'di mawtikum*)—or from their stupor, according to most interpretations—so they might give thanks.

30. Q 7:143: When Moses asked God to show Himself to him, God replied, "You will never see me (*lan tarani*)." Cf. al-Rabi' 3:34: "Al-Hasan [al-Basri] said, 'You will never see Me,' [meaning] 'It is never possible [literally "appropriate," *yanbaghi*] for a human being to see Me.' Al-Rabi' b. Habib said, '*Lan* is one of the words indicating deprivation of hope among the grammarians and philologists, meaning that no one will ever see Him in this world or the next.'"

Why would you limit its intensification if not out of ignorance of the station of knowledge?

Admit that you have rejected rational proof and have covered the unveiled sun of the text!

Doesn't your Lord say, "You will never see me"? So stop asking!

Yet you say, "I will see you, though the manner is unknown!"

Is that not evident obstinacy? Go on—before you is an unavoidable punishment!

Is there the slightest doubt in the verse of *Surat al-An'am* [6:103], or the verse of *Surat al-A'raf* [7:143]? Beware of altering God's word!

Is there any ambiguity in these two verses that can lead you to imagine that one can deny them and affirm what one wishes?

No! But sheer caprice led you to lift the prohibition, causing deviation and turning it into mere embellishment!

Out of misfortune the efforts of whole communities have gone astray, and you have mimicked them in the pursuit of their whims!

Did you catch a glimpse of the light of God's self-manifestation and declare the essence of the True Reality unveiled?

Glory be to Him, the attributes of Whose perfection transcend all the attributes that are attached to origination!

The mountain crumbled at the manifestation of His Reality, and Moses fell into a swoon at its crumbling!

Don't you know that the manifestations of His glory were terrifying to the one who asked for the impossible?

They requested what was impossible for the qualities of His essence and were seized by God's wrath!

Do you deny His leveling of a mountain as a sign from Him in rebuke to the Jews?

Let's suppose that God did reveal Himself, as you say—so where in His sign is the place of "without how"?

Your vision would be destroyed by the rays of God's manifestation! You indulge in fantasies that would destroy you!

If you deny His manifestation in the greatest sign, beware of straying by treating Him with disdain!

His majesty, beauty and perfection: do you see Him in His essence or in an act related to an attribute?

Don't you know that your Lord is able to do anything through His power except manifest His essence?

What do you think is meant by "Your Lord comes" (Q 89:22) [on the Day of Resurrection]? Does it mean in His essence, or the unveiling of the command of resurrection?

Nothing comes but His command and His great power, while all things in creation are brought to a halt.

Do you think He Himself will come with His angels in His essence, surrounded by the shadows of clouds (Q 2:210)?

Will anything come besides His seizing them and the pain of His wrath for their scornful rejection of Him?

Do you shamelessly take refuge in the veil of not saying how He can be seen, or is His form finite?

Do you imagine that those who are veiled from His gardens and the witness of His mercy and favor

Are kept by that veil from seeing His essence? Either you err or you must worship a protective veil!

Does the veil increase or decrease, or is it level, so you can see it from any direction?

Tear off your veil, you who say your Lord has a body! How thick is the veil of your ignorance!

Turn instead to glorify the essence of the Real by the light of the one to whom He gave revelation, and beware of claiming to see Him!

Glorify God's qualities beyond those of creatures, and cast off the qualities of heresy!

If you long for other guidance, the path of straightness [Ibadism] is the desire of those who sincerely seek Him (*al-mutasawwifa*)

Our sect (*nihlatuna*) belongs to God, how blessed is its path (*ni'ma sabiluha*), in its roots and its branches; it does not violate His Book (*mushafahu*)!

It is the very message revealed by the Trustworthy Spirit to the trustworthy guide—all else is vain!

We do not worship what can be seen; all perceptible things are originated and composite.

Rather, we worship God, of Whom we know in truth that we will never see Him.

Our inability to perceive Him is true perception, not the perception of our substances that have form!

Our abstraction of His attributes and essence are just as He declared Himself to be abstracted—we will never see Him. We declare Him to be One, affirming His singularity in His essence, acts and attributes.

We declare Him to be too great to be seen by eyes or hearts, whether in this world or the next.

In our religion we decline to follow the authority of men, who are not immune from error in their distortions;

We follow the doctrine that accords with the root, of one who has proven its truth in knowledge.

You have slipped away from the source of guidance—admit your blindness and deviance!

You have strayed from the path of Abu Bakr and 'Umar and Ibn Wahb (*Adlalta siddiqiyyatan 'umariyyatan wahbiyyatan*), which offers sure guidance,

The path of Badr and Uhud, which did not appoint 'Amr [b. al-'As] as arbiter over their Qur'an, so that he might distort it!

This path has drunk the water of the river[31] from the cup of its Prophet, a chilled cup mixed with what is right!

Do not claim the disgrace of the permissibility of vision; reason suffices to refute the possibility of seeing Him!

Cut short your overweening ambition; to desire the impossible is disobedience.

Hold to the truth of "You will never see me," which absolutely negates the possibility of vision for all time.

Look at the nature of the impossible, because if something is impossible, it cannot happen.

If it could happen, impossibility would have no meaning, and the Jews would not have trembled and fallen into a swoon.

It is ancient knowledge that the mountain did not stay firm at the time it was shaken.

If you claim that this prohibition applies only to this world, but that it can occur in the afterlife,

We say you have affirmed that God can change, if you suppose His attributes will change at that time!

His perfection belongs to His essence and is not temporary—

31. A reference to the battle of Nahrawan. In his poem, "Al-Fath wa-'l-ridwan fi 'l-sayf wa-'l-iman" [Conquest and Pleasure in the Sword and Faith] (in al-Rawahi n.d.), al-Rawahi lauds the people of Nizwa, who (he says) all long to drink from the waters of Nahrawan, meaning they share in the zeal the early Khawarij who were slaughtered by 'Ali at Nahrawan, and are willing to share their fate.

no, and His attributes are not altered.
The attributes of our eternal Creator do not change, and the passing of ages will not alter Him.
No change will ever come to Him that could allow you to see Him.
Glory be to Him! His perfection is infinite, for it has no beginning!
Turn from your path! Your eye cannot turn its gaze toward anything that does not have form,
Only to a direction which sets finite limits for a substance bearing an accident that enables it to be situated;
Otherwise, vision is rationally impossible, and we see your talk of it as mere distraction!
Between me and you, the Book has ordained that we follow guidance, and you are foolish!
Do not make the unity of God the object of fancy; the object of truth in it is the essence of knowledge
How remote is true knowledge from your hearts, if the holiness of the Master is subject to "without how"!

S: I know for certain that belief in the possibility of seeing God is the result of poor choice (*su' al-ikhtiyar*) and of hearts deviating from guidance and leaving the path of truth, and that God may not be perceived by any of the senses or by the intellect, from all eternity and forevermore (*min al-qidam ila 'l-abad*). But enlighten me regarding what their theologians, like Fakhr al-Din al-Razi and others, mean when they say, "When a human being sees Him, it is a comprehension (*idrak*) regarding the essence of the Most High God, similar to the relationship that eyes have to objects that are seen in the external faculties. We do not say that its locus is the eye or anywhere else"; and al-Ghazali's saying, "Our opponents merely deny the vision [of God] because they do not understand what we mean by it, and they think that we mean a condition comparable to that experienced by a person when he looks at bodies and colors. God forbid! We confess the impossibility of that concerning the reality of God Most High."

T: They are retreating from the idea of seeing God in a physical manner and imply that the essence of the True Reality will be unveiled in a conceptual manner, so that perception leads to knowledge of His essence. These theologians only took this path as a refuge, fleeing from the implications of seeing with the eye, but both paths lead to perception and comprehension of the essence of God, Who is far too exalted for that. This is one of the traps that lead people astray in their investigations; one must beware and protect oneself from such a subterfuge, and we do not accept it from them. The essence of the Exalted Reality is absolutely too splendid and mighty to be perceived by the intellect, and no creature has knowledge (*ma'rifa*) of the true nature (*kunh*) of the Glorified Reality (*al-haqq subhanahu*). The farthest human knowledge can go by logical proofs is to know that the Glorified One exists, is living, is knowing, is powerful, has a will, exists from all eternity, remains forever, has no body or accident, and so on for the rest of His attributes. If what they say about intellectual perception were possible, it would also be possible to perceive Him with the five senses, because they have made Him perceptible by two bodily senses: they say that one may hear His eternal, essential speech,[32] but we do not, except in the sense that one must deny that He has any defect, and they say that He may be seen—which is what we are discussing—and the truth is that the Most High cannot be perceived by senses or by intellect—I mean that His essence is not intelligible.

S: What is the correct response to what Sa'd [al-Din al-Taftazani] said: "If the intellect is released from bondage and one does not judge it impossible to see God as long as he has no proofs against it, and the principle is that there are none, then the burden of proof is on whoever claims that it is impossible"?

T: We reply to this, and to other such sayings that pass arbitrary judgment on the rules of logic, that the intellect cannot accept the possibility of seeing God, because one of the conditions of perceptibility is that the object of perception be in a place and direction and be in front of the viewer, and that the distance between it and the viewer be neither too near nor too far, and that the rays of the viewer's eyes connect with the object of perception, and all of that, as we have already explained, is impossible concerning the Most High God.[33]

S: I know, esteemed teacher, that they affirm that God can be seen without direction or inhabiting (*hulul*) [a place] or being in front of the viewer or any dis-

32. In fact, Sunni scholars have held diverse opinions on this subject, as explained in Part One (38–40).

33. Al-Sanusi wrote that believers will be able to see God "without a direction or facing a certain way," without the use of physical organs of sight, just as knowledge of God does not require a directional orientation (Kenny 1970, 76).

tance or any contact with the rays of sight, but that it is a vision that transcends rational judgment with respect to the vision of a creature.

T: In that case, what Sa'd says—and he is one of their great scholars (*min a'azim muhaqqiqihim*)—that the intellect does not judge it impossible to see God, is invalidated. They say that it is a vision that lacks what is necessary for vision, which either contradicts the affirmation of vision, arbitrarily judges against reason, and dismisses what is actually true (*mukabira li-'l-waqi'*), or transforms it into intellectual vision (*al-ru'ya 'l-'ilmiyya*). If they mean knowledge of His reality, that is beyond the ability of creatures; if they mean knowledge of the existence of the Most High and of the rest of His attributes, that is true and we gladly concede that point, for no one disputes it.

Lesson 3: What Is Necessary for God, What Is Impossible for Him, and an Interpretation of Comparability (*Ta'wil al-Tashabuh*)

S: What is the meaning of God's nearness (*qurb*) to His creatures?[34]

T: God's nearness to His creatures and His distance from them are not like the nearness and distance of created things to each other. The use of the word *dana* (He drew near)[35] concerning the Most High does not mean that He adhered (*yaltasiq*) to anything, for adherence is an accident that characterizes bodies (*'arad min khususat al-ajsam*), and our Lord is neither a body nor an accident. Nearness (*dunuww*) concerning Him is a metaphor implying the nearness of His mercy, knowledge, and power, and that each of these attributes surrounds all things. The Most High is not described by nearness in the sense of adherence to a thing (*mulasaqat shay'*) or contact with a thing (*al-ittisal bi-shay'*), nor when He is described as distant does this mean separation (*al-infisal*), because contact and separation are accidents that require substances (*jawahir*), bodies, and things that have volume (*al-mutahayyizat*), and God is too majestic for that. It is possible that His nearness to His creatures can be interpreted as His being known

34. Q 50:16: "We [God] are nearer to him than his jugular vein."

35. Q 53:4–10 describes one of the Prophet Muhammad's visions: "It is naught but revelation that is revealed; One Mighty in Power has taught him, the Lord of Strength. He rose to the highest horizon, then He drew near (*dana*)."

by them by evidence (*bi-'l-dalil*), but not with respect to the essence of the Most High, only with respect to His existence and His attributes. It is possible to interpret His distance from His creatures as His being imperceptible (*ghayr mahsus*) to them. In either case, the metaphor holds. When we say "He drew near" (*dana*), we mean that He is known by evidence, and when we say "He is far" (*na'a*), we mean that He cannot be perceived by the senses. It is possible to interpret (*ta'wil*) His nearness in the sense of the Most High's nearness to the attributes of perfection—divinity, lordship, and oneness—by which He is described, and to explain His distance as His distance from attributes of deficiency, like origination and other attributes of creatures. What is meant by His nearness to the attributes of perfection is that He is worthy of them (*ta'ahulluhu la-ha*), and what is meant by His distance from the attributes of deficiency is that He is not suited for them. The metaphor holds (*al-majaz bi-halihi*) because of the requirement that a thing be near that to which it is suited, and that it be far from that to which it is not suited, so the relationship is one of rhetorical necessity (*al-luzum al-bayani*), not rational or ordinary necessity. It is possible to interpret nearness as His nearness to His allies (*awliya'ihi*) by making it easy for them to obey Him, and to interpret distance as His distance from His enemies by not making it easy for them to do this (*bi-'adam tawfiqihim la-ha*). It is possible that nearness means His response to the prayer of one of His allies, and distance means that God is too exalted to respond to the petitions of His enemies. The Most High said, "If my servants ask about Me, I am near. [I answer the prayer of the suppliant when he calls on Me, so they might hear My call and believe in Me and be rightly guided]" (2:186).

S: What is the meaning of the existence of the One Whose name is holy (*taqaddas dhikruhu*) in every place?[36]

36. Cf. al-Rabi' b. Habib (n.d., 3:28): "Jabir [b. Zayd] said: Ibn 'Abbas was asked whether there is any place in which God is not present (*Allah hal yakhlu minhu makan*). He said, "The Most High God said, 'There is no secret conversation of three people but I am their fourth, nor of five but I am their sixth, nor any number less nor more but He is with them wherever they are' (Q 58:7). The Mighty and Majestic One has informed us that no place is devoid of His presence and that He witnesses every place, is present (*hadir*) in every place in knowledge (*ihata*) and control (*tadbir*)." When Nafi' b. al-Azraq asked Ibn 'Abbas what God is like and where He is (*kayf huwa wa-ayn huwa*), Ibn 'Abbas replied (ibid., 3:22)—after pronouncing a curse on him for his impudence—"Nothing is like God (*la kayf la-hu*)! He is unlike the creation; He created the creation and He is the creator of their

T: Our glorified Lord's existence in places does not mean that He inheres in them in the manner of substances, composite things, and accidents. He Whose majesty is glorious is not a thing like other things, and He is not subject to time or circumstances, because dependence on circumstances is one of the attributes of composite things and accidents. The Glorified One's existence in places is by bringing things into existence, originating them, having perfect knowledge of them, adding to them (*al-ziyada fi-ha*) or diminishing them (*al-tanqis min-ha*), maintaining their existence until their appointed terms are over, exterminating them at the times He has determined, witnessing them, and by the impossibility of describing Him as absent from them. The Glorified One, by virtue of His essence, is too great to have any need for them at all (*ghani li-dhatihi 'an al-ihtiyaj ilayha mutlaqan*), whether by inhering (*hulul*), residing (*qarar*), attainment (*tawassul*), or by asking for help (*isti'ana*), for these conditions and attributes belong to originated things and are impossible for the Eternal One (*al-Qadim*) Whose existence is necessary (*al-wajib al-wujud*) by virtue of His essence (*li-dhatihi*), may He be glorified and exalted. He is not absent from anything, and nothing is absent from Him, because the originated thing is an artifact (*san'a*) of His knowledge and preservation, and is beneath His sovereignty (*qayyumiyyatihi*), control (*tadbirihi*), power (*bayna yadayy qudratihi*), and will (*iradatihi*). In that sense it is said that God is in every place, in all things, in every creature, in every world, and in the heavens and in the earth, not with respect to circumstances or inhering or residing. It is not said that He is in this world (*al-dunya*) or in the next (*al-akhira*), or in the night or in the daytime, or in a year or in a month, or in a day or in any moment, for time does not pass over Him, and He is not in bodies without accidents, or in accidents without bodies, or in accidents and bodies together.

S: What do the people of truth say about [God's] hand, right side, eye, face, leg, side, coming, bringing, and descending, which are attributed to Him in the Qur'an and Hadith?[37]

---

likenesses (*kayfiyyatihim*) and He is in every 'where' (*ayn*)," which, the text explains, means He is in every place (*bi-kulli makan*).

37. Al-Rawahi's response to this question is not dissimilar to that of the Ash'arite theologian al-Juwayni (al-Juwayni 2000, 86–91).

T: There is much talk on this subject, and the corporealists (*al-mujassima*)[38] have much to say on this, some of which leads to unbelief, and some of which leads to hypocrisy and going astray. The upshot of what they say is that the Karramiyya, a Shiʿite sect,[39] described Him as having two hands and a face (*atlaqat ʿalayhi lafz al-yadayn wa-'l-wajh*). They said, "We do not go beyond saying this; we do not interpret it or explain it, we merely confine ourselves to saying of Him what the text says." Al-Ashʿari said that God's limbs are attributes subsisting in the essence of the Creator, without saying that God has a body. The corporealists say that the Most High God has two hands that are His members (*ʿudwan la-hu*), and likewise for the face and the eye. They affirm that He has two legs that hang down from His throne, and two thighs that He will uncover on the Day of Resurrection, and a foot that He will place in hellfire, so that it will be filled with it. They affirm this in its actual meaning, not just as an expression, and as a reality, not a metaphor. No statements of interpretation, anthropomorphism, or corporealism have been attributed to Ahmad b. Hanbal at all; he just said that one should not interpret these expressions, and one should use the expressions used by the Book and the Sunna and not delve into their interpretation, citing God's words, "No one knows their interpretation except God" (3:7).[40] Most of his companions say the same.

Our companions, however, may God have mercy on them, and the Muʿtazila, and all those who practice *Kalam* theology deny all this of the Most High, and

38. Those who said that God is a body, a position rejected by all surviving Muslim sects.

39. Contrary to what al-Rawahi says, the Karramiyya were not Shiʿite. Ibn Karram's ideas are known only through heresiographies, who usually place him among the "corporealists" or the "anthropomorphists" (*mushabbiha*), although al-Ashʿari placed him among the Murji'a. He is said to have taught that God had a body of finite proportions in certain directions, enabling Him to come into contact with His throne (Bosworth 2002).

40. This verse reflects the interpretive difficulty posed by Arabic's lack of punctuation and subsumption of pronoun subjects in their verbs. Concerning ambiguous verses of the Qur'an, 3:7 says either (1) "None knows its interpretation but God and those who are firmly rooted in knowledge. They say: 'We believe in it; it is all from our Lord'"; or (2) "None knows its interpretation but God. Those who are firmly rooted in knowledge say, 'We believe in it; it is all from our Lord.'" The first version holds that some people are able to interpret the ambiguous passages, but the second version limits such understanding to God alone, and commends those who simply affirm their faith without trying to understand such passages.

interpret [anthropomorphic] expressions in the Qur'an, such as "to what I made with My two hands" (38:75) and "I neglected my duty concerning God's side" (39:56), and other similar expressions, as metaphors. They interpret them correctly in a way that is permissible in the Arabic language. They explain God's hand (23:88, 36:83, 67:1) in a way that is appropriate for God's attribute, as a metaphor for His power, and His right hand (39:67) as a metaphor for His power and might; and His eye in His words "floating before Our eyes" (54:14) in the sense of preservation, and in His words "so you [Moses] may be brought up before My eye" (20:39) in the sense of "My command and My knowledge." They interpret God's face (2:115 and elsewhere) as His essence, and His leg (68:42) as a metaphor for a weighty, terrifying matter (*al-amr al-shadid al-ha'il*) that He reveals to His creation on the Day of Resurrection, and they make His side a metaphor for obedience to His commands and prohibitions. They interpret His coming (*maji'*) in the words "your Lord comes with angels, row upon row" (89:22) as the coming of His command, His decree that distinguishes right from wrong, and His just judgment. They interpret His coming (*ityan*) in the words "Are they waiting for God to come to them?" (2:210) as the coming of His command and decree.

Expressions in the authentic hadiths that without interpretation would suggest a likeness between God and creatures, like His descending, in the words of the Prophet, "God descends to the lowest sky every Friday night and asks, 'Is there anyone who repents, so I might forgive him?'" (Al-Muttaqi 2001, no. 38295), they interpret in a manner that is appropriate for the Most High, which is the descent of one of His angels, who calls on God's behalf and informs us of God's desire. Likewise the "image" of God mentioned in the Prophet's words, "God created Adam according to his image" (al-Bukhari no. 6227), they interpret to mean the form of Adam in God's eternal knowledge according to which He knew He would create him, making the pronoun ["his" in "his image"] refer to Adam.[41] Likewise, the foot mentioned in the Prophet's words, "On the Day of Resurrection, when the people of Paradise are in bliss and the people of the Fire are in hell, and the Fire will ask, 'Are there any more?', the Overpowering One (*al-Jabbar*) will place His foot in it and the Fire will say, 'Enough, enough'" (al-Nawawi

41. Cf. al-Juwayni (2000, 90–91).

1994, 17:182), they interpret the foot (*al-qadam*) to mean the people whom God sends ahead (*yuqaddimuhum*)[42] into the Fire, meaning that He knew from before that they would be inhabitants of the Fire. Likewise, the leg mentioned in the report (*riwaya*), "until God places His leg on it," they interpret to mean the large number of people.[43] There are other similar examples. These examples are useful and comprehensive as illustrations of how the people of straightness and truth interpret anthropomorphic descriptions of God whose literal meanings must be excluded from God. This is the truth (*'ayn al-haqq*), and all else is deviation.

S: Does any monotheist dare (*yatajasar*) to say that God is in a direction (*li-'llahi jiha*)? What do the people of truth say about that?

T: The people of truth and straightness, may God have mercy on them, and the Mu'tazila and all theologians who have ascertained the truth (*al-muhaqq-iqin min al-mutakallimin*) say that God is not in any direction or place, and that such things require corporeality (*al-jismiyya*) or having accidents (*al-'aradiyya*), which are linked to corporeality. Since it is impossible for Him to have a body or accident, He cannot have a direction. The philosophers agree with this. The Karramiyya and the Hashwiyya say that the Most High God is in the direction "above." This is the teaching of Hisham b. al-Hakam,[44] 'Ali b. Mansur, Yunus b. 'Abd al-Rahman, Hisham b. Salim al-Jawaliqi, and many of the People of Hadith. Muhammad b. al-Haysam, a theologian of the Karramiyya, taught that the Most High is an essence that exists alone, separate from (*munfarida bi-nafsiha 'an*) all other existents and does not inhere in anything the way accidents do or mix with anything the way bodies do; that He is unlike (*mubayin*) creatures, but He is in a direction "above," and between Him and the Throne is an infinite distance. This is what the theologians relate from him, and this is specious (*fasid*), because it is impossible to have an infinite thing between two finite limits. These apostates

42. "Foot" (*qadam*) and "send ahead" (*qaddama*) both have the same Arabic root: *q-d-m*.

43. "Leg" (*rijl*) and "man" (*rajul*) both have the same Arabic root: *r-j-l*.

44. See ch. 3, n. 13. According van Ess (2002), Hisham b. al-Hakam gave up the concept of God having a form and merely ascribed to Him an ideal geometrical shape which he called a "body" (*jism*) in the philosophical sense of the word. He conceived of God as a regularly shaped mass of light which emits rays as means of perception. This could no longer be called anthropomorphism, but since he used the word *jism* which, under a perspective different from his, evoked the idea that God is composite, he was labeled a corporealist (*mujassim*).

(*al-malahida*) have positions and statements that take them outside the pale of Islam, as we will explain in detail in this treatise.

S: Has any monotheist said that originated things inhere in (*tuhillu*) the essence (*dhat*) of the Creator, and is someone who says such things a monotheist?

T: A sect that claimed to be Muslim did teach this—although this teaching of theirs makes them unbelievers—and they are the Karramiyya.[45] [They said] that originated things inhere in His essence, for when God originates a body He also originates an idea (*ma'nan*) that inheres in His essence, and that is origination; so the body is originated at the same time (*muqarinan*) as the idea or right after it. They said, "This idea is His word 'Be' and it is what we call creation, which is different from what is created." God Most High said, "I did not allow them to witness the creation of the heavens and the earth or the creation of their own selves" (18:51). They replied, "But He has allowed us to witness their essences (*dhawatiha*) which indicate that they were created by something else." Their chief theologian (*mutakallimuhum*), Ibn al-Haysam, explicitly wrote in his book, *Al-Maqalat,* that originated things subsist in God's essence (*bi-qiyam al-hawadith bi-dhat Allah*). He said that when God commands or prohibits or wills something, His command, prohibition, and will come into existence after not having been, and they subsist in His essence, because His speech is heard from Him and likewise His will comes into existence from Him. He said, "The subsistence of originated things in His essence does not mean that He is originated, because origination means a succession of opposites (*ta'aqub al-addad*) that cannot be impeded (*la yasihh an yata'attal minha*), whereas opposites cannot successively pass over the glorified Creator (*al-Bari' subhanahu la yata'aqab 'alayhi 'l-addad*)." Abu 'l-Barakat al-Baghdadi wrote in his book, *Al-Mu'tabar,* that originated things subsist in the essence of the glorified Creator and that divinity cannot be affirmed except by admitting this (*la yasihh ithbat al-ilahiyya illa bi-dhalika*). He said, "The theologians say He is too transcendent for that, but it is necessary to transcend this transcendence (*al-tanzih 'an hadha 'l-tanzih huwa 'l-wajib*)." This is *kufr* and apostasy (*ilhad*) concerning the essence of the glorified Creator. Our companions and the Mu'tazila and most theologians say that this is incorrect, and that it cannot be said of God Most High; rather, it is impossible according to both reason and revelation,

45. Al-Rawahi's response is comparable to that of al-Juwayni (2000, 27–28).

because that would make the Necessary Being contingent—indeed, it would mean that He Whose stature is glorious is originated! There is a great deal of writing on this subject in the books of theology; consult them if you wish.

S: What are the nine words that cannot be asked (*al-tisʿatu 'l-alfaz al-mumtanaʿ al-su'al bi-ha*) concerning the Most High God?

T: In order to facilitate memorization, and out of a desire to increase benefit and guidance, and out of sincere devotion to God's exaltation, I composed a poem on this topic in the following verses:

When (*mata*), how (*kayf*), how much (*kam*), does (*hal*), what (*ma*), who (*man*),
which (*ayy*), where (*ayn*), and why (*li-ma*): Keep these nine from God,
and do not ask them.
"When" (*mata*) is a condition of time, and conditions are originated; my Lord
existed before originated things, from all eternity.
"How" (*kayf*) is a question about conditions, and He is too glorious to be
subject to conditions.
"How much" (*kam*) is only used of things that can be counted, and the unity
of our Lord is self-evident to any rational being.
"Does" (*hal*) is a request for proof, and it accompanies
doubt, and there is no doubt in God, so do not ask "does."
"What" (*ma*) is a request for detail concerning a truth, and the knowledge of
God's essence is impossible for creatures.
"Who" (*man*) is a request for distinction of one from others, and that means
comparing (*tashbih*) the Most High to other similar beings.
"Which" (*ayy*) is to designate something that shares qualities with others in a
common matter, such as "Which of the two of them is better?"
"Where" (*ayn*) implies a place that is receptive to a thing that occupies
space (*mutahayyiz*), and God cannot be described as occupying space
(*al-tahayyuz*) in a locus (*fi mahall*).
"Why" (*li-ma*), with a *kasra* on the *lam* and a *fatha* on the *mim*,[46] is a question
about causation (*al-taʿlil*), and God is exalted beyond causes.
So glorify God's perfection beyond these, for they are attributes of creatures,
who are limited by their deficiency.

46. *Kasra* is the vowel "i" that follows the letter *lam* (L) in the word *lima* ("where"), and *fatha* is the vowel "a" that follows the letter *mim* (m).

S: What are the attributes of God Most High that the accountable person (*al-mukallaf*) must know because God cannot be known without them and whoever is ignorant of them or of any part of them does not know God?

T: The perfections of the True Reality, our Lord Most High, are infinite (*la tatanaha*). The accountable person must know twenty such attributes, which are in four categories:

(1) The first category is the essential attribute (*al-sifa 'l-nafsiyya*), which is God's essential existence (*al-wujud al-dhati*), expressed by His essential identity (*al-huwiyya*) and by the existence that is particular to the Most High (*al-wujud al-khass bi-hi ta'ala*) in the sense of His existence by virtue of Himself (*bi-ma'na wujudihi li-dhatihi*), not an existence that is caused (*mu'allalan*) and dependent (*mutawaqqifan*) on any cause that would bring Him into being; His existence, may He be glorified, does not admit nonexistence (*la yaqbal al-'adam*), whether in the eternal past (*azalan*) or the eternal future (*abadan*). An essential attribute is an affirmative attribute (*al-sifa 'l-thubutiyya*) that indicates a description of the very essence, without any additional qualifications, as when one describes a substance (*jawhar*) as a substance, an essence (*dhat*), a thing (*shay'*), or an existent (*mawjud*).

(2) The second category are the negative attributes (*al-sifat al-salbiyya*), which are any attribute that implies the negation of something unsuited to the Most High. They are:

(a) existence from all eternity (*al-qidam*), which means that the existence of God Most High is not preceded by nonexistence, because the Eternal One (*al-Qadim*) cannot have any beginning to His existence;

(b) perpetuity (*baqa'*), which means that there can never be an end to His existence, because the proof of the necessity of His existence in the eternal past also proves that it can never come to an end;

(c) difference from originated things (*mukhalif li-'l-hawadith*), whether they be before existence, like the things that have not existed from all eternity, or those that are attached to the blessings of the afterlife; this difference implies the exclusion from the Most High of substance or accident or being described as entire (*kulliyya*) or being a part (*juz'iyya*) or by qualities that are linked to such concepts;

(d) self-subsistence (*qiyam bi-'l-nafs*), meaning that the Most High does not need anything else for His existence, whether a locus (*mahall*) or a particularizing agent (*mukhassis*)—that is, something that would cause and necessitate His existence (*al-mu'thir wa-'l-mujib*);

(e) unity (*wahdaniyya*), meaning the unity of the essence and the attributes (*wahdat al-dhat wa-'l-sifat*)—that is, the absence of an equal to Him in these two things (*'adam al-nazir la-hu fi-hima*). These are the five negative attributes.

(3) The third category consists of qualifying attributes (*sifat al-ma'na*), which are concepts for which we have expressions (*al-mafhumat al-i'tibariyya*), as I explained to you, not the real things (*al-ma'ani 'l-haqiqiyya*) that the Ash'arites believe are added to the essence (*za'ida 'ala 'l-dhat*). These are seven:

(a) power (*qudra*), which is an eternal essential attribute through the expressed concept of which every contingent being is brought into existence and nonexistence when it attaches (*tata'allaq*) to them according to His will;

(b) will (*irada*), which is an eternal attribute in the sense discussed above (*bi-ma'na ma marra*), the function of which (*sha'nuha*) is to particularize (*takhsis*), so that each contingent thing is given particular qualities that are possible for it when it [God's will] attaches to it [each contingent thing];

(c) knowledge (*'ilm*), which is an essential attribute in the sense discussed above, by which objects of knowledge are known (*tankashif*) from all eternity and forevermore when it attaches to them;

(d) life (*hayat*), which is an eternal attribute in the sense discussed above, entailing soundness of knowledge and issuance (*sudur*) of act;

(e) hearing (*sam'*), which is an eternal attribute in the sense discussed above and attaches either to things that are heard or to things that exist, as I explained earlier;

(f) sight (*basar*), which is an eternal attribute in the sense discussed above and attaches either to things that are seen (according to one opinion) or to things that exist (according to another opinion) and has total comprehension, as I explained earlier;

(g) speech (*kalam*), which is an essential attribute indicating that God could never be silent or incapable of speech, for defects are impossible for the Most High. The attribute of speech means that the Most High commands, prohibits, informs, and so forth. Verbal expressions (*al-'ibara*), writing (*al-kitabiyya*), and symbols (*isharat*) indicate this attribute: if it is expressed in Arabic, it is the Qur'an, if in Syriac it is the Psalms (*al-Zabur*), if in Hebrew it is the Torah, and if in Greek it is the Gospel (*al-Injil*). All these things that are named are the same, even if the expression differs.

4. The fourth category consists of adjectival attributes (*sifat ma'nawiyya*), that is, the names of the Most High that are linked to the aforementioned seven attributes: the Living (*al-Hayy*), the Knowing (*al-'Alim*), the Powerful (*al-Qadir*), the Willing (*al-Murid*), the All-Hearing (*al-Sami'*), the All-Seeing (*al-Basir*), and the Speaking (*al-Mutakallim*), splendid is His majesty (*jalla jalaluhu*).

Every accountable person must know these twenty attributes and which of them attach to contingent things and which do not. The attribute of life and the negative attributes do not attach to anything at all. This is evident concerning the negative attributes; as for life, this is because it is an attribute entailing comprehension and issuance of act in the sense that it is a rational condition for them and without it these do not exist, though its existence does not necessitate their existence or nonexistence. Existence (*wujud*) and eternity (*qidam*) are like life, according to those who consider them essential attributes (*sifat dhatiyya*), although the predominant opinion is that God's existence is the same as His essence and eternity is one of the negative attributes. The attributes that attach to contingent things are knowledge—because it implies an object of knowledge, whether that object of knowledge be necessary or possible, as knowledge is linked to both—and likewise hearing and vision, according to one opinion, and also speech. Knowledge implies (*yaqtadi*) an object of knowledge that is revealed by it; power implies an object of power that it brings into existence or into nonexistence; will implies something the particularization of which is desired; speech inherently (*li-dhatihi*) implies a meaning that it indicates; hearing inherently implies something that is heard; and vision inherently implies something that is seen. All these, as has already been explained, are verbal expressions or meanings, not real things additional to the essence of the Glorified One (*amr za'id 'ala dhatihi subhanahu*). One must believe that the eternal power (*al-qudra 'l-azaliyya*) attaches appropriately (*tata'allaq ta'alluqan suluhiyyan*) to something that does not of necessity exist or not exist, in the sense that from all eternity it is fit (*saliha*) to be brought into existence or nonexistence, according to the attachment of the eternal will to these two conditions in what is an effectual attachment (*ta'alluqan tanjiziyyan*) from all eternity. It is the attachment of an originated thing that is receptive to the attachment of the will by actual origination (*bi-'l-huduth al-hali*). Will is like power in that they are both attached to things, even if they differ in the aspect of the attachment, because power only attaches to possible things to bring them into existence or nonexistence, whereas will attaches to them to give them their particularities. Hearing, comprehension, and vision all attach to both what is necessary and what is only possible.

S: Esteemed teacher, may God be pleased with you! You have filled my heart with the light of monotheism concerning what constitutes monotheism and its foundations. But I still need to investigate (*tahqiq mabahith*) matters that I must not ignore, the true nature (*kunh*) and reality (*haqiqa*) of which I have not grasped. Is my esteemed teacher ready to explain them to me and guide me through their obscure aspects?

T: Indeed, I am ready to respond to your requests cheerfully and to comply with your wish to study any subject you do not understand. To what subject do you refer?

S: One of the things I have not studied, the reality of which has escaped my understanding, is your saying that [God's] existence is the same as [His] essence. This is very confusing to me, and I can only understand it with your help.

T: Leave the explanation of this luminous truth to others! Know that the existence of the Most High Creator is indicated by manifest signs (*a'lam al-zuhur*), so that He is manifest in what is hidden (*zahir fi butun*) and concealed in what is manifest (*batin fi zuhur*), and we can only infer His existence (*yustadall 'ala ithbatihi*) from two luminous signs, each of which is a true indication: the first is existence (*al-wujud*) and the second is the existent (*al-mawjud*). The proof of His existence from existence itself is the way of the best theologians, both of our school and other schools (*al-mudaqqiqin min mutakallimi ashabina wa-ghayrihim*). They base their proof on the fact that what we call existence is something that is shared: it is added to the quiddities (*mahiyyat*) of contingent beings but the existence of the Necessary Being is not added to His essence (*dhat*) and His essence cannot be without existence. The only possible result is that His essence is the same as His existence (*lam yabqa illa an takun dhatuhu hiya 'l-wujud nafsuhu*). They affirm the necessity of that existence and the impossibility of nonexistence ever occurring to it in any way. They do not need to contemplate (*ta'ammul*) anything other than existence itself in order to affirm the

Glorified Creator. If you look in the volumes on theology, you will clearly see that [God's] existence is the same as [His] essence. The proof of His existence through what has been brought into existence rather than existence itself is a proof based on His acts and the effects of His power (*al-istidlal fi-af'alihi wa-athar qudratihi*). That is the way of most theologians (*al-jumhur min al-mutakallimin*), and it has already been described.

The way of the Islamic philosophers (*al-falasifa 'l-islamiyyin*) in proving the existence of the Necessary Being is the first way. [Abu] 'Ali b. Sina said that it is higher and nobler to prove His existence by existence itself because it does not need anything besides His essence. He supported this statement by citing a verse from the Glorious Book that indicates this: "We will show them Our signs in the horizons and in yourselves so the truth will be clear to them" (41:53). Ibn Sina said, "This is the way of some theologians (*qawm min al-mutakallimin*) and others who prove God's existence through His acts. The rest of the verse says, 'Is it not enough that your Lord is a witness over everything?' This is the proof for those who know the truth (*al-siddiqin*), who seek their proof for Him in Him"[47]—that is, those who affirm His Lordship through His existence alone, and whose proofs do not depend on His acts.

S: I would like you to summarize what necessarily belongs to our glorified Lord (*ma yajib li-rabbina subhanahu*), what is impossible for Him, and what is possible for Him, how splendid is His majesty.

T: What is necessary for our Lord is whatever affirms His perfection and the nonexistence of any deficiency, which is impossible; examples of this are knowledge, power, and will. What is impossible for the Most High is any deficiency and the opposite of the twenty aforementioned attributes. Our religion requires (*yajib shar'an*) belief in the impossibility that anything could negate these essential, negative, and adjectival attributes (*al-sifat al-nafsiyya wa-'l-salbiyya wa-'l-ma'nawiyya*) and the impossibility of attributes that would negate what is necessary for the Most High. What is possible concerning the Most High is anything the existence or nonexistence of which would not imply a deficiency

47. In SA someone has written (in Arabic) on a paper inserted into the manuscript: "Note that the wording is not the same in the text," presumably meaning that al-Rawahi's quotation of Ibn Sina is not exact.

in Him, like creating (*al-khalq*), annihilating (*al-ifna'*), restoring to life (*al-i'ada*), bringing into existence (*al-ibda'*), and providing sustenance (*al-razq*). Learn this principle, which encompasses the essentials of belief in God (*hadha 'l-asl al-jami' li-jawami' al-tawhid*), for the science of theology revolves around it (*madar 'ilm al-kalam 'alayhi*). May God grant us and you true knowledge of His unity.

Lesson 4: The Names of God Most High and What They Are Called

S: Esteemed teacher, may God reward you! I seek your guidance to the path of the true creed concerning the names of God (*asma' Allah*). Are they the same as He Himself (*hal hiya huwa*) or are they other than He? What is the truth of this matter?

T: The community of Muhammad (*al-umma*) agrees (*ijtama'at 'ala*) that God exists from all eternity (*lam yazal*), and that His names are as mentioned in His Book: the All-Merciful (*al-Rahman*), the All-Compassionate (*al-Rahim*), the King (*al-Malik*), the Holy One (*al-Quddus*), the Lord of Peace (*al-Salam*), the Keeper of faith (*al-Mu'min*), the Watch-Keeper (*al-Muhaymin*), the All-Strong (*al-'Aziz*), the Overpowering (*al-Jabbar*), the Self-Aware in His Greatness (*al-Mutakabbir*),[48] as the Mighty and Majestic One informed us in His Book. They agree that God is the Creator and all other things are created. Beyond this they disagree.

The Mu'tazila and the Nakitha, and those who agree with them, say that the names are expressions (*alfaz*) by which God informs about Himself, just as we refer to ourselves by our names. Their proof is that a name is an intelligible expression (*al-lafz al-ma'qul*) in Arabic deriving from an act, and it is usually grammatically indefinite (*yajri 'alayhi al-tanwin*), like knower (*'alim*), knowledgeable (*'allam*), merciful (*rahim*), ever-merciful (*rahim*), and all-merciful (*rahman*). No one can deny that this corresponds to the indefinite active participle in Arabic, analogous to the words *entering, leaving, rising, descending,* and so on. These groups confine themselves to saying that God's names are these verbal expressions and they claim that God's names are created. Their proof for this is the word of the Most High: "God has the most beautiful names" (7:180). They say

48. When describing a person, *mutakabbir* means conceited, but no amount of pride is conceit when describing God. I have decided to follow Kenneth Cragg's felicitous translation of this word (Cragg 1988, 87). Except for the first two, all the names mentioned here are from Q 59:23.

this is a feminine plural, and the word *has* indicates possession (*lam al-tamlik*), whereas aggregation, feminine gender, and plurality must be denied of God, who is Mighty and Majestic. [They also base their doctrine on] the words of the Prophet, on whom be blessing and peace: "God has ninety-nine names, one hundred minus one. Whoever counts them (*man ahsaha*) enters Paradise" (al-Suyuti 1981, no. 2353). A sound mind knows that it is impossible for God to be counted, but the names can be counted, which indicates that they are just words used by human beings.

Our companions and those who agree with us in the rest of Muhammad's community say that the names of God are He Himself and not distinct from Him, but that their verbal expressions (*al-alfaz*) are the words and acts of those who name them. The expressions serve the meanings, and the name is what is called a meaning (*ma'nan*), not the verbal expression heard in speech. The name is what is indicated by naming, and the verbal expression and the naming are the act of the speaker (*al-lafiz*) who names in order to indicate the name of the one who is named. The name does not derive from the verbal expression, but is indicated by the naming. If someone says "Zayd," his speech is a naming (*qawluhu tasmiya*), and what is understood from it is a name, and the name is what is named in this case; the description (*al-wasf*) and the attribute (*al-sifa*) are tantamount to the name and the naming. The description is the speech of the one who describes, and the attribute is what is indicated by the description.

The aforementioned Mu'tazila and Nakitha equated the naming and the name, and the description and the attribute; by doing so, they committed a terrible blasphemy. They said the Most High Creator in the eternal past had no attribute or name, because the name and the attribute are the speech of those who name Him and the verbal expressions of those who describe Him. Whoever claims that God did not have from all eternity the attribute of divinity as a meaning—though not as a verbal expression—has left the [true] religion and contradicted the consensus of the Muslims.

No rational person doubts that someone's "name" (*ism*), for example, Zayd—and by this we mean the letters *hamza, sin, mim* [i.e., the letters that make up the word "name" in Arabic] and other similar letters in whatever language is used—and the name that you say, for example, "Zayd," which consists of the letters *za', ya', dal,* or the name "Bakr" which you say, which consists of the letters *ba', kaf, ra'*, and other names [that may be said], is not the same as the one who is named.

How could the letters that are spoken be the same as the essence of the one who is signified by them? The verbal expression is made up of distinct sounds that have no power and differ among the different nations and cities, and sometimes are multiple and other times just one.

What is named is not like that. The verbal expression "name" (*ism*), which is the letters *hamza, sin,* and *mim* according to the language that is used, is not used to mean what is named. When God says, "Raise the name of your Lord in praise" (Q 87:1), this does not mean "raise the essence of your Lord in praise," but "raise in praise the name itself that you speak." Just as His essence and attributes are too exalted to have any deficiencies, likewise the verbal expressions that are given to them are too exalted to be tainted by obscenities or bad manners. This is also true of the verbal expression of a name given for emphasis, such as "Raise the name of your Lord in praise," or any allusion (*kinaya*) to the glorification of the essence, such as "Peace be on the noble assembly and sublime presence (*al-janab al-munif*)" or "Peace be on your assembly" or "on your presence (*'ala hadratik*)." Something may be added to any reference to what is named "your Lord." When the Most High says, "What you worship other than Him are only names" (Q 12:40), it means "in your worship you did not reach an essence that deserves worship, only verbal expressions that have no essences to worship, because they are not fit for that, as if they were nonexistent." As for "He taught Adam all the names" (2:31), what is meant are the verbal expressions, not the things that are named, although after that He says, "Then He showed them to the angels and said, 'Tell me the names of these.'" The "them" in "He showed them" means the things that are named by saying their names and known by mentioning the names. Afterward He indicates the things that are named by saying "these."

Furthermore, the words of the Most High, "Blessed be the name of your Lord" (55:78), do not constitute proof that the name is the same as the thing that is named, because blessing is used in the sense of having great stature, and just as a thing that is named can be described this way, so can the name. Although these interpretations (*ta'wilat*) contradict the literal meaning of the source (*al-asl*), to claim that the name means the same as what is named contradicts it even more. Some say that "name" means the verbal expression and the letters that constitute it, but it can also mean what is named, and to prove this they cite these verses from the Qur'an and say that "name" in these verses is used to signify what is named. Everyone agrees that the "names" in a verse like "He has the most beautiful names" (59:24) mean the verbal expressions that are uttered, not the essence, because God's essence is one [whereas the names are many]. It has been reported that God has ninety-nine names, and there is no doubt that if what were meant by the verbal expression is what is named and signified by it, that cannot be true in this case because of the impossibility of the unity of the signifier and the signified.

If you say, "Zayd got up," there is a word spelled *za', ya', dal,* and that is the signifying name (*al-ism al-dall*), and there is the signified (*al-madlul*), which is the one (*al-dhat*) who is described as getting up, and that is the one who is named. If what is meant by the verbal expression are the letters, this still applies, for if you say "Zayd" is subject to grammatical declension (*mu'rab*) or that it is in the nominative case (*marfu'*), the word "Zayd" in your speech is a name and what is named by it is the verbal expression "Zayd" that you speak, for example, when you say, "Zayd got up." But the phrase in this case does not transcend the rules pertaining to verbal expression without some indication.

When we say, "The names and attributes of God are He Himself," we mean that what is signified by them is the glorified and exalted Necessary Being; we do not mean that the names and attributes that we utter are God Himself—God forbid!—but that the meaning that is signified by saying "Allah," "the Creator," "the Provider," "the Knower," "the Powerful," and so on, is the Necessary Being. When we say that His attributes are He, such as "Creator," "Provider," "Knower," and "Powerful," we mean that they do not signify an essence or something added to God's essence and inhering in it (*halla fi-ha*), because that would entail a multiplicity of eternal beings (*ta'addud al-qudama'*), and that His attributes are all to be categorized as attributes of essence and that He is a locus for them, which would also necessitate His being a locus for the attributes of act as well. We do not deny that "the Creator" signifies His creating, "the Provider" signifies His provision [for His creatures], "the Knower" His knowledge, and "the Powerful" His power, but all these verbal expressions signify the Necessary Being whose existence requires these attributes.

Al-Ash'ari said that the names of God are either His essence, like His name "Allah," or are other than He, like "the Creator," "the Provider," and other attributes of act, and that this would mean that the meanings contained in their corresponding verbal nouns (*ma'aniha 'l-masdariyya*), like *creating* and *providing,* are other than God, not that what is signified by the verbal expression "the Creator" and "the Provider" is other than God; it is neither He nor other than He (*imma la nafsuhu wa-la ghayruhu*), like "the Knower," "the Powerful," and the other attributes of essence. That is, the meanings contained in the verbal nouns are neither He nor other than He. It is said that if someone says, "By God! (*wa-'llah*)," one understands this to be an oath, and if someone says, "In the name of God (*bi-'smi 'llah*)," one understands this to be an invocation of good fortune and blessing, because of their usage according to custom, and because the oath is in God [Himself], not in His name "Allah," which is a verbal expression. It is also said that what is expressed by "By His face (*wa-wajhihi*)" is other than God, but oaths cannot invoke anything but God. One can read about this in the books of rules about oaths in the Qur'an; "face" signifies God's essence and attribute, and so do the names.

Some of the Hanafis said that when one says "in the name of Allah" and means to swear by the name, it is an oath, whether what is meant by the name is what is named or whether "the name" was intended as something additional. They say that if someone says "in Allah" (*bi-'llah*), there is no benefit of generalization (*al-ijmal*) and specification (*al-tafsil*); "in the name of Allah" is said to attain the point (*tahsilan li-'l-nukta*) of generalization or specification and to indicate a general invocation (*al-ta'mim*), because blessing or help may be sought from all His names, for they may be invoked (*yuqsad bi-ha*) for blessing (*al-tabarruk*), help (*al-isti'ana*), and other such things in view of their signifying a signifier (*bi-''tibar dalalatiha 'ala 'l-dall*).

A name is generalized if it can refer to other than the Most High, but it is specified in its attribution to God Most High if it is specifically meant to refer to His name. Generalization is also in the name if it can mean any one of the names of the Most High, and specification is in its attribution to the name which is the verbal expression of majesty (*lafz al-jalala*), which is your saying "Allah." The first aspect applies if the intention in saying "Allah" is the Necessary Being, and the second applies if the intention is the verbal expression—that is, the name that is this verbal expression—in which case the attribution is for clarification. What is meant may be God's essence, in which case by the name you mean the One Who is named, according to the teaching of some. In that case when you say the word "Allah" you mean "the Compassionate, the Merciful," two descriptions that refer to a name, not to "Allah," except by way of exaggeration or common usage.

One scholar allowed that what is meant by "the name" are the three names, "Allah," "the Compassionate," and "the Merciful," because all three are intended.[49] So "the name" means three names, whether one means only these three names or other names as well and limits oneself to the three in order to make a point that required these three in particular.

The benefit of generalization and specification is for the speaker to see the meaning in two different forms, one that is ambiguous and the other clear; two types of knowledge are better than one, and by this the meaning is more firmly established in the soul, because God created our souls in such a way that if something is mentioned in a veiled manner and then clarified it has greater impact and the pleasure of knowing the meaning is perfected because of what had been left inexplicit, since pleasure is greater if something is obtained after it has been desired and sought.

Furthermore, one does not say "in Allah" as an exaggerated form of glorification and courtesy, as when one says, "Peace be on your exalted assembly" or "on your noble presence" to mean "on you." If what is intended by a name is the verbal expression and what is intended by "Allah" is the Necessary Being, then the addition of a name is really in order to immerse oneself in the meaning (*li-'l-istighraq bi-ma'na*) of the definite article that is attached to all the names of the Most High, or to point to the whole contained in a single name (*li-'l-jins fi dimni fard*)—not regarding Him (*la min hayth huwa*), as that cannot be said (*idh la yumkin al-nutq*), let alone come first (*fadlan 'an an yaqa' ibtida'an*).[50] The dif-

49. This is because the complete invocation spoken before eating or engaging in any task is *Bi-'sm Allah al-Rahman al-Rahim*, "In the name of God, the Compassionate, the Merciful," but one might say *Bi-'sm Allah*, "In the name of God," for short.

50. In Arabic, the definite article ("the") is attached to a single noun not only to specify a particular person, place, or thing, but to create a generic noun. In contemporary English, we typically use the indefinite plural to create a generic noun, as when we say "Women live longer than men." The corresponding Arabic would literally read, "The woman lives longer than the man." When the definite article is attached to one of God's names, however, it cannot refer to a generic, because God is unique. Some of His names can apply only to Him (the Creator, the All-Knowing, the All-Powerful, the All-Merciful), and others can be used by others without the definite article: we may describe someone as wise (*hakim*), but only God is The Wise (*al-Hakim*).

ference is that immersion is a way to enter into each one of His names (*madkhal li-kull fard min asma'ihi*) at the level of saying them one by one. It is as if you are saying "in the name of the Necessary Being, the Compassionate, the Merciful" when you say "Allah" or "the Compassionate" or "the Merciful" or "the Giver" or "the Provider" or "the Helper," and so on. It is better to say each name rather than referring to them all collectively (*huwa awla min al-jins*), because a holistic term (*al-jins*) does not benefit a person with the same level of understanding. We said that it is not possible to utter a single name in which a holistic meaning is contained, because the reality [of the distinction between the names] is only conceived in the mind and has no objective reality (*innama tutasawwar dhihnan la kharijan*), and the intention here is to seek blessing by mentioning all the individual names. This blessing is obtained only by immersion [into the meaning of each one], not through a holistic term, even if we say that it is better to praise God with a more holistic term, because the goal of praise is to affirm the particularities of His individual names, and the affirmation of the whole is an affirmation of [the particularities] by providing evidence (*bi-tariq al-ihtijaj*). [This is so] because, although it is true that some of the names of praise can be predicated of someone other than the Most High,[51] the totality [of God's qualities] is not indicated by [such a name], because the meaning contained in that individual [name] can also be said of someone else. The essence of praise (*mahiyyat al-hamd*) is instantiated (*tujad*) in an individual name found in someone else, just as it is instantiated in what is affirmed of the Most High. One cannot say, "Let's make the intention of praise immersion by affirming each individual name of praise one by one, since the affirmation of individual attributes entails the affirmation of the whole, because the whole in the sense of the essence (*al-mahiyya*) is actualized in the individual. So let it be actualized by immersion in each individual name of praise, because there is no basis for preferring to affirm a specific individual name by affirming the whole rather than affirming the whole

51. Some of God's names, like *al-Hayy* ("the Living") or *al-Qadir* ("the Powerful"), are adjectives that can be used to describe other beings, though in a more limited way. But the instantiation of a name in a nondivine being does not yield the totality of the meanings contained in the divine essence.

by affirming the individual names." On the contrary, we say that what makes it preferable is that the names be grasped because they are infinite, so it is more appropriate to specify the whole as an indication of the individual names, rather than specifying the individual names as an indication of the whole, so as to draw conclusions from it concerning them.

If by using a name one means what is named, and if by saying "Allah" one means the Necessary Being, then the addition [of "the name" to "Allah" in the phrase "Praise the name of God"] is rhetorical: it indicates the One Who is named, Who is God. If what is meant by the name is something other than what is named, and if by saying "Allah" one means the verbal expression, then the addition [of "the name" in "Praise the name of God"] is still rhetorical: "the name" means your saying "Allah." If this is what is meant by "the All-Compassionate, the All-Merciful," then the verbal expression in this regard is clearly intended for the same purpose. If what is meant by these two names ["the All-Compassionate" and "the All-Merciful"] is the Necessary Being to Whom mercy is ascribed, it is unclear how one can exchange what is signified by the essence (*al-dhat*), which is the All-Merciful, the All-Compassionate, for what is meant as a verbal expression, which is your saying "Allah," and how He would be qualified by it (*wa-kayf yun'at bi-hi*).

The answer is that it is customary (*dhalika istikhdam*) to say the name of majesty [*lafz al-jalala*, i.e., "Allah"], meaning its letters with the pronoun restored to it (*wa-urida bi-hi hurufuhu wa-u'ida 'alayhi 'l-damir*),[52] not in the sense of the verbal expression but to mean the essence, or that the dependence (*isnad*) of mercy on the pronoun of the name of majesty is a rational metaphor (*majaz 'aqli*) for the dependence of what is signified on the signifier. Naming is the mention of the name and also designates (*tutlaq*) the application of a name to something (*wad' al-ism li-shay'*); so it is known by that designation, by making the verbal expression a signifier of its meaning. So it is said, but it is a definition without firm boundaries, because it encompasses both the act [of naming] and the word

52. I am not sure what al-Rawahi means by the pronoun (*damir*) restored to the name Allah. *Damir*, usually translated as "pronoun," is related to *idmar*, "concealment," a term used by Arab grammarians when speaking about an unexpressed but existing grammatical element. Perhaps al-Rawahi means that the *alif* at the beginning of the name Allah, which is not pronounced in ordinary speech when preceded by a vowel, must be pronounced in this case.

[the name]. A definition is useful only if it defines something according to its original meaning and is a symbol of something (*'alama 'ala shay'*), whether an act, a letter (*harf*), or a noun (*ism*). Perhaps this is what the scholar who said this meant. Many of the Shafi'ite theologians say naming makes the letters of a name a metaphor. And God knows best.

Chapter 5

AFFILIATION (*WALAYA*) AND DISSOCIATION (*BARA'A*)

Lesson 1: Affiliation (*Walaya*): Its Types and Its Regulations

S: It is as clear as day (*qad wadaha 'l-subh*) for anyone with two eyes; I have comprehended most of the important things that are necessary for our majestic Lord and those that are impossible for Him, which you have laid out perfectly. By God, you are a guide to what is good! My heart remains eager to learn what are the next requirements of monotheism, without which it cannot be sincere or complete. Guide me to this in a convincing manner, even if it is by allowing the whole to be a key to the gates of the particulars of its laws.

T: How high is your ambition in comprehending useful knowledge, and how beautiful is your earnest desire for guidance! No act is purer than exerting oneself in such activity! Because of the extent of your thirst for religious knowledge, I humble myself before God, that I might spare no effort to enlighten you and take you on the way of straightness and guidance—the guidance of God, from Whom come help and success.

Know, and may God teach you, that among the inseparable and immediate obligations for any accountable person who has affirmed the oneness of God Most High is to distance himself from those who rebel against God—to hate them, denounce them, and keep away from them—and to draw near to those who obey Him: to love them, praise them, and pray for God's forgiveness for them, pleasure in them, and mercy on them, whether they are living or dead. The first obligation is comprehensively indicated (*yujma'*) by the word *dissociation* (*bara'a*), and the second is comprehensively indicated by the word *affiliation* (*walaya*).

S: Are there any indications (*dala'il*) of this necessary, immediate, and comprehensive obligation to observe these two duties?

T: You have found an expert! There are so many indications for the necessity of affiliation and dissociation in the Book of God and the Sunna of His Messenger, on whom be God's blessing and peace! Among the indications in the Book of the necessity of affiliation is God's word, "Ask forgiveness for your sin and for those of the believing men and women" (47:19); and the words of the Most High describing the Companions of the Messenger of God, "compassionate among themselves" (48:29); and the word of the Most High, "Help one another in righteousness and piety" (5:2); and the word of the Most High, "The believers, both men and women, are affiliates (*awliya'*) of one another" (9:71).

Among the indications of the necessity of dissociation from those who rebel against God are the words of the Most High, "Whoever among you affiliates himself with them (*wa-man yatawallahum*) is one of them" (5:51), which indicates that whoever affiliates himself with an unbeliever (*mushrik*) is himself an unbeliever, and whoever affiliates himself with a hypocrite is a hypocrite; and "Do not affiliate yourself with a people with whom God is angry" (60:13); and "Believers do not affiliate themselves with infidels instead of with believers" (3:28); and "You will not find a people who believe in God and the Last Day [loving (*yawadduna*) those who oppose God and His Messenger, even though they be their fathers, or their sons, or their brothers, or their kinsfolk]" (58:22).

Among the indications in the Sunna of the necessity of affiliating oneself with believers are [the Prophet's] words, may God bless him and grant him peace, "The strongest of ties in Islam is affiliation in God and hatred in God" (al-Haythami 2001, 1:117–18, *Kitab al-Iman* [1], *bab* 34, no. 309), or in another transmission, "love in God (*al-hubb fi 'llah*), which is the essence (*haqiqa*) of faith." Another is his saying, "Whoever gives, prevents, loves, and hates for God's sake has perfected the characteristics of faith" (al-Suyuti 1981, no. 8308).

Regarding dissociation are his words, may God bless him and grant him peace, "God has cursed the one who introduces a new thing into Islam or who offers protection to the one who has done so" (al-Rabi' b. Habib n.d., 1:13, no. 42); "Anyone who cheats us is not a believer" (ibid., 2:45, no. 582); "I dissociate from anyone who tells omens or oracles or requests an oracle" (ibid., 3:3, no. 747); "Anyone who shaves his head and wails [in grief] is not one of us" (Abu Dawud 2000, *Kitab al-jana'iz* [21], *bab* 29, no. 3132); and other comparable Qur'anic verses and hadiths. Indications of the necessity of one of these two pillars indicate the necessity of the other, because a command to do something necessarily entails the prohibition of its opposite, and vice versa.

The *umma* has agreed on the necessity of affiliation and dissociation in general, but there are disagreements on the permissibility of affiliating with particular individuals. Our companions [the deceased Ibadi scholars], may God have mercy on them, affirm affiliation and require it if there exists a condition that necessitates it, such as faithfulness in religion. Some of our theological opponents do not require it at all, while others require it only with those individuals concerning whom there is an explicit text stating that such a person is among the people of paradise, without requiring it regarding other people.

One of the indications of its necessity are the [Prophet's] words, may God bless him and grant him peace: "The Muslim has the right to receive six courtesies from his brother: that he give him the greeting of peace when he meets him, that he visit him when he is sick, that he accept his invitation, that he attend his funeral when he dies, that he bless him if he sneezes[1] and that he wish for him whatever he likes for himself" (al-Tirmidhi 2000, *Kitab al-adab* [39], no. 2955).

The indications of the obligation to dissociate from some individuals are also indications of the obligation to affiliate with some individuals, and vice versa. It is necessary to deem an unbeliever anyone who is ignorant of the necessity of affiliation and dissociation in general, or anyone who affiliates with all people or dissociates from all people or suspends judgment concerning all people. If someone affiliates with one-third of the people, dissociates from one-third of the people, and suspends judgment (*waqafa*) concerning one-third of the people, he is an unbeliever, although some of our scholars in the Maghrib suspend judgment concerning whether to deem him an unbeliever. Anyone who affiliates with infidels despite their infidelity is an unbeliever; this is also the case if someone dissociates from the Muslims despite their adherence to Islam or suspends judgment concerning them despite their adherence to Islam. If someone unconditionally (*bi-la taqyid*) affiliates with members of the community of Muhammad (on whom be God's blessings and peace) who commit acts of disobedience, he is an unbeliever

1. The proper Arabic response to a sneeze is, "May God have mercy on you," to which the proper reply is, "May God guide you and make you prosper."

(*ashraka*); if he does so with reservations, he is a hypocrite and an infidel (*nafaqa wa-kafara*). If he dissociates from the monotheists (*al-muwahhidin*), they should dissociate from him. If he says, "I dissociate from all of them," there are two opinions, the best of which, in my opinion, is the first [that one should dissociate from him], because the people of affiliation are included in the category of the monotheists. If he dissociates from those who practice a particular craft or have a particular attribute or defect, such as those who are deaf, or carpenters, or those who are miserly, he is a hypocrite. If he says, "I dissociate from human beings" or "from the Muslims, unless I am not allowed to do this," there are two opinions concerning whether one should dissociate from him, although it is blameworthy not to do so (*'ala 'adamiha min-hu huwa khasis madhmum*).

If someone says, "I dissociate from the prophets and messengers [of God], unless I am not allowed to do so" or "unless they are Muslims," he is an unbeliever. Anyone who dissociates from an affiliate (*wali*) and adds "unless he is an affiliate" is subject to dissociation, and the exception he made does not benefit him. Whoever dissociates from someone who should not be subject to dissociation, like a child or animal or tree, is an infidel. Anyone who dissociates from the people of affiliation is subject to dissociation. Anyone who dissociates from those who adhere to affiliation and dissociation in a general way should be left in the state of affiliation if he is an affiliate, unless he dissociates from them for a reason that does not deserve dissociation, like the practice of a particular craft or occupation.

Whoever dissociates from the jinn is a hypocrite and whoever dissociates from all jinn is an unbeliever, because he has included those whom God said had come to faith.[2] If someone dissociates from the angels or from one of the angels or from the religion or paradise or hellfire or the resurrection of the dead or the judgment or from the Creator of all things—God forbid!—he is an unbeliever. Ignorance of the general obligation of affiliation and dissociation is a characteristic of unbelief (*irtikab khaslat shirk*) because such a person is an infidel (*jahid*)

2. Q 72:1–2: "Say: It has been revealed to me that a group of the jinn listened [to the recitation of the Qur'an] and said, 'We have heard a wonderful recitation, guiding to the right way, so we have believed in it and we will not assign anyone to our Lord as a partner.'"

or someone who treats everyone the same way (*musawin*), and the regulations for dealing with unbelievers apply to him. Anyone who does not affiliate with anyone or dissociate from anyone, or who affiliates with all of humanity and jinn or dissociates from all of them or suspends judgment concerning all of them, has no religion.

S: What is the literal meaning of *walaya* (affiliation)?

T: It means nearness (*al-qurb*) and doing things for others (*al-qiyam li-'l-ghayr*) by commanding, helping, taking interest in their well-being (*al-ihtimam bi-'l-masalih*), keeping them safe, and keeping in touch with them (*al-ittisal*). Among us [Ibadis] and among our people (*qawmina*) there is affiliation in the sense that our Book is one and we have agreed on the roots of the law (*asl al-sharʿ*), and there is no harm in disagreement on its branches. This pertains to affiliation with them as a group, although they are still subject to dissociation if they do forbidden acts. This is the basis of affiliation according to God's law (*al-walaya 'l-sharʿiyya*) concerning both the Creator and those He has created, although the Creator cannot be said to take an interest in something (*la yusaf bi-'l-ihtimam*) [so as to take an interest in the well-being of His affiliates]. The [initial] letter *waw* [of the word *walaya,* meaning "affiliation"] takes a *fatha* [is followed by an "*a*" vowel; if it takes a *kasra* [is followed by an "*i*" vowel], that [forms the word *wilaya,* which] means "having the power to rule and command." Furthermore, *walaya* is [grammatically] transitive, whereas *wilaya* requires the use of the preposition *over* (*ʿala*). Some say it can take either a *fatha* or a *kasra;* there are two opinions on this (Atfayyish 1980a, 32).

S: What does it mean according to God's law (*ma hiya sharʿan*)?

T: Regarding believers, it means having compassion for them and asking for forgiveness for them because of their adherence to Islam and their obedience, and to praise them with love in the heart. Regarding the angels, it means having compassion on them and loving them, without asking for forgiveness for them. There are two opinions concerning whether affiliating with the prophets is like affiliating with the believers or like affiliating with the angels.[3]

3. One cannot ask forgiveness for angels, because they cannot sin. Atfayyish (1980a, 32) said that prophets' immunity from error is not the same as that of angels, who have no ability to discern right from wrong.

S: What is the literal meaning of dissociation (*bara'a*)?

T: The root meaning of *bara'a* is *bur'* (convalescence) and *bur'a'u* (innocent).[4] *Tabarru'* (ridding oneself of something) means removing oneself from something the proximity of which is disliked, or ridding oneself of something painful. Therefore, one says, "I recovered (*bari'tu*) from the sickness" and "I got rid (*bari'tu*) of someone" or "I got rid of him" (*bari'tu min-hu* or *tabarra'tu min-hu*). In general, the root meaning of *bur'* is the release of something from something else, whether in the sense of recovery, as in "The sick person recovered from his illness and the debtor from his debt," or in the sense of bringing something into being from something else, as in "God created (*bara'a*) Adam from clay."[5]

S: What does it mean according to God's law?

T: It is the opposite of *walaya* and what is meant by it. If you dissociate from someone, you distance yourself from him and are released from the rights that a believer owes to another believer, just as if you had a loan and are released from it.

S: What makes dissociation obligatory?

T: It is obligatory if someone commits grave sins, and persistence in minor sins is a grave sin (*wa-min-hunna 'l-israr*).

S: What are the aspects (*wujuh*) of persistence?

T: There are four aspects: (1) commission of a sin; (2) turning away from repentance; (3) believing the person will commit the sin again; and (4) believing the person will not repent. These last three can only be known if the sinner discloses his refusal to repent or his belief that he will commit the sin again or that he will not repent. If someone tells him, "Repent!" and he keeps silent or occupies himself with something other than repentance, one should not pass hasty judgment against him that he is persisting in the sin; one can only judge

4. A rare plural form of *bari'*, used in Q 60:4. The root meaning of *bara'a* is "innocence," but it also implies "washing one's hands" of something bad, hence dissociation from something.

5. The Qur'an consistently uses the word *khalaqa* (create) rather than *bara'a* when referring to God's creation of Adam from clay, although the divine name *al-Bari'* (59:24, 2:54) is interpreted as "the Creator," or "the One who brings [everything] into being." The verb *bara'a* is used with reference to God bringing forth a record of human deeds in their "books" on the day of judgment (57:22). The usage of *bari'a, bara'a,* and *tabarra'* in the sense of renunciation, avoidance, or innocence (in the sense of being innocent of someone else's sins, i.e., avoiding them) is much more common in the Qur'an: 2:166–67, 6:19, 6:78, 8:48, 9:1, 9:3, 9:114, 10:41, 11:35, 11:54, 26:216, 43:26, 54:43, 59:16, and 60:4.

that he persists in the sin if he replies, "I will not repent." According to God's law, one cannot say that someone is persisting in sin if he does acts of obedience, although 'Isa b. Ahmad allowed this [if someone errs in] matters of belief (*fi 'l-tawhid*), [even if he performs his religious obligations], and the Qutb holds a similar teaching regarding all acts of obedience,[6] and in *Al-Su'alat* ["Questions"] [by Abu 'Amr 'Uthman al-Sufi] it says that, etymologically, every omission of a religious obligation can be considered perseverance in sin (*yutlaq lughatan 'ala kulli iqama*). The Qutb says:

> The correct answer is the permissibility of applying [the notion of persevering in sin] to the commission of an error in a matter of faith, and by analogy (*bi-'l-qarina*) to all other acts of obedience; it is as if you say that he persisted in [error in a matter of] faith or in recitation [of the Qur'an]. The aspect of preventing its application is ambiguity in the meaning of the word "persistence" in God's law. It means commission [of an error] without repentance while saying something similar, which can create ambiguity concerning its meaning and can make someone think that *'ala* ("on") means *'an* ("from," "concerning"). (Atfayyish 1980a, 33)

You know that there is consensus concerning the general principles of affiliation and dissociation, and that it is obligatory to affiliate with some individuals and types of individuals and dissociate from others, according to our sect, by indications from the Book and Sunna, and consensus on matters entails the obligation of both [affiliation and dissociation]. Whoever rejects the bond (*'aqd*) of affiliation deserves execution, according to some, because he has violated the consensus of our companions.

S: Is there agreement that whoever does not affiliate with the Muslims as a group and does not oppose the infidels as a group should be judged an unbeliever, or are there divisions in this matter?

T: Some say he is an unbeliever, and others say he is an unbeliever if he denies [the obligation of affiliation and dissociation] but is only a hypocrite if he [acknowledges their obligation but] fails to act accordingly or if he is ignorant of

6. That is, even if someone performs some acts of obedience, if he fails to perform other obligatory acts one should dissociate from him.

their obligation. Others say he is an unbeliever if convincing proofs are brought against him (*in qamat 'alayhi 'l-hujja*).

S: How does one affiliate with the prophets and angels, on whom be blessing and peace?

T: You affiliate with them as a group, and you specifically affiliate with our prophet Muhammad, Adam, and Gabriel, on whom be God's blessings and peace. Affiliating with the angels means loving them for their obedience and praying that God would have mercy on them by granting them things they like, such as strengthening them to do acts of obedience, just as they pray that He will give the believers what they like. It is well known that the angels have no passions, but only long to worship God and take delight in that. They do not delight in pleasant aromas, although the literal meaning of the hadith is that they do take pleasure in that; perhaps what is meant is that they dislike putrefaction, as pleasant aromas are compatible with its lack, not that they literally take pleasure in it. That is more appropriate than saying that although they do not take delight [in material things], one may make an exception concerning pleasant aromas (ibid., 34).[7]

Anyone who does not know that our Prophet is human (*adami*) is an unbeliever, not whoever does not know Adam—to say so goes against the consensus of our companions, because there is no proof (*hujja*) for this. If there is proof concerning the name of a prophet or an affiliate or someone who is praised for a particular attribute, it is obligatory to affiliate with that person; our companions say that whoever does not affiliate with such a person is an unbeliever, although the Qutb said he is only an unbeliever if he denies [his or her worthiness] (Atfayyish

7. I do not know of a hadith that mentions the angels' predilection for pleasant aromas, but Muslim has a number of hadiths indicating that people should not come to the mosques with the odor of garlic or onion on them; two of them say this is because "the angels are harmed by the same things as people" (Muslim 2000, *Kitab al-masajid* (5), *bab* 1, nos. 5 and 7; Muslim 1977, *Kitab al-salat,* ch. 211, nos. 1145 and 1147). In a commentary on a hadith in *Sahih Muslim* indicating that angels do not enter a house where there is an image or a dog, al-Nawawi (1994, vol. 5, *Kitab al-libas wa-'l-zina* [37], *bab* 26) wrote that one of the reasons angels do not enter a house where there is a dog is because dogs smell bad, and angels hate bad odors. Ibadi teachings favor a rational approach to the spiritual realm and deny a literal interpretation of Qur'anic verses and hadiths that appear incompatible with reason. Rationally speaking, since the angels are made from light, one cannot say they have senses of the type possessed by those whose bodies are made of clay; so they cannot take delight in aromas, which would depend on the sense of smell.

1980a, 34). For example, if someone sees in the Qur'an that Mary is praised, it is obligatory to affiliate with her specifically; no other woman is specifically named. This implies a rejection of the Christian belief in her divinity and an affirmation of her servanthood (*'ubudiyya*) [i.e., her humanity], because an indirect allusion to women is more courteous (*al-kinaya 'an al-nisa' ajmal*). If someone says, "That is like Mary," the word "like" implies imaginary individuals (*al-afrad al-dhihniyya*), even if, in objective reality, there is none but Mary. Another example is if someone reads in the Qur'an about the Companions of the Cave (18:9–22) and those who were burned in the ditch (85:4), likewise it is obligatory for him to affiliate with them as a group (*ijmalan*). Or if he reads in it that a man from Pharaoh's family hid his faith (40:28), it is obligatory for him to affiliate with that man without knowing his name. Likewise if he reads in it about a servant to whom God gave mercy from Him and knowledge from His presence (18:65), [it is obligatory for him to affiliate with him without knowing his name] unless a convincing proof is made concerning him, such as a proof that this servant is al-Khadir,[8] in which case it is obligatory to affiliate with him by name (Atfayyish 1980a, 34).

[This is also the case] if proof is given from an oral source (*bi-'l-sam'*), whether from the Qur'an or reliable reports [from the Prophet or his Companions] (*akhbar*), and this proof rests on the testimony of two trustworthy persons, or one trustworthy person, or by many (*tawatur*)—there are different opinions—and the *tawatur* is a report transmitted by a large group of people from one to the other in a continuous chain of people who could never agree on a falsehood, not a heresy (*ilhad*) or the propaganda of a particular sect (*madhhab*); it is a chain of three, four, five, twelve, twenty, forty, or seventy, according to different opinions. A person who is named in such a text [as one of the people of paradise] must either be kept (*ma'sum*) from grave sins—which would mean he is an angel or a messenger of God—or from dying in a state of sin. Likewise, anyone whom God calls "happy" is kept from dying in a state of sin, though we do not know this

8. Al-Khadir or al-Khidr, "the Green One," according to legend, drank from the waters of eternal life (hence he is always "green," in the full bloom of youth), and appears in Sufi literature as an immortal mystical guide who appears in various guises. Although the identity of this special servant of God who has knowledge of hidden things is not revealed in the Qur'anic story of Moses' strange encounter with him, he is commonly identified as al-Khadir.

about him unless the text says this about him explicitly. The Qutb said, "Anyone who forgets a prophet other than our Prophet, or an angel or divine attribute or a religious regulation is excused, though this opinion differs from that of most of our companions" (Atfayyish 1980a, 34–35).

S: What is the ruling concerning affiliation with the subjects of a just imam?

T: It is obligatory for anyone who knows of his imamate to affiliate with them as a group, as long as none of them manifests a grave sin. Some scholars say that such a person is considered an affiliate but is not seen as trustworthy, meaning that you should affiliate with him but not accept his testimony, because he is considered an affiliate merely because he is a subject of a just imam, but such an affiliation is not adequate to make an individual just and worthy of giving testimony if he is not in and of himself trustworthy. Such people are included in the general affiliation because of their obedience to their imam, which is at root obedience to God and one of the religious obligations He imposes on His servants. For this reason they deserve this type of affiliation which resembles affiliation with a collectivity. They say you may attest to the credibility of someone who is not in a state of affiliation, like someone who is a treasurer, and that it is also desirable to affiliate with an individual among them if only because of the clothes he wears, even if you know he has committed a minor sin, or a sin concerning which you do not know whether it is minor or grave, as long as you do not know him to have committed a grave sin. This rule applies both to the time of the imam and after his death. One may accept the testimony of that individual until he commits a grave sin; then, if he is asked to repent and does so, [continue in affiliation], and if he refuses, dissociate from him. That is the sound opinion, although the more common opinion is that if he is needed as a witness, it is not necessary to ask him to repent. Some say that one should only affiliate with him if one has witnessed his faithfulness, or if one is [reliably] informed of such (ibid., 35).

S: Why are the imam's supporters (*jama'a*) called a *bayda*?[9]

T: They are called such (*summiyat bi-bayda bi-fath al-ba'*) in the name of the imam, because he is the *bayda* of the town, that is, the unique individual (*wahiduhu*) to whom the people gather and whose word is accepted. Alternatively, in

9. The root meaning of *bayda* is *whiteness,* and it can mean "an egg," but it also means "the main part, substance, essence, or best part of something."

light of the possessive construct of the phrase "*jama'at al-imam*" [the imam's supporters], one could consider it an extension by association, that is, they are the supporters of the imam, who is the *bayda* (*aw taqdiran li-'l-mudaf ay jama'at al-bayda wa-hiya 'l-imam*). Or one could say they are the *bayda* of the fight (*al-qital*) because they gather to defend God's religion, or because of their strength they may be called the *bayda* of the fight. [They are like] the egg (*bayda*) of a bird in sweetness, because of their purity and the whiteness of their faith, or because we must be united in a single word and doctrine.[10] The Muslims of Nizwa are called the *bayda* of Islam because it is the capital of the imams and the place where the Muslims gather.

S: Does one affiliate with a person who converts to Islam (*kayf walayat dakhil fi 'l-Islam*)?

T: It is obligatory to affiliate with a person who enters Islam, even if he converts at the hand of one of our theological opponents, as long as he does not commit a grave sin that requires dissociation, according to the best opinion, though some say one should suspend judgment concerning him if he converts after the appearance of the people of injustice until he dissociates from them, even if he converts at the hand of someone concerning whom one is suspending judgment. Another opinion is that one should suspend judgment concerning him if he converts at the hand of one of our theological opponents until one sees evidence of faithfulness in him. There are various opinions on this matter (Atfayyish 1980a, 35–36).

S: Should one affiliate with one of our theological opponents if he enters our sect?

T: It is necessary to affiliate with him if he is merely following received teaching (*muqallid*) and can be excused (*ghayr qati' li-'l-'udhr*) [for having been in that sect]. On the other hand, if he was a scholar who exercised his reason (*mujtahid*) and had no excuse [for belonging to that sect], one cannot affiliate with him until he repents from each heresy (*bid'a*) he embraced, one by one, and confesses the sin in such heresies in the presence of all who knew of these heresies from him,

10. Al-Rawahi follows Atfayyish (1980a, 35) up to this point, but adds the specification concerning the Omani town of Nizwa.

even if by means of a letter. If he does not know where the person is [before whom he demonstrated heretical beliefs or practices], one may accept his repentance, for the gate of repentance is always open, and he is cautioned concerning it.

If one of our theological opponents says, "My affiliate is your affiliate, and my enemy is your enemy," this is accepted from him in a general way. If he says, "My affiliate is your affiliate and my enemy is your enemy" and there is a specification preceding or following this statement, or if it carries the sense of "You must affiliate with whomever I affiliate with, and you must hate whomever I hate," or if he keeps to the apparent meaning—that is, "I have no affiliate but yours and no enemy but yours"—indeed that is better, because to say "I have no affiliate but your affiliate and no enemy but your enemy" is a negation of having any affiliate except your affiliate, or enemy except your enemy, whereas "Your affiliate is my affiliate and your enemy is my enemy" is a denial that he would deny your affiliate his affiliation, or deny your enemy his enmity, not a denial that he would have no affiliate but yours (ibid., 36).

S: How do I affiliate with a particular person?[11]

T: Affiliate with him if you see that he is faithful or if you know that he is faithful through the report of someone of our sect, because there is consensus that the characteristic that necessitates affiliation in general is faithfulness, and because of the words of 'Umar b. al-Khattab and 'Amr b. al-'As, "We will affiliate with anyone in whom we see goodness."[12] This saying is also transmitted as a hadith [from the Prophet]. The Prophet's words, "A Muslim has [the right to expect] six [courtesies] from his brother" until [the conclusion of the hadith], "to bless him when he sneezes, and to like for him what he likes for himself" (al-Tirmidhi 2000, *Kitab al-adab* [39], no. 2955), [are not relevant to the question of affiliation and dissociation], because these six are the right of every monotheist, but we do not say that one should affiliate with every monotheist. Some say that

11. The teacher's answer to this question is an abridged version of Atfayyish (1980a, 37–39).

12. F (56, n. 1) notes that the original wording from 'Umar b. al-Khattab is "We will say good things of anyone from whom we know good, and we will speak ill of anyone from whom we know ill" (al-Rabi' b. Habib n.d., 2:68, no. 700), but it is not clear that this is the saying to which al-Rawahi refers. I have not found any such report.

this hadith applies only to affiliates; we say that these six courtesies are owed to an affiliate even if he is not faithful.[13]

God's word, "Fight all the unbelievers" (9:36), does not mean that one should apply affiliation with a group to every individual, just as unbelievers are killed as a group, not individually (*wa-la afradan*),[14] because we say that what is meant by "all" (*kaffa*) is each individual because [it occurs at] one time (*li-ttihad al-waqt*).[15] The meaning of "Love for a monotheist what you love for yourself" is that you should work to bring him to faithfulness (*al-jary fi jalbihi li-'l-wafa'*), while praying for good for him, commanding [good] and prohibiting [evil], and working on behalf of his earthly interests. If he is an affiliate, you increase your love for him in affiliation.

The meaning of blessing a person if he sneezes is to say an appropriate prayer for him, even if it be as little as "may God strengthen you." This is not because of the words of the Prophet (on whom be God's blessing and peace), "May God have mercy on Abu Dharr,"[16] because that is not an indication of obligation [to bless people when they sneeze], as it is possible that what was meant was [a prayer that Abu Dharr be given] perfect faith in addition to his reward, as it is possible to give, prevent, love, and hate for other than God, just as one may love for selfish reasons—for example, because a person has benefited him—or hate a person because he has been unjust to him, or give something to a person because he has given something to him.

I told you that most scholars of our school agree (*'an jumhur qawmina*) that there is no obligation to affiliate with specific individuals unless there is an

13. Atfayyish (1980a, 38) says "owed to a monotheist" instead of "owed to an affiliate," and this obviously makes more sense.

14. Atfayyish (1980a, 38) says, "Just as we kill unbelievers as a group, although they are [killed] individually (*wa-law afradan*)."

15. Atfayyish (ibid.) says "not because [it occurs at] one time (*la ittihad al-waqt*)."

16. Atfayyish (1980a, 38) adds here, "nor because of [the Prophet's] words, 'Whoever loves for God, hates for God, gives for God and prevents for God perfects his faith'." Al-Rawahi's omission of this second prophetic saying makes his subsequent reference to perfect faith and doing things for selfish reasons very unclear. Concerning the Prophet's saying "May God have mercy on Abu Dharr," this was after Abu Dharr sneezed, to which the appropriate response is "May God have mercy on you." However, as Atfayyish and al-Rawahi indicate, the Prophet's saying this after Abu Dharr sneezed does not make it an obligation to say it whenever a monotheist sneezes.

explicit text concerning them, or in the opposite case, [there is no obligation to dissociate] from specific individuals about whom there is no explicit text.[17] Some say it is necessary [to affiliate with someone] if this person is said to be one of the people of paradise, as [for example] if [the Prophet] said, "God, have mercy on Zayd; he is one of the people of paradise." Some say there is no obligation to affiliate with individuals concerning whom there is an explicit text [that they are among the people of paradise]. There is no basis for calling some of our companions *kuffar* if they affiliate or dissociate with stipulations (*bi-'l-sharita*), unless someone says that because of a certain stipulation he would not pray for him (*la-hu*) or over him (*'alayhi*) [when he dies], because he is commanded to pray for him. If one prays for someone and then attaches a stipulation, he is not praying with conviction but with doubt; he is neither affiliating nor dissociating.

It is correct to say that anyone who delays affiliation or dissociation after they become obligatory is a hypocrite, for they are both obligatory acts of obedience unless there is an explicit text [that would remove this obligation], so they are both requirements of faith (*fa-huma tawhid*). Some say that whoever neglects these requirements or is unaware that they are obligatory is an unbeliever, and that whoever denies that they are obligatory is a hypocrite, but that is not correct: it is better to say that whoever denies that they are obligatory is an unbeliever than to say this of someone who neglects to do them.[18]

There are two opinions concerning the status of one who denies or is ignorant of the obligation to affiliate with or dissociate from someone about whom there is no explicit text, or who is ignorant of the reward for doing these obligations, or a disobedient person who is ignorant of it. Anyone who affiliates with or suspends judgment concerning someone about whom there is an explicit text

17. This clearly refers to people who lived at the time of the Prophet or earlier, not people one may encounter today. There are prophetic sayings that name certain of his Companions as among the people of paradise, and the Qur'an specifies Abu Lahab and the pharaoh who ruled Egypt at the time of Moses as among the people of hellfire.

18. Not only Ibadis, but also Sunnis and Shi'a, hold that negligence is not as grave as unbelief. Sunnis hold that anyone who disbelieves in a tenet of faith (e.g., that prayer is obligatory) is an unbeliever, but that a person who believes in the tenet of faith but fails to act accordingly is a negligent, but believing, Muslim. Ibadis say such people are hypocrites or *kuffar ni'ma* (ungrateful for God's blessings) and should not be seen as Muslims or as believers.

saying that he is one of the people of evil, or who dissociates from or suspends judgment concerning someone about whom there is an explicit text that he is one of the people of good, is an unbeliever; if there is no explicit text, he is a hypocrite.

One should not dissociate from someone who affiliates with someone before witnessing his faithfulness and without the testimony of trustworthy individuals and without [knowing that the person has] a reputation for faithfulness, or because the person has a single good attribute, or from someone who dissociates from a person without evidence of grave sin, or who affiliates with a person because of two good attributes, but it is not good to do these things.

S: What is the rule concerning affiliating with and dissociating from children who have not yet reached maturity?[19]

T: Affiliate with children who have not reached maturity, because our Lord bestows mercy and does not unjustly punish anyone, and because every infant is born according to the original human nature (*fitra*) [as a Muslim],[20] and because [the Prophet], on whom be God's blessings and peace, after having suspended judgment concerning the children of hypocrites and unbelievers, saying, "God knows best what they were doing"(Bukhari n.d., *Kitab al-jana'iz* [23], *bab* 92, no. 1384), [later] informed us that they are among the people of paradise. In another hadith, he said "I asked my Lord about those who have no awareness (*al-lahin*), and he gave them to me as servants of the people of paradise" (al-Suyuti 1981, nos. 4606 and 4598), meaning the children of unbelievers and hypocrites, because the children of Muslims are with their parents and are not servants. The Most High said, "We unite them with their offspring" (52:21).

The most commonly held opinion in our sect (*al-mashhur 'indana*) is that one affiliates with the children of those who are in affiliation and suspends judgment

19. The teacher's answer to this question is taken from Atfayyish (1980a, 39–41). The age of maturity is later defined as fifteen or seventeen.

20. The Qur'an says, "Set your face toward the religion, being upright, following the nature (*fitra*) according to which God created people" (30:30). This verse, and a famous hadith (al-Bukhari n.d., *Kitab al-jana'iz* [23], *bab* 92, no. 1385) in which the Prophet says every child is born a Muslim, and it is his parents who make him a Christian, Jew, or Zoroastrian, are seen as indications that Islam accords with human nature, and that everyone is born a Muslim. We may note that on this point the Ibadis diverge from the radical Khawarij, who saw the children of unbelievers as part of the community of unbelievers, and killed them along with adults.

concerning others. Others hold that one should suspend judgment regarding all [children], or that children should be grouped with their parents, so an unbeliever's child is [considered] an unbeliever. There is no proof for that [opinion] in "They will not beget any but immoral, unbelieving offspring" (Q 71:27), because what is meant are those who reach maturity and then commit immoral acts; Noah said this by way of speculation concerning them, but he would not reject the child of a woman who had brought him up the mountain out of the water, if this had happened. It is said that God made their wombs barren for seventy years before the flood, and some say for forty years.

The judgment in "When they disbelieved, We drowned them" (Q 25:37) is for their disbelief (*takdhib*). Our theological opponents might say that this verse applies to all of them, but this objection is not sound, because a child cannot disbelieve. It is not true that the Prophet said—although it has been transmitted from him—"The children of the unbelievers are with their parents in hellfire" (al-Haythami 2001, *Kitab al-qadar* [31], *bab* 28, no. 11941), or that on the Day of Resurrection a fire will be set for them and for the children of the hypocrites, and whoever rushes into it will be saved,[21] because it is too late when the accounting comes—all of these are false sayings, unlike the first two. When the Prophet, peace and blessings upon him, told ʿAli to embrace Islam when he was eight years old, what he meant was to do the deeds of a Muslim and to believe what they believe. The most common teaching is that accountability (*al-taklif*) begins at the time when one can distinguish right from wrong.

It is obligatory to affiliate with the child of an affiliate by his affirmation that the child is his son in his presence, or by the testimony of a trustworthy person, or some say by the testimony of two trustworthy people besides him—there are different opinions—or by the acknowledgment that he was born to his bed, or by the testimony of one or two trustworthy individuals simply that he was born—there are different opinions on this—or by the testimony of three trustworthy people of the community if they attended the birth. By such people's testimony one may confirm lineage, the appearance of the new moon, death, marriage,

21. Among eight different hadiths given by Ibn Hajar al-ʿAsqalani (1970, *Kitab al-jana'iz, bab* 92) concerning the children of unbelievers, the seventh is that they will be tested on the Day of Judgment by being presented with a fire, and that those who enter it will find it cool and not be harmed.

calamity, the existence of a true imamate, and deviations (*amyal*), if there is no cause for objection or doubt.

A person may be given affiliation even if he is sinful (*wa-law fasiq*), in addition to his child, if he intends to repent from his immorality. One suspends judgment concerning the slaves of an affiliate if they are children, whether or not he has granted them freedom, and also concerning the children of his slaves, his mother's bastard son if his mother is an affiliate, and the son of a Muslim woman who was born while she was an unbeliever, although some say they should all be given affiliation. One should affiliate with one's own child slave, and if the slave is freed one should suspend judgment concerning him, because he was given affiliation because of his attachment to his owner, not because of his own virtue, and his ownership has ceased—there are different opinions on this.

If two affiliates testify that someone is the son of his mother, he is not given affiliation until they say, "He is so-and-so, son of so-and-so, a Muslim woman, whose husband is unknown or whose husband is an unbeliever or a slave." Some say that a slave's son is not called the son of his mother, even if she rejected the marriage after knowing he was a slave. Perhaps what is meant is that an unbeliever married a Muslim woman or a slave without the permission of his master; in that case, the marriage is null and void, and the lineage is not confirmed. The son of a free man and [someone else's] slave woman is a slave and belongs to the slave woman's master, unless the master stipulates that he is free, in which case the child is free. The son of a concubine is free.[22]

A child should be treated as a monotheist if one of his parents is a monotheist, if the father is a monotheist and the mother is one of the People of the Book, or if they were both monotheists and the father later commits apostasy, or if they were both unbelievers and later she embraces Islam;[23] that is the correct opinion. The more commonly held opinion in our school is that the child takes his

22. Not only is the child born free, but no social stigma attaches to him or her. Many of the sultans of Zanzibar were born to concubines.

23. A Muslim man may marry a Jewish or Christian woman, but a Muslim woman may only marry a Muslim man; the marriage of a woman who embraces Islam and is married to a non-Muslim is automatically nullified. Note that Ibadis consider Jews and Christians to be unbelievers, but they nonetheless allow a Muslim man to marry a Jewish or Christian woman, despite the Qur'an's prohibition against marrying unbelieving women (2:221).

father's status in all circumstances, whether or not she is a monotheist or one of the People of the Book; there are two opinions on this matter.

One should affiliate with the [slave] child who is set free by an affiliate and a nonaffiliate, if they both had a share in him. One should suspend judgment concerning a child whose paternity is shared, that is, his mother had sexual relations with two men during a single cycle of purity, whether through marriage or concubinage, and the date of conception is unknown; if she becomes pregnant after having relations consecutively with two men in a single cycle of purity, paternity is attributed to the second man, not the first. [One should also suspend judgment concerning a child whose paternity is shared] if they had relations with her at the same time; the one who had relations with the mother is one of two partners in owning her, or is one of two men who contracted marriage with her and his identity is unknown.[24] This also applies in a case in which two women gave birth to babies in a dark place, for example, and it is unknown which woman gave birth to which child; or to a single child, and it is unknown which woman is his mother if they both claim him. Some say one should suspend judgment concerning the children of someone who turns back to unbelief or hypocrisy after faithfulness, while others say they should be retained in affiliation, or that one should affiliate with the children of someone who turns back from faithfulness to hypocrisy [but not to unbelief], and one should suspend judgment concerning the children of others [who turn to unbelief], or vice versa—there are many opinions. The best opinion is to suspend judgment [with children] after [their father abandons the stipulations requiring] affiliation, because it follows logically (*li-annaha bi-'l-tab' hunna*).

One should suspend judgment concerning an affiliated child when he reaches maturity until there is evidence of his faithfulness, at which point he should be given affiliation, or until he commits a grave sin, at which point one should dissociate from him. The Qutb said it is better to affiliate with him if he affirms [belief in] the obligatory doctrines until it is known that he has committed a grave sin, and he should remain in a state of affiliation if it is unclear whether or not he has

24. All of these hypothetical cases would be extremely abhorrent in Islamic law, which prescribes a waiting period of three menstrual cycles for women before remarriage after widowhood or divorce, in order to avoid any confusion concerning paternity. Nonetheless, al-Rawahi's point is that the child born from immoral acts is not judged by those acts.

reached maturity, but if he says, "I have reached maturity," he should be considered mature. Anyone who is insane remains in the condition he was in before his insanity (Atfayyish 1980a, 41).

If the child of an affiliate is absent, the child remains an affiliate as long as it is unclear whether he has reached maturity, through the testimony of trustworthy people or by reaching the age of maturity, which is seventeen, or fifteen according to the source we will cite. Some say one should look at his age-mates, while others say he remains an affiliate as long as his maturity is not established by the testimony of trustworthy individuals, even if one hears from someone else that he has fathered children—but that is not sound, unless one argues that begetting children is not proof of maturity—because we are not sure if he is alive, so how can we stop affiliating with him if his maturity is in doubt? But if we hear from trustworthy people that he fathered a child, that is proof of maturity, just as if they testified that he is alive. Maturity is at age seventeen or fifteen, or when sperm is produced, or when there are other signs of maturity. If they say he has grown up or reached maturity or that religious requirements are obligatory for him, then he is mature. No one knows the exact onset of maturity or the exact time of prayer or true weight and measure, except God the Glorious.

S: What does it mean for a person who is accountable [before God] to affiliate with his own self?

T: It means that you avoid disobeying God, have true repentance, declare your regret [for sin], persevere in true determination not to commit anything hateful to God or to abandon any of His commands, that you wish good for yourself and have mercy on yourself, and that you ask God's forgiveness and seek the success that comes from Him. You can only truly affiliate with yourself by avoiding what God has prohibited and obeying His commands, because the one who disobeys God causes his soul to perish, which is exactly what an enemy does to his enemy.

S: What is the root meaning of affiliation?[25]

T: The root meaning of affiliation is agreement on the truth. Those who are in agreement are affiliates, even if one of them does not know the other, or even if he appears to dissociate from him. Dissociation is the opposite. An affiliate must be someone of whom one hears or sees good things. If one hears something concern-

25. The teacher's response is taken from Atfayyish (1980a, 42–43).

ing someone on the testimony of trustworthy witnesses that requires dissociation or that is incompatible with affiliation, if that person was previously an affiliate, meaning if he does something bad, like failing to act according to the Prophet's attested practices or persisting in doing reprehensible things, such a person is not an affiliate, even if he seems pleasant. Likewise, if one hears from [trustworthy witnesses] what requires affiliation but sees him do what is incompatible with affiliation, he should not be given affiliation, even if one is not repulsed by him—though if one is repulsed by him for God's sake because he seems to command evil, even if it is uncertain, such as commanding dissimulation, he should not be given affiliation; or if he is living with his father who profits from usury, and you do not know that he lives off money that is not his father's, [he should not be given affiliation]; and all other prohibited acts are of the same order. The saying that affiliation requires the agreement of the heart pertains to what a person seems to be, but you should consider the Prophet's words, "And did you examine your heart?" (al-Nawawi n.d., 1:339–40, no. 590–91). This clarifies the matter.

A person is given affiliation if one has seen faithfulness in him by being in his company, or if one has not personally seen him do good things like fulfilling his obligations toward his wife and his slave but one assumes he is faithful in this, or if one sees him doing something good like washing impurity in preparation for prayer, along with other things, then he is given affiliation because of the indication provided by his washing [for example] that he is someone who does good deeds and does his religious obligations; there are two opinions on this matter.

A person is given affiliation by the testimony of [his worthiness] from two free men who are affiliates, or by the testimony of one free man who is an affiliate and two free women who are affiliates. That is the correct interpretation, as in all other cases of giving testimony, except that women are not allowed to testify in the case of *hudud*. Some scholars say that the testimony of a single man is adequate, and some say the testimony of a single trustworthy woman is adequate to establish the worthiness of a person for affiliation or, on the other hand, to establish that a person should be subject to dissociation. Some say one may choose between affiliation and suspending judgment in the case of a report from only one man, while others say one may choose if the man informed him without being asked. Some object to both these opinions, because affiliation is not subject to choice; rather, once it is established that a person deserves affiliation, it is immediately obligatory to affiliate with him unless there is evidence to the contrary.

A person should be granted affiliation if one is informed about him after questioning, just as in law the attestation of a person's honor is rejected before it is requested but is accepted after it is requested, although in this case one may reject it if one is informed without asking, but it is not obligatory to do so. Some say the testimony of a single free person is adequate, whether that person is male or female, but there are different opinions on that point. A person is given affiliation by reputation if there is no evidence to the contrary, meaning that one only knows good about him and someone whose status is unknown does not say anything bad about him. So understand!

S: What is "information" (*khabar*), and what is the difference between that and legal testimony?

T: One speaks of "information" (*khabar*) in the case of a matter that is undisputed, such as being informed that the time of prayer has come, or the time to break the fast, or any matter for which God's law does not stipulate the number and honorable record [of witnesses], or what is told without intending it as legal testimony and without saying, "We testify." Anything that requires the legal judgment of two honorable witnesses is called testimony. Alternatively, the terms may be seen as interchangeable.

S: Summarize for me the rules for affiliating with the Prophet's Companions.

T: We affiliate with all the Companions except those who clearly committed a grave sin in the matter of the sedition (*al-fitan*) that occurred among them. We also affiliate with those who suspend judgment concerning them because they are unable to understand the truth, because it is obligatory for those who do not understand the truth to suspend judgment, unless it is clear that such a person is capriciously suspending judgment after coming to understand the truth. We do not suspend judgment concerning those who were aware of what 'Uthman and 'Ali were doing and were present at the time they were doing reprehensible things, unless he considered what was wrong to be right, or considered what was right to be wrong; that is not to be tolerated. The Companions are not like other people because the Prophet explicitly spoke well of them.[26] One should not suspend judgment concerning them as one would concerning other people, such as

26. There are many hadiths on the virtues of the Prophet's Companions—indeed, there is an entire *kitab* by that title (*fada'il ashab al-nabi*) in al-Bukhari (n.d., 767–91).

if the imam deviates or dies, or if he is removed from the state of affiliation; [the Companions] remain in a state of affiliation.

S: Is it permissible to be ignorant of imams of power (*a'immat al-sultan*) and imams of exemplary learning (*a'immat al-qudwa fi 'l-'ilm*)?[27]

T: It is permissible to be ignorant of Imams Abu Bakr al-Siddiq, 'Umar b. al-Khattab, 'Abd Allah b. Yahya Talib al-Haqq al-Kindi, Abu 'l-Khattab 'Abd al-A'la, al-Julanda b. Mas'ud, 'Abd al-Rahman b. Rustam, the just Rustamid imams, and others, as well as all the leading scholars of the religion, whether their names are unknown or their names are known—like 'Abdallah b. Abad and Jabir b. Zayd—whoever fights the leaders of deviance or defends the religion, unless there is proof otherwise. That is the correct opinion. The more commonly held opinion, taken from Abu Khazar, is that it is impermissible to be ignorant of them, and it is obligatory to affiliate with them and to affiliate with the leading scholars, although there is no proof (*hujja*) in the Qur'an or Sunna that this is a religious obligation that would remove all possibility of excuse or that there is no possibility of disagreement on this. The truth lies in one of these opinions.

Some scholars in our school say this concerning the leaders, that even if our colleagues are faithful [in other matters], if they dissociate from [the leaders], one cannot accept two words from them.[28]

Perhaps what Abu Khazar meant—may God have mercy on him—are those of whom one cannot be ignorant, who are the first scholars (*mujtahidun*) who defended the religion, like 'Abdallah b. Abad, but knowing their names is not required in such a way as to take this as a proof. It is reported concerning Abu Khazar that he wrote from Egypt to Abu Salih Janun, in response to a query [on this], that it is impermissible to be ignorant of all of those whom the Messenger of God called people to follow.

S: Is it permissible to be ignorant of those who contradict the truth we hold?

T: No, it is not permissible to be ignorant of those who contradict our doctrine; rather, it is necessary to know them in a general way, that they do what is prohibited and contrary to what God revealed as the [true] religion, on which there can be no

27. The teacher's response is taken from Atfayyish (1980a, 44).

28. Atfayyish (1980a, 44): "Even if thousands of our companions came and dissociated from them, it would not be accepted from them."

disagreement, even if one does not know the point of contradiction or those who are doing the contradicting, or if one does not know if there is a contradiction.[29]

Lesson 2: Dissociation: Its Types and Its Regulations

S: I know the literal definition of dissociation (*bara'a*)—distance from something—and what it means legally: hatred and denunciation (*la'n*)[30] for those who deserve it. What are its regulations for individuals (*al-ashkhas*) among us [Ibadis]?

T: It is obligatory to dissociate from individuals among us if there is a cause (*li-wujud 'illa*) that requires dissociation from a group (*bara'at al-jumla*), such as committing a grave sin, because of the words of 'Umar b. al-Khattab and 'Amr b. al-'As, "We will dissociate from anyone we see doing evil," which is also transmitted as a hadith. The obligation does not derive from God's words, "Do not take the unbelievers [as affiliates instead of the believers]" (4:144), or "Do not affiliate with a people [with whom God is angry]" (60:13), or "Whoever affiliates with them [is one of them]" (5:51), because the prohibition of affiliation does not invariably imply dissociation, because there is an intermediary position: to suspend judgment. It is well-known that the prohibition of something is a command to do its opposite, and vice versa, and what is meant by its opposite is what contradicts it. This applies when the opposite can mean only one thing, as is the case with movement and rest. Neither does proof lie in the Prophet's dissociation [of people], because not everything he did is obligatory; it is only obligatory if he commanded it (Atfayyish 1980a, 45).

29. Cf. Atfayyish (1980a, 44). It is strange to say that it is not necessary to know the leading Ibadis but it is necessary to know their theological opponents. He probably means that it is important to know that there are people who oppose Ibadi doctrine and that any such opposition is religiously prohibited, even if one does not know any specifics.

30. Although *la'n* can mean "curse," al-Salimi explicitly prohibits cursing (*shatm*) those who go astray (A. al-Salimi 2003, 28). As we shall see, al-Rawahi says that courtesy should continue to be observed with those from whom one has dissociated. Use of the term *la'n* may have prompted Sunnis in Zanzibar to say that the Ibadis curse the Prophet's Companions, an accusation strongly rebutted by 'Ali b. Muhammad b. 'Ali al-Mundhiri (1866–1925), an Ibadi scholar and judge in Zanzibar (al-Mundhiri 1980, 21–22).

S: I know that it is obligatory to dissociate from individuals if there is a cause that requires dissociation from a group. Please explain dissociation from a category and the regulations attached to it.

T: Dissociation from a group is comparable to affiliation with a group. It is obligatory to dissociate from unbelievers as a group. Anyone who dissociates from all people or affiliates with all people, or who treats one group of affiliates differently from others, or who dissociates from [everyone who belongs to a type of being], such as all jinn or people or angels, or who is unaware that God has commanded affiliation with the group or dissociation from it or that there is reward for doing this, is an unbeliever—unless we are speaking of someone concerning whom it is permissible to be unaware until one has proof. Dissociation from a group is only obligatory if there is infidelity (*kufr*), for wherever infidelity is found, dissociation is obligatory, and likewise affiliation [is obligatory if there is no infidelity]. Someone who is not subject to dissociation but then does something requiring dissociation of anyone who does such a thing becomes subject to dissociation, because God's judgment is the same whether it concerns a group or an individual.

Just as we are obligated to dissociate from a particular individual or group, we are obligated to dissociate from those about whom there is an explicit text if there is proof of the necessity of dissociation from them. The Qur'an specifies types (*anwa*ʿ) like the people of Noah,[31] individuals like Pharoah,[32] Goliath (Q 2:249–51), and Abu Lahab,[33] groups like those who spread the lie (*ʿusbat al-ifk*),[34] and individuals who are not mentioned by name, such as the king who seized every boat (18:79) or the one who disputed with Abraham (2:258), or like

31. Who rejected Noah's prophetic exhortations (Q 11:25–49, 54:9–15, and Sura 71).

32. Who oppressed the Children of Israel and rejected Moses' prophetic exhortations, in passages too numerous to cite.

33. An uncle of the Prophet who was one of his most ardent opponents. Sura 111 denounces him.

34. The Prophet's favorite wife, ʿA'isha, was accidentally left behind after a rest stop during a journey, and was found by a young man, who brought her back to town on his camel. Rumors spread that they had had an adulterous affair. The Qur'an exonerated her: "Surely those who concocted the lie (*al-ifk*) are a party (*ʿusba*) from among you" (24:11). The verses that discuss this, however (24:11–20), do not tell people to dissociate from those involved in the slander.

Noah's wife[35] and Lot's wife.[36] Anyone who reads these texts about their evil in the Qur'an, or hears it and understands it or is informed about it, must dissociate from them as a group, and unless there is a convincing proof shown to him concerning a particular named individual, he must dissociate from each individual by name, whether that person is mentioned in the Qur'an or in the text of a sound hadith, or whether one knows it because it is reported by many people. Otherwise, one should not mention him except with what is said about him in the Qur'an, the knowledge of which leads to this obligation. It is not permissible to dissociate from someone mentioned in a text by name if it is not explicitly given in the text, because perhaps that is not the person's name. Some say the testimony of one or two trustworthy witnesses is enough to specify the person's name—there are differences of opinion on this (Atfayyish 1980a, 45–46).

S: What should I do if the imam is unjust, and among his subjects are some who follow him and others who abstain from fighting for him (*al-qa'id 'anhu*)?

T: Dissociate from [the imam] and from those who follow him and oppose you—they are to be blamed. Continue your affiliation with those who do not follow him if they were previously affiliates, because it is permissible to abstain from fighting under unjust rulers, whether they obey the religion or act contrary to it—[one may even affiliate with those who] are subjects of an unbelieving ruler, as long as the Muslim observes his religious obligations, even if in secret (Atfayyish 1980a, 46).

S: What is the rule for an apostate (*al-murtadd*)?

35. Nothing explicit is said in the Qur'an about Noah's wife, but when Noah cried to God because his son was among those who were drowning in the flood (11:45), God replied that the young man was "not from your family; he is [from] an unrighteous deed" (11:46). Most exegetes have understood from this that Noah's wife committed adultery, from which the boy was born.

36. The Qur'an says that when God destroyed Lot's city because of their sins and failure to repent, "We delivered him and his followers, except his wife; We decreed that she be among those left behind" (27:57). In the story of the destruction of Sodom and Gomorrah in Genesis 19, the angels warned Lot and his family not to look back at the cities as they fled, but Lot's wife looked back and became a pillar of salt (Gen. 19:26). Scholars of biblical criticism believe this to be "an old tradition to account for bizarre salt formations in the area such as may be seen today on Jebel Usdum" (Metzger and Murphy, 24).

T: One must dissociate from him, and if possible he should be killed at any time if he does not repent. Hadith commands in general that he be killed,[37] but 'Umar b. al-Khattab, may God be pleased with him, stipulated that he should not be killed until he has been called on to repent for a period of three days; then, if he does not repent, he is killed (Atfayyish 1980a, 46).

S: Why did 'Umar make this stipulation, when the hadith requires killing him without [stipulating that he should be] called to repent?

T: Do you doubt 'Umar's expertise in the Sunna and his regard for Islam? By God, 'Umar was uniquely endowed by God, along with Abu Bakr! 'Umar was one of God's great gifts to the community—anything he and his companion said or did was a *sunna* from the Messenger of God, on whom be God's blessing and peace, taken from him and clarifying his words or a matter brought for judgment, either something suggested to them or an understanding from them, because the Prophet said, "Follow the two caliphs who come after me, Abu Bakr and 'Umar."[38]

There is nothing in his saying "Kill whoever changes his religion" that prevents calling on him to repent, even if he did not say this; perhaps the apostate will be reminded of his faith or become afraid. There is no harm in waiting three days to call him to repentance before executing the penalty against him; rather, it is a precaution to be certain of his apostasy, to remove any hesitation he might have had to repent and submit to Islam, or to confirm his unbelief. Perhaps during the days that he is called to repent he might be admonished, and [God's] kindness might reach him. On the whole, there is nothing in calling a person to repent that contradicts the intention of the hadith or subverts it.

37. According to a hadith (al-Bukhari n.d., *Kitab al-diyyat* [87], *bab* 6, no. 6878), "The blood of a Muslim who confesses that none has the right to be worshipped but God and that I am His Messenger cannot be shed except in three cases: in retaliation for murder; a married person who commits adultery; and someone who reverts from Islam (apostate) and leaves the Muslims." For a discussion of apostasy and its punishment in Islam, see Heffening 1999. For contemporary Muslim critiques of its logic and contemporary application, see Talbi (1998) and An-Na'im (1990, 86–87, 109, 150, 183–85).

38. Al-Suyuti (1980, no. 1318): "Follow those two who are after me, Abu Bakr and 'Umar." The commentary is by al-Munawi (1994). A similar hadith is found in al-Tirmidhi (2000, *Kitab al-manaqib* (45), *bab* 16, no. 4023): "Follow the two who are after me, Abu Bakr and 'Umar."

S: What is the rule concerning his wealth and his children?

T: Some say his children are not taken [into slavery] and his wealth is not plundered, while others say his children are taken and his wealth is not plundered, and still others say [his children] may be taken and [his wealth] may be plundered because he attached himself to the Abode of War—there are different opinions. There are also two different opinions as to whether one may enslave his offspring up to the fourth or third generation. Some of our companions interpret the third generation to mean the apostate's grandson. The Qutb said, "This is not explicit" (Atfayyish 1980a, 47).

An apostate's child is one of the orphans of the Muslims, and some say so is the apostate's grandchild. [An apostate's] grown son should be killed if he declines to embrace Islam, and his wealth belongs to the people of the religion he embraced and should be distributed by the imam or his representative among them, according to what seems best to him in the country in which he resides first of all, whether or not he is killed. Apostasy is like death.[39] Some say his wealth should be given to his Muslim heirs, whether children or adults, but that is a weak opinion, because a Muslim may not inherit from an unbeliever, and an unbeliever may not inherit from a Muslim. The holder of this opinion would have to prove that they are more deserving of it, following the model of the estate of an unbelieving Muslim or his possessions in the Abode of Islam, even if he is still living. Whatever he owns in the Abode of War, he acquired after his apostasy; if he dies in the Abode of Islam, it goes to his heirs who are unbelievers, or it reverts to the state treasury—there are different opinions.

The rule regarding an apostate is the same as that for someone who worships idols: no *jizya* is accepted from him, no peace can be made with him, any animals he slaughters are impermissible for a Muslim to eat, a Muslim cannot marry him or inherit from him, and nothing will protect him from the sword except his embracing Islam, no matter what religion he converted to besides Islam, because of the hadith, "Kill anyone who changes his religion." If he wishes to embrace Islam, it is sufficient for him to give the testimony of faith that the Messenger of God used to require (Atfayyish 1980a, 46–47).

39. That is, the rules for the distribution of the wealth of an apostate are the same as the distribution of the wealth of a deceased person.

S: What is the rule regarding the religious duties performed by an apostate before his apostasy?

T: Whatever good deeds he did before his apostasy are null and void, even if he repented for an offense. There are different opinions on whether a person who returns to Islam must redo his religious obligations or only the *hajj* after its conditions have been met, or if its conditions have already been met when he repents, or whether he need not redo any of his religious acts, or whether he will be rewarded for the good deeds he did before his apostasy if he dies as a repentant Muslim and does not redo them—this is the correct interpretation—or whether he must redo the religious obligations that he had done before his apostasy (ibid., 47).

S: What is the rule regarding his ritual purity?

T: He is impure (*najis*). If he wishes to embrace Islam, he must wash his entire body, and he must also wash anything that his body's moisture touched, or some say only anything that has impurity on it[40]—there are two opinions.

S: What is the rule regarding the bad deeds he did while an apostate, if he returns to Islam?

T: God turns those bad deeds into good deeds, just like the bad deeds of a hypocrite who repents from his acts of rebellion. His turning his bad deeds into good deeds might mean that he gives him the power to do good deeds after his repentance (ibid.).

S: Must the hypocrite who repents redo the good deeds that he did during his persistence in hypocrisy?

T: No, there is consensus that he need not redo them, but they are counted as a loss, and he is deprived of the reward for those deeds. He must only make up any fasting and prayer he failed to do, and he must atone for anything that requires atonement.[41]

40. The rules of ritual purity in Islamic law distinguish between greater impurities (*najas*, literally "filth") and lesser impurities (*hadath*, "something which occurs"). *Hadath* requires ritual ablutions (*wudu'*) before one may prayer, but *najas* requires a full body bath (*ghusl*). All Islamic legal schools consider seminal emission and menstrual blood to be a source of greater impurity. Some schools also feel that anything touched by a dog is *najis*, and there are other sources of *najas* as well.

41. See Chelhod 1999. Atfayyish (1980a, 47) adds, "By consensus the hypocritical monotheist does not redo them, but he receives no reward for them if he does not repent."

S: What is the rule regarding an apostate's wife?

T: She is prohibited to him, just like the wife of someone who is found to have an attribute of unbelief, who is like an apostate in the previously mentioned rules. If this attribute existed ever since he came of age, he is treated under the law like a person whose natural disposition is to be an unbeliever (*hukm al-shirk al-fitri*). Some say the wife of someone with an attribute of unbelief is not prohibited to him if it is a minor fault, and that he is considered a monotheist in matters of inheritance, slaughtering animals, and burial (ibid.).

S: How does the repentance of an apostate become valid?

T: By professing the three statements of faith,[42] while practicing dissociation from the deviant religions that contradict Islam, as is required of any unbeliever who repents. Some say it is enough to say, "There is no god but Allah [and] Muhammad is the messenger of Allah," because, if he is God's messenger, then everything he taught is [automatically] true, since he was sent to all beings (Q 21:107) and since the Qur'an is from God. Still others say that this applied only to the time of the Prophet, peace and blessings upon him—there are different opinions (ibid.).

S: What is the rule for someone who opposes our school and follows our opponents?

T: One should dissociate from him, and only if he has insulted our religion should we kill him, as we killed Khardala at the command of Jabir b. Zayd when he abandoned our faith and followed the ways of our opponents and began to insult our religion; so Jabir issued a *fatwa* that killing him was the best jihad. *The Indication and Proof* (Abu Ya'qub Yusuf 1997) says that Khardala killed a Muslim, and the blood of one of our theological opponents and those who leave our sect may be shed only in the case of outright attack, not merely belief in and profession of a religious doctrine that is inexcusable. Our people say that killing is not permitted because of an insult unless it is an insult to the Qur'an or the Prophet, on whom be God's blessings and peace, because when someone

42. The three statements of faith (*al-jumal al-thalath*) are: "There is no god but Allah," "Muhammad is the messenger of Allah," and "What Muhammad taught is true." The profession of faith (*shahada*) among Sunni Muslims is said to consist of the two "words" (*kalimatan*), which are the first two of these three statements, in which the second is sometimes "Muhammad is his servant and messenger."

told [Abu Bakr] al-Siddiq, "We will kill this person because he insulted you," he replied, "We do not have the same rights as the Messenger of God, peace and blessings be upon him." One can argue (*la-na 'l-hujja*) that the Qur'an and the Messenger, on whom be peace, are the source of the religion, and insulting the religion is an insult to these two; our religion, praise be to God, is God's religion, taken from the Qur'an and the tongue of the Messenger, on whom be God's blessings and peace. Al-Siddiq did not kill the one who insulted him because he had merely insulted him as a person, not the religion, as indicated by his response, "We do not have the same rights as the Messenger of God" (Atfayyish 1980a, 48).

S: For what reason should I dissociate from a person?

T: Dissociate from anyone who has committed a grave sin or persists in committing a minor sin, or a sin concerning which the scholars do not know whether it is small or great in God's eyes.

S: Can one know a minor sin from a grave sin?

T: According to our companions in the east, this can be known; our people and the Nukkar agree on this. Our companions in the west say it cannot be known.

S: On what kind of sins is there disagreement among us as to whether they are minor or of unknown status?

T: An example that some give is beating on a tambourine without singing and not in a gathering, although others say this is a grave sin, and others say that it is only a grave sin if one sings with it or if one does this in a gathering—there are different opinions.[43]

Another example is telling a lie to someone other than God, though some say that is always a grave sin, and that is the commonly accepted and correct opinion. Others say a lie is a grave sin only if it leads to bloodshed or the corruption of wealth, and yet others say if it is added to truthful speech it is a minor sin, otherwise it is a grave sin—there are different opinions.

43. Muslim opinions regarding the permissibility of music range from those who prohibit all types of music as something that stirs the passions and distracts from religious devotion, to those who encourage it as something that promotes joy and spiritual experience. In between there are many distinctions, some saying singing praises to God and the Prophet are permissible but other types of songs are not, some saying that percussion instruments are acceptable, but other instruments are not, and so on (Shehadi 1995; Shiloah 1999).

Another example is slapping someone without leaving a mark, though some say that is always a grave sin, and that is correct—there are two opinions on this.

Another example is entering the bathroom in the dark without clothes, or going about naked in the daytime in a place where one cannot be seen, though some say that doing this at nighttime is a minor sin.

Another example is entering someone's house without permission, or slander, though some say these are both grave sins, and that is correct; any other opinion is wrong because of explicit texts in the Qur'an and Hadith, but there are two opinions on this.

Another example is stealing something of little value, or slighting a customer in weighing by the amount of a single date, though others say they are both grave sins, and that is correct because of hadiths that say so, but there are two opinions on this (ibid.).

S: Why do the Ibadis of North Africa say that one cannot know what sins are minor?

T: They say this subject is wider than the desert, and that divine wisdom made them unknown so we would be cautioned against doing them, which closes the door to all sins, and that if they were specified as forgiven, people would destroy themselves through disobedience to God, and that would lead to people having less fear of God—God forbid!—so specifying them is unwise.

It is also said that minor sins are forgiven if one avoids grave sins, and a person does not know whether he will die while avoiding grave sins or not, so it is better to avoid all sins, lest he rely on the forgiveness of minor sins by avoiding grave sins—but who knows, perhaps what is predestined will overtake him and he will acquire [commit] a grave sin and die without forgiveness.

Such sins include playing the flute, drums, and all musical instruments used for amusement, but beating a drum for a reason other than amusement, such as to call people together or warn them or to announce a marriage, is not a sin, nor is it a sin to beat a drum when someone is bitten by a snake, in order to keep him from fainting, without any expectation that he would enjoy it (ibid., 48–49).

S: I know that seeing a person committing a sin that requires dissociation is the way in which there is no doubt, but what secondary ways are considered adequate by God's law to require dissociation and constitute convincing proof for the withdrawal of affiliation?

T: The ways considered adequate are merely means of transmission of information, and these means differ with regard to their evidentiary power, but not with regard to their adequacy as proof. The strongest is a report from multiple sources; next is reputation; and finally, a report from two affiliated men or one affiliated man and two affiliated women. This is commonly accepted, and we act according to this. Some say it is enough to take the word of a single affiliated man, or even a single affiliated woman.

S: If I see someone persisting in a sin, and the scholars do not know whether it is minor or grave, or if I have proof that he is persisting in doing it, how should I treat him and those who affiliate with him?

T: You must dissociate from him and from anyone who persists in sin, because if the sin is minor, persistence makes the sin no longer minor, and if it is grave in God's sight, a person who commits grave sins is even more deserving of dissociation!

S: According to those who do not accept the testimony of a single trustworthy affiliate, what is the status of someone who dissociates from someone based on only that testimony?

T: He condemns himself, because he has impugned a Muslim and has dissociated from him and withdrawn his affiliation without proof.

S: If I hear the sound of sin being committed but cannot see it, but my heart is certain that it is a particular person, what should I do?[44]

T: There are two opinions on this. The first says you should dissociate from him if your heart is certain that it is a particular person, and the second says you should not dissociate from him without seeing him do it with your own eyes—but you may believe in your heart that whoever did that sin is an enemy, if he is accountable before God, in order to exclude a child or an insane person [from dissociation]. You should do the same if the sounds are made by one of the jinn: you should not dissociate from the *jinni,* because the one making the sound might be a child or an insane person, who would not be accountable before God, since he is not in his right mind.

44. The teacher's answer to this question as well as parts of his answers to the succeeding questions concerning the jinn and Iblis are taken from Atfayyish (1980a, 49), and parts concerning Iblis are also taken from Atfayyish 1981.

S: Let's suppose that one of the jinn appears and interacts with us in such a way that he is not invisible. What is his status then?

T: His status is just like that of a human being, except that he cannot exercise the greater imamate over human beings, though he can over other jinn.

S: Where are the happy jinn in the afterlife?

T: They are in the deserts of paradise, and we will see them, but they will not see us.

S: What is the origin of the jinn?

T: They are the offspring of Iblis [Satan], may God curse him. He is *al-Jann,* their father. Some claim that *al-Jann* is a righteous man and is their father

S: If someone says that Iblis is an angel, is he an unbeliever?

T: Yes, it is said that he is an unbeliever, but the Qutb, may God have mercy on him, explicitly says that he is not an unbeliever, because one could interpret God's words, "All the angels prostrated except Iblis" (38:73–74) to mean that the exception is linked with the fact that he was one of them, or it could mean simply that the cursed one was a single *jinni* among a number of angels that did not include him, but he happened to be among them and was included in God's words, "So they prostrated," and then was excepted as if he were one of them.[45] It is also possible that the exception is what separates him from them, and that he—may God curse him—is not an angel who went bad, but that he is of a different species who are the jinn, and then he deviated from his Lord's command, and before he went astray he used to worship in the angels' courts and wherever he liked, until the misery ordained for him caught up with him—we seek refuge in God from such a thing!—and he entered the rank of infidelity in such a way that he became chief of those who will be miserable. Oh God, by your honor, do not expel us from the circle of your mercy, in this world or the next!

Whether the exception [of "except Iblis"] separates him from them or includes him among them, there is no harm in saying that whoever says that Iblis is one of the angels is an unbeliever, because angels are immune from disobedience to God: "They do not disobey God's commands and they do what they are

45. Q 2:34, 7:11, 17:61, 18:50, and 20:116 say that when God commanded the angels to bow before Adam, "they all bowed except Iblis," which would lead one to think he was an angel, but 18:50 also says, "He was one of the jinn, so he transgressed the commandment of his Lord."

ordered to do" (66:6),[46] because if he were really one of them he would not have disobeyed God when He commanded him and he would have done what he had been commanded, as they did. May God protect us by His grace and mercy from Iblis and his soldiers and their trickery!

One might say that a verse like "When we told the angels to prostrate before Adam, they all prostrated except Iblis—he declined and waxed proud and was among the infidels" (2:34) means that Iblis was one of them, because he was included in the command, and because the Most High reported that He only commanded the angels. Iblis was among those commanded, as indicated by God's words, "What kept you from prostrating when I commanded you?" (7:12), and He did not separate His command to him from His command to the angels, which [arguably] means He knew that he was one of them, and that the exception indicates that he was among them and was responsible to do what they were responsible to do, but he declined and waxed proud and disobeyed the blessed and Most High God, who became angry with him and cursed him and transformed him into an accursed demon. So when the Most High says in *Surat al-Kahf,* "except Iblis, who was one of the jinn" (18:50), this means that he became one of the jinn, just as when He said, "He was one of the unbelievers" it meant that he became one of the unbelievers.

Some might ask how Iblis could be an angel when angels do not procreate, because procreation is between a male and a female, and there are no females among the angels, as indicated by God's denial addressed to those who judged them to be females, and the negation of femaleness implies the negation of procreation, whereas Iblis has so many offspring! The Qur'an clearly states that he has offspring (18:50), so how could he be an angel when angels do not have offspring? One might reply that he only came to procreate and have offspring after he was transformed and his form changed to that of someone who procreates, and all the transformations did not last more than three days, after which he could no longer

46. This verse refers specifically to the angels who will guard hellfire in the afterlife. There is no Qur'anic text that explicitly says that angels are immune from sin, although all Muslim sects hold this to be true, and also say that the angels are made from light, although this is not mentioned in the Qur'an (these doctrines derive from Hadith). One could even argue that the angels' protest when God announced His intention to create a viceroy on earth (2:30) is proof that they are not immune from at least minor sins.

procreate or beget offspring, but the cursed one asked for a respite until the Hour [of resurrection of the dead], and he was given that (15:36–38).

Furthermore, although it is common in spoken language to use an exception that does not imply inclusion, it does not occur in proper Arabic, as used in the Qur'an; whatever is contrary to pure Arabic is unlikely to be used in Qur'anic rhetoric. Some say that the angels who were commanded to prostrate were just one set, the guardians of the jinn, and were called *al-jann,* and that God sent them to earth to drive the jinn from the earth into the oceans, islands, and mountains.[47] The Qutb, may God have mercy on him, wrote: "This is not true, nor is it true that Iblis was an angel among them. The closest thing to that is that he was born from jinn who lived before him, and they are not angels, and the angels fought them and imprisoned him, so he worshipped with the angels. The commonly held doctrine is that he was the first of the jinn. It is said that these were angels of the earth, because the matter had to do with the rule of the earth." He also said, "Anyone who says that the angels of the earth can disobey God like the children of Adam is wrong" (Atfayyish 1981, 7:367).

The correct opinion is that the command was addressed to all the angels, as indicated by the emphatically inclusive language in God's words, "So the angels prostrated, all of them" (*kulluhum ajmaʿun,* 38:73), and that the exception of Iblis among them is an exception symbolically linking him to them because he was among them, worshipping as they were, so it came to be as if he were one of them and was called "angel" as a borrowed figure of speech (*majazan bi-ʾl-istiʿara*).

It is also possible that the exception is unlinked. Some of our companions say that anyone who claims that Iblis is one of the angels is an unbeliever because God the majestic and glorious said, "He was one of the jinn." The Qutb said:

> He is not an unbeliever, because it is a [possible] interpretation of the exception, because exception contains a principle of linkage, and he interpreted God's words, "He was one of the jinn," to mean that he was one of them in doing evil deeds and in belief and speech, but that he was one of the angels in origin, body and type, just as when we say "ʿAmr is a demon" or "he is an animal." So when he says, "Iblis is God's enemy and is one of the angels, but he acted corruptly like the jinn," the discussion with whoever says this turns on the immunity of

47. In Arab folklore, the jinn inhabit desolate and uninhabited places.

angels from sin. The truth is that they are immune from sin, because the Most High said, "They act according to His command" (21:27),[48] i.e. they do nothing that He does not command. He is not one of the angels, because God's words, "He was one of the jinn," obviously mean that he is one of them, and that his lineage lies among them. That is what the words say and that is their most obvious meaning, whereas the previously mentioned interpretation interprets this as a metaphor and is contrary to the obvious meaning, and metaphorical interpretation should not be adopted without clear similarity (*bi-la qarina*).

Our people (*qawmuna*) claim that Ibn 'Abbas reported that one group (*qawm*)[49] of angels procreated and were called jinn, and Iblis was among them. Our companions say that anyone who says that the angels are male or female is an unbeliever, as is anyone who says that they procreate. Some say such a person is not an unbeliever if he says this about individuals among them or a type among them, only if he says this of all of them, because a person who says this [about some of them] is interpreting the words of Ibn 'Abbas that they claim are from him. A person can only be called an unbeliever for saying this only about individuals among them or a group among them if he is obstinately contradicting the Qur'an or is ignorant, not if he is basing his interpretation on what was transmitted from Ibn 'Abbas. Likewise, an accusation of unbelief against someone who says that Iblis was one of the angels applies only to someone who is ignorant or who obstinately contradicts the Qur'an, not to someone who relies on what is transmitted from Ibn 'Abbas, for example.

Likewise, concerning the immunity of the angels from sin, one may say that not all the angels are immune from sin, but most of them are, just as most humans are not immune from sin, but a few of them are. It is possible that the jinn were ordered to prostrate just as the angels were, and that this is omitted in the text, so that it should be read as "When we ordered the angels and the jinn to prostrate before Adam, they prostrated," meaning that the angels and the jinn all prostrated except Iblis, in which case the exception would be linked [to the group].

If you say, "How could the jinn prostrate, when they are evil?", I would say that the believers among them prostrated in obedience and sincerity, and the

48. This is a strange verse choice, because the Qur'anic text here is speaking of prophets, not angels. The verse quoted previously as proof of the angels' immunity from sin, 66:6, is a better choice.

49. Atfayyish (1980b, 1:451) says *naw'* ("type"), rather than *qawm* ("people," here translated as "group"). It is unclear who are "our people," as they made a claim that is contradicted by "our companions," the Ibadi scholars.

> polytheists and hypocrites among them did it with loathing in their hearts and without sincerity.
>
> If you say, "What indication is there that part of the text is left out, and that it should read 'When we told the angels and the jinn'?", I would say that what indicates this is that an exception is made of Iblis, and because if the great ones, who are the angels, were commanded to prostrate, it is even more appropriate for the lesser ones, who are the jinn, to be commanded to do so. (Atfayyish 1980b, 1:451–52)

If you would like to know more about this, read the Qutb's commentaries, in which there is healing and guidance.

S: What is the meaning of the saying "Affiliating with our imams means dissociation from the imams of others," and vice versa, that dissociation from the latter means affiliation with our imams?

T: Why is that confusing to you? If you affiliate with the imams of our mission (*da'watina*), which calls people to the straight path, that affiliation implies dissociation from imams of those who oppose the [true] religion and call people to deviance and heresy; and vice versa, if you dissociate from the imams of deviance because of their opposition to the Muslims, you affiliate with the imams of the Muslims. You can also say it the other way around, that affiliating with the imams of deviance implies dissociation from the imams of guidance, even if one affiliates with both, because if one deems the deviants to be correct in spite of their deviance, then one deems the imams of guidance to be wrong in deeming the deviant to be deviant, despite their guidance. To say that the deviant is correct, and to find error in the one who is guided because he deems him deviant, is the essence of dissociation from the one who is guided.

Although it is a good deed to affiliate with the affiliates of God, the sin of affiliating with God's enemies while affiliating with His affiliates is greater and overwhelms the good deed, so this good deed is lost, as if it never happened. It is void, as if it had never existed; it is not considered and it receives no reward and has no good in it. There is no way out of it by playing around with the religion and mocking the most important pillars of faith. One cannot say, "Good deeds take away bad deeds" (11:114), because we say good deeds take away bad deeds only if they are practiced continuously, with repentance; they cannot be considered and have no power in removing bad deeds without repentance. What really removes bad deeds is repentance. This is one of the blessings of the all-merciful Forgiver (*al-Tawwab*), that He has made good deeds take away minor sins if the one who commits a minor sin forgets to repent, not by way of persisting in committing it, because persistence turns it into a grave sin. If someone forgets to repent and persists in committing a minor sin, or if he commits a sin that is grave from the outset, it is not in God's religion that a good deed can remove it—it remains as it is without true repentance, and its removal is made sure by following repentance with good deeds. This is the truth, so rely on it, even if there are sayings in Ibadi books like *Al-Diya'* (al-'Awtabi 1990–1993) and *Al-Taj* (al-Thamini 2000) that say that [God] counts good deeds more than bad deeds, such as "Anyone who does a good deed erases the bad deed that follows it," and "If he repents, the reward of his good deed is restored to him," and "Whatever comes last is counted, whether good or evil." The sayings of the Muslims are the truth.

S: If someone calls himself an enemy of God from whom one must dissociate, or if someone else calls him that and he is pleased with that, and he is mature and rational, or if someone else like his son is called this and another person dissociates from him because he thinks he is indeed an enemy of God and he is a contemporary of that person and is in his company, is he unjust to him by dissociating from him?

T: Some say that he is not unjust to him, because he has allowed dissociation from himself by calling himself this, and anyone subjected to dissociation after exposing himself to dissociation is not treated unjustly by that dissociation. The correct opinion is the one on which the Qutb relies, which is that he is unjust by dissociating from him because he did not investigate the matter but acted in haste and neglected [the duty of investigation], but the person treated this way receives no reward for the injustice he has suffered, because he opened himself to suspicion. There are two other opinions, one that it is impermissible to dissociate from him, and a second that one condemns oneself by doing so (Atfayyish 1980a, 50).

S: If someone says, "I am a Hanafi" or "a Maliki" or "a Mu'tazili," must one dissociate from him?

T: If your heart is certain that what he means is that he follows the Hanafi or Maliki school in religion, and there is no ambiguity about whether he means that his tribe is the Banu Hanifa or that he is saying that he belongs to the pure religion (*al-din al-hanif*), and there is no uncertainty as to whether he means that he belongs to the Maliki tribe, you must dissociate from him. If there is any uncertainty, one must avoid imposing Qur'anic penalties (*hudud*)—and dissociation is a Qur'anic penalty (*hadd*) that is not carried out if there is any uncertainty (ibid., 50).

S: Should one dissociate from a person who bears the characteristics and signs of our theological opponents?

T: There are two opinions on this.

S: What is the regulation for calling a person from whom one has dissociated to repent?[50]

T: It is desirable, because it is a call to God, a revival of the religion, and a manifestation of its teachings.

S: What is the regulation for calling an affiliate to repent if he commits a sin?

T: It is obligatory. Anyone who does not call him to repent if he commits a grave sin is a hypocrite, and anyone who does not call him to repent after a minor sin or a sin the status of which is unknown commits a sin, according to the most obvious interpretation.

S: If I witness an affiliate commit a grave sin, or if trustworthy witnesses inform me of such, which do I do first—dissociate from him or call him to repent?

T: There are two opinions on this. The correct opinion is to dissociate from the person first, and the second opinion is to call the person to repentance first, and if he repents, there is no need for dissociation, but if he does not, you must dissociate from him. Those who hold this opinion make an exception for adultery and say that dissociation comes first in that case and, likewise, in the case of unbelief, dissociation comes first, because it is even worse than adultery, and is worse than any evil deed.

S: Can one imagine any grave sin worse than worshipping others besides God?

T: Yes, one can imagine a grave sin worse than polytheism, and worse than all grave sins, and that is to despair of God's acceptance of one's repentance from polytheism.

S: Why is no excuse accepted from some people, like Pharaoh and Iblis?[51]

50. The discussion concerning calling sinners to repentance is taken from Atfayyish (1980a, 50–51).

51. According to Q 10:90–92 and 40:46–47, Pharaoh repented as he was drowning, but his repentance was not accepted.

T: This is a harsh rebuke (*zajr wa-taghliz*), but it is not certain that repentance would not be accepted from them (*la tahqiq*).

S: If I have given affiliation to a judge or a governor, should I dissociate from them based on the report of trustworthy people that they have acted corruptly?

T: Dissociate from them, and may their eye not be blessed (*wa-la na'imat 'ayn*) [with the vision of one of God's affiliates], according to sound opinion.[52] Some say one should dissociate from them until they are present and allowed to defend themselves, and others say one should never dissociate from a Muslim until he is present and can defend himself, and that one should dissociate from him if he dies, because he is not present [to defend himself] (ibid., 51).

S: Must everyone call to repentance an affiliate who commits a sin, or just one person?

T: The scholars seem to say (*al-mafhum min kalam al-'ulama'*) that every individual who affiliates with that person must call him to repent if he commits a sin, and that Zayd cannot do it for 'Amr, although in *al-Diya'* it says that it is enough for one person to do so, praise God. The first opinion means that if Zayd calls him to repent when he sins and he does not repent, 'Amr should not hastily dissociate from him until he also calls him to repent, and so on for all those who are affiliated with him, as long as he does not repent. According to *al-Diya'*, if one person calls him to repent and he does so, everyone else retains him in a state of affiliation (ibid.).

S: If I have affiliated with someone as part of my affiliation with the *bayda*[53] and he sins, must I call him to repent?

T: No, it is not obligatory.

S: If I call an affiliate of mine to repent when he sins and he repents of that sin and then commits the same sin again, what should I do?

T: You should continue to call him to repentance until Satan is the loser—that is the correct opinion. Some say you should do it up to three times, and beyond that you need only dissociate from him.

52. My translation here is based on an explanation given by F (71, n. 1): "This is an imprecation (*du'a' bi-'l-sharr*) meaning 'May God not let the eye of any of His enemies rest on those He loves.'"

53. That is, the person is one of the core supporters of a just imam and one does not know him personally, but "affiliates with" him as part of the obligation to affiliate with all the core supporters of the imam.

S: What if he commits a different sin after repenting?

T: There are two opinions on this. The sins that require calling a person to repent and dissociation from him, even if they vary, are like a single sin.

S: If I call him to repent and he does so, and then says, "I did not repent," what should I do?

T: Judge him to be an enemy of God. He does not receive affiliation or suspension of judgment, as he deserves dissociation.

S: If I call him to repent and he says, "I repent from all my sins," is this sufficient, or must he specify each one?

T: Some say it is not sufficient until he specifies the sin of which he is repenting; others say it is always sufficient; and others say that if he is asked to repent of a sin he committed while considering it permissible, he must specify the sin of which he is repenting—there are different opinions on this.

S: If I am suspending judgment concerning someone who then commits a grave sin and repents of it before I dissociate from him, what should I do?

T: Some say you should continue to suspend judgment; others say you should dissociate from him, and if he repents after dissociation you should continue to dissociate from him—so they say. The Qutb says:

> Perhaps this is in order to keep from shifting from dissociation to suspension of judgment, but in my opinion that is baseless: how can one dissociate from a person over something of which he has repented, when the door of repentance is never closed? No one can say, "God did not accept his repentance," because that is unknowable, nor "I do not accept it," because no one has the right not to accept it, nor "When he committed a grave sin his immorality was clear to me, so I judged that he had done or would do other sins or repeat the grave sin [I observed]," because it is wrong to dissociate from someone based on mere speculation. The correct course of action is to return to suspending judgment concerning him after dissociating from him. How can one keep from shifting from affiliation or dissociation to suspending judgment, and thereby oppose a matter on which the scholars have consensus, that the door of repentance is always open? We are merely assuming that someone we have seen do an evil thing has done or will do other evil things, but we cannot be certain of that. How can we dissociate from him based on mere speculation? 'Umar's saying "We thought there was evil in him" (Ibn Hanbal 1998, 62, no. 286) is proof of what I say. What we saw him do has been voided by his repentance—although [not] if

you investigate and it is clear to you that such a shift is prohibited, because you would have to turn your back on what you know, for example, if you are suspending judgment concerning someone with whom you are affiliated or from whom you have dissociated, not for due cause or because the person had done something the reality of which you do not know, like the case of al-Harith and 'Abd al-Jabbar, may God have mercy on them: they were found killed in Tripoli in North Africa, and the sword of each of them was in the body of the other, and no one knew who had killed them.[54] The man who killed them led people to think that each of them had killed the other, in order to promote dissension and conflict. The Ibadis of the west, and some of those of the east, retained both of them in a state of affiliation, and some suspended judgment concerning them until the Ibadis of the west agreed to retain them in affiliation. Then I read in a history book that 'Abd al-Rahman b. Habib [al-Fihri] marched against them in the year 131 [748–749 CE] and killed them both, or perhaps his soldiers killed them, may God curse him, and he placed the sword of each of them in the body of the other.

As for the question at hand, going back to suspending judgment in this case is not turning one's back on what one knows, because what I knew of the person's grave sin had apparently been erased through his repentance, although God alone knows his secret thoughts. Then, after having exhausted the capacity that the merciful and compassionate God granted to me, I must act in accordance with the opinion of one of the scholars of Nafusa, which is: "Whoever dissociates from a man on the basis of something he did, and knew nothing about the man but that deed, and then the man repented of that deed, he must return to his original suspension of judgment concerning him." He explicitly permits this. Between my words and those I quoted concerning what happened in Nafusa are many years, and God knows best. (Atfayyish 1980a, 51–52)

That is the end of the Qutb's words, may God have mercy on him. There is also another opinion on this, and that is that one should dissociate from him even if he has already repented.

S: How do the Qutb's words apply to what 'Urwa b. al-Zubayr said: "If you see a man do a good deed, love him for it and know that he has other deeds like

54. Al-Harith b. Talid al-Hadrami and 'Abd al-Jabbar b. Qays al-Muradi were two leading Ibadis who died around the year 748–750 CE.

it. If you see him do a bad deed, hate him for it and know that he has other deeds like it"?

T: There is nothing in 'Urwa's words that requires dissociating from someone concerning whom you are suspending judgment if he commits a grave sin and then repents of that particular sin, because [in this case] "know that" means "assume" and he did not say that the man repented, and because interpreting his words in their most obvious meaning, which would be to affiliate with someone based on a single characteristic, is impermissible. What 'Urwa meant by "love" is love without religious affiliation (ibid., 53).

S: If a person repents of a sin for which I dissociated from him, should I affiliate with him immediately or wait some time until my heart is certain [of the genuineness of his repentance]?

T: You may wait before renewing affiliation with someone who did something prohibited after calling on him to repent, and after he repents until you are sure he is continuing [in his repentance], and you may continue to dissociate from him after his repentance until your heart is certain [of the genuineness of his repentance], as a precaution, despite the words of Muhammad b. Mahbub as narrated by Abu Ishaq [Ibrahim b. Qays]: "You may affiliate with him the moment he repents"(ibid., 52; Abu Ishaq 1984, 34).

S: If one of two affiliates tells me that the other dissociated from him without due cause, should I maintain my affiliation with him?

T: His words, "He dissociated from me without due cause," are an accusation of a grave sin, and you must call on anyone who accuses your affiliate of a grave sin to repent. If he repents [all is well], but if not, dissociate from him. If he limits his words to "He dissociated from me" without adding "without due cause," do not dissociate from him, because of the possibility that that person did so because the other did something requiring dissociation. Those who say the evidence of a single affiliate is adequate would allow you to dissociate from him if one affiliate testifies to you that he has dissociated from the other. Undeserved dissociation is wrong (*hadath*), and you cannot be sure whether his dissociation from him is for just cause. It would appear, then, that what your affiliate did is wrong, and proof has been shown to you, so understand. This is based on the testimony of a single affiliate, whereas the best way is to be certain of the truth in matters of religion. In my own opinion, it is best not to destroy the affiliation of your affiliate by executing the penalty of dissociation on the basis of such evidence. If you believe [his testimony], the one who so testifies comes under suspicion, because the one concerning whom he is testifying is also an affiliate, so be careful. May God help us and you in such treacherous circumstances (Atfayyish 1980a, 53).

S: If someone concerning whom I am suspending judgment says to me, "This person dissociated from me," what should I do?

T: Dissociate from the person who says this, because he is not an affiliate, nor is he trustworthy, and he has accused an affiliate of a grave sin.

S: If someone concerning whom I am suspending judgment says, "This person and that person dissociated from me," and they are both affiliates, or if he adds, "because I did such-and-such," on what basis is he deserving of dissociation?

T: Dissociate from him and call on him to repent if he is an affiliate, because of what he said, not because of what is attributed to the two affiliates. According to *Al-Su'alat* [by Abu 'Amr al-Sufi], one should not dissociate from someone concerning whom one is suspending judgment if he says "This person and that person dissociated from me" and they are both affiliates, unless he adds "because I did something" that requires dissociation. The Qutb said, "It is not evident, because it is not a stipulation of dissociation that the two affiliates mention the cause—by God, unless the account [of his doing something requiring dissociation] is weak, in which case it is a stipulation. What a person says about himself is more persuasive" (ibid., 53).[55]

S: What if he says, "One of this group and one of these two people dissociated from me"?

T: You should dissociate from him and call on him to repent if he is in a state of affiliation, unless there is something in the group or in the two people that requires dissociation or suspending judgment.

S: If I have two affiliates, and one of them does something and the other dissociates from him, so the first one likewise dissociates from the second, what should I do?

55. It would seem that what Atfayyish means is that a person does not have to inform someone from whom he is dissociating why he is dissociating from him, unless he has simply heard a rumor about something that person did; in that case, it is necessary to verify the truth of the story from the person who allegedly did the deed requiring dissociation. If a person testifies concerning himself that he has done something requiring dissociation, then one must dissociate from him. But if someone merely says that someone else has dissociated from him without mentioning the cause, the hearer need not do anything.

T: Keep your affiliation to both of them. You are not required to dissociate from them or to call them to repent—at least not if you do not know the truth of what happened between them. If your affiliation with one of them is firmer than with the other, he and his affiliation are proof for you concerning the matter of which they inform you that requires dissociation from the second person.

S: If an affiliate says to me, "This deed is a grave sin or infidelity," and then he does it himself, how should I treat him?

T: If he is a trustworthy affiliate or if you believe him and do not know the legal ruling concerning that deed, then turn to God and dissociate from him (*fa-ibra' ila 'llah*); otherwise, do not. In dissociating from him, if you know that the ruling concerning that deed is that it is not grave and not infidelity, there are two opinions. The reason for dissociating from him is because he intended to commit an act of infidelity, as some have said concerning someone who says that water or saliva is wine, and then drinks it. The second opinion is that one should not dissociate from him if it is clear that the deed is not infidelity (ibid., 53–54).

S: If I learn from a scholar that a certain deed requires dissociation from the one who does it, or if he judges that a person who does such a deed must be punished by a particular *hadd* penalty or executed, and then I see someone doing it, how should I treat him?

T: Act according to what you learned from the scholar. If the deed precedes your learning about its status from the scholar, do not pass judgment on him without the testimony of two trustworthy men, because in that case they are witnesses of it; or you may judge according to what you learned from a single scholar, if you ask him about it after the deed was done—there are two opinions (ibid., 54).

Lesson 3: General Questions Related to Affiliation and Dissociation

S: What is the meaning of God's affiliation to and enmity for people [literally, "His servants"]?

T: His affiliation is His pleasure, and His enmity is His wrath, which means His punishment and His reward, or His knowledge of what reward and punishment are required. It can also mean His helping (*tawfiq*) or not helping people toward obedience, or preparing reward or punishment. The most correct interpretation is that it is His helping people toward obedience, or His abandoning them—we seek refuge in God from His enmity! There are various opinions.

S: Are the two [God's affiliation and enmity] reversible?

T: No, they are not reversible. The person who [will be] happy [in the afterlife] is God's affiliate, even while committing a sin, and the person who [will be] miserable [in the afterlife] is God's enemy, even while obeying Him.

S: Does anyone say they are reversible?

T: The Nukkar and [their leader, Ahmad] b. al-Husayn, said so—may God keep them far from us!

S: What made them say something so repulsive?

T: What mishap could be greater than whatever made them say this, and what disaster could be greater than the one that ensnared them! Their doctrine required them to say that the Exalted One, Whose majesty is glorious, is ignorant, because they said that, on the one hand, He is ignorant of what happens until it happens, and, on the other hand, they say that His knowledge is contrary to what His knowledge has ordained! That is folly and well outside the bounds of the wisdom of the Most High, Who is full of majesty and glory and is the wisest of all—He is exalted far beyond such nonsense! The glorious God knows what has been and what will be. One cannot say that God knows what has not been and what will not be, but neither can one say that He is ignorant of it; it is possible to say that if it existed He would know it, or that it would come into existence because of His knowledge.

S: May God be pleased with you! You have guided me to what is brighter than the sun! So what does it mean for us to affiliate with our Most High Lord?

T: We affiliate with our Most High Lord by following His commandments and keeping away from what He has prohibited.

S: What right does an affiliate have from the one who affiliates with him?

T: He must love him and love for him what he loves for himself, hate for him what is hateful to himself, and honor him and help him.

S: And the opposite holds for the person from whom one is dissociated?

T: Indeed, it does. The one who deserves dissociation is hated and despised because of his enmity to God and his sin.

S: What prayers should be said for one's affiliate, and what prayers does the enemy deserve?

T: Pray for good for your affiliate, in this world and the next. Do not pray for good in the afterlife for an enemy of God, but one may wish him well in this world, as a way of circumvention, and as compensation and protection.

S: It occurs to me that affiliation takes the form of phrases uttered in prayer, and that this is also true of dissociation. Is that so?

T: What you are thinking is undoubtedly correct.

S: If someone addresses another person as "Muslim" or "righteous one" or "pious one" or similar phrases, or says to him, "You are one of the inhabitants of paradise," do these phrases and their like indicate affiliation?

T: These phrases do indicate affiliation, but they are not enough for affiliation, because they contain no prayer—even if one says, "May God give you long life," it is only affiliation if one adds "in paradise." Likewise, if someone says, "May God reward you," that is not affiliation until he adds "with the reward of those who do good." Some of the prayers that indicate affiliation are "May God widen your grave and make it illuminated and cool" and "May God make death easy for you"—although on this there are two opinions; some object that God might make death easy for an infidel as a reward for what good he has done in this world, so he might arrive at the afterlife without any good deeds to his account, and the believer may suffer at death in order to arrive at the afterlife without sin. The death of a believer or anyone else might be quick, but he might suffer more in that brief time than someone else who takes a long time to die. There are two opinions on whether prayer that punishment in the grave be lightened is a sign of affiliation.[56] The correct interpretation is that it is not, because the Prophet, on whom be blessings and peace, tore apart a palm-leaf stalk and threw half into the grave of a man who was guilty of slander, and half into the grave of a man who did not clean himself after urinating, in the hope of alleviating their suffering somewhat, as long as the stalk had moisture in it (ibid., 55).

S: If a hypocrite does an act of obedience, is it permissible to say he is one of the people of obedience (*min ahl al-ta'a*), or that he is fit for obedience (*ahl li-'l-ta'a*)?

T: No, it is not allowed, for if he were one of the people of obedience, he wouldn't be a hypocrite. This single act of obedience, unless it is an act of

56. There are Qur'anic verses that indicate that the angel of death pulls the souls out of an unbeliever roughly but is gentle with believers. Belief in the punishment in the grave for unbelievers awaiting the resurrection of the dead on the Last Day is derived from Hadith. For a full discussion of this topic, see Smith and Haddad 1981.

repentance, does not remove him from his hypocrisy, and it is lost because he persists in hypocrisy (ibid., 56).

S: Should I not say to someone who is not an affiliate, "May God welcome you" or "May God strengthen you" or "May God increase your reward and may His blessings be on you"?

T: You should not say these things to anyone other than an affiliate, because they suggest affiliation. Some say you can say them meaning a worldly reward, while having an inner aversion to saying this, because just as it is impermissible to empower an enemy of God to disobey God, likewise it is impermissible to pray that he would be strengthened or blessed or welcomed by God. The best interpretation is just to say, "Welcome" (*ahlan wa-marhaban*), without intending or suggesting anything regarding the afterlife. The most commonly held interpretation is that it is even prohibited to say "welcome," but all of these are different opinions. Say "May God make you prosper (*aslahaka*)" if you mean a worldly compensation, and "May God give you health" if you mean health in this world.

In my opinion, it is permissible to pray for prosperity (*salah*) and health while meaning the prosperity of his religion and healing him from the commission of sins through guidance. The permissibility of doing this revolves around the speaker's intention, and in this case the intention is correct and the goal is something God deems good. So for example, if by saying "May God heal you" you mean healing from God's justice in the afterlife, that would mean nothing but affiliation. So look to the state of the person for whom you pray—if he is an affiliate, you are on target, but if he is an enemy, God cannot affiliate with him. Likewise if you say, "May God make your destiny narrow" and you mean disgrace in the afterlife or the narrowing that pertains to an infidel, that is entirely dissociation. So look to the state of the one to whom you address such hostility, and do not say such a thing to an affiliate of God (ibid.).

S: Is it permissible to appear to pray for good in the afterlife for an enemy of God, but without intention? If it is permissible, why is it?

T: It is permissible if there is an alternative implication in what you are saying, or if you intend to address your speech to an affiliate of God. This is only in circumstances in which this is beneficial—not to multiply words—or will repel harm, and in situations in which one must hide one's true beliefs (*mawadi' al-taqiyya*), in which case words can have a double meaning, one that is apparent and one that is hidden. An example of this is if you say to him, "May God raise your status (*rafa'a 'llah sha'naka*) in the afterlife," and what you mean by "raising" is removing his status,[57] or if by "the afterlife" (*al-akhira*) you mean another (*ukhra*) town, and other such expressions that can have a double meaning.

S: I found that the Messenger of God said, "God, do not bestow a blessing on an infidel who lives near me, for which I might love him (al-Muttaqi 2001, 2:211, no. 3810)." And he said, "Hearts are drawn to love those who are kind to them (*jubilat al-qulub 'ala hubbi man ahsana ilayha*)" (al-Suyuti 1981, no. 3580). If an enemy of God is good to me, undoubtedly his kindness will cause my soul to incline toward him and love him. Does such a natural inclination harm me?

T: Natural love does not harm you unless it becomes religious affiliation.[58] There is nothing wrong with being polite to someone while inwardly maintaining religious dissociation from him. The Prophet only asked his Lord not to give any infidel who lived near him something that would make him love him because of the Prophet's perfect devotion and desire to be affected by God alone, in worship and in love. The Messenger of God was pleasant, gentle, and perfectly courteous to everyone, but that did not impugn his complete dissociation from God's enemies. There is no harm in good etiquette, gentleness, kind words, living courteously with other people, and observing proper speech, as long as it does not extend to affiliation with the person for whom God requires enmity. Likewise, there is no harm in giving gifts and financial assistance or helping God's enemy escape from injustice and helping him in a just and pious cause, as long as such assistance does not strengthen his ability to disobey God or perpetrate injustice against a person or his wealth or lead to any injustice against a Muslim or the private property of the Muslims or anything of that sort. While being courteous, you avoid doing for the one from whom you dissociate anything that requires affiliation or that leads to it, in act or speech, but do good and observe manners with the just and the unjust; and God knows best.

S: Should I greet a person from whom I dissociate, comfort him in his sorrows, and congratulate him on occasions of joy?

57. *Rafa'a* can mean either "raise" or "remove."

58. The distinction al-Rawahi makes here between "natural" love and the love of religious affiliation appears to contradict the definition of *walaya* given by 'Abd al-'Aziz al-Thamini (1986, 2:115): "The reality of *walaya* is love in the heart/soul (*bi-'l-janan*), mentioning with the tongue, inclination in the heart (*al-mayl bi-'l-qalb*) and the limbs."

T: If he is a monotheist, give him the greeting of peace and shake his hand, if your heart is safe from religious love (*al-hubb al-dini*), and comfort him in his sorrows. If he is an unbeliever, do not greet him or comfort him except with an appropriate expression and by commanding God's pleasure and giving good admonition. If he gives you the greeting of peace, just reply, "And on you."[59]

S: If he is a hypocritical monotheist or one of our theological opponents and he gives me the greeting of peace, do I reply with the same greeting I would give to God's affiliates, responding in kind or with a greeting that is better than his?

T: If you like and you feel it is necessary, you may say "And on you be peace and the mercy and blessings of God" instead of "And on you," while meaning things in this world. God the Mighty and Majestic said, "Return their greeting with what is better" (4:86). Greeting is general, and the law (*al-shar'*) has chosen the greeting of peace and other similar greetings. If he says, "May God make your evening good" or "Good morning," you may expand on his greeting or shorten it. For example, you could reply, "May God make your evening good and give you good health." Every sort of greeting is permissible and should be responded to or added to in an appropriate manner. If you console him by saying "May God reward you greatly and remove your sorrow," and you mean in this world, no harm is done. It is best to avoid such expressions and use other less suggestive words of consolation, for there are many alternatives in speech (Atfayyish 1980a, 57).

Lesson 4: Suspending Judgment and Its Regulations

S: Is suspending judgment[60] from someone with whom neither affiliation nor dissociation is permissible a religious obligation in the same way that affiliation and dissociation are when they are appropriate?

59. The greeting "Peace be upon you" (*Al-salamu 'alaykum*) is used exclusively among Muslims, to which the appropriate response is "and on you be peace" (*wa-'alaykum al-salam*), or, even better, "And on you be peace and the mercy and blessings of God" (*wa-'alaykum al-salam wa-rahmat Allah wa-barakatuhu*), because the Qur'an tells Muslims to return a greeting with a greeting that is better than it (4:86). A curt "And on you" would be noticeably short of the standard of politeness expected between Muslims, but is suggested here as a minimal courtesy that could be observed with those deemed "polytheists," which would include Jews and Christians.

60. The discussion on suspending judgment is taken from Atfayyish (1980a, 58–59).

T: It is obligatory for a person who is accountable before God to suspend judgment when appropriate, just as it is obligatory to affiliate or dissociate when appropriate.

S: When is suspending judgment appropriate, and what makes it obligatory?

T: It is appropriate and obligatory when you do not know whether something someone has done requires affiliation or dissociation, or if there are two opinions on it, or if there are two contradictory obligations in which one does not overrule the other. In the case of such ignorance, you must dissociate from him until you know the rule for that deed, whether it requires affiliation or dissociation.

S: What is the basis for the obligation to suspend judgment?

T: It is based on the Book and the Sunna. From the Book are the words of the Most High, "Do not form an opinion on something of which you have no knowledge" (17:36), and "My Lord has forbidden indecencies, whether evident or hidden, and sin and unjust oppression, and that you associate with God others to whom He has not given authority, or that you say about God what you do not know" (7:33). And in the Sunna are the Messenger's words, "Suspend judgment concerning what you do not know."[61]

S: If two men curse each other or fight each other and I do not know which of them is right and who is wrong, what should I do?

T: Leave each of them in the condition in which they already were with you, whether in affiliation, dissociation, or suspending judgment. That is with regard to their status with you. As for what they are doing, suspend judgment and do not decide that it is right or wrong. If it becomes clear to you which of them started the cursing or fighting, you must dissociate from him; at that point, you may not suspend judgment concerning what he did, because you know that it is something that requires dissociation.

S: If I see someone do something and I don't know the rules for that act, and I know that I have kept the one who did it in the condition in which he was before (affiliation, dissociation, or suspending judgment), and I am suspending

61. A similar hadith may be found in Ibn Maja (2000, Introduction, bab 8, no. 57), in words addressed to Mu'adh b. Jabal when he was sent to Yemen: "If a matter is unclear to you (*in ashkala 'alayka amr*), suspend judgment (*fa-qif*) until you have clarified it."

judgment concerning what he did, as to whether it was right or wrong, am I required to ask about the judgment of the law on that act?

T: You are not required to ask about the judgment on that act, although some claim that you are. But if you wish to ask, do so without naming the person who did the act; just ask as if you were wishing to learn the rule regarding that act, without attributing it to a specific person. For example, you could say, "What is the rule concerning someone who does such-and-such?" or "What is the rule concerning an affiliate who does such-and-such?" Because if you identify the one who did the deed and, for example, it is polytheism or adultery, whoever hears what you say must dissociate from you unless you bring three witnesses in a case of adultery, in which you are the fourth witness, and they confirm your testimony, and you say before you report the matter, "These three say the same as I," or, in a case of polytheism, if there is a second person who gives the same testimony as you. If one of them is not a valid witness, or if you do not say "They say the same as I," the one who hears your allegation must dissociate from you as well as from the three who confirm your testimony in a matter of adultery, or the single person who confirms what you say on a matter of polytheism, if you do not say "They say the same as I" or "This one says the same as I," because your testimony would then be null and void. They must also say the same thing, if their testimony is valid. If you identify the accused, and the sin is a grave sin that falls short of polytheism or adultery and the accused is an affiliate, your accusation would be a sin that would require dissociation from you, unless you have someone else with you who gives the same testimony and you are both valid witnesses and you say "This person says the same as I" before you give your report.

S: If the person I am asking says, "The person who did this is an infidel," should I dissociate from him?

T: No, why would you do that? His infidelity is based only on hearsay, not on the testimony of an eyewitness. And you must say "I am asking," lest you become obligated to dissociate from the person you are asking by not dissociating from the person who committed the grave sin. That is what the scholars say, and the Qutb, may God have mercy on him, said: "This is so you explicitly tell him that you are not dissociating from the perpetrator, although you know that the deed is a grave sin, or so it is clear to the person you are asking that you are an affiliate of the perpetrator or that you are suspending judgment regarding him, although you know that the deed is a grave sin. It is not required for you to say 'I am asking,' as some have said. You should then ask a second scholar, and if they issue a joint opinion that the deed is a grave sin, then you must dissociate from him" (Atfayyish 1980a, 59).

S: What is the status of someone who affiliates with someone because of a deed the rule for which he does not know and it is a grave sin, and of someone who for the same reason abandons affiliation or dissociation, and of someone who dissociates from him because of that deed?

T: His correct status is hypocrisy. Some say he has disobeyed God, and others say he has committed an error that does not lead to perdition—there are different opinions (ibid.).

S: If the deed is permitted or disapproved or is a minor sin, and on the basis of that someone affiliates, dissociates or suspends judgment, what is his status?

T: His status is the infidelity of hypocrisy (*kufr al-nifaq*), unless he believes it to be permitted or reprehensible or prohibited; in that case, his status is the infidelity of unbelief (*kufr shirk*). Likewise, if he believed a minor sin to be unbelief, or if he believed it to be the beginning of unbelief, his status is the infidelity of hypocrisy (ibid., 59–60).

S: If someone applies one of the three judgments to all people, what is his status?

T: He is an unbeliever (*mushrik*).

S: Is the one who hears him do this excused?

T: Some say he is excused if he does not dissociate from him regarding his affiliation with all people, but not if he does not dissociate from him regarding his suspension of judgment concerning all people or dissociation from all people. So they say, but the Qutb says: "The most obvious interpretation is that either he must be excused for all the stances the other person takes, or he must be subjected to dissociation for all of them. What is required is that one dissociate from him in all these cases. The argument that the speaker applied the same judgment to all but only meant some, and that since he is a monotheist the one who heard him do this must be excused in all cases, although they did not excuse him in all cases, is unsound" (ibid., 60).

S: Why did Imam Aflah b. 'Abd al-Wahhab say, "Do not dissociate from a believer until he is present and can defend himself"?

T: The imam was truthful and righteous, may God be pleased with him! He said this because of the hadith in which Abu Dharr did something reprehensible, and the people said, "Messenger of God, Abu Dharr is an unbeliever (*ashrak*)!" In other words, this is how it appeared to them, and they were asking about it. He replied, "Abu Dharr is not an unbeliever,"[62] meaning that he would wait until he came to say, "My heart is not at peace with the faith," at which point he could judge him to be an unbeliever. God forbid that Abu Dharr would ever commit sedition or fall into temptation! He had said something the people found repugnant, but his heart was at peace with the faith. And the words of the Messenger, God's blessings and peace on him, "Abu Dharr is not an unbeliever," are an assurance that Abu Dharr is happy [in the afterlife]. So the hadith is a proof for the imam, may God have mercy on him.

S: If someone dies as an affiliate, should testimony that he was an infidel be accepted?

T: There are two opinions on this, but the witnesses against him are not subject to dissociation.

S: Why are the witnesses not subject to dissociation?

T: How can they be subject to dissociation, when they are one of the proofs of God? Those who feel that one should dissociate from the person against whom they are testifying feel this way because proof has been given against him, and since he has passed on to his Lord, one cannot wait for him to defend himself. The Messenger of God said concerning the dead, "They have passed on to their Lord."[63]

S: If someone says to someone else, "You adulterer!" or "You unbeliever (*mushrik*)!", and the second replies, "You are the adulterer," or "You are the unbeliever," what should I do with them?

T: Dissociate from both of them in God (*ibra' ila 'llah min-huma*), though some say you should not dissociate from the one who replied to the person who called him this. Anyone who calls a monotheist an unbeliever is himself an

62. I have not been able to locate this hadith.

63. I have not been able to locate this precise hadith. There are many transmissions of a similar hadith, "They have passed on to [the deeds] they sent before," for example, in al-Bukhari (n.d., *Kitab al-jana'iz* [23], *bab* 97, no. 1393).

unbeliever, so if the second person replies, "You are the unbeliever," he would be telling the truth and one should not dissociate from him for telling the truth.

In my opinion it is correct to deem an unbeliever (*tashrik*) anyone who calls a monotheist an unbeliever, if the judgment is based only on his theology (*'ala tawhidihi*), not like those who deem disobedient members of the people of the *qibla* to be unbelievers. If a person says to an affiliate, "You infidel (*ya kafir*)!" and he replies, "You are the infidel!" there is no harm to the one who replied, because he is telling the truth. The Messenger of God said, "If a man says to his companion, 'You infidel!' one of the two is an infidel, and the one who said it first is more unjust" (al-Rabi' b. Habib n.d., 1:18, no. 65; cf. al-Bukhari n.d., *Kitab al-adab* [78], *bab* 73, no. 6103). He spoke of them collectively when he said, "One of the two is an infidel," and then he made a distinction between them by saying, "The one who said it first is more unjust." What he meant by "more unjust" is "unjust," because one cannot think that the person who replies is unjust, only the one who declared the other to be an infidel (Atfayyish 1980a, 60–61).

S: If an affiliate says to another, "One of us is an infidel," what should I do with him?

T: Dissociate from him in God, because he is either declaring that he is an infidel, or he is accusing his affiliate of being an infidel, and both cases require dissociation.

S: What if he says to a group of people who are in a state of affiliation, "One of you"—or "one of them—is an infidel"?

T: Dissociate from him for saying this.

S: What if an affiliate of mine directs a word of general infidelity such as "infidel" or "profligate" or "deviant" at a person who is in an affiliated group, and the person who is in the affiliated group responds in kind, what do I do with the one who responds?

T: Do not dissociate from the person who responds, because he is defending himself and proof does not stand on the testimony of a single individual. If two or more affiliates say "You infidel" or something like that, you must dissociate from the person who is in the affiliated group, even if he does not respond. If he is accused of something specific, such as "You thief" or "You drinker of wine," dissociate from him if he responds.

S: If two affiliates quarrel in front of an arbiter, and during the quarrel one says something to the other, such as "You have wronged me," or if he makes this claim when they are not quarreling, or if the second says, "You accused me of being unfair" or "a liar" or "unjust," or if he says to witnesses something like "You have testified that I acted unjustly," or if he says to the arbiter, "You have judged me to have acted unjustly," as if he is demanding proof that has not yet been given, how should I treat them?

T: Keep them both in affiliation. There is nothing in this that requires dissociation from them, for such a case does not constitute slander; it is only self-defense and a demand for proof. The Messenger of God said, "A truthful person (*sahib al-haqq*) has the right to speak" (al-Bukhari n.d., *Kitab al-wakala* [40], *bab* 6, no. 2306). Some say one should dissociate from a person who says this, and the Qutb said, "and that is better" (Atfayyish 1980a, 61); and God knows best.

S: What if they go beyond proper bounds in their allegations and say something that requires dissociation, how should they be treated?

T: Dissociate from the one who went beyond proper bounds and said something requiring dissociation, and the judge and witnesses should dissociate from them if the litigants accuse them of injustice or unfairness, if the judge and witnesses have been wrongly accused.

S: What if I dissociate from someone who commits a grave sin, because of [that sin], and then he commits another, must I renew my dissociation, or does it remain as it is?

T: You do not need to renew your dissociation unless you have forgotten the first one or have forgotten that he is in a state of dissociation, even if the second sin is polytheism. If you forget why you dissociated from him, retain him in dissociation, and you are pardoned what you forgot. If you forget from whom it is you dissociated, you are not pardoned, according to the authoritative opinion [*'ala ma sahhahu*]. The Qutb says, "Really, he should be pardoned. One scholar said this, and it is related that he retracted his opinion and was treated roughly for his retraction" (ibid., 62).

Chapter 6

HOW TO DEAL WITH PEOPLE WHO ARE NOT OF MUHAMMAD'S *UMMA*

Lesson 1: The Six Religions and the Regulations Concerning Them

S: I found that God mentioned in His Book six religions (*milal*).[1] Explain these six religions to me.

T: Indeed, God mentioned six religions, of which He has prescribed (*shara'a*) only one, and that is Islam. Iblis, God curse him, prescribed Judaism, in opposition to the religion of Moses, on whom be peace, Christianity, in opposition to the religion of Jesus, on whom be peace,[2] Sabaeanism, in opposition to both of them, Zoroastrianism, and the religion of those who deny God's existence or are ignorant of Him or deny that He alone is worthy of worship. All of these except Islam are religions of unbelief (*shirk*), and anyone who follows a religion other than Islam is an unbeliever (*mushrik*). Each of these religions has regulations that pertain specifically to it. All those who follow any religion other than Islam after the mission of our prophet Muhammad, on whom be God's blessings and peace, are unbelievers if they have heard of him and not believed in him, or if they follow the Torah and the Gospel without believing in him. The seventh religion is idol-worship (*al-wathaniyya*).

1. This chapter follows the organization and wording from Atfayyish 1980a, 62–72.

2. Although the Qur'an recognizes Moses, David, and Jesus as prophets to whom God gave a scripture comparable to the Qur'an, it accuses the Jews and Christians of distorting the truths these prophets brought. The Qur'an sees the religion of all the true pre-Muhammadan prophets as Islam, and explicitly says that Abraham, his son (usually thought to be Ishmael), and Jesus' disciples called themselves *muslimun*—that is, "Muslims" or, more generically, in submission to God (2:128 and 3:51).

S: Which of these religions were true before the coming of our messenger Muhammad, God's blessings and peace on him?

T: Take the answer to your question from God's word: "The believers, the Jews, the Sabaeans, and the Christians, whoever believes in God and the Last Day and does good deeds, has no reason to fear, and they will not grieve" (5:69). This verse indicates that the Jews (*al-Yahud*), the Christians (*al-Nasara*), and the Sabaeans (*al-Sabi'un*) were originally following the truth before the coming of the Prophet, but they became unbelievers by introducing new things into their religions, like Sabaean angel-worship, or violating the commands of the Torah and the Gospel and not believing in God's Messenger, on whom be blessings and peace.

S: What is the origin of these three names?

T: The Jews were called *al-Yahud* because of their distortion (*tahawwud*) in their recitation of scripture,[3] or because they said, "We have turned (*hudna*) to You" (7:156), meaning "We have repented." *Al-Yahud* might also mean the followers of Judah (*Yahudha*), Jacob's son, whose name is better known by dropping the *alif* and ignoring the dot over the letter *dhal*.[4] The Christians are [allegedly] called *al-Nasara* because they said, "We are God's helpers (*ansar*) (61:14), but that explanation is improbable. It is more likely that they are called such because they settled in a village called Nazareth (*Nasira*).[5] The Sabaeans are called *al-Sabi'un* because of their turning (*subu'*) from one religion to another, or because they chose only the pleasant parts (*mata'ib*) of the Torah and Gospel, or because they said, "We are correct" (*sa'ibun*), from being on the mark (*isaba*), and *sa'ib* was

3. Western scholars believe the Arabic *al-Yahud* is taken from the Aramaic word for "Jews," but here al-Rawahi (following Atfayyish) treats it as an Arabic word and tries to find its root. The word *tahawwud* in its modern usage means "to convert someone to Judaism," but the linkage here to distortion in recitation (*qira'a*) of scripture refers to the Qur'an's accusations that the Jews misquoted scripture or took its words out of context (4:46).

4. The *alif* is the lengthening of the "a" at the end of Yahudha, marked in transliterations of Arabic into Latin letters as a dash over the letter. The letter *dhal,* which makes a hard "th" sound as in the English world "this," is distinguished from the letter *dal* (the "d" sound) only by a dot over it. If the *alif* is dropped, Yahudha becomes Yahudh, and if the dot is ignored, Yahudh becomes Yahud.

5. Most contemporary scholars agree that the name pertains to Nazareth, not because the disciples settled there (which they did not), but because Jesus was known as Jesus of Nazareth.

changed to *sabi'*. It is not from their saying "We hit the mark" (*asabna*)[6] because that has a four-letter root (*ruba'i*), whereas *al-Sabi'* is from a three-letter root, because *al-Sabi'un* came with a *hamza* after the letter *ba'*,[7] not the other way around as in "he hit the mark" (*asaba*).

S: What does it mean for them to choose the pleasant parts of the Torah and the Gospel?

T: They took litanies (*awrad*) and superfluities (*nawafil*) in isolation, and occupied themselves only with these. If they had changed any of the religious obligations or rules about what is permitted and prohibited, God would not have denied that they would have fear and grief if they believed and did good deeds.

S: Why are the Zoroastrians called *Majus?*

T: They are called by the name of their chief in the Farsi language, which is *Maka'us,* which means having much hair on the ears.[8] It was Arabized by replacing the letter *kaf* [the "k" sound] with a letter *jim* [the "j" sound], and eliding the *hamza* [glottal stop] to it because of the *damma* [the "u" sound] which removes the *hamza*. They worship fire, the sun, the moon, and the stars. They married their close relatives (*maharim*) and ate carrion.[9] It is said that they had a scripture and lost it entirely, so it was taken away. Because of the likeness of

6. *Asabna* would indeed mean "we are correct" or "we have hit the mark," but it is not from a four-letter root, so perhaps a different vocalization was intended than that given in the manuscripts I consulted. I am not aware of any four-letter roots using these consonants. Nonetheless, he is right to say that *al-Sabi'* (root *s-b-'*) is not from the same root as *asaba, isaba,* or *asabna* (root *s-w-b*).

7. The *hamza* is the glottal stop marked by an apostrophe when Arabic is transliterated into Latin letters. The *hamza* is considered a consonant in Arabic. The letter *ba'* is transliterated into Latin letters as *b*. Short vowels are not considered letters in Arabic, so from the perspective of Arabic grammar the letter *ba'* in *al-Sabi'un* is followed by a *hamza*.

8. The name *Majus* applied originally only to a priestly caste in the pre-Islamic Persian empire, but came to be used in Arabic for Zoroastrians in general. The "Magi" or "wise men" who are said to have come seeking the newborn king of the Jews in Matthew 2:1 are likely a reference to this group. In Old Persian the pronunciation was *magush* (Morony 1999). Abu Ishaq Ibrahim Atfayyish, the editor of Atfayyish 1980a, notes that he has never come across the word *Maka'us*. I am unaware of any source linking the *Majus* to hairy ears.

9. *Maharim* are relatives whose kinship is too close to allow marriage according to Islamic law. The Qur'an also prohibits eating carrion (2:173) and requires that animals that are eaten be slaughtered in God's name.

their scripture to that of the People of the Book [the Jews and Christians], they were allowed to pay the *jizya*.[10]

S: Who are the unbelievers, according to the Qur'anic verse [5:69]?

T: The unbelievers are idol-worshippers and others who deny the Divinity (*al-uluhiyya*), and those who deny His attributes (*al-mu'attila*), materialists (*al-dahriyya*), those who attribute creation to natural causes (*al-tabayi'iyya*), and those who deny the resurrection of the dead and the messengers (*munkiri 'l-ba'th wa-'l-rusul*); there are different types and sects.

S: What is meant by "those who have believed" (2:9 *et passim*)?

T: They are the Muslims who follow God's messengers and His laws, from Adam, peace be upon him, until the Day of Resurrection.

S: Is it necessary to know these religions and the regulations pertaining to them?

T: In the opinion of shaykhs 'Amrus, 'Abd al-Rahman b. Rustam, Abu Khazar, Ibn Zarqun, Abu Ya'qub Yusuf b. Ibrahim, and others among those who realized the truth among our companions—and that is the correct opinion—knowledge of the religions and the regulations pertaining to them is not required until it is proved otherwise. Some others deem an unbeliever anyone who does not know them and the regulations pertaining to them, and others say this only of someone who does not know the religions. To know them means knowing that they are religions of unbelief, or knowing that idol worshippers and Zoroastrians are unbelievers, because a person who is ignorant of the polytheism of those who say there are multiple gods is not excused. The Sabaeans said that light existed from all eternity and that good was begotten from it, and likewise darkness begat evil. According to this opinion, it is not necessary to know that they say this, and such a statement does not explicitly state that they believe in multiple gods. Some say that what is required is to know that they have rejected God, and that the Jews, Christians, and Sabaeans are infidels (*kafirun*), while others say that they are unbelievers (*mushrikun*), and others say that they are hypocrites—but that is not an appropriate thing to say about them, because of the obligation to know that rejection of a prophet or anything like that is infidelity (*kufr*) and a grave

10. Paying the *jizya* can be considered a privilege in that it allows people to practice their own religion, be exempt from military service, and be protected by the state.

sin and rebellion against God, but there is no certainty that it is unbelief (*ishrak*) until that is proven; there are different opinions on this.

S: What are the regulations that pertain to monotheists?

T: The regulations pertaining to them are all one: the testimony of honest members of other [Islamic] sects (*'udul al-mukhalifin*) is allowed, except concerning crimes that require a *hadd* penalty or [matters pertaining to] spiritual affiliation and dissociation, or anything that involves accusing the Muslims of infidelity. That is the correct opinion. Others say this is allowed only if they have conquered us, and others say their testimony is never allowed at all—there are different opinions. Their testimony concerning marriage and divorce in all its types is not invalidated if there is an objection, unless the objection pertains to the honesty of individual witnesses, [which is relevant] whether they belong to our sect or to theirs. Their testimony is unconditionally permissible in cases of intermarriage with members of other sects and members of our own sect who have committed grave sins, except for someone who intentionally killed someone and did not repent; in such a case, the rule is that the woman, her guardian, the witnesses, and the person making the contract are all condemned to death if they knew of the murder, but the marriage remains valid. A person who gives his female ward who is an affiliate in marriage to a man of another sect does not commit infidelity, although it is wrong to do this because he causes her to turn to the other sect. Some say that such a person does commit infidelity, if he forces her to convert to his sect. The Qutb commented, "This is very weak. How can his infidelity depend on an outcome?" (Atfayyish 1980a, 64). There are various opinions on this.

Their slaughtered animals are permissible for us to eat, and we can inherit from each other and interact in other ways, except that they are in a state of religious dissociation. They should not be allowed to renovate a mosque, and neither they nor people of our sect who commit grave sins nor those concerning whom one is suspending judgment should be called believers or Muslims, unless what is meant by this is that they are monotheists, lest one give an impression of religious faithfulness. One scholar wrote that it is permissible to call them "believers" or "Muslims" in all speech and regulations, except matters concerning affiliation and dissociation or explicit mention of their sect.

It is not permitted to accept the testimony of grave sinners of our own sect or of those concerning whom judgment is suspended, though some scholars say that those who commit grave sins may give testimonies in matters not relating to their sin, provided that the matter does not concern affiliation or accusations of infidelity. Others say that the testimony of a person concerning whom judgment is suspended may give testimony—there are various opinions. The testimony of a slave is not permissible, even if he is an affiliate, and neither may one accept the testimony of an affiliate who has a bad character, although some say it is permissible to take the testimony of a person who has committed a grave sin in a matter other than his sin. Al-Rabiʿ said that neither may one accept the testimony of an affiliate who has perjured himself if he repents after the *hadd* penalty has been executed (cf. Q 24:4). Nor may one accept testimony concerning property from the stewards who are entrusted with it, even if they are said to be entrusted with other property as well.

Any unjust person among us or among the other [Islamic] sects should be called to abandon his injustice. If he repents, no further action should be taken against him. If he does not, it is obligatory to fight him until he returns to obedience to God's command. The imam must call our theological opponents to the truth and to affiliate with our allies and dissociate from God's enemies—that is, those individuals and groups from whom we dissociate in conformity with our teachings. If they repent, he should call them to be governed by our laws and to do what is right; if they refuse, he must fight them.

We do not take any monotheists as slaves and we do not plunder their wealth. We do not kill any wounded monotheist or pursue him if he flees, unless he has a stronghold or bodyguard from which he seeks protection. This is in keeping with Hadith. It is always a grave sin to flee from fighting oppressors, just as it is in fighting against unbelievers (*al-mushrikin*), unless it is for tactical reasons or to join a group (cf. Q 8:15–16), unless the enemy is more than twice our number, according to the correct opinion. Some say it is permissible [to flee], and that the rule [that the enemy must be more than twice the number of the Muslims before Muslims are allowed to flee] pertained only to Badr; there are two opinions on this. But if the Muslims persist in fighting against more than twice their number and the fighting becomes intense, it is not permissible for some to flee, unless it is by unanimous agreement.

We do not take weapons or animals that belong to monotheists or any of their war supplies, like bullets or gunpowder, or their provisions, in order to appropriate them for ourselves, though we may take them in order to weaken them; but once there is peace, we must return it to them or to their heirs. We keep it as a trust and safeguard it from being squandered. But it cannot be returned to them unless they have repented or been weakened; otherwise, we will keep them from taking it, but we do not possess their property. One scholar claims that it may be sold and its value distributed among the poor who have participated in the war. The author of *Al-Mawaqif,* [al-Iji,] rebuked our sect because of the writer who deemed this permissible, because it leads to allowing us to take the wealth of a monotheist as plunder. There is no harm in this, because in every sect there are things that some scholars accept and others reject, but our scholars do not act according to this, and the one who deemed it permissible did not intend to treat it as plunder, but saw it as a way of strengthening the poor who fought in the war and are more deserving of it. Our companions should not be blamed because of the opinion of one of them, and they do not act according to it, though if the owners of the property are unknown, the Muslim poor are more deserving of it. The Qutb said, "I do not accept this principle. Rather, if they [the owners] are unknown, their poor are more deserving of it" (Atfayyish 1980a, 65).[11] Another scholar of our sect said that whatever is taken from them should be buried.

S: If a tyrant intends to do me bodily harm, what should I do?

T: If you are sure of his intention, you must fight him. If those who are fighting you are more than three, you may flee, because of God's words, "If there are one hundred steadfast men among you, they will vanquish two hundred" (8:66).

S: If I am sure that his intention is to take a little of my wealth, am I required to fight him?

T: You must fight anyone who intends to harm your body or your wealth, no matter how little.

S: What is the rule concerning someone who speaks ill of the Muslim soldiers, whether it be true or false?

11. That is, some Ibadi scholars suggested it should be given to the Ibadi poor who participated in the war, but Atfayyish said it should be given to the poor of the non-Ibadi Muslim community from which it was taken in the first place, because it is a rule that Ibadis must not seize the wealth of other monotheists.

T: Kill him if you can, because he intends to undermine (*tazalzul*) Islam.[12] Kill anyone who alters the regulations [of Islam], and the hypocrite who[se destiny] is in the lowest depths of hellfire (Q 4:146).

S: Tell me who is the hypocrite who is in the lowest depths of hellfire.

T: It is said that it means either a profligate (*al-fasiq*) or an unbeliever who appears to be a Muslim, but inwardly harbors unbelief. You know from what I previously told you that the second aspect in particular characterizes him.

S: Will the profligate be punished in the same way as the unbeliever?

T: God save us from the punishment they will endure! It befits God's justice that the profligate will be punished only for abandoning his obligations and doing what is prohibited, and that his punishment be less than that of the unbeliever; that is the correct opinion. Don't you see that the punishment of the People of the Book is less than that of idol-worshippers and those who reject God, because of [the truth that] they have? On the other hand, some say that the profligate will be punished in the same way as the unbeliever. The Qutb said:

> The reasoning behind this opinion is that his belief in God's oneness and whatever good deeds he has done thwart him, according to the hadith that [punishment] will begin with corrupt carriers of the Qur'an. They will say, "It begins with us?" They will be told, "The one who knows is not like the one who does not know."[13] [This is also indicated by] the hadith, "A single woe to the one who does not know and does not act, and woe sevenfold to the one who knows and does not act" (cf. al-Suyuti 1981, no. 9657). Some say that the fact that they are punished first does not necessarily mean that they are less than (*taht*) the unbelievers, and the hadith multiplying the woe [to those who know and do not act] is considered in relation to those whose profligacy is less than theirs. I am certain that the hypocrities who are mentioned in the Qur'an are those who hid their unbelief and appeared as Muslims. I have clarified this in my commentary on Tabghurin. (Atfayyish 1980a, 66)

12. Atfayyish (1980a, 66): "It is permissible to kill someone who falsely speaks ill of the Muslim soldiers while they are fighting, or even if what he says is true but [said] with the intention of undermining Islam."

13. I have not been able to locate this hadith.

Lesson 2: How to Interact with People of the Book

S: How should the imam treat the leading men (*umara'*) of the People of the Book—the Jews, Christians, and Sabaeans?

T: The imam should invite them to embrace Islam, according to sound opinion. Some say he should invite nomads (*ahl al-badiya*) one by one, and if he does not know their language a trustworthy person should translate for him—which is sound—or two trustworthy people; there are two opinions.

S: What is the rule pertaining to them if they reject Islam?

T: He calls on them to pay the *jizya* tax from their hand in a state of subjugation (cf. Q 9:29).

S: If they agree to this, what are the regulations regarding them?

T: The animals they slaughter are permissible to the Muslims,and Muslim men may marry their chaste, free women, though ʻUmar b. al-Khattab, may God be pleased with him, said it was disliked to do so, as there are many Muslim women available.

S: Does such a marriage carry any stipulations?

T: It is stipulated that a woman of the People of the Book whom a Muslim man wishes to marry must take a bath to wash herself of all impurities, must remove her pubic hair, and must avoid wine, pigs, and the cross.

S: You said that a Muslim may marry chaste women among those who are free, as if this excludes others.

T: Indeed, it excludes slave women. There are two opinions as to whether someone who considers it permissible to marry a slave woman is a hypocrite. It also excludes prostitutes, but it is permissible to marry a woman who was someone's mistress, although she must be kept from this afterwards. Whoever marries a slave girl is a hypocrite, but any children born of that union carry his lineage. Some say that whoever does not prohibit contact with pigs, but only the consumption of pork, is a hypocrite, as is anyone who permits marriage with a woman of the People of the Book who is kin through breastfeeding, even if she was not raised in the husband's home.[14]

14. In Islamic law, breastfeeding creates kinship, regardless of who does the breastfeeding. Q 4:23 states that a man may not marry a woman who breastfed him or a woman who nursed from the same woman as he.

S: If a woman of the People of the Book concedes the correctness of the imam's ruling concerning the people of her religion, though her family and her people fight the imam, what is her status?

T: She is not herself fighting the imam, so she may be married, and any animal she slaughters is permissible to eat. On the other hand, a woman who is actively involved in fighting may not be married, and the animals she slaughters may not be eaten. Some say she may be married because she is a chaste, free woman of the People of the Book, and some also say it is permissible to eat animals slaughtered by People of the Book who fight the imam, because the Messenger of God, peace and blessings be upon him, ate the meat of the poisoned ewe slaughtered by the Jews who fought him, and other such examples. It is said that the meat of animals slaughtered by Sabaeans is not permissible to eat, even if they pay the *jizya,* because they are not People of the Book.

S: Are the people of protection (*ahl al-dhimma*) made to wear a sign (*sima*) that distinguishes them from Muslims?

T: If they enter into protection by paying the *jizya,* Jews must wear a *zunnar* around their waist, with which they must provide themselves. Some say they must wear it around the hem of their garments, and some say they must wear lead rings and bells that they hang around their neck. The Qutb said, "This is weak because of the prohibition against clanging cymbals" (ibid., 67).[15] There are different opinions on this.

S: What is the *zunnar?*

T: The *zunnar* is a coarse, colored cord worn around the waist over the clothes. It is the color of the sky, which they claim enables them to remember God, and they do not dislike it.

S: What is the sign of the Christians?

T: They continue to carry their small sticks, as is their custom.

15. The so-called "covenant of 'Umar" stipulates restrictions on the *ahl al-dhimma,* which include the wearing of distinctive garments and a prohibition against ringing church bells or making other loud sounds as part of their religious rituals. The extent to which these regulations have actually been applied varies tremendously over time and space. It is ironic that this topic is being discussed here in the traditional manner in a text written under European colonial rule. This was the case for both Atfayyish, who lived in French-ruled Algeria, and for al-Rawahi, who lived in British-administered Zanzibar.

S: How does a woman of the *dhimma* tie her *zunnar?*

T: They said it was underneath her clothes, and that it had a distinctive sign, unless she dangled it on top of her clothes so it would show, and the latter is the preferred opinion.

S: What is the sign of the Sabaeans?

T: They wear one of the two symbols of the People of the Book, because the regulations pertaining to them are the same.

S: How does the imam treat their houses of worship?

T: Either they are all destroyed or only those that were built after Islam are destroyed; there are two opinions.[16]

S: What do you mean by "after Islam"?

T: After their country has been conquered. According to the first opinion, the houses of worship they built before the conquest should be destroyed, but not according to the second opinion.

S: They manifest reprehensible behavior and things that pertain to infidelity. Should they be allowed to continue to do these things?

T: No, they should not be allowed to do such things in public at all. The imam's honor requires him to prevent them from publicly doing things like drinking wine, eating pork, inviting people to join them in their infidelity, insulting Islam, or blaspheming the prophethood or apostleship of our master Muhammad, on whom be God's blessing and peace.

S: If a Muslim spoils the wine or its vessels inside the homes [of the People of the Book], what should be done to him?

T: He should be fined for what he spoiled inside their homes, though some say he should be fined for what he spoils, whether it be inside or outside their

16. The more commonly accepted rule among Muslims in general is that the protection afforded to the *ahl al-dhimma* includes protection of their houses of worship, but they are not allowed to build new ones or repair existing ones. In actual practice, however, non-Muslims have usually been allowed to do so with government permission. There is often a large discrepancy between the theoretical restrictions on the People of the Book and actual practice, although the government of Saudi Arabia prohibits the practice of all religions besides Islam, in keeping with the notion that Arabia itself is sacred ground and should be limited to Muslims. In contrast, Sultan Qaboos b. Sa'id of Oman donated five plots of land for the building of Hindu temples in Oman to accommodate the large Indian population in that country, although Hinduism is technically not a religion of the Book.

homes, and whatever fine or punishment is deemed permissible by the people of integrity should be imposed on him, even if this is imposed by their people of integrity.

S: I suppose that the imam prevents them from doing certain things, but I do not know exactly what.

T: Yes, you suppose correctly. He prevents them from wailing over their dead, or lighting fires in the paths that Muslims take or in their markets, or putting their dead near these places. They are prohibited from buying slaves captured by the Muslims; preventing any of their co-religionists from embracing Islam, if he wishes to do so; decorating their rings with Arabic writing; bearing arms; doing what they call prayer in a congregation, even if it is in buildings that were used for this purpose before Islam; calling people to prayer; ringing cymbals or bells, unless it is done quietly in their churches; making usurious sales; riding horses (though there is no harm in their riding mules or donkeys with pack saddles, not high saddles); raising their buildings up higher than the buildings of the Muslims,[17] unless it is on property that is highly elevated, though some say they should not be allowed to own such property; having any authority over Muslim affairs, presiding over Muslim assemblies or sitting with them, as a precaution against having curses pronounced on them, or even accompanying Muslims on the road, unless one of them has leased out his riding animal or is being hired as a guide or porter, on condition that he walk in front of it in fear and disgrace so he can care for you, for there is no good in accompanying a cursed person.

[They are prohibited from] living in the region of the Hijaz; displaying their books in Muslim markets, clubs, or roads; displaying the cross, and if anyone does display it, it should be broken over his head; and eating, drinking, conversing, or sitting with Muslims, because it is dangerous to sit with someone whom God has cursed and detested—and it subjects one to His vengeance, God forbid! They are prohibited from occupying themselves with anything that inevitably requires raising the voice, like buying and selling, lecturing, or being asked about something important. They are prohibited from entering mosques, places

17. We might note that Sayyid Barghash (ruled 1870–1888), the sultan of Zanzibar who most zealously supported Ibadism, nonetheless allowed the building of prominent Anglican and Roman Catholic cathedrals in the center of town.

intended for prayer, and religious assemblies like those held for *dhikr,* prayers of petition, mutual consultation regarding Muslim affairs, or Qur'an recitation, or any place visited for the sake of blessing. If they [try to] enter, they must be prevented, and if they persist, they must be beaten.

S: Are they prohibited from reading the Qur'an and other books?

T: There are two opinions on this. One is that they should be prohibited from openly reading the Torah and the Gospel, and they should keep to narrow passageways and not initiate the greeting of peace. If a Jew or unbeliever gives the greeting of peace, there are two opinions. Some say one should answer, "And the same to you." The Qutb said, "Perhaps the person meant well in saying this, and one may pray for good for him in response. The most obvious thing to do is to respond, 'May you get what you deserve for your unbelief'" (ibid., 69).

This answer is also fitting for someone who is in your company or who seeks your protection and is not one of the *ahl al-dhimma.* It is prohibited for an unbeliever to do anything that is prohibited for a *dhimmi,* and they must be compelled to embrace monotheism if they call others to embrace it, or if they say to someone else, whether of their own religion or of another, "Why don't you believe, when you have seen it [the same teaching] in the Gospel or the Torah?", or if they command people to say the word of faith ["There is no God but Allah, and Muhammad is the Messenger of Allah"], or if they write it, or if they deem it correct, or if they agree with it up to a certain point, or if they say the [Islamic] prayer, or if they give the call to prayer or face the *qibla* specifically or generally for their prayers or to call on God, or for an important matter, seeking blessing from it, but not if they decline to say the word of faith or merely quote someone else saying it, or if they deem it erroneous or ridicule it. They are prohibited from wearing turbans or Muslim shawls and headgear.

S: If they refuse to pay the *jizya,* how should they be treated?

T: They are considered enemies and the imam must fight them, capture them, and plunder their wealth. Then their food and slaughtered animals and marriage to their chaste, free women are prohibited. That is the custom that has been followed. Some say that their slaughtered animals are still allowed even if they refuse to pay the *jizya* or fight against the Muslims, because they are still People of the Book.

S: What is the rule regarding the prey caught by their trained dogs?

T: It is the same as the rule for their slaughtered animals.

S: Is it permissible for the imam to make peace with them?

T: It is permissible for him to make peace with them, either before or after fighting breaks out, according to what he sees as being in the best interests of the Muslims.

S: What is the rule for Zoroastrians?

T: They are like the People of the Book except concerning their slaughtered animals and marrying their women, if they pay the *jizya.*

S: What is the status of someone who deems it permissible to marry a mature woman who is not of the People of the Book?

T: He is an unbeliever, because the Most High said, "Do not marry unbelieving women until they believe" (2:221).

S: What is the status of someone who deems it permissible to marry a prepubescent girl [from among the unbelievers]?

T: Whoever deems it permissible to marry a prepubescent girl from among them is a hypocrite, if he does not consider her an unbeliever and she is one of the People of the Book who are at war with the Muslims or who refuse to pay *jizya,* or if she is a Zoroastrian or any other kind of unbeliever, because it is obligatory to suspend judgment concerning children. Those who affiliate with all children of the unbelievers allow marriage to a girl [from among them], even if her people are at war with the Muslims or she is not one of the People of the Book, because one cannot say that she is at war.

S: When can one say that a *dhimmi,* whether one of the People of the Book or a Zoroastrian, has broken his covenant [with the Muslims], and what should be done to someone who breaks the covenant?

T: He breaks it by refusing to pay the *jizya* or by refusing to observe any of the stipulations required of the *dhimmi,* or by speaking about Muslims' private parts, or by showing favor to infidels, or beating a monotheist or killing him because of his religion, or by having relations with a woman who is a monotheist, or by marrying her.

S: What is the rule pertaining to such a person?

T: He should be killed or enslaved. Some say he should be forced to convert to Islam, and if he refuses, then he should be killed or enslaved.

S: How should the imam treat atheists and idol-worshippers?

T: He must call them to embrace Islam in the way previously explained. If they refuse, he must fight them and enslave them and seize their goods. Some say the Quraysh tribe should not be enslaved,[18] and some say no Arab should be enslaved out of respect for the Prophet, on whom be blessings and peace, and for his lineage. Others say they all may be enslaved, as indicated by the enslavement of the Hawazin and the capture of al-ʿAbbas, may God be pleased with him, and his being required to get ransom for himself and his brother's son, ʿAqil [b. Abi Talib]. That is the correct interpretation, but there are different opinions. Arab tribes that are not linked to the Prophet's lineage may be taken captive, like Ghassan, Lakhm, and Judham.[19]

Those wounded in battle who are not monotheists should be killed, but children should not be killed, though if they fight one must defend oneself, and if they are killed in the course of such action, no harm is done. Women are not killed, unless they join in the fighting. Men who are too old to fight should not be killed unless they are giving the command to fight.

S: What is the wisdom in capturing children?

T: Some say it is to draw them to Islam. Others say it is to enslave them and enrich the treasury. Others say it is to enslave them because their fathers have been killed. The Qutb said, "This is not a general rule" (Atfayyish 1980a, 70). My own opinion is that perhaps there is wisdom in all of these, and God knows best.

Lesson 3: The *Jizya*

S: What is the *jizya?*

T: The *jizya* is paid by someone in a covenant relationship with the Muslims. It is done as a declaration of this covenant and as a punishment executed against him by the religion.

S: How much is it?

T: Its amount is whatever the imam sees fit, in addition to offering hospitality for three days and nights for them to collect it, though some say one should only pass through Christian territory but may spend the night among Jews, who

18. This discussion is purely theoretical, because the entire tribe of Quraysh, to which the Prophet belonged, had embraced Islam by the time of his death.

19. These were Arab kingdoms in the northern Arabian peninsula before the Muslim conquests.

must provide a place to sleep, shelter, and fire. Others say the Jew pays ten *dirhams* per year, and the Christian pays twelve or fifteen, and others say that the wealthy Jew and Christian should pay forty-eight, while the person of average wealth should pay half that, and the poor person should pay half again; there are different opinions. The Sabaean and the Zoroastrian pays whatever the Imam deems most appropriate among these different opinions. The Qutb, may God have mercy on him, said:

> Investigation proves that 'Umar and other Muslim leaders did not intend to set a specific amount for every individual for all time, but always assessed the tax on every people according to their circumstances, the time in which they lived, and the need of the Muslims. Don't you see that the people of Alexandria said to 'Amr b. al-'As, "Set the *jizya* for us," and he replied, "No, even if you gave me enough to fill the house from the foundation to the roof! If we are in need, we will be exacting with you, and if we are in ease, we will be easy on you." Don't you see that 'Umar issued one ruling for the people of Syria, according to what the shaykh related, and he gave a different ruling for the people of Kufa than he did for others? If the people knew of one ruling they thought it was applied everywhere for all people, but it was not like that, as indicated by the difference among them. (Atfayyish 1980a, 71)

By "the shaykh" he means Shaykh Isma'il [b. Musa al-Jaytali], may God have mercy on him, because he wrote in his *Qawa'id* that 'Umar, may God be pleased with him, wrote to 'Uthman b. Hunayf in Kufa that the wealthy should pay forty-eight *dirhams*, and those who had less should pay twenty-four, and those who had yet less should pay twelve *dirhams*. He said this in the presence of the Companions, and no one objected. The value of the *dirham* in relation to the *dinar* is that twelve *dirhams* equal one *dinar* except in matters of *zakat,* for which ten *dirhams* equal one *dinar.* If they wished, they could pay the *jizya* in *dinars* at the rate of twelve *dirhams* for one *dinar.*

S: Is the requirement of the *jizya* general or are only particular individuals required to pay it?

T: No, there is no *jizya* on women, children, slaves, old men, or insane people. There are two opinions on whether it is required of monks or those who are bankrupt.

S: What do God's words (9:29) "[until they pay the *jizya*] from [the] hand" (*'an yad*) mean?

T: "From the hand" is a circumstantial phrase (*hal*) attached to the pronoun in "they pay," that is, from a willing hand, with the meaning that they are submissive. Or it could mean that they submit it with their own hands and do not send it with someone else. For that reason it is forbidden for them to appoint a trustee to do this. Or it could mean "from [their] wealth," and therefore it is said that it should not be taken from a poor man. Or it could mean from a hand that has conquered them, which means they are powerless and humbled. Or it could mean that it is from a grace bestowed upon them, because keeping them alive through payment of the *jizya* is a great grace. Or it could mean from the *jizya,* meaning in coins that are passed from hand to hand.

S: What is the meaning of God's words (9:29) "while they are subjugated" (*wa-hum saghirun*), and what is the wisdom in attaching subjugation to them?

T: It means while they are humbled. Ibn 'Abbas, may God be pleased with both [him and his father], says that when the *jizya* is taken from someone, he should be slapped on the neck (*tawajja'a 'unuquhu*). *Wajja'tuhu 'unuqahu waj'an* (I slapped his neck with a slap) means "I hit him."

The wisdom in slapping his neck and in attaching subjugation to him and not just taking the *jizya* is that the Most High linked their paying the *jizya* with His words "while they are subjugated," so in order to spare the blood of one of the People of the Book it is not enough for them just to pay the *jizya,* but they must do it in humiliation and subjugation. The reason for this is that any rational person naturally recoils from bearing humiliation and subjugation, so if he is given time to witness the glory of Islam and to hear the proofs of its soundness, while witnessing the humiliation and subjugation of infidelity and its people, it is obvious that this will draw him to Islam. That is the goal of prescribing the *jizya.*

The goal of imposing the *jizya* is not to reinforce the People of the Book in their infidelity, but to take it to spare their blood and to give them time, in the hope that perhaps they will become aware during this time of the excellences of Islam and the strength of its proofs, and turn from infidelity to faith. They have the scripture in their hands, so perhaps they will think about it and observe the truth of Muhammad, on whom be blessings and peace, in his claim to prophethood. So they are given a respite, not to affirm their position or because of pleasure in it. This is the sound opinion with regard to the wisdom of subjugating them.

Some say they are merely affirmed in their false religion by our taking the *jizya* out of respect for their ancestors who died in the truth of the law of the Torah and the Gospel, but that opinion is worthless.

S: How is the bankrupt person treated, since it is obligatory for him [to pay the *jizya*]?

T: His face is coated with milk or his body with honey—there are two opinions—and he is bound and exposed to the sun, so he will suffer from its heat and from flies and ants.

S: What is the wisdom in this humiliation, when there is no compulsion in religion (Q 2:256)?

T: Glory be to God! The scholars who prescribed this were not heedless of the fact that there is no compulsion in religion! But this is done to force him to pay the *jizya,* not to force him to embrace the religion. He will see the glory of Islam with his own eyes, so if he wishes to ennoble himself and escape from the humiliation of infidelity, he has the ability to do this. He really brought this suffering on himself through his own choice, because he can escape it through his tongue declaring God's oneness, and then he is released to go his way. It is obvious that the punishment suggested by both opinions is harsh, but, as I explained earlier, the bankrupt person does not pay the *jizya,* but that is not lucky because of what follows. The Qutb, may God be pleased with him, said, "The sound opinion is that he has no obligation to pay the *jizya,* because no obligation is imposed beyond a person's ability. Rather than binding him, it would be better to make him do work that would equal the amount of the *jizya*" (Atfayyish 1980a, 71).

S: What are the permissible limits on a ruler (*sultan*) of the Muslims in collecting the *jizya?*

T: The limits are these: he may not oppress those from whom he takes the *jizya;* he must provide for the poor of the people who pay the *jizya* from the money collected in the *jizya,* and for the poor of the people [Muslims] who pay *zakat* from the money collected in *zakat.*[20] No one may collect the *jizya* except the imam, and if someone else collects it, it should not be used; though some say anyone who is able to protect them from oppression may collect it; there are two opinions on this. Some say that unbelievers may use money that they have

20. Atfayyish (1980a, 71) adds here, "even if they are not Ibadis."

taken as a religious obligation from monotheists, though most do not agree with that opinion. Those who permit unbelievers to use this also permit the use of money obtained from the price of wine or pigs, and they also permit taking goods plundered from grave sinners who belong to the people of the *qibla,* or some say those who commit any sin, small or great, in addition to the price of tobacco if the person who sells it belongs to a group that considers tobacco use permissible.[21]

21. Ibadi scholars prohibit smoking.

Chapter 7

KNOWLEDGE AND ACTION[1]

Lesson 1: The Foundations of Religious Practice, Knowledge, and Action

S: What are the foundations of religious practice (*qawa'id al-din*)?

T: The foundations of religious practice are four things, from which four others are derived.

S: What is the first foundation?

T: It is knowledge. One must know at what time things are done, like the obligation to affirm the faith when one reaches maturity and rationality, and that one prays the noon prayer after the sun has reached its peak, and that fasting is done at the onset of Ramadan. One must know of the prophets and angels, what is permissible, and what is prohibited, by being presented with evidence. One must know how God is described, by having it explained and by asking about it. One must know about equivalence in action, though some say it is not necessary to know it, but that saying is weak. One must know what pleases God, what He has commanded and prohibited, what is erroneous, and what is correct. One should also know what things are collective duties that require only a sufficient number of people to do them.[2]

S: What is the basis for making knowledge obligatory?

T: All three roots of the law[3] are a basis for making the seeking of knowledge obligatory. The entire *umma* agrees on the obligatory nature of seeking necessary

1. This chapter, which is probably incomplete, closely follows Atfayyish (1980a, 72–76).

2. A collective duty (*fard kifaya*), such as the obligation to defend Muslim territory, is distinct from a duty imposed on every Muslim (*fard 'ayn*), such as prayer.

3. The three roots of the law are the Qur'an, the Sunna, and consensus (*ijma'*). Al-Rawahi presents proof from consensus first, followed by a Qur'anic verse, and then a hadith from the

knowledge; God Most High said, "So ask the people of remembrance, if you do not know" (16:43); and the Prophet said in a sound hadith, "The search for knowledge is a religious obligation on everyone who has reached puberty."[4]

S: Perhaps the command in the verse and in the hadith is simply meant to encourage people to seek knowledge?

T: Not at all! Keep to your own limits, and beware of these explanations, which I fear will lead you to rely on dubious arguments! In truth, I assure you, when the command came, it was because of obligation! If it were an isolated instance and there were no second proof-text, you might say it was merely to encourage people. This is our teaching and the teaching of all our theological opponents concerning isolated commands.

S: What is the proof for this allegation?

T: Turn your eyes to the words of the Most High: "May those who oppose His command beware" (24:63) and "He deviated from the command of His Lord" (18:50). If you look in comparable verses you will find that the Glorious One says that sedition, immorality, reproach, and blame all result from opposing and failing to obey His command. Would these calamities fall on those who oppose His command if the command were meant only as an encouragement? You see that He Whose praise is glorious made clear what happens to those who oppose His commands, without telling us that the command is obligatory, but He tells us, "If you don't do this, you are an infidel" or "you will be punished" or something of the sort, so understand or come learn! Yes, it is possible that when the Most High says "They oppose His command" He means just one of His commands, with the implication that it is the opposite of prohibition. In the hadith, "If I command you to do something, obey as well as you can," his saying "as well as you can" indicates that obeying is an obligation linked to the command in his words "if I command you." If he commands us, we are obligated to obey his commands. The outcome is that the command is an obligation so you will act according to it, as you would with other commands.

Prophet. The roots of Islamic jurisprudence (*usul al-fiqh*) include a fourth root, *ijtihad*, (systematic individual reasoning), but *ijtihad* is not binding, so it is not included here.

4. I have not found this precise version. The more familiar version is "The search for knowledge is obligatory for every Muslim" (Ibn Maja 2000, Introduction, *bab* 17, no. 229).

S: If, while I am praying, I happen to think of something the knowledge of which cannot be delayed, such as whether a certain attribute is affirmed of God or negated of Him, or whether a situation requires affiliation or dissociation, or whether I should affirm prophethood and the mission of God's messengers or not, what should I do, when the circumstance requires that I not be diverted from prayer?

T: Stay where you are and complete your obligation, in spite of the matter that is in your heart, and complete your prayer. That is the sound opinion, though some say prayer is corrupted by denying an attribute of God or by affirming something of God that should be denied, and others say it is corrupted by all these things.

S: If I affiliate with someone or dissociate from someone in my heart while in that situation, is that sufficient to receive a reward?

T: No, it is not.

S: If a person in prayer knows the meaning of one of God's attributes in a general way but does not know whether or not God may be described by it, what is his status?

T: If he knows the meaning of an attribute that is affirmed of God but does not know whether or not he should affirm it, or if he knows the meaning of an attribute that must be denied of God and does not know whether or not to deny it, that is unbelief (*shirk*), which negates his ablution as well as his prayer. He should look into the matter or ask about it, and then renew his ablution and prayer, but he need not do a full body bath.[5]

S: If he does not know the meaning of the attribute, what is his status and what should he do, such as if he does not know the literal meaning of *al-Muhaymin* ["the Vigilant"], so he suspends judgment, may he describe God with it or not?

T: He does not need to do anything to complete his prayer, and he is not required to ask about it afterward. Some say that he is not required to ask about it at all, whether the question occurs to him during prayer or any other time. If he

5. A full body bath (*ghusl*) is required after major ritual impurity, but only ritual ablution is required after minor impurity. Although al-Rawahi calls such ignorance unbelief, he clearly does not consider it as serious as idolatry, which would require a full body bath before prayer.

knows the meaning and does not suspend judgment, his prayer is sound, and he should remember that "there is nothing like Him" (Q 42:11).

S: If he is asked about a particular trait that constitutes unbelief, must he know that it is an act of disobedience, a grave sin, and [a sign of] infidelity, for which there are severe consequences? If he does not know this, what is his status?

T: He is a hypocrite. He need not know that it is unbelief (*shirk*) if no proof of that has been given to him of this, unless it is belief in multiple gods; in that case, if he does not know that it is unbelief, he is an unbeliever. Some say that if he does not know that it is infidelity to abandon Muhammad, the Messenger of God, he is an unbeliever. Likewise, there is an opinion that it is obligatory to know that affirming his prophethood is part of monotheism, and if he does not know this he is an infidel, though others disagree.

S: Is it generally obligatory to know through asking that a person who permits what God has prohibited is an infidel, and that whoever prohibits the grave sins of hypocrisy but then judges someone who does them to be a Muslim, as if he considered them permissible, is an infidel?

T: There are two opinions on this.

S: If someone judges something to be prohibited but does it in spite of his judgment that anyone who does this is not a Muslim, or if the perpetrator of a deed he considers prohibited does not know what the Muslims say about this, is he an infidel, or is his status less severe than that because of the weakness of his knowledge or because of doubt?

T: There are two opinions on this.[6]

S: According to sound opinion, is it obligatory to know that a person is an infidel if he persists in his ignorance of or forgets an attribute of a prophet or messenger of God, or of an angel, or his knowledge of religious affiliation or dissociation, or a religious law, or if he does not remember the Qur'an, to the point that he cannot distinguish it from poetry, or if he cannot remember it, although he distinguishes it from poetry?

6. The two opinions are: (a) that such a person is an infidel, or (b) that he has not gone as far as infidelity. I have followed the texts of R and F on the teacher's response here. N and SA say, "In our opinion, this is not necessary," which seems like an odd response to the question, as it is unclear what it is that would not be necessary.

T: Ignorance of his infidelity in the sense of ingratitude for God's blessings (*kufr ni'ma*) is impermissible, although some say that the only aspect of the Qur'an one may not forget is to act according to what is in it, even in the case of someone who has memorized it. This is contradicted by the hadith, "I have never seen a sin greater than forgetting the Qur'an" (cf. al-Suyuti 1981, no. 5421; al-Muttaqi 2001, no. 2833). The apparent meaning concerns abandoning the memorization of the Qur'an, though some say that what is really meant is acting according to what it says, and that the failure to act according to the dictates of the Qur'an is a sin greater than that of earlier religious communities who failed to act according to what was in their books, and it is a greater sin than failing to act according to what is in the Sunna.

S: If someone forgets the Qur'an because of an illness, is he not excused?

T: He is excused for anything that is beyond his capacity.

S: Then is it obligatory to learn prosody in order to distinguish between the Qur'an and poetry?

T: We do not say that it is obligatory, but one should know prosody and rhymes in order to distinguish the Qur'an from poetry. Prosody teaches us that speech is poetry only if it has a meter that is intended to be read as poetry, and what God created in the Qur'an goes beyond what is allowed in poetic meter. He knows poetic meter, but did not wish to recite poetry.[7] That is a brief clarification.

S: I asked you, dear teacher, about the obligation of knowledge, in a general way, by asking you about the infidelity of someone who permits what God prohibits, and so forth, and I understand your answer. If it is known more specifically that Zayd deems something permissible [that God prohibits], or that he persists in doing it, or forgets his knowledge of it, must one say he is an infidel?

T: It is not required to say he is an infidel until he knows that what he has done is a grave sin or a sign of unbelief. Some say it is obligatory to declare anyone who permits what is prohibited or persists in a minor sin or forgets his knowledge to be an infidel.

7. In the early years of his prophethood, some accused Muhammad of composing poetry, but the Qur'an vehemently denies that it is poetry (21:5, 36:69, 37:36, 52:30, 69:41) and implies that its composition is too miraculous to be of human origin (10:38, 11:13).

Lesson 2: The Obligation to Link Knowledge with Action (*al-'Amal*)

S: Is knowledge beneficial without action, or action without knowledge?

T: No, there is no benefit in one without the other. If you know something is a religious obligation and know how to do it in all its aspects but do not do it, how can you benefit from something you have failed to do, when you are commanded to do it? Likewise, if you know you are commanded to do it but you do not know how to do it, so you do it incorrectly, how can you benefit from doing what is incorrect? Rather, know in order to act, and act in a sound way according to what you know, in order to be called great in the kingdom of the heavens (*li-tud'a 'aziman fi malakut al-samawat*). Do not fail to act according to what you know, or your punishment will be double. Do not be without knowledge and action, or you will die the death of an unbeliever (*fa-tamut mawta jahiliyya*).

S: If I do something in ignorance, but happen to act according to what is commanded, does that act benefit me?

T: Others have spoken concerning a person who in ignorance does what is commanded. Some say that his deed is not sound; some say that it is, but he is sinful; some say he is doomed; some say that what he does is bad; there are different opinions.

S: What is the meaning of the words of the Maghribi scholar, Ibrahim b. Ibrahim, may God have mercy on him: "Knowledge without action is sound if it concerns religious obligations other than faith (*tawhid*), as long as its time has not come"?[8]

T: What the shaykh says is sound. Indeed, a person's knowledge is sound even if the time comes and he does not do what is required—that is, before the time. By soundness of knowledge we mean that it is beneficial. If he acts according to it afterward, he benefits from the act as well, except in matters of faith, because knowledge of faith does not precede an action: if you know it and do not deny it, you have completed the action in your heart. But the most common opinion is that such a person receives no reward until he declares his knowledge.

8. I have not been able to identify Shaykh Ibrahim b. Ibrahim or to locate this saying, but al-Darjini (2:413, 428, 439) relates accounts from an Ibrahim b. Ibrahim dating from the fifth/eleventh century.

What I mean is, merely knowing something in the heart without declaring it with the tongue is not beneficial or rewarded. You know that belief in God's oneness is both knowledge and act at the same time, and that the heart cannot know God's oneness without doing what is in concordance with that knowledge. Another exception to what the shaykh says must be made for acting without knowledge.

S: Can one say concerning the People of the Book, or others who affirm the existence of God, that they know God or remember God?

T: No, one cannot say such a thing—how ignorant they are of God Most High!—lest it be imagined that they know Him in a sound fashion. The knowledge of the Arabs in the Age of Ignorance was corrupt and unsound, for they claimed to worship idols in order to draw near to God (Q 39:3). If they truly knew Him, they would have drawn near to Him in sincere worship, not by worshipping others, but they compounded their ignorance.

[End of text][9]

9. The fact that this chapter ends abruptly and does not pursue the last two sections of Atfayyish 1980a, which up to this point al-Rawahi had been following faithfully, may indicate that the author passed away before completing the text. The other two dimensions of religious practice that Atfayyish discusses on pp. 76–80 are intention and fear of God (*wara'*).

PART THREE

ʻAbd al-ʻAziz al-Thamini al-Musʻabi on God's Power and Human Acts, from *Kitab Maʻalim al-Din*

[*Maʻalim al-din* means "The Characteristics of Religion." The book is divided into parts called "characteristics" (*maʻlam*, plural *maʻalim*), which are subdivided into chapters called "observations" (*marsad*, plural *marasid*), which are further subdivided into sections called "goals" (*maqsid*, pl. *maqasid*). The following selection comprises the seventh section (*maqsid*) of chapter (*marsad*) 3 and the entirety of chapter (*marsad*) 4 of part (*maʻlam*) 3, "On Matters Pertaining to God" (*fi 'l-ilahiyyat*). Page numbers from volume 1 of the published Arabic text are inserted in brackets.]

[261] Chapter 3

ON THE NECESSITY OF THE ABSOLUTE ONENESS OF GOD MOST HIGH

Section 7: Demonstrating That God Creates Human Acts

If you understand the preceding concerning the necessity of the absolute oneness of God Most High, you will know that one may use the proof of mutual prevention (*dalil al-tamanu'*) to demonstrate that the Most High is the one who brings human acts (*af'al al-'ibad*) into existence, without any effect from human power on them. Rather, [human power] comes into existence only at the moment of [the act for which it is created]. This is in opposition to the Mu'tazila, in their claim that human power is what produces (*hiya 'l-mu'aththira fi*) the acts according to their choice, and that the eternal power (*al-qudra 'l-qadima*) has no effect at all on those voluntary acts, and neither does it flow according to the will of God Most High.

The way to prove [that God creates human acts] is the proof that a multiplicity of gods necessarily implies the affirmation of God's impotence when His will is not implemented—which is exactly what the teaching of the Mu'tazila entails, for they have said that the attachment of human power and will to the act prevents the attachment of the power and will of God Most High to that act, although that act is one of the possible things that have been conclusively proven to be necessarily attached to the power and will of God Most High, through a general attribution of [His power and will] to all [possible things]. This act, therefore, is [262] subject to both human power and will and the power and will of our Lord, because of what you know of the generality of the attachment of God's power and will.

The Qadariyya claimed that what produced and influenced human acts and inhered in them is the weaker of the two powers and more feeble of the two wills, human power and will. This despicable doctrine is nothing other than an affirmation that the Most High has a partner in [the act] and that the Most High should, on the contrary, be described as impotent and overpowered by another. For this reason, the Messenger of God, may God bless him and grant him peace, called them the Magians of this *umma* (al-Rabi' b. Habib n.d., 3:10; Abu Dawud 2000, *Kitab al-sunna* [41], *bab* 17, no. 4693), for what their teaching requires is not considered a [genuine Islamic] doctrine. Since it is a defamation of His divinity and an affirmation of His deficiency and of the nonexistence of His essence to assert that God is made impotent through the effective power of the will of another god, how could the effective power and will of a human being make Him impotent?

They are not helped by their response, which is that it is not necessary that the Most High have no power over an act produced by a human being, because the Most High is capable of bringing it into existence by stripping the person of power over it and of will for it, and by making it an act of coercion, like the act a person who is shivering, because we say that it is absolutely impossible for God to be overpowered or unable to bring any possible thing into existence. This answer of theirs requires that the Most High be unable to bring the act of the person into existence, unless the person is stripped of power and will. So, according to them, that possible act is beyond His power and He is unable to bring it into existence, and He is overpowered by the power and will of the person, although their aforementioned answer does not accord with their corrupt principle that God must do what is good and best, because it is impossible for Him to strip the person of the power He created for him after making him accountable; indeed, He must help him by making [good] acts easy for him.

If you understand this, you know that the correct teaching is that of the majority (*al-jumhur*), and is indicated by [263] the obvious meaning of the Book and Sunna, and was agreed upon by the early Muslims (*al-salaf*) before the appearance of heresies: that God is the Creator and all else is created, that the Most High has no partner in His dominion, and that having an effect on things and the power to bring things into existence are His characteristics and cannot be affirmed of anything else.

It is reported that al-Juwayni said that originated [human] power does affect acts, but not independently [of divine power], as the Mu'tazila said; rather, human power affects acts according to the measure determined by God Most High and in the manner He intended. Al-Baqillani and al-Isfarayini also said that human power affects the particular quality of the act, but does not bring it into existence, although al-Baqillani said that it is a particular quality, whereas al-Isfarayini, who denied the modes (*al-ahwal*), said that the particular quality is only an aspect and expression. Some of the Ash'arites chose the teaching of al-Baqillani and distinguished between the aspects of production (*ikhtira'*) and acquisition (*kasb*), in that the movement, as a movement, is attributed to the act of God Most High in terms of its production and being brought into existence.[1] This requires that He know it in all its aspects, and that the movement not act upon the essence of the Most High, nor is He described by it in the sense that it subsists in Him; nor can one say that He moves by it because He brought it into existence and produced it.

The act is attributed to the human being in terms of its particular qualities, such as prayer, for example, or illegal seizure or theft or adultery, and human power has no effect except in that aspect; there is no stipulation that the person know all aspects of the act. His body is the locus of the act and of his acquisition of it, and the act is attributed to him, so it is said that he is moving or at rest or praying or illegally seizing or stealing or committing adultery, and so forth. If a command is attached to it and the act accords with it, it is called an act of obedience and of worship. If a prohibition attaches to it and the act opposes it, it is called an act of disobedience and a crime. That is the aspect concerning which the person is commanded through words that are addressed to him, ordering him to pray and fast and not to commit illegal seizure or theft, and it [is this aspect] that makes an act worthy of reward, punishment, praise, or blame. However, concerning its coming into existence, there is no difference between voluntary and involuntary acts.

[264] That is what this group says, and it is more balanced than the teaching of the Mu'tazila, because they affirm things according to their realities in nonexistence, in the sense that [they say that] the reality of a nonexistent possible thing and its essential characteristics (*awsafahu 'l-nafsiyya*) are fixed in the mode of its

1. Ibadis, Ash'arites, and Maturidites all say that God creates human acts, which are subject to human "acquisition" in the case of voluntary acts.

nonexistence, as has been explained; existence, according to them, is added to the essence, which is shared by each mode and is an intermediary between existence and nonexistence. So the one who does an act does nothing concerning things except bring it into existence, which is a mode concerning which there is no intelligible distinction according to the difference of realities. Command and prohibition do not attach to a specific mode, but to particular characteristics and expressions. Acts are either good or bad according to these characteristics, and these entail praise or blame.

According to them, acts that are commanded or prohibited are not determined for a person; what is determined for a person are things for which there is no human accountability. In this way they differ from the teaching of al-Baqillani, whose opinion meets the demands of both reason and revelation, as indeed do the opinions of all three of them, although what al-Juwayni reports concerning the teaching of al-Baqillani and al-Isfarayini drifts into the teaching of the Mu'tazila, but without going so far as their heinous belief or [on the other extreme] so far as requiring people to do what is impossible for them, with the assessment that human power has no effect on anything at all, as the majority say, whereas the Mu'tazila say to us that the outcome of obligation according to this estimation is "Act, you who have no act: do what I am doing," although that is weak.

What al-Baqillani and his companions rely on in attributing all possible things to God Most High is their possibility; the particular characteristic of one is no better than another [in this regard]. This is an extension of what they attributed to the human being, for this aspect is either possible or not. If it is possible, it must be linked to His power. If it is not possible, its attribution to any power is impossible. The compulsion[2] from which they fled is forced upon them, because in that case one cannot imagine an intention to bring it into existence in view of its impossibility (*'ala hiyaliha*), so the act is not produced from the person [265] as long as God Most High has not done the act in that body (*dhat*).[3] On the

2. The text reads *al-khabar,* "information" or "report," which does not make sense in this context. I believe this word should be *jabr,* "compulsion," the spelling of which is distinguished from *khabar* by the placement of a single dot.

3. *Dhat* is a word that often translates as "essence," but *dhat* can also mean a person's physical body, especially in late medieval writings of the Maghrib.

other hand, when He does the act in that body, one cannot imagine the person abandoning it, as they claim. So compulsion is forced upon them. Al-Isfarayini is forced into this even more, because he says that this aspect is just an expression in the mind, so how can one intend to do something that has no objective existence (*wujud fi 'l-kharij*)?

In sum, there are five opinions on this question: (1) that of the majority, which is that human power has no effect at all, and comes into existence only at the time of the act; (2) that of al-Juwayni; (3) that of al-Baqillani and his followers; (4) that of the Compulsionists (*al-Mujbira* or *al-Jabriyya*), who deny that the human being has any choice concerning his acts; and (5) that of the Mu'tazila.

Note: Our companions say that a [voluntary act] does not issue from a person unless these five conditions are met: (1) God wills it and creates it for him; (2) human power to act occurs at the time of the act, not before it or after it; (3) the person wills it and acquires it; (4) God helps (*i'ana*) him to do it if it is an act of obedience; (5) God abandons him to it if it is an act of disobedience. More investigation of this follows.

Chapter 4

ON WHAT IS POSSIBLE CONCERNING THE MOST HIGH

[By "possible,"] I mean what is neither necessary nor impossible, but is possible for Him. This chapter is divided into sections.

Section 1: The Doctrine of Acquisition

A person who is subject to the law must believe that God the Glorious created human beings (*al-'ibad*) and created their acts and created reward and punishment for these acts, and that they acquire (*iktasabu*) their acts and do them, [266] and are not compelled or forced to do them. There is disagreement concerning the definition of an act, insofar as it is [their] act. The best definition of it, according to the principle of our companions and those who agree with them on this, is that it is an accident[1] brought into being at the same time as the capacity (*istita'a*) to do it. This matter is referred to as "acquisition" (*kasb*), which is one of the obscure topics of study in theology (*min ghawamid mabahith 'ilm al-kalam*).

The truth is that a person does not create his [or her] own acts, but merely acquires them by the necessity of the attachment of accountability to them (*darurat ta'alluq al-taklif bi-ha*). We know by demonstration (*bi-'l-burhan*) that there is no creator but God Most High, and we know of necessity that power that is originated for a person (*al-qudra 'l-haditha li-'l-'abd*) attaches to some of his deeds, such as getting up, but not others, such as falling. The effect of the originated power is called "acquisition." Although we cannot completely understand it, it

1. In the philosophical sense of something that is nonessential, transitory, and changeable.

is said that a person's acquisition of an act occurs at the same time as his power and will, without his affecting anything or bringing anything into existence; he is merely the locus (*mahall*) for the act.

Acquisition does not make necessary the existence of the act for which a person is given power, although it does necessitate the ascription of the act to the person doing it. Because of this ascription, the person is variably described according to the deed: good if it is an act of obedience and bad if it is an act of disobedience, because a bad deed done intentionally and willfully is bad, unlike the creation of evil, which does not negate a praiseworthy benefit; indeed it may be both, because it is established that the Creator is wise[2] and that He does not create things without a praiseworthy outcome, although we may not understand it. So anyone who imagines that the Most High does evil must understand that there may be wisdom and good in His creating them, just as there is in the creation of ugly, harmful or painful bodies—unlike the acquirer, who may do good or evil. Therefore we say that the acquisition of evil after its prohibition is evil, foolish, and deserving of blame and punishment.

One cannot say, "The Most High's independence in creating acts is proven, and a single object of power cannot come under two different powers, as is necessary by your assertion that the act is both created by God and acquired by the person who does it," [267] because we say that since it has been demonstrated that the creator of the act is God, and it is necessary that the power and will of the person enter into some acts, such as the movement of anger, but not others, such as shivering, we need to avoid this difficulty by saying that God Most High creates the act and the person acquires it. It has been established that the application of a person's power and will to an act is limited to acquisition and that God, as the one who brings the act into being, is its creator. Therefore, a single object of power (*al-maqdur al-wahid*) is subject to two different powers from two different aspects; it is subject to human power from the aspect of acquisition. This determination of meaning is necessary, although we cannot say more than to summarize by saying that human acts are created and brought into being by God at the same time as human power and choice. We may distinguish between acquisition and creation

2. The published text, which is very flawed, says *hakama,* "judged," but I assume that it should be *hakim,* "wise."

by saying that acquisition occurs with an instrument, and creation occurs without an instrument.

Those who say humans are compelled to act say that humans have absolutely no choice concerning what they do; rather, they are compelled to do them and are an instrument for them, just as a knife is an instrument for cutting and a tree is an instrument for wind—rather, like a string attached to the air, twisted by the wind to the right and then to the left, powerless to oppose or resist it. According to them, animals are like inanimate things in relation to their acts and have no power over them, either to produce them or to acquire them. The fallacy of this argument is obvious, for we necessarily judge that we choose some of our acts, such as extending our hand to take something, and are compelled toward others, such as shivering. They are compelled to hold that human beings are not accountable for anything they do, and that it is literally and legally inappropriate to ask them to do something or to prohibit it or praise or blame or reproach them for doing it, and that there should be no surprise over their disbelief, as expressed by "How can you disbelieve in God?" (Q 2:28). All this is false, by the consensus of the monotheists.

One cannot say, "You must believe in compulsion, since you do not assign to human beings any effect in their acts," because we say that the compulsion of which one should beware is what we can sense (*hissi*). The compulsion that we understand with our intellect, on the other hand, is the removal of [268] [the attribution of] creation from human beings, for all [Muslim] sects agree on this—indeed, that is faith itself. Just as whatever God Most High wills to occur from a person necessarily occurs through his choice, the necessity of its occurrence through choice is inevitably actualized because of that choice, a truth that no one denies.

Note: Some say that the meaning of choice is that when it occurs to a person to do something and he hesitates to do it and abandons it, there arises from his hesitation an inclination toward preferring one alternative over the other. This inclination is called "will," and the preference is called "choice." If he suddenly tries to do something and prefers it, the One who brings it from nonexistence into existence is God, who is glorified and exalted.

Section 2: Human Power Comes into Being with Its Act

Know that we only speak of a power belonging to a human being at the time of the act that is its object because of the necessary distinction you find between the movements of coercion (*idtirar*) and of acquisition. This characteristic (*hukm*), which is conjunction, is not permanent insofar as it is a power, but rather insofar as it is an accident (*'arad*). One of the characteristics of accidents is that they pass into nonexistence after the time of their existence, and it is usually (*fi 'l-akthar*) impossible for them to remain beyond that time in order to exist in another, as has been explained earlier. If the impossibility of their remaining is established, it is clear that originated power cannot exist before [the act for which it is created], because if it existed before the act, it would have to pass into nonexistence at the time that the act that is its object comes into existence, in which case it would come into existence through a nonexistent power, which is impossible. To affirm that means that if the power is nonexistent, the existence of its opposite, impotence, is possible, in which case the act would be subject to a person's power at a moment when he is impotent, which would mean that he is unable to do it. So something would happen that at the time of its occurrence is the result of an impotent power, which is impossible.

One of their scholars who has reflected on the impossibility of the existence of power to act before the act said that if this is taken only with respect to the impossibility of the endurance of accidents, then the power is not really a cause of the act's coming into existence, nor does it affect it. If it does not bring the empowered act into existence, [269] it is possible for it to exist before the act that it is empowered to do, then pass into nonexistence, and then a similar power could come into existence. In that case, the power that comes into existence at that time is attached to the act, and the power that existed before the act is [also] attached, so one could say that this power was attached to the act before it passed into nonexistence and ceased to exist, and its attachment to it ceased to exist, and a similar power came into existence.

It is as if someone knew by true information that Zayd would come into existence tomorrow at sunrise, for example. Then we could renew his knowledge that this would happen at the known time, until its occurrence at the time he was told it would occur. So the [knowledge] that comes into existence at that point, attaching to the previous existence [of knowledge], attaches to Zayd's coming into existence at the specified time. So the object of knowledge is attached to both of them, one earlier and one later.If it were possible for something that is the opposite of knowledge to occur at the time that an object of knowledge comes into existence, such as bewilderment, neglect, ignorance or doubt, then, at the time that the object of knowledge came into existence, it would be unknown by knowledge that occurs at the same time, although it attaches to the knowledge that existed before the object of knowledge came into existence. So a consideration of its lack of attachment to the one who knew of it beforehand at the time it comes into existence enables us to understand that an empowered act is not attached to a preexistent power at the time that it comes into existence. This does not prevent its preexistence, especially since we have said that [the power] does not affect [the empowered act], but merely attaches to the empowered act, without producing an effect on it. Since we say that knowledge can attach to an object of knowledge before it comes into existence, what is to prevent power from attaching to an empowered act before the act? A person can sense in himself, before he does something, the difference between his act of shivering and something he does when he is healthy. That is simply because he finds an essential attribute attached to the act before it occurs, and then similar powers are renewed until the time the empowered act comes into existence.

Proof for the assertion (*ithbat*) of originated power is that we can imagine two movements going (*mutajarradatayn*) in the same direction (*jiha*) and having similar force (*jabr*), but one of them is coerced (*idtirariyya*) and the other is acquired (*iktisabiyya*). There is no doubt that we find a necessary distinction between the two movements, but this distinction cannot be due to a difference in the movements themselves, because they resemble each other and belong to the same person who is doing these movements; what can be discerned concerning both is the same. So the distinction must be due to an additional attribute in the mover. It cannot be due to a mode (*hal*), because a mode cannot be examined by itself in a substance, as modes [270] cannot be discerned by themselves, but would have to be distinguished by another mode subsisting in it, and that by another mode, and so on, which would result in an infinite series. The distinction [between the two movements] cannot be due to the soundness of the construction [of the body of the mover] because that is not [necessarily] lost in a coerced movement, for example, if someone else is moving the person's hand, despite the distinction, in which case the attribute would be an accident. Furthermore, this attribute must be something that either requires life or does not. The second [alternative] is wrong, because it would have no attachment to movement, and because it is shared between two things, so it is not the basis of the distinction between the two movements. So it must be the first, something that carries this stipulation. This [attribute] cannot be knowledge or life or speech, because all of these exist with both movements in the case of bewilderment. So it must be an accident with a relation and attachment to the movement. This is what we call "power." Although we and the Mu'tazila disagree concerning whether it is one of the attributes that exist from the start, we agree that it is one of the attributes that have attachments (*annaha min al-sifat al-muta'allaqa*).

Section 3: Accountability Attaches to Acquisition

What is meant by "acquisition" is nothing but the attachment of this originated power in the locus of the empowered act, at the same time as the act, without producing any effect. Acquisition is the attachment of legal accountability and entails the attainment of reward and punishment. So the teaching of the Compulsionists (*al-Jabriyya*), is wrong, because compulsion implies necessity and the nullification of the locus of accountability and the aforementioned entailment [of reward and punishment]. For this reason, it is a heresy (*bid'a*) that impacts the contract (*'aqd*) of faith.

The teaching of the Mu'tazila is also wrong, which is that a person produces (*yakhtari'u*) his own acts according to his will by the power that God Most High created (*khalaqa*) for him by the enabling He has given him (*bi-wasitat iqdarihi la-hu*). They agree with us that it is created by the Most High,[3] because if it were created [by the person] that would entail an infinite series [of creators], and the falsity of that has already been explained in the proof of God's oneness and the impossibility of His having a partner.

The doctrine of acquisition occupies a position between those two corrupt teachings. The attachment of accountability, meaning that the empowered act comes into existence with the originated power, is required by the law in the matters for which the human being is held accountable, because in the case of an empowered act without [271] human power, like the movement of shivering, for example, our glorified Lord graciously removes accountability from us, whether negatively by prohibiting it or positively by commanding it. A person who falls from a high place cannot be prohibited from falling at the time that this occurs,

3. The later Mu'tazila, however, did say that humans create their own acts.

though someone may wish this of him by telling him, "Don't fall on it." Nor can he be commanded to fall by telling him, "Fall on it." Likewise, the person who shivers can neither be commanded to do that movement nor prohibited from it, although if the Glorious One reversed accountability or made everyone accountable, that would [still] be good,[4] because the power of the accountable person has no effect on anything, but the Most High in His wisdom deemed what is fixed by the law to be most appropriate, as has been explained.

In sum, these acts that are created by God Most High have legal implications (*nasabaha 'l-shar'*) when they come close (*'inda iqtirabiha*) to originated accidents like power and will, entailing the attainment of reward and punishment or something else, meaning whatever reward has been set for it, according to whether, with the intention of obedience, one has done something obligatory or recommended, or not done something that is prohibited or reprehensible, and punishment for doing something that is prohibited or failing to do what is obligatory, or the absence of reward and punishment for doing something that is permitted or reprehensible or for failing to do something that is recommended or for failing to do something that is reprehensible, without the intention of obedience. What we asserted earlier does not negate this, because it is an example that need not be restricted, and because the abandonment of obligatory duties is categorized as prohibited and the abandonment of recommended acts is categorized as reprehensible.

Judgment concerning individual felicity and misery [in the afterlife] exists from all eternity without any cause for it except that God Most High does what He likes and judges as He wills. The outcome of the teaching of the Compulsionists (*al-Mujbira*), which results in stupidity and weakness of intellect, goes against the Shari'a, because it removes accountability for acts for which there is usually no possible alternative (*didd*), whether through existence or nonexistence. Accountability usually exists for what is easy for a person to do or not to

4. According to this theological perspective, anything God does is good, because goodness is defined by what God does, not by human judgment of what is good. So even if God commanded what we perceive to be evil and prohibited what we perceive to be good, or if He made people accountable regardless of their ability to obey His commands, that would still be good. God is therefore gracious when He removes accountability for things over which we have no power.

do. What a person does has no definable effect on anything, contrary to the claim of the Mu'tazila.

There is no distinction between acts for which the law makes people accountable and those for which it does not make people accountable, [272] except the presence or absence of acquisition. If all acts were equal, as the Compulsionists say, the legal distinction between them would be nullified, and accountability for doing them would also be nullified—that is, for an act that is within the capacity of the accountable person, not any other act. In that case, no acts would ordinarily be within human capacity, so there would be no accountability for anything, because of the words of the Most High, "God does not place an obligation on a soul that is beyond its capacity" (2:286). Their teaching nullifies the Book of God, the Sunna of the Prophet, and the consensus [of the *umma*].

Section 4: Human Power Cannot Nullify God's Power

There are two other pitfalls in the doctrine of the Mu'tazila, in addition to the previously mentioned proof of the impossibility of the impotence of the eternal power. One of these is that it requires that a possible thing be impossible. The second is that it gives more weight to that which has less (*tarjih al-marjuh*),[5] which is obvious from their aforementioned arguments. Concerning the first, it is said that a human act is possible before the power is created for it, and every possible thing is subject to the power of God Most High. The result is obvious: if He creates a power for a person, the Mu'tazila say that at that point the possibility that the act could come into existence by the power of God Most High ceases by what He has established for the person, and it becomes impossible for it to come into existence by [God's power]. So what was possible with respect to the power of the Most High has become impossible with respect to it.

One cannot say that [the empowerment of] an accident is impossible for Him due to a cause, namely the attachment of originated power to it, or that it is impossible for a single act to be brought into existence through two different powers.

5. This is because the Mu'tazila say that human power (which has less weight) over an act means that God's power (which has more weight) does not affect the act, so what has less weight predominates over what has more.

The impossibility of something with regard to an accident does not affect its possibility with regard to the essence, because we say that there is no good reason for it to be impossible. Their allegation requires that the impossibility apply to the essence, because the originated power that they see as impeding the attachment of the eternal power to the act cannot impede it; rather, what is correct, according to both reason and revelation (*'aqlan wa-naqlan*), is the reverse.

They say: It remains possible concerning the act of a person that he could be stripped of the power to do it. We say: In that case, the act cannot be due to human power. Furthermore, according to your principle [273] of [God's] obligation to do what is best, stripping a person [of power to do an act] would not be possible after a person has been ordered to do it.

They say: If a person's power has no effect on his act, he cannot be rewarded or punished for doing it. It is known that the latter is false, so therefore so is the former. Their interdependence is proven by the fact that if the act is not an effect of his power, there would be no difference between him and his body and all other bodies in the world,[6] and if his accidents were joined together, their union would have no effect on him. Just as there would be no reward or punishment for this act, because he has no effect on any aspect of it, likewise there would necessarily be no reward or punishment for any of his acts, because he has no effect on any aspect of them. We say: Their interdependence is prevented by acquisition, which is sufficient for a person to attain reward and punishment for his act, and what you say does not make acquisition of the act impossible.

They say: How can a person be praised or blamed for what he does not do? In that case, people could have a basis for making a plea in the afterlife, and God Most High has said, "So the people may have no plea against God [for punishing them] after the Messengers [had warned them]" (4:165). We say: This concerns the first type [of act], and that results from his acquisition of it. They are also obligated by what we already said of their teaching, namely that they say that originated power has an effect on voluntary acts, although they agree with us that the Most High is the creator of that power and is the one who calls it into being by creating desire in the person and the power to decide to do it, and other

6. That is, a person's relationship to his own acts would be no different from the relationship of any other person or thing to his acts.

such causes of the act. If the causes of its existence are from the Most High, and with these causes the act becomes necessary and unavoidable, then the person is forced to do the act; God has forced him and made him do it by creating for him all the causes and things on which it depends, so that, given the existence of these causes, the person has no way to avoid doing the act. In addition, the Glorified One knows what act of obedience or disobedience the person is doing, [274] so the disobedient person would also have a plea [before God] according to their principle [that God must do what is best for His creatures], by saying, "Lord, why did You create desire in me? Indeed, why did You create me, since You knew that I am not one of those who are able to obey You? And since You did create me, why didn't You cause me to die when I was little, before I reached the age of accountability? And since you did cause me to reach it, why didn't you make me insane, not a commander of the earth from heaven, for that would be easier for me than enduring torture [in hellfire]. And since You made me rational, why did You make me accountable, when You knew that accountability would not benefit me in any way? Indeed, it is more disastrous for me than anything else!"

Fakhr [al-Din al-Razi] said, "One of the most clever of the Mu'tazila said, 'These two questions are the enemies of our school. Were it not for them, we would hold the place of honor [among theologians] comparable to the rank of chess among games.'" What he means is that the answers to these two questions would solve all the problems introduced by the Mu'tazila. The answers come from two directions: first, that God Most High knows that whatever He brings into existence must occur, and that whatever He will not bring into existence cannot occur; second, no preponderance of impetus exists that prevents an act (*lam yujad rujhan al-da'i imtana' al-fi'l*); if that were necessary, a problem would arise against them on these two issues.

This is what Imam Suhar al-'Abdi meant when he said, "They should be asked about [God's] knowledge [of what people will do], for if they affirm it, they also affirm [His] creation [of their acts],"[7] referring to His words "God knows all

7. At least one of the earliest Muslim groups identified by the heresiographers as upholding human power over their own acts, the Shabibiyya, allegedly felt that God's knowledge of what people will do would remove their free will, so they felt compelled to say that God does not know what people will do. Most of the Qadariyya and Mu'tazila, however, denied this linkage between God's knowledge and His power.

things" (Q 2:282) and "God is the creator of all things" (Q 13:16), "for they are two general questions concerning their attachment to human acts. Neither of them has anything to distinguish it from the other in this regard, for if you say this, and that whatever God knows He will not bring into existence cannot occur, that goes against your teaching, and your companions will disagree that God has knowledge of a possible thing that will not occur, so what about something that is innately impossible (*fa-ma zannuka bi-'l-mumtani' al-wuqu'*)?" We have already answered this question concerning the attachment of [God's] knowledge [to human acts]. By what is innately impossible, he is speaking comprehensively (*ma huwa shamil*) concerning that possible thing.

Note: Know that when the Glorified and Exalted One habitually gives a person the desire [to do something], followed by the power [to do it], so that he does not feel that he is forced to do the act [275] that comes to him, no matter how determined (*mahma sammama 'azmahu*) the person may be to do the act, God the Glorified helps him by creating it and creating the power to do it, whether it be an act of obedience or disobedience, as the Most High said: "Whoever desires this fleeting life shall soon receive in it whatever We will; We bestow Our gifts on whomever We please. But then We have prepared hell for him, where he will burn, disgraced and rejected" (17:18). He also said, "We bestow the bounty of your Lord on all—on these and those" (17:20). This bestowal (*imdad*) is arranged according to their desire, if He wills, and that bestowal is called help (*'awn*) and abandonment (*khidhlan*). So if you say that you interpret abandonment as a failure to help, in what sense is this a bestowal? I say it means that when the Glorified One does not help a person, but lets him have what is ruinous to his soul while creating that in him, He has bestowed on him [the state implied by the Prophet's prayer,] "God of majesty and generosity, do not leave us to ourselves (*la takilna 'ala anfusina*) for an instant (*tarfat 'ayn*)" (cf. Abu Dawud 2000, *Kitab al-adab* [42], bab 110, no. 5092) and by that bestowal the person appears to bring his act into existence, so fantasy and imagination have no doubt about that. Many have entered into that [fantasy and imagination], and were it not for the fact that God, by His grace and generosity, has supported the minds of the believers and torn away the veils of fantasies that darken the mind and exposed them to the suns of knowledge by which they understood the truth of the matter, they would be like others.

Therefore, some of them have interpreted the meaning of acquisition as the attachment of reward and punishment to a deed, in esteem, law, custom and intellect, and for this reason it is appropriate for a person be praised or blamed for his acts. But if we look to the inner meaning, as has been stated, and to the truth of the matter, it is not correct to make his act a rational cause of something. The Qur'an and the Sunna sometimes refer to human acts in the manner of "Enter the Garden because of what you have done" (16:32), and sometimes in the manner of "None of you will enter the Garden because of what he does."[8] Because one can find texts coming down on both sides of the issue, and in consideration of the obscurity of what is meant by acquisition, it is said that the scope of human volition (*al-jaza' al-ikhtiyari*) is narrower (*adaqq*) than a hair in the thought of al-Ash'ari.

Our shaykh[9] (may God love him greatly!) said, "What is affirmed for us in this matter is that we attribute to God Most High what He has attributed to Himself, namely creation, and to the human being what He attributed to him, namely acquisition. We refrain from describing that acquisition in such a way that would [276] lead to a doctrine of compulsion, because of the words [of the Prophet], peace and blessings be upon him, from our glorified and exalted Lord: 'Determination (*qadar*) is my secret. No one may know my secret.'"[10] Therefore, some of them say, "The human being is compelled (*majbur*) in the form of choice (*fi qalib mukhtar*)," which links the Qur'anic verse and the hadith in a number of ways:

First, it expresses the aspect of human acts found in the Qur'anic verse, which makes them the cause of reward, because of the appearance of choice a person has, which is not expressed in the hadith, which shows the hidden aspect of compulsion in human acts, which makes them like necessary acts, like the movement of the person who shivers, or colors and foods, and other such things that are not the cause of reward or punishment.

Second, it expresses human agency, because he appears to choose the act, although the reason the verse affirms this is because, legally speaking, human acts are the cause of reward, whereas the reason the hadith denies that works are the cause of reward is that, rationally speaking, human acts are not the cause of

8. The printed text reads "because of his knowledge" (*bi-'ilmihi*) rather than "because of what he does" (*bi-'amalihi*), but this is undoubtedly an error produced by switching the order of the letters *lam* and *mim*. Variants on this hadith can be found in the collections of al-Bukhari, Muslim, Abu Dawud, al-Tirmidhi, and Ahmad b. Hanbal.

9. Abu Zakariya Yahya b. Salih al-Afdali (d. 1202/1787).

10. I have not been able to find the source of this *hadith qudsi*.

reward. So the denial and the affirmation are not of the same thing; rather, the denial is of a rational cause, and the affirmation is of a legal cause.

Third, the meaning of the Qur'anic verse, "Enter it because of what you did" is [that it is] a mercy from God, and the meaning of the hadith is that no one enters Paradise because he deserves it because of what he did.

Fourth, the meaning of the verse is "Enter it because of what you did," although guidance and acceptance are only due to God's favor, so in fact no one enters it because of deeds alone.

Fifth, the hadith can be taken to mean only entering Paradise, whereas the verse can be taken to mean the attainment of ranks within it.

Sixth, "because of" in the verse means "in exchange for," whereas in the hadith it implies a causal relationship.

Seventh, the meaning of the hadith is that good deeds, insofar as they are human acts, do not allow the doer to enter Paradise unless they are accepted, and since that is so, and the matter of acceptance [277] belongs to God Most High, only those whose deeds are accepted by Him receive His mercy. The meaning of the verse is "Enter it because of what you did," namely an act that is accepted. In this case there is no contradiction between the verse and the hadith.

Ibn al-Banna'[11] al-Marrakushi said, concerning acquisition, "Everyone finds in himself the ability to advance toward something (*al-iqdam*) or refrain from it (*al-ihjam*). A person does not advance or refrain because he knows what God wants concerning this; rather, he advances or refrains because of what his own soul wills and desires, and because he is able to do so. After the fact, he knows that he was compelled to make that particular choice (*majbur fi 'ayn ikhtiyarihi*), but not beforehand. The direction from which he advanced or refrained (according to his understanding) is acquisition, and the direction from which the act actually occurred is compulsion. Both are correct (*haqq*): acquisition from the mode of being God's viceroy (*khalifa*), and compulsion with respect to reality (*min wajh al-haqiqa*). Accountability, reward and punishment are all placed by God Most High on acquisition with respect to the human being (*min wajh al-khalq*), not on compulsion with respect to reality."

11. The text reads Ibn al-Naba al-Marrakushi, but this is undoubtedly a misprint, requiring only the switching of the order of two letters in Arabic.

That is what he said. This is enough to guide a person to the path of guidance. It is best to avoid delving into obscure questions and their answers and argumentation with opponents, for although it was once a theological battle in need of defense, today it is a struggle (*jihad*) without enemies, and it tarnishes the purity of the hearts of God's friends, because much investigation into futile matters disturbs the purity of the light of truth in the darkness of the hearts, and that is one of the greatest defects.

[278] Section 5: Human Power Has No Effect on Anything

You know that originated power has no effect on any possible thing; it attaches [to them] without effect; its relationship to them is like the relationship of knowledge to its object. [Human power] merely attaches to its object in the locus for which it is created (*bi-mahalliha*) and does not go beyond its locus; there is no relationship between [the empowered act] and [human power], whether of effect or of anything else.

You know that the Mu'tazila say that a person produces (*yakhtari'u*) his own acts, although they agree with us that the originated power does not attach directly to anything except the empowered act, which is in the locus of the originated power, although they think that in the locus there is a cause that brings into existence something outside the locus of human power. They claim that the cause and the thing that is caused are both objects of human power at the same time, one directly and the other through the mediation of the cause. They do not speak of the generation of secondary effects (*tawallud*) in the locus of the originated power, except abstract knowledge (*al-'ilm al-nazari*), which they say is produced as a secondary effect by reflection (*al-nazar*) in the locus of the power over it.

According to their teaching, the generation of a secondary effect means that an originated thing is brought into existence by means of something produced by originated power. This does not contradict what we said earlier about the acknowledgment of secondary causes. They took this teaching from the philosophers concerning natural causes, according to what was said earlier, that nature (*al-tabi'a*) has an effect on its object,[12] as long as no impediment exists to pre-

12. That is, that causes necessarily produce certain effects.

vent it. According to them, necessary intelligence (*al-'aqliyya 'l-wajiba*) is not like knowledge, because of characteristics belonging to its essences (*li-ahkam li-dhawatiha*),[13] because nothing can prevent it, as was already explained. So the Mu'tazila took this teaching and called it generation [of secondary effects] (*tawallud*). They did not place secondary causes (*al-sabab al-muwallad*) on the same plane as rational causes (*al-'illa 'l-'aqliyya*), because an impediment may prevent a secondary effect.[14] They also changed the expression, so the source of their teaching would not be obvious; they said it is the act of the one who has produced the secondary cause.

If this were true, it could not produce a result, because a single effect cannot result from two causes (*mu'aththirayn*); of necessity, the effect of the cause on it prevents the effect of the power [that produced the cause] on it. To say that the person affects it by means of a secondary cause deflects the result of what is said, as has already been demonstrated, to mean that it is the act of its cause. Likewise, according to them, the exalted Creator [279] [does not produce][15] human acts; rather, people produce their own acts, and their acts are not acts of God Most High, because they do not allow the attribution of human acts that are evil to Him. Their assertion of secondary causation compels them toward the very thing from which they were fleeing, namely that, according to their teaching, a secondary effect is the act of the one who produced its cause.

One cannot say that the Mu'tazila were all in agreement concerning secondary causes, since al-Nazzam, who was one of them, attributed secondary effects to the glorified Creator, not in the sense that He did them, but in the sense that He created bodies according to natures and characteristics that require the origination of temporally produced effects arising from those natures and characteristics. He did not say that they are the act of the person who produced their cause.

Hafs al-Fard[16] said that [a secondary effect] occurs as a construct of the locus of [human] power and is determined by the choice of the person who produced

13. The text reads *al-ahkam li-dhawatiha,* but I believe this should be *li-ahkam li-dhawatiha.*

14. A primary cause necessarily produces its effect, but this is not the case with secondary causes.

15. It appears that a verb has been omitted from the text. The context would favor this translation.

16. The published text mistakenly reads Hafs al-Qird (the difference in writing being a single dot).

the cause, so it is the act of the of one who produced the cause, like cutting, bloodletting and slaughter,[17] but not if it does not involve the choice of the person who produced the cause, like the rush of air caused by rapid propulsion (*al-indifa'*) or something similar; the rush of air is not his act.

They also disagree concerning the time that human power no longer attaches to a secondary effect. Some said that it remains determined (*maqdur*) by the original act as long as the occurrence of something that is produced by the act is a cause that necessitates the occurrence of the effect; after this point, the effect of [human] power ceases. Others said that it only ceases to be determined [by the original act] when the secondary effect occurs and comes into existence, not when only the cause [of the secondary effect] occurs.

They also disagree concerning whether human color and foods can be secondary effects of human acts. Thumama b. Ashras said that these secondary effects are acts without an actor, but that would nullify proof for the affirmation of the Maker.[18] Mu'ammar, the author of *Al-Ma'ani,* said that all accidents occur in the natures of bodies, except will.

According to them, there are four types of secondary effects: force (*i'timad*), proximity (*mujawara*), reflection (*nazar*) that generates knowledge, and fragmentation (*waha'*), which is the separation of generated parts due to pain (*iftiraq al-ajza' al-mutawallida li-'l-alam*). Al-Jubba'i and his son [Abu Hashim] disagreed on whether the secondary effect is the force or the movement [produced by the act]; al-Jubba'i favored the latter, and his son [280] the former. According to the Mu'tazila, forces are due to the pull of muscles and the strength of the connection of nerves to limbs. All this is from the teaching of the naturalists (*al-tabayi'in*).

The result of the foregoing is that they disagree on the cause of pain. Some say it results from a force of one thing on another through a blow or cutting. Abu Hashim leaned toward this but then turned against this idea and settled on the answer that force produces the separation of parts, and he called this separation

17. That is, slaughter is caused by bloodletting, which is caused by cutting; the person who cuts produces the cause of slaughter, and the slaughter is his act.

18. The cosmological argument for the existence of God is based on the idea that all things are produced by a cause. The idea that an act can exist without an actor undermines this classic linchpin of theology.

fragmentation; he said[19] that force generates fragmentation, and fragmentation generates pain. So if God creates pain[20] in a body without the separation of parts or force, scholars agree that it is necessary (*daruri*).[21]

The difference in their opinions concerning colors and foods has to do with what happens when color is caused by the act of a dyer or washer, possibly from washing after boiling with bleach or other such things: is this an effect generated from a human act or did God simply create this without any human effect or act? The same question arises concerning foods that are prepared by cooking, or drinks and pastes (*ma'ajin*) that are prepared from several ingredients, or other such things that are described in medical books. One of the things that makes them say that colors are secondary effects from human acts is that if the juice produced from fresh, ripe dates is stirred in a *natiq*, which is the vessel [used for this], as is done for all juices, its color changes only when it is stirred. Most do not accept this as a secondary effect of human action. A small group of the Mu'tazila of Baghdad and Basra said that it is a secondary effect by extension, through analogy (*li-qiyasihim*).

The Mu'tazila also disagreed about whether or not it is possible for the acts of the glorified and exalted Creator to generate secondary effects. One group said no, because the power of the Most High is effective over the generality of all things. Another group said it is possible, because one cannot exclude the possibility that something that can occur from God Most High will produce a secondary cause that in turn produces an effect, unless there is an impediment; the issuance of a secondary cause is not an impediment, unless that is evident, so it must produce a secondary effect. That is a summary of what they say about secondary causation.

[281] Section 6: Against the Generation of Secondary Effects

You know from the foregoing, by decisive proof (*al-burhan al-qat'i*), that all originated things depend on the Creator, and that there is no effect from anything but Him on anything, whether in whole or in part. That is a refutation of what

19. The text reads "we say," but the context makes "he says" more likely. The difference in Arabic orthography is in the placement of dots.

20. The published text adds a *hamza*, making it *al-ma'* (water) instead of *alaman* (pain). This is undoubtedly incorrect.

21. That is, not the result of a human act.

they teach about secondary causation. There is no harm in our indicating some of the corollaries that necessarily derive from their insistence on the existence of an effect from two things, namely originated power and the act empowered by it, which is the secondary cause, because they claim that the secondary effect is produced of necessity once the secondary cause exists, and that the secondary effect is the act of the person who did the original act through originated power. This teaching leads to the absurd conclusion that there can be an act without a doer who willed it or feels that he has done it.

If a person shoots an arrow and he falls down dead before it reaches its target, but then it reaches it and hits a living person, who is wounded by it, who continues to experience pain until he finally dies, for example, this bleeding (*sariyat*) and the pains [according to the Muʿtazila] are the deeds of the one who shot the arrow, whose bones had [perhaps] already disintegrated (cf. al-Juwayni 1950, 233; al-Juwayni 2000, 127). There is no absurdity greater than attributing a killing to a dead man, given the elimination of what is required for the dead person to act; otherwise, there would be no proof for the existence of an act when the doer is alive. The existence of an act when there is no one to do it makes it impossible to formulate a proof for the existence of a Maker from the existence of originated things. Even if they say that the act does indicate an actor, their teaching does not require the existence of an actor at the time that the act takes place.

The correct response is that an act must be attributed to an actor, and its issuance (*suduruhu*) cannot be attributed to a person at a time that he cannot act, since its issuance from him requires that his condition be [sufficiently] sound [to perform the act], and prevention (*al-imtinaʿ*) eliminates soundness. This also requires that the death which follows the pains be a secondary effect from the one who caused the pain. To attribute to the shooter what happens to the victim after the pains that occur as a consequence of his act is tantamount to attributing the subsequent death to him. As has already been stated, they have no way to avoid this. Al-Jubba'i had no way to avoid this and had the audacity to rend the consensus of the *umma* by attributing the victim's death to the shooter who caused the pain, whereas the *umma* agrees [282] that the glorified Creator is the One Who gives life and death. Al-Jubba'i said the giver of death is someone else. If a person can give death, then he must also be able to give life, as that is the opposite of giving death, and according to the Muʿtazila power is over a thing and its opposite. They argue that secondary effects must be attributed to the person who did the original act, if these effects accord with the person's intention and motive, just like the act that is directly caused by originated power.

The response to them is that events follow others according to [God's] habit (*bi-hasab majra 'l-'ada*); their habitual sequence does not prove that one of these events has an effect on the other.[22] If this is rejected, then the root, to which one makes an analogy, and the branch, which is the thing being compared [to the root], are of equal value, falling upon the lack of proof for secondary effects, according to most scholars.

Another thing that contradicts their doctrine is their argument that we find that things happen according to motives and intentions. [Through this argument] they have helped us to prove that there is no secondary causation. Some examples [the Mu'tazila give to prove that secondary effects occur according to human motives and intentions] are satiation and quenching of thirst when we eat or drink; illness, health and death, according to most of the Mu'tazila; the heat produced from rubbing one body forcefully against another; the sparks flying from a firesteel when it is struck; the understanding of speech; the feeling of embarrassment or fear when speech is understood; and causing someone to feel embarrassed or afraid [when one speaks] (cf. al-Juwayni 1950, 234; al-Juwayni 2000, 128). Some of them say that satiation, quenching of thirst and heat are secondary effects produced [of necessity] by their causes, though most of them do not say this, and they are those who are right (*wa-'l-muhassilin min-hum*).

This first group alleges that bodies can be produced by secondary causes, although they are not, according to consensus, the type of thing that can be produced by human power. This is because if the flying of sparks from a firesteel when it is struck is a secondary effect, because it occurs according to human intention, then all other bodies should be able to generate such effects, because they are comparable. If they claim that the fire was hidden within the body, which then moved, and that the cause of the secondary effect was the movement of the body, not the existence of a body, no rational person could accept this, for there is nothing in flint or a firesteel before they are struck. Likewise, if one cuts

22. For example, God is in the habit of creating wetness of ground after creating the falling of raindrops. The Ibadis, like the Ash'arites, do not see this habitual sequence as proof that the wetness of the ground was caused by the falling of rain.

open a piece of wood like *markh*,[23] for example, with a saw, there is no fire in it, but when it is rubbed it appears.

If they reply that in these cases there are no secondary effects in these [283] matters for which they have made them necessary, they say this only because they cannot deny that one may intend a certain amount of food to produce satiation, yet it may not, or for a certain amount of water to quench one's thirst, yet it may not, or to injure someone by striking him, and yet he may not be injured. Likewise, a physician may treat a sick person so he might recover, and he may [not] recover.[24] Likewise, one may strike something with the aim of producing a spark, but it is possible that no spark will be produced. The same applies with trying to make someone understand or feel embarrassed or afraid, and with the heat produced from rubbing. So the effect is not caused by these things.

One should say to them: It has thus been established that there can be no extending (*itrad*) the effects of human power in the examples you have given, like shooting, wounding, lifting and carrying a heavy body, and other things that are in dispute. Concerning shooting, a person shoots and sometimes hits his mark, and sometimes does not; the wound may bleed, or it may heal without bleeding. A person who wishes to lift and carry something may succeed in doing so sometimes, and not succeed other times.

The teaching of the Muʿtazila concerning the movement of heavy things is that a heavy thing is moved to the right and to the left, not by pushing against it and lifting it, or, if someone wishes, lifting it and carrying it. They disagreed concerning this: the earlier Muʿtazila said that the pushing that moves it to the right and to the left then lifts it upward, but [Abu] Hashim and his followers said that is incorrect; rather, more movements are needed besides those that move it to the right and left, because what we depend on to produce a secondary effect is what we feel from the process, according to our motives and intentions,[25] and

23. According to Lane (1863–1893), *markh* is a certain kind of tree that quickly emits fire, has no leaves or thorns, and grows in small water-courses and hard grounds. Wooden instruments for producing fire were made from it. He identifies its Latin name as *Cynanchum viminale*.

24. "Not" does not appear in the published text.

25. The published text reads *qusurina*, "our inadequacies," but in all other instances the word "motives" (*dawaʿi*) was paired with "intentions" (*qusud*), which is undoubtedly correct in the current instance.

there is no doubt that we find that a person who has the power to move something to the right and to the left may not be able to lift it, so such a movement must not be sufficient for lifting.

They also disagreed concerning a group that lifts a heavy object, and what each individual in the group independently carries. Al-Ka'bi and 'Abbad al-Daymari[26] and their followers said that each one carries parts not carried by the others, and that no two people share in carrying a single part. Other Mu'tazila said that [284] each one of them affects each part, resulting in sharing. This is the teaching of most of them, but what they all say on both issues is false.

If we hold to the true teaching, which is to nullify the principle of secondary causation and to say that all contingent things depend a priori on God Most High, then there is no problem. If we accept it for the sake of argument, the teaching of the earlier scholars on the first issue is false by what Abu Hashim said, though what he says is also wrong, because it entails the conjoining of two comparable things (*ijtima' al-mithlayn*), because he said that there must be more movements, which is impossible. For the sake of argument, we may accept the possibility that two comparable things may be conjoined, but one should say to him: If the lifter produces one movement in this heavy object, it cannot be lifted except by moving it, for the person must undertake a movement in a body while it remains at rest (*sakin*) in its location (*bi-hayyizihi*). That would nullify the reality of the movement, because movement requires expulsion (*tafrij*), which is impossible. So the stipulation of more movements in an upward direction, in such a manner that it is moving in all directions, is a stipulation of something that will happen without stipulating it, which negates the reality of the stipulation.

As for their disagreement on the second problem concerning a group carrying a heavy object, if each one of them carries it independently, someone who held the first opinion, according to which no part is carried by any particular one of the carriers, or it is unclear [which of them is carrying it], said to 'Abbad: "If it is unclear [which of them is carrying it], then it would be impossible to lift the part concerning which there is no clarity, because the meaning of its lack of clarity is that it is taken up as a whole, or rather that the effect is on any one of its parts, not this particular part. This is impossible, because the whole does

26. The published text reads al-Damiri.

not exist except in one of its members; it has no separate existence. So if one of its individual parts is taken, that is an effect on a particular part, and that is the second section, which is what follows. If it is taken in only one of its individual parts, then the thing is nonexistent and is not a thing, in which case it could not be lifted. If the effect on it is particular to that part, it is also impossible to lift a particular part of it; it is no better than specifying any other part, because if the outcome is that it is receptive by itself, the carrying is of all the parts, so in what sense can one part be taken [285] by itself without any other? That is because if the carrying of none of the bearers is independent of that of the whole group, the aspect of specifying the part that is carried becomes clear, for example, if it is something that follows its head, because one cannot carry more than it. It would be similar for another part. The other, unlike what can be carried independently, has no way of being specified in that case." When he said this to 'Abbad, [the latter] said, "I don't know how one can specify the part you mentioned."

One should say to those who hold the second opinion: Is the secondary effect of the act of one of the bearers the same as the secondary effect of the act of another of them, or not? If so, a single effect would be caused by two things, which is impossible. If not, then the lifting of the body is accomplished by one of them, in which case the addition of the others is pointless. So those who say this are delivering a purely fantastical judgment.

One should say to those who say that the effect of each one of them is on each part: Concerning the secondary effect on this part from the act of Zayd, for example, is it the same as the secondary effect from the act of 'Amr? In other words, is the lifting caused by Zayd the same as the lifting caused by 'Amr, or is there an effect on this piece from one person's lifting of it, and another effect from another person's lifting of it? In the first case, a single effect would result from two causes, and in the second case the lifting of the body is by only one of the two effects.

If you look in the books of jurisprudence written by our companions, you will find that they speak of secondary effects in some matters of jurisprudence, but not in matters of doctrine, because to believe in that is pure fantasy, leading to bewilderment and corruption, because the outcome is the necessity of positing a single effect existing between two causes, and the existence of an act without an actor, or an actor who has no will or sense of what he has done, or other such impossibilities discussed here at length.

[286] Section 7: God Is Not Obligated To Do What Is Best

We have already said that the glorified and exalted God created human beings, and created their acts, and created reward and punishment for those acts, without any requirement on the Most High to do what is good or best for them. Otherwise, it would be necessary that there be no accountability or trial in this world or the next, for all acts, whether good or evil, beneficial or harmful, equally point to the overwhelming nature of His power, the wideness of His knowledge, and the execution of His will. None of that, neither perfection nor deficiency, reaches the essence of the Most High. God exists and nothing is with Him; He is now as He always has been. The Glorified One honors whomever He wishes in an inexplicable manner with different types of favors out of sheer grace, not because of an inclination toward him, or because he deserves this in such a way as to make this obligatory on Him. Likewise, He imposes on whomever He wishes indescribable types of torment, not in order to relieve His anger or because of some harm He has suffered from the person.

These acts are indications to us of the existence of the Glorified One, as has been explained. If He were obligated to do what is good for human beings, He would not have imposed obligations on them. Nor is He obligated to do what is best for them; if that were so, He would not have created the infidel or the poor person, because it would be better for them not to be created, rather than be tormented in this world and the next. It would be best for human beings if He created them in Paradise.

In general, if God were obliged to do what is best, He would not test people at all. Al-Ash'ari debated this point with al-Jubba'i.[27] If you know that all acts are equal with respect to God Most High, that He freely chooses whatever He does (*wa-annahu mukhtar fi jami'iha*), and that nothing is rationally obligatory for Him and that the sayings of our companions concerning the necessity of reward

27. This refers to the famous example of three brothers that al-Ash'ari allegedly put to his teacher, al-Jubba'i, in order to point out the flaws in the Mu'tazilite doctrine that God must do what is best for His creatures. Watt (1973, 305) pointed out that the story is likely apocryphal, because al-Jubba'i, unlike his predecessors among the Basran Mu'tazila, denied that God must do what is best, and by al-Ghazali's citation of this story as a criticism of Mu'tazilism, without saying that it had previously been used by al-Ash'ari.

and punishment point only to a necessity required by His wisdom, then you know the impossibility that any act of the Most High be for a purpose (*li-gharad*), because if He had a purpose in doing something, it would not be obligatory for Him, and as long as there is no purpose that causes it, then the words "Your Lord creates and chooses what He pleases" (Q 28:68) become understandable.

Furthermore, [if an act of God had a] purpose, it would either be eternal, which would necessitate the eternity of the act, whereas its origination has already been proven, or [God's purpose] would be originated, in which case it would depend on another purpose, and there would be an infinitely regressing series of purposes, which would result in originated things that have no beginning, and [287] we have already proved that such a notion is false.

Furthermore, the purpose would either be a benefit to Him or to the person, both of which are impossible. Concerning the first, that would necessarily mean describing His exalted essence by originated things, and that there is a deficiency in His essence that is perfected by His act. The second alternative [must also be rejected], because of the lack of obligation on Him to do what is good or best, and because the person's goal is simply to obtain pleasure or to repel pain, and God Most High is able to make that benefit reach the person without the mediation of an act. It would also mean that a thing is caused by itself or [by another cause, which is then caused by another cause, resulting in] an infinitely regressing series of causes, because [otherwise] the implication would be that this benefit is for itself.

We demonstrate this by saying: What is the thing that makes the creation of that benefit necessary, or that it must come into existence by means of an act? If someone says, "Because it is a benefit," this requires that a thing be caused by itself, because it becomes its own goal. If someone says, "For an additional purpose," we have already written a response to this, that this would require an infinite series of causes, and that the meaning of the purpose include the act, according to a wisdom that rationally impels its coming into existence in such a way that it would mean a deficiency if He did not do it, so He is required to do the act.

Alternatively, the act has no purpose or cause; rather, the act is not obligatory for Him, because that would mean that something has overpowered Him and that He has no choice, as we explained earlier. The choice is what results in His doing or not doing the act, whereas if there were a purpose for the act, He could not choose not to do it, and you know that the Most High must have the power to choose. So it is wrong to say that any one of His acts has a purpose that leads Him to do it. The Most High said, "Your Lord creates and chooses what He pleases" (Q 28:68).

Just as you know the necessity of denying that the acts of the Most High have a purpose, you must also know the necessity of denying this regarding His laws (*ahkamihi*). What the scholars of jurisprudence say concerning the motives for laws (*'ilal al-ahkam, ration legis*) is simply a way of saying that the imposition of the law confers a benefit (*huwa bi-'l-ja'l al-shar'i tafaddulan*), not to say that there is a rational motive (*la bi-'l-hukm al-'aqli*) to which the law is responding. Therefore, in discussions of the motives for laws, like that of Ibn al-Hajib, who said that "motive" can mean the impetus (*al-ba'ith*) for a law, what he meant is the impetus for the person who must follow this law, [288] not the impetus for the Most High in commanding obedience to it.

Likewise, concerning expressions in the Qur'an and Sunna that can give the impression that they are speaking of causation (*al-ta'lil*) in the sense of purpose (*al-aghrad*), as in the words of the Most High, "I only created jinn and people so that they might worship Me" (51:56), the *lam* [translated here as "so that"] is placed there only to indicate the outcome (*al-sayrura wa-'l-'aqiba*).[28] Like it are His words, "So he might be an enemy and a sorrow to them" (28:8).[29] Or it can be placed like a guarantor of a loan, in accordance with what was said elsewhere.

The Mu'tazila who accept the idea of purposes that necessitate [God's acts] and judgments give a specious argument when they say, "If an act or judgment occurs without a purpose, then what issues from it is necessarily foolish and futile, but the Most High is wise, so that is impossible for Him. Therefore, it is impossible for Him to act or make a judgment without a purpose."

We say there is no necessity [of folly and futility when acts and judgments are without purpose], because folly, according to custom, is an expression of ignorance of what is beneficial and of weak-mindedness. The foolish person may even

28. Although al-Thamini's interpretation is possible from a philological point of view, it is unlikely that this is what the Qur'an means, since the Qur'an clearly states that most jinn and people do not worship or serve God.

29. This is in the story of Pharaoh's wife finding the infant Moses in a basket on the river and taking him into her household.

do something that is harmful to himself or that kills him instantly or eventually, while he is unaware, or while he is aware, but because of his ignorance and weak-mindedness he prefers an empty pleasure that cannot endure over mighty ends that remain. As for futility, this is customarily applied to an act that is done in bewilderment and aimlessness (*'adam al-qasd*). None of this has any necessary relationship with the denial of purpose (*nafy al-gharad*), because we say that the glorified Creator has no purpose in anything He does, although all His acts accord with His knowledge and will, and nothing we do can harm Him (*la yalhaquhu darar min qibalina*), nor do His deeds renew His perfection. Indeed, He is the One who has no need of anything for His essence or His perfections, from all eternity and forevermore. The wisdom attributed to the Most High is an expression of His knowledge of things and His ability to strengthen (*ihkamiha*) and perfect them (*itqaniha*). These require knowledge and power, not purposeful action.

Concerning whether His wisdom and creating are attributes or actions, I discussed this in the commentary.[30] If you understand this regarding the acts of the Most High, then understand His laws in a similar way, for they also accord with His knowledge, and no deficiency in them reaches Him (*la yatatarraqu ilayhi min qibaliha naqs*), regardless of how it appears to His servants. If the Mu'tazila interpret folly and futility as purposeless, we can, for the sake of argument, accept [289] this, but we reject exceptionalism (*mana'na 'l-istithna'iyya*). In sum, we reject the application of these two words to this affirmation with regard to the Most High because they have a meaning that is impossible for Him, although, as we said, they customarily indicate this, not because they indicate a denial of purpose, as they say.

Note: Know that the Mu'tazila say that God must do what is good and best for His servants. They also say that graciousness is incumbent on Him (*awjabu 'l-lutf*), that is, He must create something that inclines a person to obey His command, without having it reach the point of coercion. They say that He must give the person who is subject to His commands a sound mind (*kamal 'aql*), and empower him, and remove from him any obstacles that might prevent him from doing what he is commanded to do, so that if He fails to do that, they must oppose

30. Perhaps he means *Al-Nur* (1306/1888–1889), his commentary on Abu Nasr Fath b. Nuh al-Malusha'i's theological poem, *Al-Nuniyya*.

Him and demand that He give them what is their right. Our Lord is too exalted for that! The Messenger of God spoke the truth about them when he said, "The Qadariyya are God's opponents concerning [His] determination [of things]" (cf. al-Muttaqi 2001, no. 569). Both reason and revelation declare their doctrine to be a lie, as you know.

Section 8: God's Knowledge of What People Will Do Does Not Compel Them to Do These Things

Once you know that all acts depend on (*mustanida ila*) God Most High from the outset, without intermediary, and that no one else has any effect on any aspect of them, you will know that all acts are equal with respect to God; none of them may be called good with respect to His essence or His attribute, nor can any of them be called bad. There is, therefore, no room for the mind to understand any of God's laws, for they have no cause (*sabab*), as you know. So what is good according to the Shari'a pertains only to what they are commanded to do (*illa ma qila fi-hi if'aluhu*). Likewise, nothing is bad except what is prohibited (*illa ma qila la taf'aluhu*), as has already been explained.

The Mu'tazila say that voluntary acts are rationally good or bad, and that some of them are necessarily understood by the mind, like the goodness of beneficial truthfulness and faith, and the evil of harmful lying and unbelief, and that others are not rationally comprehensible through reflection, like the goodness of telling the truth [290] when it brings harm, and the evil of telling a beneficial lie, and others that cannot be understood without the teaching of the law, like the goodness of fasting on the last day of Ramadan, and the evil of fasting on the first day of Shawwal. They say concerning this type of law that the lawgiver [the Prophet] brings information from the mode of the locus, not that he establishes a law, like a wise man who informs people that a particular land is hot or cold, for example.

They also disagree among themselves. The earlier Mu'tazila said that deeds are inherently good or bad, and some of them said this is because of a characteristic that attaches to the deed. For example, fasting breaks lust, which leads to a lack of corruption, whereas adultery includes the mixing of lineages,[31] which leads to the birth of illegitimate children. Another group of them distinguished between evil and good by saying that evil is bad because of its attribute (*li-sifatihi*), whereas good is good because of its essence (*li-dhatiha*). Their proof is that all essences are equal, and the distinction between them is only because of their attributes, so if a deed were bad because of its essence, its evil would attach to the Most High. Al-Jubba'i and his followers said that the mind approves and disapproves [of an act] because of an aspect (*wajh*) and consideration (*i'tibar*), so the beating of an orphan is approved if it is for purposes of discipline, and disapproved if it is for some other reason.

The refutation of all this is in what was said earlier: that human beings have no effect on any aspect of their acts, so their obligation or prohibition are not good because of human reason. The laws of the Shari'a are all based on the fact that these deeds are commanded because they entail reward or punishment, or do not entail reward or punishment, as has already been explained. If deeds were described as good or bad because of their essences or because of a necessary attribute, God would not have ordered the unbelievers to believe, and this last is false by consensus.

The clarification of the dependence (*al-mulazama*) [of judgment concerning acts on God's will alone] is that the Most High knew that the unbeliever would not believe, so to order him to believe is to order him to do the impossible, which is bad [from the perspective of human reason]. Furthermore, if a deed is good or bad because of its essence or because of a necessary attribute, it would never vary, sometimes being good and sometimes being bad, or else opposites would be conjoined, as if somebody says, "Tomorrow I will tell a lie," which could be either true or false. [291] In other words, if his saying this is good, because he told the truth, but it is [also] bad, because it necessarily entails the occurrence of its corollary, telling a lie, which is bad. There is no doubt that it would be good for him to go against his word and avoid what is bad.

To say that a good deed is always good and a bad deed is always bad necessitates in daily speech the conjunction of the characteristics of inherent good and

31. *Ikhtilat al-ansab*: I am assuming that the text, which reads *ikhtilat al-insan* ("mixing of the human being"), is in error.

evil, which are necessarily contradictory—the good cannot be bad, because of the inherent contradiction in their meaning, according to usage and understanding, as Saʿd [al-Taftazani] said, that good and bad are equal because they are opposites.

It can also be explained another way, that the person [who said he would lie the next day] must either lie the next day or tell the truth: in the first case, evil attaches to him because he lied, and good attaches to him because he told the truth in what he said in the first place, and goodness must attach to what is good. So in what he said the second day what is good and what is not good (*al-hasan wa-'l-la hasan*)[32] are conjoined, and that is the conjoining of opposites. In the second case [if he tells the truth on the second day], the goodness of what he said on the second day attaches to him, because he told the truth, and its evil attaches to him because he told a lie on the first day, so two opposites are conjoined. This conjoining of opposites occurs in the first three [Muʿtazilite] opinions, but not in the fourth, [that of al-Jubba'i and his followers,] because in this case a deed is not simultaneously being described as good and bad, but through different considerations, for example, the conjoining of paternity and prophethood in a single person through two distinct attributions.

Section 9: Divine Law Has No Rational Foundation

The corruption of the Muʿtazilite doctrine that the laws of the Shariʿa concerning human acts can be rationally discerned, even without a prophetic mission, can also be clarified by admitting, for the sake of argument, the principle of the rational necessity of deeming something good or evil because of the contradiction between different perspectives, in order that the corruption of their opinion on this matter may become manifest. If we consider gratitude to the Most High for His blessings on us before the coming of the law, according to them reason would make gratitude to [292] the Most High obligatory, without requiring the coming of a lawgiver, because knowledge of the Most High and the knowledge that He bestows blessings are rationally comprehended without the law, as are the goodness of thanking the One who bestows blessings and the evil of ingratitude to

32. The published text reads "what is good and what is better" (*al-hasan wa-'l-ahsan*), but this is probably an error.

Him. Therefore, the obligation to give thanks and the prohibition of ingratitude are understood without the law.

We will say to them: This obligation to give thanks before the Shari'a must have a benefit, because if there is no benefit to it, then it is not good until it becomes obligatory. But the affirmation of a benefit before the coming of the Shari'a is absurd, because either its benefit goes to the person who gives thanks, or to the Lord Who is thanked. If it goes to the person, the benefit is either immediate or postponed, or all the allotments [of benefit] are void. The falseness of its going to the person immediately is because the immediate impact on him is only fatigue. The falseness of its going to him later is because, according to consensus, the intellect had no ability to understand the affairs of the afterlife before the coming of the law. The falseness of its going to the Lord Most High is because He transcends any renewal of His perfection; indeed, in His essence He has no need of people and their deeds. This point of view is rational and repels the obligation of giving thanks and contradicts their point of view which makes it obligatory, which is the comprehension that the Most High bestows blessings.

If they say, "We do not accept that there is no benefit to giving thanks before the coming of the Law; indeed, there is a benefit to the person, and that is safety from the punishment that could be imposed for turning away from giving thanks," we say that likewise it is possible for the act of giving thanks to be punished, for two reasons:

First, he has caused fatigue to someone who belongs to God Most High and has done this without His permission. In this he is like someone who thanks a king who has enabled him to receive a blessing, in that he causes the king's servant fatigue by giving thanks for it without his permission. There is no doubt that by thanking the king for this blessing, he has exposed himself to punishment.

[293] Second, it is a matter of an extremely generous king giving him a little piece of barley bread, for example, while he has treasure-houses of different types of food and infinite wealth, and it would not diminish him in any way for him to give him from his stores. Then that poor, needy person mentions the king and praises him in social gatherings for giving him this piece of barley bread. He would deserve punishment from the king for mocking him and thinking little of him, making him out to be a coward by praising him for something that imposes no burden on him at all. There is no doubt that all the blessings of this life and the next are like nothing compared to the greatness of God Most High and the wideness of

His dominion and majesty. So it is clear to you by this that for reason to enter into the laws of God Most High concerning acts with the scale of approval and disapproval is to enter with a faulty scale that will make its owner turn back exhausted.

If you say, "All this clashes with what you have affirmed before from the teaching of your imams, who agree with the doctrine of the Mu'tazila," I say, as for its clashing with it, you are right; what I have affirmed here is the teaching of the company of our companions, as well as the Ash'arites. As for the teaching of some of our imams being the same as that of the Mu'tazila, this is incorrect, as I have already explained, because of the evident difference between the two schools: the Mu'tazila say that the judge is reason and that the law is an affirmation of rational judgment, and that it does not bring anything that differs from this, whereas the teaching of those imams is that judgment belonged to reason before the coming of the law, but after it comes, the law is the foundation, and it may bring something that does not accord with human reason. So there is a difference.

Another thing that demonstrates the denial of the principle that good and bad can be rationally known is that we say, regarding someone with respect to whom all acts are equal, that nothing he does can be deemed good or bad. Acts are equal with respect to the Creator; nothing He does can be deemed good or bad, because if an act is deemed good, this requires a preference for doing it over [294] not doing it, and if it is deemed bad, this requires a preference for abandoning it over doing it, but deeming them equal negates any preference. This is why we said previously that what is preferred in contingent things is simply whatever the Most High wills.

The demonstration (*bayan*) that all acts are equal with respect to Him is that the Glorified One transcends benefit and harm. If we are able to do something that causes us no harm, and if by not doing it no benefit escapes us, then there are no repercussions from our doing it or not doing it. All acts with respect to the Most High are like this supposed act with respect to us. Furthermore, if all acts were not equal with respect to Him, it would be better for Him to bring them into existence than not to bring them into existence, which would lead to His perfection being due to His acts, and you know that He is perfect in His essence and in His attributes, which are the same as His essence, not by His acts. So the conclusion is that with respect to the Most High, nothing is either good or evil. And God grants success (*wa-bi-'l-lahi 'l-tawfiq*).

Glossary

Biographical Dictionary

References

Index

GLOSSARY

ʿAbbāsids: a dynasty of caliphs who were descendants of the Prophet Muḥammad's uncle, al-ʿAbbās. They ruled from their capital, Baghdad, from 132–656/750–1258.

Abode of Islam and Abode of War: Traditional Islamic sources divide the world between the "Abode of Islam," ruled by Muslims, and the "Abode of War," which is outside the domain of Islam and is therefore subject to attack. The radical Khawārij deemed all who did not join their community to belong to the Abode of War.

Abū: "father of"; it was customary among the Arabs to refer to a man not by his own name, but as the father of his eldest son. In the genitive grammatical construction, Abū becomes Abī, hence ʿAlī b. Abī Ṭālib means ʿAlī, son of Abū Ṭālib.

acquisition (*kasb*): Ibāḍīs, Ashʿarites, and Māturīdites use this term with reference to voluntary human acts; God creates the acts, and humans, by virtue of the exercise of their will, "acquire" them, or acquire the power to do them.

ahl al-dhimma: the "people of protection," that is, non-Muslims who live under Muslim rule and pay the *jizya*.

ahl al-istiqāma: "the People of Straightness," an Ibāḍī term for their own sect.

Āmīn: "Amen," recited by Sunnīs in prayer after the recitation of the Fātiḥa.

Ashʿarism/Ashʿarites: a Sunnī theological school founded by Abū 'l-Ḥasan al-Ashʿarī in 300/912, according to Muslim sources. The teachings of this school were the basis of the curriculum in the Niẓāmiyya colleges founded by the Seljūq vizier, Niẓām al-Mulk (the first of which opened in Baghdad in 459/1067), leading to the predominance of Ashʿarism in the Middle East.

attributist: a term coined by Wolfson to signify a theologian who believes that God's attributes are real things that inhere in His essence.

Azāriqa/Azraqites: an early, violent sect of the Khawārij, followers of Nāfiʿ b. al-Azraq (d. 65/685). Their doctrines include: the permissibility of killing unrepentant sinners, who are deemed apostates from Islam; migration away from other Muslims; administering difficult tests to those who wished to join them (such as killing a "non-Muslim" relative); "excommunication" of Muslims who did not make the migration to their group; and the licitness of killing the women and children of their enemies.

Azd: an Omani tribe, large numbers of which lived in Baṣra, Iraq, and were active in the early Ibāḍī movement.

'azzāba: town councils that developed among Ibāḍīs in North Africa after the end of the Rustamid Imāmate.

Badr: the first great battle between about 300 Muslims of Medina and 1,000 pagans of Mecca, on 21 Ramaḍān 2/17 March 624; it was a decisive victory for the Muslims, leading to expectations of future victory.

barā'a: dissociation. In theory, Ibāḍīs are supposed to dissociate from everyone except observant, righteous Ibāḍīs.

Baṣra: a city in southern Iraq originally built during the caliphate of 'Umar b. al-Khaṭṭāb (13–23/634–644) to house Arab soldiers in the newly conquered territory, it played a major role in political and theological developments for several centuries in early Islam. It is the city where the Ibāḍī sect originated.

bi-lā kayf: "without how," the Sunnī doctrine that anthropomorphic descriptions of God must be accepted without explanation or rationalization. Frank (1992, 25) says that the denial of *kayfiyya* in God is not a renunciation of reason, but an affirmation of God's transcendence and lack of comparability to created things.

bint: girl or daughter.

Bū Sa'īdī dynasty: rulers of Oman from (de facto) 1154/1741 or (de jure) 1167/1753 to the present day, and rulers of Zanzibar and other parts of the Swahili coast until January 1964.

caliph (*khalīfa*): "deputy" or "successor," this was the title given to the ruler of the Islamic empire until the Mongol conquest of Baghdad in 656/1258, after which the Mamluks of Egypt retained a member of the 'Abbāsid family as titular caliph until the Ottoman conquest of Egypt in 923/1517, after which the title was surrendered to the Ottoman sultan, who retained it until the caliphate was formally abolished by the Republic of Turkey in March 1924. "Caliph" carries a sense of religious legitimacy, whereas "sultan" does not. The first four caliphs, who ruled from Medina after Muḥammad's death, were known among Sunnī Muslims as the Rightly-Guided Caliphs (9–40/632–661). They were followed by the Umayyad dynasty, which ruled from Damascus from 40–132/661–750, and the 'Abbāsid dynasty, which ruled from Baghdad from 132–656/750–1258. The title was also used by the Fāṭimids and some other rulers in North Africa and Muslim Spain, and continues to be used by the king of Morocco.

companion/*ṣāhibī*, pl. *ṣaḥāba*: the Muslims who lived in the time of the Prophet.

dhimmī: one of the *ahl al-dhimma*.

dhikr: the remembrance of God, frequently commanded in the Qur'an. It is customary for many Muslims to do *dhikr* after their formal prayers, through the recitation of standard phrases ("Glory be to God," "Praise be to God," and "God is greater"). Sufis developed rituals of *dhikr* involving the repetition of "There is no god but Allah" and certain of God's names. Many of al-Rawāḥī/Abū Muslim al-Bahlānī's poems are reflections on God's names, and are also called *dhikr.*

dīnār: a gold coin first struck in the year 72/691–692.

dirham: a silver coin in the Islamic monetary system from the time of Muḥammad through the 'Abbāsid caliphate.

fajr: dawn, or the prayer said at dawn, before sunrise.

Fātiḥa: the seven-versed opening chapter of the Qur'ān. The *Fātiḥa* is recited at the beginning of each *rak'a* in Muslim ritual prayer.

Fāṭimids: an Ismā'īlī Shī'ī dynasty that conquered North Africa beginning in 297/909, founded the city of Cairo, Egypt, in 359/970, and ruled until ousted by Ṣalāḥ al-Dīn al-Ayyūbī (Saladin) in 567/1171.

fatwā: a nonbinding legal decision issued by a scholar (a muftī) in response to a question.

fiqh: Islamic jurisprudence, the process by which God's law is discerned. There are four "roots" or sources of jurisprudence (*uṣūl al-fiqh*): the Qur'ān, Sunna, *ijmā'* (consensus), and *ijtihād* (systematic individual reasoning through analogy).

fitna: trial, temptation, or sedition. The "great *fitna*" is the civil war that erupted in the Muslim community after the death of 'Uthmān b. 'Affān (35/656).

ḥadd,* pl. *ḥudūd: punishments for particular offenses specified by the Qur'an or Ḥadīth; because these are considered offenses against God's ordinances, *ḥudūd* punishments cannot be altered. Some say the *ḥudūd* are limited to punishments specified in the Qur'an, which are four: *sariqa* (theft), *qat' al-ṭarīq* (highway robbery), *zinā* (fornication or adultery), and *qadhf* (unproven accusation of *zinā*). Sunna provided punishments for two more offenses that are often included among the *ḥudūd*: *sukr* (intoxication) and *ridda* (apostasy from Islam).

ḥadīth: a narration of something the Prophet Muhammad said or did; the initial letter is capitalized if the reference is to the corpus of such narrations rather than a single narration. Ḥadīth is the source of Sunna, the second "root" of Islamic jurisprudence, and is of crucial importance for the interpretation of the Qur'ān. It adds considerably to Islamic doctrine as well. Ḥadīth was originally an oral tradition; it was first committed to writing in the late eighth century, and the "canonical" collections date from the mid-ninth century. Muslims have long recognized that ḥadīths were forged, and established a mechanism for critiquing ḥadīth authenticity through examining the chain of transmission (*isnād*) attached to each narrative; authenticity was determined on the basis of the reliability of the transmitters. Ḥadīths are then judged to be "sound" (*ṣaḥīḥ*), "good" (ḥasan), "weak" (*ḍaʿīf*), or "forged" (*mawḍūʿ*). Six collections of Ḥadīth have "canonical" status among Sunnī Muslims, but only the collections of al-Bukhārī and Muslim b. al-Ḥajjāj are considered completely "sound." Western-trained academics tend to be skeptical of the authenticity of many ḥadīths that were traditionally accepted as sound.

ḥadīth qudsī: divine sayings found not in the Qur'ān but in Ḥadīth.

ḥāl: see mode.

Ḥanafī: a Sunnī legal school that predominates in Iraq, Turkey, and Central and South Asia.

al-Ḥārithiyya: a subsect of the Ibāḍiyya that allegedly broke from Abū ʿUbayda by accepting the doctrine of free will.

Ḥarūrā': a village near Kūfa, Iraq, where the first Khawārij went after seceding from ʿAlī's army at the battle of Ṣiffīn in 37/657.

Ḥashwiyya: a contemptuous epithet applied to those who reject the use of reason in theology and insist on a literal interpretation of the Qur'ān and Ḥadīth's anthropomorphic descriptions of God.

Hawāzin: an Arab tribe that fought against the Muslims at the battle of Ḥunayn, shortly after the Muslim conquest of Mecca in early 8/630.

Ḥijāz: the center section of the west coast of the Arabian peninsula, location of Mecca and Medina.

hijra: migration; if spelled with a capital *H,* it means the emigration of the Prophet and the Muslims from Mecca to Medina in 622 CE, the starting point of the Muslim calendar. Some of the Khawārij felt that "true" believers must imitate the Prophet's example and leave the society of the "unbelievers."

ḥudūd: see *ḥadd.*

Ḥusayniyya: an Ibāḍī subsect, followers of Aḥmad b. al-Ḥusayn (early third/ninth century) of Tripoli, Libya. They held that no one who believes in God can be called a polytheist, even if his beliefs contradict those of Islam. There were still some Ḥusaynīs living east of the Jabal Nafūsa in Libya in the sixth/twelfth century. They allegedly remerged with mainstream Ibāḍism in the seventh/thirteenth century through the influence of Abū Yaḥyā Zakariyya b. Ibrāhīm al-Bārūnī.

hypocrite (*munāfiq*): in the Qur'ān this means those who outwardly profess Islam while inwardly disbelieving and conspiring against the Muslims. Ibāḍīs apply this term to non-Ibāḍī Muslims and to sinning Ibāḍīs.

Ibāḍīs: called "moderate Khawārij" by non-Ibāḍīs, Ibāḍīs define themselves as a moderate Islamic school that is not Khārijite at all. They restrict the use of the terms "Muslim" and "believer" to piously observant Ibāḍīs, but do not condemn sinners or non-Ibāḍīs as unbelievers or apostates, who are deemed guilty of the unfaithfulness of hypocrisy (*kufr nifāq*) or ingratitude for God's blessings (*kufr ni'ma*).

ibn, pl. banū: "son of," abbreviated as *b.*

***ijmā'*:** consensus of the Muslims, one of the roots of Islamic jurisprudence.

***ijtihād*:** systematic individual reasoning in jurisprudence. It is one of the four roots of jurisprudence in all sects of Islam, although its role varies among the different Muslim schools and sects. In classical Islam, *ijtihād* was employed only for legal problems on which there was no consensus and for which there was no explicit ruling found in the Qur'ān or Sunna. It operated by means of analogy with a precedent found in the Qur'ān or Sunna, when the purpose of the preceding ruling could also be applied to the new situation. For example, since a ḥadīth allows coitus interruptus in order to prevent conception, other forms of contraception might also be allowed.

imām: it literally means "leader," and is the title used by Ibāḍīs and Shī'a (and sometimes by Sunnī political theorists) for the rightful head of the Muslims. Whereas the Shī'a believe that the imām is chosen by God from the Prophet's household, specifically 'Alī b. Abī Ṭālib and his descendants, the Ibāḍiyya believe he should be chosen for his piety, without regard to tribe or lineage. Modern Sunnī Muslims often use "Imām" as an honorific for respected religious scholars, but Ibāḍīs do this only rarely, and seemingly only since the twentieth century. With a lower-case *i*, an imām is anyone who leads a group of Muslims in prayer.

imāmate: the rule of an Imām. In Ibāḍism, there are four types of imāmate: the hidden or secret imāmate (*imāmat al-kitmān*); the imāmate of defense (*imāmat al-difā'*), which is an emergency appointment of someone as imām in order to repel an invading enemy; the activist imāmate (*imāmat al-shirā'*), when at least forty men have pledged to die in order to establish a righteous imāmate; and the declared imāmate (*imāmat al-ẓuhūr*), that is, one that exists openly after enemies have been defeated.

***isnād*:** the chain of authorities that authenticates a ḥadīth.

***isti'rāḍ*:** the policy pursued by radical Khawārij of assassinating those they believed to have renounced Islam by committing grave sins without repentance.

al-Jabal al-Akhḍar: the "Green Mountain" region in Oman's interior that is the heart of Ibāḍism in that country, where, until the modern period, the two major towns of scholarship were Nizwā and Rustāq.

jinn: a species that, according to the Qur'ān, was created before human beings, from flames of fire. Jinn and human beings are both commanded to believe in God and obey Him, and are subject to reward for obedience and punishment for disobedience.

Jirba/Djerba: an island off the southern coast of Tunisia, home to an Ibāḍī community.

***jizya*:** the "poll tax" levied on non-Muslims who live under Islamic rule.

***kāfir*, pl. *kuffār*:** this word is usually translated as "unbeliever," which does not reflect Ibāḍī usage (see *kufr*); in this work it is translated as "infidel."

Karrāmiyya: an allegedly anthropomorphist sect named after Abū 'Abdallāh b. Muḥammad b. Karrām (ca, 190–255/806–869), an Arab resident of Persia who was an ascetic and popular preacher. Ibn Karrām's theological ideas are expounded in his book, *'Adhāb al-qabr* ["punishment in the grave"], in which he expressed the view that Munkar and Nakīr, the two angels who, according to Ḥadīth, will question people in the grave after their deaths and give them a foretaste of their eternal reward or punishment according to their answers, are the same as the two guardian angels that are at the right and left shoulder of each person. This work is no longer extant, and its contents can only be known through citations in other works. He is also accused of anthropomorphism—that is, interpreting anthropomorphic expressions concerning God in the Qur'an in their literal sense, saying that God is a substance (*jawhar*) and a body (*jism*) of finite dimensions. The Karrāmiyya flourished in the central and eastern Muslim lands until the Mongol invasions of the early thirteenth century.

Kaysāniyya: a Shī'ī sect that existed in the late first/seventh and early second/eighth centuries, recognizing as the fourth imām Muḥammad b. al-Ḥanafiyya, a third son of 'Alī b. Abī Ṭālib by a second wife of the Ḥanafī tribe, not by the Prophet's daughter, Fāṭima. Like many of the early Shī'a, they allegedly said that God can change His mind, a doctrine known as *badā'*.

***khalīfa*:** deputy, successor, or vicegerent. In the Qur'ān, God creates Adam (and, by extension, humankind) to be His deputy or vicegerent on the earth, to rule the world on His behalf. For its use as a title of the Muslim ruler, see "caliph."

Khawārij or Khārijites, sing. Khārijī/Khārijite: an early sect that approved of 'Uthmān's assassination and broke with 'Alī at the battle of Ṣiffīn in 37/657, when he agreed to subject his dispute with Mu'āwiya to arbitration. The name "Khawārij" means "those who go out," and has been variously interpreted to mean those who left 'Alī, those who left the Muslim community, or those who wage war against rulers they deem unjust. The Khawārij were subdivided between the activists, who advocated rebellion, and the quietists, among whom the Ibāḍīs may be counted. The most radical Khawārij felt that any Muslim who commits a grave sin and does not repent is an unbeliever (*mushrik*) who has renounced the faith and deserves death; they denounced the majority of Muslims as unbelievers and declared the necessity of a new *hijra* (emigration) away from the society of these "polytheists." These radical groups were gradually eliminated, but they had given the name "Khawārij" such notoriety that the Ibāḍīs reject being called Khawārij at all.

***khuṭba*:** the sermon delivered during the Friday congregational prayer.

kitmān: "concealment," a strategy among Ibāḍīs and other moderate Khawārij of living in secret dissension from the ruling authorities.

kufr: infidelity, denial, or ingratitude; this word is usually translated as "unbelief," but for Ibāḍīs only *kufr shirk* (the infidelity of polytheism) is unbelief; lesser forms of infidelity are called *kufr al-ni'ma* (ingratitude for or denial of God's blessing) or *kufr al-nifāq* (the infidelity of hypocrisy).

madhhab,* pl. *madhāhib: "way to go," a school of thought in Islam. In Sunnī Islam, the *madhāhib* are the four recognized schools of law, and non-Sunnī groups are called sects (*firqa,* pl. *firaq*), but Ibāḍīs refer to themselves as a *madhhab.*

Mālikī: a Sunnī legal school that predominates in North and West Africa.

ma'nā: a word that often means "meaning," but in the usage of Muslim theologians who affirmed the reality of God's attributes this meant something that is real, though incorporeal, though scholars also debated whether it is a body or an accident.

marfū': a technical term for *isnād*s lacking the name of the person who was the original source of a ḥadīth from the Prophet, a deficiency that impugns the integrity of the ḥadīth.

Māturīdism/Māturīdites: a Sunnī theological school founded by Abū Manṣūr al-Māturīdī (d. 333/944). It predominates in Central and South Asia.

Miḥna: the "Inquisition" prosecuted by 'Abbāsid caliphs from 218–232/833–847 to enforce the doctrine that the Qur'ān was created.

mode (*ḥāl,* pl. *aḥwāl*): a concept developed by the Mu'tazilite Abu Hāshim (277–321/890–933) to reformulate God's attributes as modes/conditions/states (*aḥwāl*), denoting "the real ontological property or attribute of the being of a thing" (Frank 1978, 23), but having itself neither existence nor non-existence. Some Ash'arites, such as al-Juwaynī, also utilized this concept, but later Ash'arites, such as Fakhr al-Dīn al-Rāzī, rejected it.

monotheist (*muwahḥid*): in Ibāḍī parlance, a monotheist is any member of Muḥammad's *umma.* Although many Muslims would recognize Jews and Christians as monotheists, Ibāḍīs consider them unbelievers (*mushrikūn*).

Muḥakkima: those who opposed submitting the dispute between 'Alī and Mu'āwiya to arbitatration (*taḥkīm*); some say that the name *Muḥakkima* derives from their slogan, "Judgment (*ḥukm*) belongs to God alone."

Murji'a/Murji'ites: early Muslims who are depicted in Muslim heresiographies as the polar opposite of the Khawārij. Their name means "the postponers," meaning that they postpone judgment of sinners until the Day of Judgment, and held that status as a Muslim is based on the profession of faith, not on observance of religious obligations. Their position is very close to that of classical Sunnī Islam, and Abū Ḥanīfa is said to have been a Murji'ite, but the Murji'a are made heretics by allegedly saying that "where there is faith, sin does no harm."

mushrik: a polytheist or unbeliever.

Muslim: an appellation that Ibāḍīs restrict to righteous Ibāḍīs.

Muʿtazila/Muʿtazilites: the first distinct theological school in Islam, it was allegedly founded by Wāṣil b. ʿAṭāʾ in the early second/eighth century as a group that said that sinners are neither Muslims nor unbelievers, but occupy an in-between status. "Muʿtazila" means "those who withdraw," but they called themselves "the people of unity and justice," to signify their two main theological positions: the absolute unity of God (rejecting the reality of God's attributes) and human free will (a position necessitated by their emphasis on God's justice). They also upheld the ability of the human intellect to discern religious truths, without the benefit of a prophetic revelation. The school's main thinkers were in Baṣra, while a separate branch was later established in Baghdad. From 218–232/833–847, the ʿAbbāsid caliphs conducted an inquisition in order to uphold the Muʿtazilite doctrine of the Qur'ān's creation, but the strategy backfired and led to the decline of the school. Muʿtazilite theology is today maintained in Zaydī and Imāmī/Twelver Shīʿism, and the "unity" aspects of their theology are also upheld by the Ibāḍīs.

Mzāb: name of a desert valley in eastern Algeria, approximately 500 km/311 miles south of Algiers, corresponding to the current province of Ghardāya. It is home to a major Ibāḍī community. At its heart are five towns: El Ateuf (al-ʿAṭf), Bou Noura (Bū Nūra), Beni Isguen (Banī Yazqin), Melika (Malīka), and Ghardaïa (Ghardāya).

Nabhānī dynasty: rulers of Oman from the mid-sixth/twelfth century until the establishment of the Yaʿrubī dynasty in 1024/1615.

Nafūsa: a limestone escarpment in northwestern Libya, home to a major Ibāḍī community.

al-Nahrawān: site of a pivotal battle on the lower Tigris River in Iraq between ʿAlī b. Abī Ṭālib and the Khawārij on 9 Ṣafar 38/17 July 658, where most of the Khawārij were massacred.

al-Nākitha: see al-Nukkār.

Nizwā: a major town in Oman's al-Jabal al-Akhḍar region, seat of the classical Ibāḍī Imāmate.

al-Nukkār/al-Nakkāra/al-Nakkāriyya: an Ibāḍī subsect whose name means "the deniers," because they denied the legitimacy of the second Rustamid Imām, ʿAbd al-Wahhāb b. ʿAbd al-Raḥmān (168–208/784–823). They are also sometimes called al-Nākitha, al-Nakkātha, or al-Nukkāth ("violaters"), because they violated their oath to ʿAbd al-Wahhāb. However, their separation from the main body of Ibāḍīs occurred earlier in Baṣra during the imāmate of Abū ʿUbayda, who expelled ʿAbdallāh b. Yazīd al-Fazārī and his associates from the Ibāḍī assembly. They allegedly believed that Muslims who hold anthropomorphic views of God are polytheists, held that the imāmate is not obligatory, and believed that the names of God are created. The Nukkār became particularly important in the Maghrib after the fall of the Rustamid Imāmate in 296/909; in the first half of the fourth/tenth century, a Nakkārī uprising nearly defeated the Fāṭimids.

People of the Book (*ahl al-kitāb*): adherents of pre-Islamic religions that are recognized as monotheistic, specifically Jews and Christians (and, according to some, the Sabaeans), who, in return for the payment of *jizya,* are allowed to practice their faith under Muslim rule, according to Islamic law. Muslim men are also allowed to marry their women. Zoroastrians were also treated as People of the Book, although Muslim men could not marry their women.

People of Ḥadīth (*ahl al-ḥadīth*): a name applied in early Islam to those who rejected theology and insisted that doctrine must be based on a literal interpretation of the Qur'ān and Sunna.

qaḍā': God's decree.

qadar: God's measurement/determination of things.

Qadariyya: the earliest group of Muslims who upheld free will. They are seen as having denied God's determination (*qadar*) of human voluntary acts. They were proto-theologians, the forerunners of the first Muslim theological school, that of the Mu'tazila, who came into existence sometime in the second/eighth century and briefly enjoyed the official sanction and support of the Caliphate in the early third/ninth century. The doctrines and identity of the Qadariyya are known only through the works of Sunnī heresiographers.

qibla: direction of prayer, for Muslims the Ka'ba in Mecca.

qunūt: an invocation that some Sunnīs perform between bowing and prostration during the second *rak'a* of the *fajr* prayer.

Qur'ān: God's word revealed to Muḥammad over a period of twenty-three years; it is divided into 114 chapters (*sūra*s) ranging in length from 3 to 287 verses.

Quraysh: the tribe to which Muḥammad belonged, it was centered on the city of Mecca and played a dominant role in Arabian politics before the Prophet's lifetime. The Sunnī political theorist, al-Māwardī (364–450/974–1058), wrote that the caliphs must come from the tribe of Quraysh (though not from any particular clan or lineage within it). This was a way of retroactively justifying the rule of the Rightly-Guided Caliphs, the Umayyads, and the 'Abbāsids.

rak'a,* pl. *raka'āt: literally bending or bowing, it is a cycle or unit of the Muslim ritual prayer (*ṣalāt*), which begins with the recitation of the *Fātiḥa* and sometimes a second passage from the Qur'ān, followed by bowing from the waist with the hands on the knees, followed by two prostrations, separated by briefly sitting on one's leg or legs. Each of the five daily prayers consists of a set number of *raka'āt:* two at dawn (before sunrise), three at sunset, and four at noon, mid-afternoon, and evening.

Rightly-Guided Caliphs/*al-khulafā' al-rāshidūn:* a Sunnī designation for the first four caliphs—Abū Bakr, 'Umar b. al-Khaṭṭāb, 'Uthmān b. 'Affān, and 'Alī b. Abī Ṭālib—the period of whose rule (9–40/632–661) is idealized as a time when both rulers and ruled were righteous, thereby glossing over the facts that only the first caliph died a natural death, 'Uthmān was assassinated through a vast conspiracy in his army, and 'Alī encountered such virulent opposition that he spent his entire caliphate trying to suppress rebellions, and was never able to consolidate his rule outside Iraq. Ibāḍīs recognize only Abū Bakr and 'Umar as entirely righteous. They say that 'Uthmān was good for the first six years of his caliphate but then committed serious sins, and 'Alī was duly selected as caliph but forfeited his right to rule by acquiescing to the request for arbitration at the battle of Ṣiffīn in 37/657.

Rustamid: name of an Ibāḍī imāmate founded in 161/778 at Tāhart in western Algeria by 'Abd al-Raḥmān b. Rustam, and lasting until 296/909.

Sabaeans (Ṣābi'a): a group mentioned in the Qur'an among those who, like the Jews and Christians, have nothing to fear on the Day of Judgment, provided they believe in God and the afterlife and do good deeds (2:62, 5:69, 22:17). Their identity is not known for sure (cf. Fahd 1999). A probably distinct group by the same name, at Ḥarrān in northern Mesopotamia, were pagan gnostics said to worship the planets.

sayyid: "master," a title that conveys nobility and is taken by members of the Bū Sa'īdī family in Oman. In Sunnī Islam, this title is reserved for descendants of the Prophet.

Shāfi'ī: a Sunnī legal school that predominates in southern Arabia, northern Egypt, Syria, Palestine, the Swahili coast, and Southeast Asia.

Sharī'a: Islamic law.

Shī'ī/Shī'ite/Shī'a: Muslim sects that believe that the ruler of the Muslims must be from the Prophet Muḥammad's family; specifically, they believe that Muḥammad designated his young cousin and son-in-law, 'Alī b. Abī Ṭālib, to succeed him. Hence, 'Alī is the first imām of the Shī'a, and subsequent imāms were/are his descendants. The major extant branches of the Shī'a are the Twelvers/Imāmīs, the Ismā'īlīs (further subdivided into smaller sects), and the Zaydīs; other branches are extinct.

shirk: polytheism, unbelief.

shurāt: a self-appellation of the Khawārij and Ibāḍīs who had pledged to die for the cause, it means those whose lives God has purchased.

Ṣiffīn: site of a famous battle near the right bank of the Euphrates in Ṣafar 37/July 657 between the fourth caliph, ʿAlī b. Abī Ṭālib, and the governor of Syria, Muʿāwiya b. Abī Sufyān, who claimed the right of revenge for the death of his cousin, the third caliph, ʿUthmān b. ʿAffān. As ʿAlī was winning the upper hand, Muʿāwiya's soldiers reportedly attached copies—or pages—of the Qur'ān to their lances, requesting that their dispute be submitted to arbitration. ʿAlī reluctantly agreed. A group of ʿAlī's soldiers opposed the arbitration, believing that the rightness of ʿAlī's cause was self-evident from the Qur'ān, that Muʿāwiya was an enemy of God by fighting ʿAlī, and that ʿAlī had committed a grave sin by agreeing to submit the matter to arbitration. They seceded from ʿAlī's camp, moved to the village of Ḥarūrā', near Kūfa, and became known as the Khawārij.

sīra: in Ibāḍī tradition, this word means a letter or epistle written by a religious scholar. In mainstream Islam, *sīra* means the biography of the Prophet.

Ṣufriyya: a moderate Khārijite sect, especially active among the Berbers in the Maghrib. They were eventually absorbed into the Ibāḍiyya.

Sunna: literally, this word means custom or "well-trodden path," and is used in the Qur'ān to describe the way that God customarily deals with human beings, but in Islam the word acquired the technical meaning of something the Prophet Muḥammad said or did, and since whatever he said or did is exemplary, *sunna* (with a lower-case *s*) also means something that is recommended. Sunna is necessary for interpreting and giving context to the Qur'ān, and it also expands considerably on the laws and doctrines given in the Qur'ān; it is the second "root" or source of law, after the Qur'ān. It is known through Ḥadīth.

Sunnīs: the majority of Muslims, estimated to be about 87 percent of Muslims worldwide.

sūra: a chapter or portion of the Qur'ān.

tafsīr: exegesis or commentary on the Qur'ān.

tanzīh: a doctrinal insistence on God's transcendence beyond similarity to created beings.

taqiyya: religious dissimulation; hiding one's true beliefs under persecution.

taqlīd: following the opinions of earlier scholars rather than engaging in intellectual speculation in theology or *ijtihād* in jurisprudence.

tashbīh: likening God to human beings; anthropomorphism.

taʿṭīl: "denuding" God of His attributes, an accusation leveled at the Muʿtazila because they denied that God's attributes are real things inhering in His essence.

tawḥīd: declaring God to be one; monotheism.

Uḥud: site of the second major battle between the Muslims and the pagan Meccans, thought to have taken place in the year 3/625.

al-ʿUmayriyya: a subsect of the Ibāḍiyya, followers of ʿĪsā b. ʿUmayr, formed in North Africa in the first half of the second/eighth century.

Umayya: the name of the most powerful clan of the Quraysh tribe in Mecca. Except for a few prominent converts to Islam, they were the core of Meccan opposition to Muḥammad until the Muslim conquest of Mecca in 8/630, after which they embraced Islam *en masse*. Many of the prominent commanders and governors of early Islam came from this clan, including the third caliph, ʿUthmān b. ʿAffān, and Muʿāwiya, governor of Syria, who founded the Umayyad dynasty in 40/661.

Umayyads: a dynasty of caliphs that belonged to the clan of Umayya and ruled the Islamic empire from their capital, Damascus, beginning in 40/661, until they were overthrown by the ʿAbbāsid revolution in 132/750.

umma: a nation or religious community, specifically those who recognize Muhammad as God's prophet.

Wahbī: an adjective deriving from the name of ʿAbdallāh b. Wahb, the first Ibāḍī imām, it may once have referred to a branch of the Ibāḍīs, but is used by Ibāḍīs today to mean the original or purest version of Islam.

Wahhābī movement: a militant, fundamentalist movement inspired by the teachings of Muḥammad b. ʿAbd al-Wahhāb (1115–1206/1703–1792), who began his public preaching in 1153/1740. The Wahhābīs conquered large portions of the Arabian peninsula in the early nineteenth century, including the Buraimi oasis of Oman. They were driven from Mecca and Medina by Muḥammad ʿAlī, the Ottoman governor of Egypt, in 1228/1813. The Wahhābīs reconquered the holy cities in 1343/1924, and established the Kingdom of Saudi Arabia in 1351/1932.

walāya: friendship, association, or affiliation. Ibāḍīs maintain *walāya* with other pious, righteous Ibāḍīs.

walī: a friend, associate, or affiliate.

Wargla/Wārgla (Ouargla): an oasis town of Algeria that has produced a number of outstanding Ibāḍī scholars.

Yaʿrubī dynasty: rulers of an imāmate in Oman from 1024/1615 to between 1154/1741 and 1167/1753.

zakāt: one of the Five Pillars of Islam, it is a tax on wealth owned at least a year. The tax is levied on money, jewelry, livestock, and crops, and is used to provide for the needs of the poor and travelers, for the upkeep of mosques and religious schools, and for the propagation of Islam. No tax is paid by those who own less than the set minimum (*niṣāb*).

BIOGRAPHICAL DICTIONARY

ʿAbbād b. Sulaymān al-Ḍaymarī/al-Ṣaymarī (d. 250/864): a Muʿtazilite of Basra, a student of Hishām b. ʿAmr al-Fuwaṭī.

al-ʿAbbās (d. ca. 32/653): uncle of the Prophet and ancestor of the ʿAbbāsid dynasty. He fought against the Prophet at the battle of Badr, was captured, and later released. Some reports say he was released for ransom, while others say he was released without ransom. He embraced Islam in 8/630.

ʿAbdallāh b. Ibāḍ/Abāḍ: the eponymous founder of Ibāḍism, who purportedly became the leader of the quietist Khawārij after the death of Abū Bilāl in 61/680–681 and broke with the Azāriqa in 65/684–685.

ʿAbdallāh b. Wahb al-Rāsibī: the first Khārijite Imām, given an oath of allegiance at Ḥarūrāʾ on 20 Shaʿbān 37/30 January 658. He was killed at the battle of al-Nahrawān on 9 Ṣafar 38/17 July 658.

ʿAbdallāh b. Yaḥyā al-Kindī: known as *Ṭālib al-Ḥaqq* (seeker of the truth), in 128/745 he founded the first Ibāḍī state, in the Ḥaḍramawt, and was able to conquer Ṣanʿāʾ, Mecca, and Medina before being killed in battle in 139/748.

ʿAbdallāh b. Yazīd al-Fazārī: an early second/eighth-century scholar who was expelled from the Ibāḍī assembly in Basra by Abū ʿUbayda b. Abī Karīma for a book he wrote, *Kitāb al-rudūd,* one of the oldest works on Muslim theology.

ʿAbd al-Malik b. Marwān: one of the most capable of the Umayyad caliphs, he ruled from 65/685 to 86/705.

ʿAbd al-Malik b. al-Muhallab: less important than his father, the Umayyad commander, Muhallab b. Abī Ṣufra (d. 82/702), he participated in his father's campaigns against the Azāriqa. Nonetheless, he may have had Ibāḍī sympathies, and is the probable recipient of a letter written by ʿAbdallāh b. Ibāḍ that has usually thought to have been written to ʿAbd al-Malik b. Marwān (Cook 1980, 63).

'Abd al-Raḥmān b. Ḥabīb b. Abī 'Ubayda al-Fihrī (d. 137/755): a great-grandson of 'Uqba b. Nāfi', he seized Qayrawān, the capital of Ifrīqiyā (modern-day Tunisia), in 129/747, and ruled as an independent governor, until he was assassinated by his own brother.

'Abd al-Raḥmān b. Rustam b. Bahrām (d. 171/788): an Ibāḍī of Persian origin, but grew up in Qayrawān (Kairouan, in present-day Tunisia). He studied in Basra with Abū 'Ubayda Muslim b. Abī Karīma, and was one of the missionaries sent to North Africa with Abū 'l-Khaṭṭāb al-Ma'ārif, for whom he served as governor of Qayrawān. He survived the battle that killed the latter in 144/761, fleeing Qayrawān into the central Maghrib, where, in 161/778, he founded a new Ibāḍī imāmate at Tāhart, six miles west of present-day Tihert in western Algeria. His imāmate was highly regarded for its justice and order, attracting migrants from other cities. When he died in 171/788, his son, 'Abd al-Wahhāb, was selected as imām, and the Rustamid dynasty ruled the imāmate until it was defeat by the Fāṭimids in 296/909.

'Abd al-Wahhāb b. 'Abd al-Raḥmān b. Rustam: the second Rustamid imām, he ruled from 171/788 to 208/824.

Abū 'l-'Abbās Aḥmad b. Muḥammad b. Bakr (d. 15 Dhū 'l-Ḥijja 504/18 June 1111): Ibāḍī scholar originally from the Nafūsa Mountains in Libya, though later he moved to southern Tunisia and Ouargla, Algeria, where he is said to have written twenty-five books on Ibāḍī law and theology.

Abū 'Ammār 'Abd al-Kāfī b. Abī Ya'qūb Yūsuf b. Ismā'īl b. Yūsuf b. Muḥammad al-Tanāwutī al-Wārjilānī (d. before 570/1174): Ibāḍī scholar of the Algerian oasis town of Ouargla, he is credited with stimulating an Ibāḍī intellectual florescence, attracting students from throughout the Maghrib, especially Jirba. His most important work is *Kitāb al-Mūjaz fī taḥṣīl al-su'āl wa-takhlīṣ al-maqāl fī 'l-radd 'alā ahl al-khilāf*, a theological synthesis in two parts, which has been compared to the writings of al-Ghazālī and al-Bāqillānī. The first part of the book is a refutation of heretics: those who believe in the eternity of the world, dualists, those who deny the mission of the Prophet (the Jews and Christians), and those who describe God in anthropomorphic terms. The second part examines the principles of speculative reasoning and major theological questions: the creation of human acts and a refutation of the Qadariyya, a discussion of the will of God and divine justice as they pertain to human acts, a refutation of the Prophet's intercession for grave sinners, an affirmation that gravely sinning Ibāḍīs are infidels but not polytheists, an exposition of the doctrine of the creation of the Qur'ān, proofs for God's existence, an explication of doctrine on the divine names, and the imāmate. His other writings include *Kitāb Sharḥ al-Jahālāt*, a commentary on a theological work.

Abū ʻAmr ʻUthmān b. Khalīfa al-Sūfī al-Mārghinī (sixth/twelfth century): Ibāḍī scholar of Wargla (Ouargla), Algeria, who traveled among the various Ibāḍī communities of North Africa to study and teach. He is best known as the author of *Al-Suʼālāt,* a collection of detailed responses to questions in theology.

Abū Bakr (d. 22 Jumāda II 13/23 August 634): nicknamed *al-Ṣiddīq* (the truthful or the one who counts as true), one of the Prophet's closest companions, the father of Muḥammad's favorite wife, ʻĀʼisha, and the one who assumed the office of caliph when Muḥammad died on 13 Rabīʻ I 9/8 June 632. His two-year caliphate was primarily occupied with putting down rebellions in Arabia and consolidating Muslim rule.

Abū ʼl-Baqāʼ ʻAbdallāh b. al-Ḥusayn al-ʻAkbarī (sixth/twelfth century): a grammarian of Baghdad.

Abū ʼl-Barakāt Hibat Allāh b. Malkā al-Baghdādī (ca. 470–560/1077–1164 or 1165): a philosopher and physician nicknamed *Awḥad al-Zaman,* "unique of his time." He wrote *Kitāb al-Muʻtabar,* dealing with logic, natural sciences, and metaphysics, a book said to be modeled on Ibn Sīnā's *Kitāb al-Shifāʼ.*

Abū Bilāl Mirdās b. Udayya (or b. Ḥudayr) al-Tamīmī (d. 61/680–681): leader of the quietist (*qaʻada*) Khawārij in Baṣra, he was executed by its governor, ʻUbaydallāh b. Ziyād.

Abū Dawud Sulaymān b. al-Ashʻath al-Sijistānī (202–275/817–889): author of one of the six canonical Sunni collections of Ḥadīth.

Abū Dharr al-Ghifārī (d. 32/652–653): a Companion of the Prophet known for his piety and asceticism. ʻUthmān exiled him from Medina because he denied that a true Muslim could own large houses and fields, at a time when many Muslims had acquired large landholdings as a result of the conquest of Iraq.

Abū Ḥanīfa b. Nuʻmān b. Thābit (d. 150/767): eponym of the Ḥanafī school, one of four remaining schools of law in Sunnī Islam.

Abū Hāshim ʻAbd al-Salām (d. 321/933), son of al-Jubbāʼī: one of the last Muʻtazila to exert a direct influence on the development of Sunni thought.

Abū ʼl-Ḥawārī Muḥammad b. al-Ḥawārī, known as "the blind" (*al-aʻmā*): Ibāḍī scholar of the town of Nizwa, Oman in the second half of the third/ninth century, where he also died at the beginning of the fourth/tenth century. He was a student of Muḥammad b. Maḥbūb and Abū ʼl-Muʼthir al-Ṣalt b. Khamīs. He wrote an important collection of answers to questions of law entitled *Jāmiʻ al-Faḍl Ibn al-Ḥawārī,* as well as the first Ibāḍī *tafsīr* written in Oman. He adopted a position of neutrality in the dispute over the deposition of Imām al-Ṣalt b. Mālik in 272/879.

Abū Isḥāq Ibrāhīm b. Qays b. Sulaymān al-Hamadānī al-Ḥaḍramī (d. 475/1082–83): an Ibāḍī commander who conquered the Ḥaḍramawt in the name of the Omani imām, al-Khalīl b. Shādhān, after the year 450/1058. He is the author of *Mukhtaṣar al-khiṣāl,* a juridical text that is an important source on Ibāḍī law. Nūr al-Dīn al-Sālimī wrote a thousand-line poetic summary of this work, entitled *Madārij al-kamāl.* He planned a twenty-volume commentary on the poem, of which he completed eighteen, entitled *Maʿārij al-āmāl.*

Abū ʾl-Khaṭṭāb ʿAbd al-Aʿlā b. al-Samḥ al-Maʿārifī al-Ḥimyarī: of Yemeni origin, he was the first Ibāḍī imām in the Maghrib, elected in Tripolitania in 140/757. One of the missionaries sent from Basra by Abū ʿUbayda Muslim b. Abī Karīma, he extended the Ibāḍī domain in Tripolitania, Tunisia, eastern Algeria, and northern Algeria, and exercised influence as far west as Sijilmāsa in present-day southeastern Morocco, and as far south as the Fezzān region of southwestern Libya. The ʿAbbāsids, led by Muḥammad b. al-Ashʿath, defeated this Imāmate in 144/761, in a battle in which many Ibāḍīs, including Abū ʾl-Khaṭṭāb, were killed.

Abū Khazar Yaghlā b. Zaltāf (d. 380/990): an Ibāḍī scholar of al-Ḥamma, near Qābis (Gabès) in southern Tunisia. He fought against the Fāṭimids, but, after defeat in battle in 358/967, he became reconciled to them and moved to Cairo. He wrote a comprehensive refutation of all theological opponents.

Abū Nabhān Jāʿid b. Khamīs al-Kharūṣī (1147–1237/1734–1822): outstanding scholar who heralded the start of the modern Ibāḍī renaissance in Oman. Not only a formidable scholar, he was also known for his mystical and talismanic powers, and was held in awe by rulers and the people alike. He wrote many works on jurisprudence and also composed a number of poems, including a lengthy, mystical ode entitled *Ḥayāt al-Mahj,* on which both he and his son Nāṣir wrote commentaries.

Abū Nūḥ Saʿīd b. Zanghīl (fourth/tenth century): Ibāḍī scholar of Tunisia and Algeria, author of a lost refutation of the doctrines of the Ibāḍīs' theological opponents, especially the Muʿtazila.

Abū ʾl-Qāsim Yūnus b. Fayṣal Abī Zakariyāʾ b. Abī Miswar Yasjā (fifth/eleventh century): an Ibāḍī scholar of Jirba, son of the man who suggested the idea of the *ʿazzāba* social organization that became characteristic of Ibāḍī communities in North Africa after the demise of the Rustamid imāmate. Abū ʾl-Qāsim Yūnus played a crucial role in organizing the religious school in the great mosque on the island of Jirba, and was known for the deft manner with which he dealt with theological questions.

Abū 'l-Rabīʿ Sulaymān b. Yakhlaf (d. 471/1078–1079): Ibāḍī scholar of Tunisia who traveled widely among Ibāḍī communities and had many students. His writings appear to be the original core of the compendium on law entitled *Al-Su'ālāt* ("questions"), attributed to Abū ʿAmr al-Sūfī. He is best known as the author of *Kitāb al-tuḥaf,* on theology and jurisprudence.

Abū Sahl Yaḥyā b. Sulaymān b. Wījman (late fifth/eleventh century): an Ibāḍī scholar of Wargla (Ouargla), Algeria.

Abū Saʿīd Muḥammad b. Saʿīd al-Kudamī: one of the greatest Ibāḍī scholars in Oman, he lived in the latter half of the third/ninth century and died in the early fourth/tenth century. He was head of the Nizwā school and took a neutral stance (*wuqūf*) in the schism over the deposition of Imāms al-Ṣalt b. Mālik and Rāshid b. al-Naḍr, and tried to bring about reconciliation between the two camps. His authority was such that he was called leader of the school (*imām al-madhhab*). He is the author of texts that remain constant references for Ibāḍīs to this day, especially *Kitāb al-Istiqāma* on the rules for association and dissociation, and *Al-Muʿtabar.*

Abū Ṣāliḥ Janūn b. Yamriyān (early fourth/tenth century): an eminent Ibāḍī scholar of Wargla, Algeria, known for his piety and miracles.

Abū Ṣufra ʿAbd al-Malik b. Ṣufra: a Maghribi Ibāḍī scholar of the early third/ninth century, author of a document known as *Kitāb Abī Ṣufra,* which Wilkinson believes to be the core of the Ḥadīth collection attributed to al-Rabīʿ b. Ḥabīb.

Abū ʿUbayda Muslim b. Abī Karīma al-Tamīmī: a pupil of Jābir b. Zayd who succeeded him as leader of the Ibāḍī community, according to Ibāḍī tradition, although it is more likely that he studied with students of Jābir rather than Jābir himself, and that he was head of the Ibāḍīs in Basra, but not of Ibāḍīs everywhere. He is credited with establishing missionary teams to propagate Ibāḍism in the provinces of Khurāsān, Oman, Yemen, the Ḥaḍramawt, and the Maghrib. Abū ʿUbayda died during the reign of the early ʿAbbāsid caliph, Abū Jaʿfar al-Manṣūr (136–158/753–775).

Abū Yaʿqūb Yūsuf b. Ibrāhīm b. Munād al-Sidrātī al-Warjilānī (d. 570/1175): an encyclopedic Ibāḍī scholar and one of the most outstanding Ibāḍī theologians. He hailed originally from Wargla (Ouargla), Algeria, but traveled widely in the African continent, often in largely unknown territories, leaving behind a record of his impressions of these areas and their peoples. He is best known for *Al-Dalīl wa-'l-burhān* (a work on theology) and

Al-ʿAdl wa-ʾl-inṣāf (on jurisprudence), and for his arrangement of the Ḥadīth collection attributed to al-Rabīʿ b. Ḥabīb.

Abū ʾl-Yaqẓān Muḥammad b. Aflaḥ: Rustamid imām who ruled from 260–281/874–894 and allegedly wrote treatises on the human capacity to act and the creation of the Qurʾān.

Abū Zayd al-Anṣārī (d. 214 or 215/830 or 831): a grammarian and lexicographer of Basra.

Aflaḥ b. ʿAbd al-Wahhāb, Abū Saʿīd: the third imām of the Rustamid imāmate in Algeria, ruling 208–258/824–872.

Aḥmad b. Ḥamad al-Khalīlī: the current Grand Mufti of the Sultanate of Oman and author of numerous publications on Ibāḍism.

Aḥmad b. Ḥanbal (164–241/780–855): founder of the Ḥanbalī school of jurisprudence, one of the four surviving schools of law in Sunni Islam. Ḥanbalism is known for limiting the domain of reason in jurisprudence more than the other schools, and for rejecting theology altogether, holding that the Qurʾān cannot be interpreted according to the mandates of human reason.

Aḥmad b. al-Ḥusayn: founder of the Ḥusayniyya subsect of Ibāḍism, he lived in Tripoli, Libya, in the first part of the third/ninth century. He wrote one of the earliest Ibāḍī treatises on theology, *Kitāb al-maqālāt,* and a work on jurisprudence known as *Mukhtaṣar fī ʾl-fiqh.*

Aḥmad b. Saʿīd Āl Bū Saʿīd (d. 1198/1783): founder of the Bū Saʿīdī dynasty in Oman. He served as governor of Ṣuḥār on behalf of the Yaʿrubī imām Sayf b. Sulṭān II (d. 1743), ousted the Persians from Oman, and was recognized as imām in 1167/1753–1754.

ʿĀʾisha bint Abī Bakr (d. 58/678): the youngest wife of the Prophet and an important source of Ḥadīth.

ʿAlī b. Abī Tālib (d. 17 Ramaḍān 40/26 January 661): a young cousin of the Prophet Muḥammad, whom Muḥammad and his wife Khadīja raised in their household because of the poverty of his father, Abū Ṭālib. ʿAlī and Khadīja were the first to believe in Muḥammad's prophethood. ʿAlī was selected as the fourth caliph after the assassination of ʿUthmān b. ʿAffān on 18 Dhū ʾl-Ḥijja 35/17 June 656, but his caliphate was marked by civil war on several fronts, including the Khārijite secession from his army over ʿAlī's agreement at the battle of Ṣiffīn in 37/657 to submit his dispute with Muʿāwiya to arbitration. ʿAlī was assassinated by ʿAbd al-Raḥmān b. ʿAmr b. Muljam al-Murādī, an alleged Khārijite from Egypt, in revenge for ʿAlī's massacre of the Khawārij at al-Nahrawān. The

Shīʿa believe that the Prophet designated ʿAlī as leader (*imām*) of the Muslims after the Prophet's death, and that ʿAlī's descendants are the only rightful imāms.

ʿAmr b. al-ʿĀṣ (or al-ʿĀṣī) (d. ca. 42/663): a leading man of Mecca who converted to Islam shortly before the conquest of Mecca, in 8/629–630. He was a wily politician, commander of the Muslim forces that conquered Egypt in 19–21/640–642, and Muʿāwiya's most important ally in his battle against ʿAlī. It was ʿAmr who, at the battle of Ṣiffīn, conceived the plan of placing leaves of the Qur'ān on the tips of the soldiers' lances in order to submit the dispute to arbitration, and ʿAmr was the arbiter appointed to represent Muʿāwiya's side, which emerged from the arbitration victorious.

ʿAmrūs b. Fatḥ al-Masākinī, Abū Ḥafṣ (d. 283/896): an Ibāḍī scholar of Jabal Nafūsa, known as the most learned scholar of his generation. He became a judge in the governorate of Abū Manṣūr Ilyās at the end of the Rustamid dynasty. He is the author of *Uṣūl al-daynūna 'l-ṣāfiya,* on theology. He died in the battle of Mānū between the Ibāḍīs of Nafūsa and the Aghlabid dynasty, which ruled Ifrīqiyā on behalf of the ʿAbbāsids.

al-Ashʿarī, Abū 'l-Ḥasan ʿAlī b. Ismāʿīl (260–324/873–935): a student of the Muʿtazilite theologian al-Jubbā'ī, he renounced Muʿtazilism and founded a Sunni theological school that is called by his name.

Aṭfayyish, Abū Isḥāq Ibrāhīm b. Muḥammad b. Ibrāhīm (1305–1385/1886–1965): great-nephew of the great Ibāḍī scholar, Muḥammad b. Yūsuf Aṭfayyish, with whom he studied in the Mzāb, Algeria. He continued his studies in Algiers and Tunis, where his participation in campaigns against French colonialism led to his expulsion from French territories in North Africa. He spent the rest of his life in Cairo, where he forged strong relationships with modernist Sunni thinkers, while also engaged in the defense of Ibāḍism.

Aṭfayyish, Ibrāhīm b. Yūsuf b. ʿĪsā (d. 1303/1886): an Ibāḍī scholar of the Mzāb valley, Algeria, best known as the older brother of Muḥammad b. Yūsuf Aṭfayyish and grandfather of Abū Isḥāq Ibrāhīm Aṭfayyish. A student of ʿAbd al-ʿAzīz al-Thamīnī in the Mzāb, he also studied in Oman, Egypt (where he studied philosophy and alchemy), the Ḥijāz, and Tunis, and taught in Morocco before returning to the Mzāb.

Aṭfayyish, Muḥammad b. Yūsuf b. ʿĪsā (1237–1332/1820–1914): the greatest Ibāḍī scholar of the Mzāb valley in Algeria, and arguably the most important modern Ibāḍī scholar, he is known as *quṭb al-a'imma,* "the Pole of the Imāms," or just "the Quṭb." He added an *alif* at the beginning of his first name, feeling it audacious to take the name of the Prophet. He completed all his studies in the Mzāb, where he began to teach at age sixteen, and was the leading scholar by the age of twenty. He had many students and exerted a tremendous influence on Ibāḍī thought in the modern period. He wrote hundreds of works in the various Islamic sciences. His most important works are: his two Qur'ān commentaries, *Hamayān al-zād ilā dār al-ma'ād* and *Taysīr al-tafsīr;* on jurisprudence, *Al-Dhahab al-khāliṣ al-munawwah bi-'l-'ilm al-qāliṣ;* on Ḥadīth, *Jāmi' al-shaml fī aḥādīth khātam al-rusul;* a defense of Ibāḍism (*Izālat al-i'tirāḍ 'an muḥiqqī āl Ibāḍ*); a history of Wādī Mzāb; a number of poetical works; and commentaries on theological works by Tabghūrīn, Ibn Jumay', and 'Abd al-'Azīz al-Thamīnī, and on works of jurisprudence by 'Abd al-'Azīz al-Thamīnī (*Kitāb al-Nīl*) and Abū Ya'qūb Yūsuf b. Ibrāhīm al-Wārjilānī (*Al-'Adl wa-'l-inṣāf*), among others. "Aṭfayyish" has been variously rendered in Latin transliteration as Aṭfayyish, Attafayyish, Iṭfayyish, or Aṭfiyyāsh. According to Madghis Madi Afulay of Libya and Brahim Bakir Bahaz of Algeria, this Berber name is actually pronounced Ṭfaysh or Ṭfayyish, but since Arabic does not allow a word to begin with two consonants, an *alif* has been placed at the beginning of the name (personal communication, Nov. 2009). I transliterate the name as Aṭfayyish, which seems, among the variants currently in circulation, to be the one that most closely resembles the name's actual pronunciation.

'Azzān b. Qays b. 'Azzān b. Qays b. Aḥmad Āl Bū Sa'īd: appointed imām in Oman by the Ibāḍī scholar Sa'īd b. Khalfān al-Khalīlī after the successful overthrow of Sālim b. Thuwaynī in 1285/1868, he also ousted the Wahhābīs from the Buraimi oasis. He was killed in battle on 8 Dhū 'l-Qa'da 1287/29 January 1871.

al-Bāqillānī, Abū Bakr Muḥammad b. al-Ṭayyib (d. 403/1013): an important Ash'arite theologian and Mālikī judge. His *Tamhīd al-awā'il wa-talkhīṣ al-dalā'il* is possibly the earliest complete manual of theology.

Barghash b. Sa'īd b. Sulṭān (d. 1305/1888): after an exile to Bombay for a plot to overthrow his brother Mājid, ruler of Zanzibar, Barghash became the last great sultan of Zanzibar and the Swahili coast, in 1287/1870. He introduced piped water, electricity, rail travel, and a printing press to the sultanate. He had a close relationship with the British, and allowed the building of the Anglican cathedral, whose bell tower dominates the Zanzibar skyline. Nonetheless, the British betrayed him, as Barghash's territories, formerly extending to the Great Lakes, were reduced to a ten-mile coastal strip as a result of the Scramble for Africa, in which Germany took Tanganyika, Great Britain took Kenya, and the Portuguese took northern Mozambique.

al-Bārūnī, Sulaymān b. 'Abdallāh b. Yaḥyā (1287–1359/1870–1940): Ibāḍī scholar and politician of Libya, he studied in Tunis, Cairo, and the Mzāb, before entering politics, first as a member of the Ottoman parliament in Istanbul, then as a leader of resistance against the Italians in his homeland in 1329/1911. He spent most of his life in exile. In Cairo, he established a number of newspapers in succession, as well as the Azhār al-Bārūniyya printing press (1324/1906), where he published a number of Ibāḍī works, including his own history of Ibāḍī imāms and rulers, *Al-Azhār al-riyāḍiyya fī a'immat wa-mulūk al-Ibāḍiyya,* and a volume of his poetry. He served as an adviser to both Imām Muḥammad al-Khalīlī in the Omani interior and to Sultan Sa'īd b. Taymūr in Muscat.

Bashīr b. Muḥammad b. Maḥbūb b. al-Raḥīl, known as Abū 'l-Mundhir: an Ibāḍī scholar of Oman in the third/ninth century, author of a treatise on the rules for fighting jihād and other works of jurisprudence and theology.

al-Bayḍāwī, 'Abdallāh b. 'Umar (d. ca. 716/1316): Sunni scholar of the Shāfi'ite school, author of an exegesis of the Qur'ān, *Anwār al-tanzīl wa-asrār al-ta'wīl,* which is essentially a condensed version of al-Zamakhsharī's *Al-Kashshāf,* with corrections made to remove the latter's Mu'tazilite viewpoints.

al-Bukhārī, Muḥammad b. Ismā'īl (194–256/810–870): author of one of the two collections of Ḥadīth considered by Sunni Muslims to be *ṣaḥīḥ* (authentic).

Ennami (Al-Nāmī), 'Amr Khalīfa (1358/1939–?): Libyan Ibāḍī scholar who received his M.A. degree in literature in Cairo and his D.Phil. in Islamic studies at Cambridge. He taught at al-Fātiḥ University and as a visiting assistant professor at the University of Michigan. He was imprisoned in Libya several times as part of Libya's "cultural revolution," and there has been no word of him since 1986. His doctoral dissertation, *Studies in Ibadhism: Al Ibadhiyah,* was in two parts, the first devoted to a summary of Ibāḍī teachings, the second an annotated translation of several Ibāḍī texts that had not yet been published. The first part of his dissertation was published privately without publication data and again by Oman's Ministry of Awqāf and Religious Affairs in 2008.

al-Fārābī, Abū Naṣr Muḥammad (d. 339/950): the first Muslim Neoplatonic philosopher.

Fatḥ b. Nūḥ al-Malūshā'ī, Abū Naṣr (seventh/thirteenth century): Ibāḍī scholar of Libya, author of a creed set to verse, *Al-Nūniyya fī uṣūl al-dīn.*

Fāṭima: daughter of the Prophet and wife of 'Alī b. Abī Ṭālib.

Fayṣal b. Turkī b. Sa'īd: ruler of Oman from 1305–1331/1888–1913.

Ghālib b. 'Alī al-Hinā'ī: he became imām of the Omani interior after the death of Muḥammad b. 'Abdallāh al-Khalīlī in May 1954, but was defeated by Sultan Sa'īd b. Taymūr in December 1955, effectively ending the imāmate, although Ghālib and his cohorts attempted for several more years to regain power. In January 1959 they were defeated for the last time, and Ghālib escaped to Saudi Arabia, where he died at age ninety-six in November 2009.

al-Ghazālī, Abū Ḥāmid Muḥammad b. Muḥammad (450–505/1058–1111): outstanding and influential Shāfiʿite legal scholar, Ashʿarite theologian, Sufi, and original thinker. He is the author of hundreds of works, most famously *Iḥyāʾ ʿulūm al-dīn* (Revival of the Sciences of Religion).

Ḥafṣ al-Fard (early ninth century): an Egyptian scholar said to be a Muʿtazilite, though some of the doctrines attributed to him are not typical of the Muʿtazila.

al-Ḥajjāj b. Yūsuf b. al-Ḥakam al-Thaqafī (41–95/661–714): the most well-known of the Umayyad governors, known for his ruthless suppression of dissent.

al-Ḥārithī, Abū ʿAbdallāh Sālim b. Ḥamad b. Sulaymān b. Ḥumayd (d. 2007): a scholar, writer, and *qāḍī* of Mudhayrib, Oman.

al-Ḥasan al-Baṣrī, Abū Saʿīd b. Abī ʾl-Ḥasan Yasār (21–110/642–728): a famous preacher, Ḥadīth transmitter and ascetic of Baṣra. Although some of al-Ḥasan's views were later repudiated by Sunni and Ibāḍī Muslims, particularly his espousal of the doctrine of free will, he is so revered that outright heresy cannot be countenanced of him.

Ḥassān b. Thābit b. al-Mundhir al-Anṣārī (d. ca. 40/659): an important poet of Medina who was known as the Prophet's own panegyrist, though he was of mature age at the time of the Hijra and had earlier written panegyrics for princes of the Ghassānid and Lakhmid kingdoms.

Hishām b. al-Ḥakam (d. 179/795–796): an important Imāmī/Twelver Shīʿite theologian of Kūfa and Baghdad in the time of Imāms Jaʿfar al-Ṣādiq (d. 148/765) and Mūsa al-Kāẓim (128–183/745–799). He elaborated the Imāmī doctrine of the imāmate that has remained operative to this day. Hishām defined God as a finite, three-dimensional body and as radiant light; He had been in no place, then produced space by His movement and came to be in a place, the Throne. According to Madelung, Hishām's doctrine that God was a body was based on an assumption that only bodies have existence. He rejected the doctrine of some other Imāmī theologians of his time that God had a shape like that of a man. Hishām held that God did not know things or events before they came into being, believing that His knowledge of them from eternity would entail their existence from eternity. He held that God's attributes (including the Qurʾān) could not be described as either eternal or originated in time. He believed that God creates human acts according to human choice. In Kūfa he jointly owned a shop with an Ibāḍī scholar, ʿAbdallāh b.

Yazīd. The caliph Hārūn al-Rashīd took an interest in his views, but found them dangerous and ordered the arrest of Imām Mūsa. Hishām thereupon went into hiding and died shortly afterwards.

Hishām b. Sālim al-Jawālīqī: a Shī'ite scholar of the second/eighth century who, according to van Ess (2002a), imagined God as a form consisting of white light, "which only changed into black when His profuse hair had to be described," and believed that God had senses comparable to human senses.

Hūd b. Muḥakkam al-Huwwārī: scholar of Algeria in the third/ninth century who wrote the earliest extant Ibāḍī commentary on the Qur'ān.

Ibn 'Abbās/Ibn al-'Abbās, 'Abdallāh (d. 68/686–687): a cousin of the Prophet, born three years before the Hijra, he is recognized as the most eminent early scholar in Qur'ān interpretation. He also had an active political career on various sides of the conflicts that divided the Muslims of his day.

Ibn Abī Sitta, Abū 'Abdallāh Muḥammad b. 'Umar (1022–1088/1614–1677): one of the most famous Ibāḍī scholars of the Tunisian island of Jirba. He studied at al-Azhar University in Cairo, where he remained for twenty-eight years (1040–1068/1631–1658), first as a student and then as a teacher. In addition to his scholarship, he was known for his deep humility and intense piety. He composed some twenty glosses (*ḥawāshī*) on major Ibāḍī works, for which reason he is nicknamed al-Muḥashshī ("the Glosser").

Ibn Abī Sitta, Abū Zayd b. Aḥmad (d. 1100/1688): Ibāḍī scholar of Jirba, Tunisia, who also studied at the Ibāḍī school at al-Azhar University in Cairo, then returned to Jirba, where he presided over a twice-weekly scholarly assembly in which he responded to the questions of other scholars and students. He is one of three scholars who wrote a gloss on Abū 'Ammār 'Abd al-Kāfī's commentary on *Al-Jahālāt,* on theology.

Ibn al-Azraq, Nāfi': eponymous founder of a violent branch of the Khawārij, the Azāriqa or Azraqites, who conquered Baṣra in 65/684, opening the doors of the prisons there and assassinating the governor. Baṣrans of the Azd tribe expelled the Azāriqa, who withdrew to the town of al-Ahwāz in Khūzistān (southwestern Iran), where they established their headquarters and continued to harass southern Iraq. Ibn al-Azraq has been described as the first theoretician of the Khawārij. He was killed in battle in 65/685.

Ibn al-Bannā' al-Marrākushī, the common designation for Abū 'l-'Abbās Aḥmad b. Muḥammad b. 'Uthmān al-Azdī (654–721/1256–1321): a Moroccan scholar who wrote works concerning many branches of scholarship, but is best known for his writings on mathematics, astronomy, astrology, and the occult sciences.

Ibn Baraka al-Salīmī al-Bahlawī, Abū Muḥammad ʻAbdallāh b. Muḥammad, called either Ibn Baraka or Abū Muḥammad: one of the greatest Ibāḍī scholars of the fourth/tenth century, head of the Rustāq school, and author of a collection of answers to questions on matters of law so famous that it is sometimes referred to simply as "the book." He is considered the first Ibāḍī to write on the principles of jurisprudence.

Ibn al-Ḥājib, Jamāl al-Dīn Abū ʻAmr ʻUthmān (d. 646/1249): a Mālikī legal scholar of Egypt.

Ibn Jaʻfar al-Izkawī, Abū Jābir Muḥammad: one of the most famous Ibāḍī scholars of Oman in the third/ninth century, a leader of the Rustāq school. He served as governor of Ṣuḥār on behalf of Imām al-Ṣalt b. Mālik, and was present at the appointment of Imām ʻAzzān b. Tamīm in 277/890. He was one of the top three scholars in Oman, of whom it is said: "Oman consulted three at that time: one was deaf (Ibn Jaʻfar), one was lame (Nabhān b. ʻUthmān), and one was blind (Abū ʼl-Muʼthir al-Ṣalt b. Khamīs)." Ibn Jaʻfar wrote a large compendium in jurisprudence, known as *Jāmiʻ Ibn Jaʻfar.*

Ibn Jumayʻ, Abū Ḥafṣ ʻAmr (seventh/thirteenth century): Ibāḍī scholar of Jirba whose translation of a second/eighth-century creed from Berber into Arabic is a primary textbook for Ibāḍī schoolchildren in North Africa and has received a number of commentaries by prominent Ibāḍī scholars.

Ibn Karrām, Abū ʻAbdallāh b. Muḥammad (ca. 190–255/806–869): an Arab resident of Persia who was an ascetic and popular preacher. Ibn Karrām's theological ideas are expounded in his book, *ʻAdhāb al-qabr* ["punishment in the grave"], in which he expressed the view that Munkar and Nakīr, the two angels who, according to Ḥadīth, will question people in the grave after their deaths and give them a foretaste of their eternal reward or punishment according to their answers, are the same as the two guardian angels that are at the right and left shoulder of each person. This work is no longer extant, and its contents can only be known through citations in other works. He is also accused of anthropomorphism—that is, interpreting anthropomorphic expressions concerning God in the Qur'an in their literal sense, saying that God is a substance (*jawhar*) and a body (*jism*) of finite dimensions. The sect that is named after him, the Karrāmiyya, flourished in the central and eastern Muslim lands until the Mongol invasions of the early thirteenth century.

Ibn Kullāb, ʻAbdallāh b. Saʻīd (d. ca. 241/855): early theologian who can be seen as a forerunner of Ashʻarism.

Ibn Māja, Abū ʻAbdallāh Muḥammad b. Yazīd (209–273/824 or 825–887): author of one of the six canonical Sunni collections of Ḥadīth.

Ibn Rushd, Abū 'l-Walīd Muḥammad b. Aḥmad (520–595/1126–1198): a Muslim Aristotelian philosopher of al-Andalus (Spain), known in Latin Europe as Averroës. His commentaries on the philosophy of Aristotle, translated into Latin, inspired renewed interest in classical philosophy in Christian Europe and the development of Scholasticism. His ideas on the harmony of religion and philosophy inspired a Christian intellectual movement that espoused the "double truth" of both theology and philosophy, and was known as Averroïsm. He wrote a paragraph-by-paragraph refutation of al-Ghazālī's *Tahāfut al-falāsifa* (The Incoherence of the Philosophers), entitled *Tahāfut al-tahāfut* (The Incoherence of "The Incoherence").

Ibn Sīnā, Abū 'Alī al-Ḥusayn b. 'Abdallāh (370–428/980–1037): known in the West as Avicenna, he was a great Muslim Neoplatonic philosopher and physician, whose *Canon of Medicine* was a major reference in medieval Europe and in the Muslim world.

Ibn Wahb, 'Abdallāh: see 'Abdallāh b. Wahb al-Rāsibī.

Ibn Zarqūn, Abū 'l-Rabī' Sulaymān: an Ibāḍī scholar of Tadiyūt, in Jabal Nafūsa, in the early fourth/tenth century.

al-Ījī, 'Aḍud al-Dīn 'Abd al-Raḥmān (d. 756/1355): a Shāfi'ī jurist and Ash'arite theologian of southern Persia, he wrote *Kitāb al-Mawāqif fī 'ilm al-kalām,* which, according to van Ess (1999), is still used for teaching theology at al-Azhar University.

'Īsā b. Aḥmad: an Ibadi shaykh of North Africa who is mentioned in passing in al-Darjīnī (n.d., 488, 491), the classic source on medieval Ibāḍī authorities of the Maghrib. There is no biography devoted to him, but he is mentioned as the source of information for some opinions of Abū 'Ammār 'Abd al-Kāfī.

'Īsā b. 'Alqama (100–150/718–767): author of the first Ibāḍī theological treatise, *Kitāb al-tawḥīd al-kabīr,* written in response to 'Abdallāh b. Yazīd al-Fazārī's *Kitāb al-rudūd.*

al-Isfarāyīnī, Abū Isḥāq Ibrāhīm b. Muḥammad (d. 418/1027): an Ash'arite theologian and Shāfi'ī *faqīh* of Nīshāpūr.

Jābir b. Zayd, known as Abū 'l-Sha'thā' (father of al-Sha'thā', his daughter, whose tomb is in Farq): born in 21/642 of the Azd tribe in the town of Farq, near Nizwā, Oman, he migrated to Baṣra, where he became an eminent authority on Ḥadīth and law. Ibāḍīs see him as the successor to Ibn Ibāḍ as leader of their sect and consider him an imām of *kitmān,* that is, one who hid his opposition to Umayyad rule. It is said that he wrote the earliest Ḥadīth collection, which is lost, though he figures as a transmitter of ḥadīths in the collections of al-Bukhārī, Muslim, and Abū Dāwūd. Ibāḍīs see him as the one who organized their sect, and therefore call him *'umdat al-Ibāḍiyya* (pillar of the Ibāḍīs) and *aṣl al-madhhab* (root of the school). Wilkinson (1982) and Cook (1981) have cast considerable doubt on the historicity of much of what Ibāḍīs say about him. Various dates have been given for his death, ranging from 93/711 to 104/722.

Jahm b. Ṣafwān (executed 128/746): an early theologian and putative eponym of a heretical sect called the Jahmiyya that allegedly believed in an extreme form of divine compulsion of human acts, and whose denial of God's attributes led to accusations of "stripping" (*ta'ṭīl*) God of His attributes.

al-Jannāwunī, Abū Zakariyā' Yaḥyā b. Abī 'l-Khayr (fifth/eleventh century): Ibāḍī scholar of Libya, author of *Kitāb al-waḍ'*, a summary of Ibāḍī teachings on theology and jurisprudence, and a small creed called *'Aqīdat Nafūsa.*

al-Jayṭālī/al-Jīṭālī, Abū Ṭāhir Ismā'īl b. Mūsā (d. 750/1349): an Ibāḍī scholar of Jabal Nafūsa whose outspoken denunciation of wrongdoings led to his imprisonment in Tripoli and his later relocation to the island of Jirba. He wrote a number of important works, especially *Qanāṭir al-khayrāt, Qawā'id al-Islām,* and *'Aqīdat al-tawḥīd.*

al-Jubbā'ī, Abū 'Alī Muḥammad b. 'Abd al-Wahhāb (d. 303/915–916): one of the most celebrated Mu'tazila, most famous as the teacher of Abū 'l-Ḥasan al-Ash'arī.

al-Julandā b. Mas'ūd b. Jayfar b. al-Julandā: the first Ibāḍī imām in Oman (132–134/750–752), elected at the beginning of the 'Abbāsid period by Ibāḍīs who had fled to Oman after the death of 'Abdallāh b. Yaḥyā "Ṭālib al-Ḥaqq" al-Kindī, imām of the Ḥaḍramawt. Al-Julandā's genealogy goes back to the Azdī rulers of Oman in the early sixth century CE, who were overthrown by the army of al-Ḥajjāj during the reign of 'Abd al-Malik b. Marwān (65–86/685–705). Al-Julandā died in battle fighting against the 'Abbāsid army, leading to the fall of the first Ibāḍī imāmate in Oman.

Jumayyil b. Khalfān b. Lāfī al-Sa'dī: a student of Nāṣir b. Abī Nabhān, he composed the ninety-volume *Qāmūs al-sharī'a* over a twenty-year period from 1260–1280/1844–1863. The first volume of this work was the first book published by Sayyid Barghash's printing press in Zanzibar in 1297/1880. Only twenty volumes of this work have been published.

al-Jurjānī, 'Alī b. Muḥammad (740–838/1339–1434): a Sunni scholar known as "al-Sayyid al-Sharīf" because of his descent from the Prophet, he was born in northern Iran near the Caspian Sea, but traveled widely in the Muslim world. When Tīmūr captured Shīrāz in 789/1387, he took al-Jurjānī with him to Samarqand, where he had discussions with Sa'd al-Dīn al-Taftāzānī. After Tīmūr's death in 807/1405, al-Jurjānī returned to Shīrāz and remained there the rest of his life.

al-Juwaynī, Abū 'l-Ma'ālī 'Abd al-Malik b. Muḥammad (419–478/1028–1085): an Ash'arite scholar known as Imām al-Ḥaramayn, "the leading master of the two holy cities" (Mecca and Medina).

al-Ka'bī, Abū 'l-Qāsim al-Balkhī (d. 319/932): chief of the Mu'tazila in the region of Transoxiana. The Sunni theologian al-Māturīdī wrote refutations of three of his books (Madelung 1999b).

al-Khalīl b. Aḥmad b. 'Amr b. Tamīm al-Farāhīdī (second/eighth century): a philologist of Omani origin who lived in Baṣra.

al-Khalīl b. Shādhān b. al-Ṣalt b. Mālik: imām of Oman from 406–425/1016–1034.

Khamīs b. Sa'īd al-Shaqṣī (d. between 1059 and 1090): Ibāḍī scholar of Rustāq, Oman, author of the influential *Manhaj al-ṭālibīn wa-balāgh al-rāghibīn,* an encyclopedic work dealing mainly with jurisprudence. He played a key role in the recognition of the first Ya'rubī Imām, Nāṣir b. Murshid, in 1024/1615.

Khardala: one of those who opposed the arbitration at Ṣiffīn, he was allegedly sentenced to death by Jābir b. Zayd for exposing the secrets of the quietist Khawārij.

al-Kindī, Muḥammad b. Ibrāhīm (d. 508/1115): Omani scholar, author of an encyclopedic work of Ibāḍī jurisprudence in more than seventy volumes, *Bayān al-shar'.*

Maḥbūb b. al-Raḥīl b. Sayf, known as Abū Sufyān (died at old age toward the end of the second century AH/beginning of the ninth century CE): a great Ibāḍī scholar and historian, a student of al-Rabī' b. Ḥabīb, and the last imām of concealment in Baṣra. During the persecution of Ibāḍīs in Iraq, he migrated to Oman, where he settled in Ṣuḥār. He is one of the transmitters of the *Mudawwana* of Abū Ghānim, and many legal opinions are attributed to him. A collection of his epistles are cited by al-Darjīnī and al-Shammākhī in their books of the biographies of prominent Ibāḍīs.

Mājid b. Sa'id b. Sulṭān: ruler of Zanzibar from 1273–1287/1856–1870.

Mālik b. Anas (d. 179/796): founder of the Mālikī school of jurisprudence, one of four surviving Sunni schools.

Marṣūksun al-Ṣāwīnī (sixth/twelfth century): a North African Ibāḍī theologian.

al-Mas'ūdī, Abū 'l-Ḥasan 'Alī b. al-Ḥusayn (d. 345/956): a scholar with Shī'ite sympathies, a traveler, geographer, historian, and author of *Murūj al-dhahab* (Pastures of Gold).

al-Māturīdī, Abū Manṣūr Muḥammad b. Muḥammad (d. 333/944): a scholar in Samarqand who founded a Sunni theological school that became important in Central and South Asia.

al-Māwardī, Abū 'l-Ḥasan 'Alī b. Muḥammad b. Ḥabīb (364–450/974–1058): a Shāfi'ī legal scholar of Baghdad who wrote several famous works on political theory, especially *Kitāb al-aḥkām al-sulṭāniyya* (The Rules of Government).

Mu'ammar b. 'Abbād al-Sulamī (d. 215/830): a leading Mu'tazilite of Baṣra and teacher of Bishr al-Mu'tamir, founder of the Baghdad school of the Mu'tazila. Mu'ammar is famous for his doctrine of *ma'ānī*, translated by Daiber as "determinant factors which are themselves determined by other determinant factors, *ad infinitum*" (Daiber 1999).

Mu'ammar, 'Alī Yaḥyā (1338–1401/1919–1980): an Ibāḍī scholar of Libya who has published a number of very extensive studies on Ibāḍī history.

Mu'āwiya b. Abī Sufyān (d. 60/680): the shrewd but capable son of Abū Sufyān b. Ḥarb b. Umayya al-Akbar b. Shams, the former ruler of Mecca, and Hind bint 'Utba b. Rabī'a, who, at the battle of Uḥud, infamously tore out the liver of the Prophet's uncle, Ḥamza, and ate it in revenge for the latter's having killed her father at the battle of Badr. The second caliph, 'Umar b. al-Khaṭṭāb, appointed Mu'āwiya governor of Syria, and he was retained in this position by his cousin, the third caliph, 'Uthmān b. 'Affān. After the latter's assassination in 35/656, Mu'āwiya led the most powerful opposition to the fourth caliph, 'Alī b. Abī Ṭālib, preventing 'Alī from establishing effective rule over most of the Islamic empire. After 'Alī's assassination in 40/661, Mu'āwiya succeeded in consolidating control over the entire Islamic empire, ruling from his capital city, Damascus, and arranging that his son, Yazīd, would succeed him when he died in 60/680, thus establishing the Umayyad caliphate, which ruled until 132/750, when it was overthrown by the 'Abbāsid revolution.

Muḥammad b. 'Abdallāh b. Sa'īd al-Khalīlī: the last effective Ibāḍī imām of Oman's interior, he ruled from 1920 until his death in May 1954. He was the grandson of the great scholar, Sa'īd b. Khalfān al-Khalīlī.

Muḥammad b. al-Hayṣam (d. ca. 407/1016–1017): according to al-Shahrastānī, he elaborated the theology and technical vocabulary of the Karrāmiyya.

Muḥammad b. Maḥbūb b. al-Raḥīl, known as Abū 'Abdallāh (d. 260/873–874): an extremely influential Ibāḍī scholar of Qurashī descent in Oman. He was among the scholars who gave their oath to Imām al-Ṣalt b. Mālik in 237/852; he dissociated from Imām al-Muhannā b. Jayfar. He served as a judge for Imām al-Ṣalt in the city of Ṣuḥār.

He believed that the Qur'ān was created, but retreated from that position due to pressure from other scholars. He became the chief scholar of his day.

Muḥammad b. Sa'īd al-Azdī al-Qalhātī, Abū 'Abdallāh (or Abū Sa'īd) (eleventh/seventeenth century): Ibāḍī scholar of the Omani town of Qalhāt, author of *Al-Kashf wa-'l-bayān,* a work on Ibāḍī theology through refutation of the doctrines of non-Ibāḍī Muslim sects.

al-Muhannā b. Jayfar al-Yaḥmadī al-Fajḥī (d. 16 Rabī' II 237/15 October 851): the most powerful of all the imāms of Āl al-Yaḥmad, possessing a fleet of 300 battleships and an army of tens of thousands of soldiers. Oman enjoyed security and prosperity under his rule. He was nicknamed Dhū 'l-Nāb (possessor of the eyetooth) because of his habit of baring his teeth when angry. During his time, the question of the creation or eternity of the Qur'ān was a subject of great controversy in Oman, threatening schism; Imām al-Muhannā prohibited discussion of the topic. He became imām on 3 Rajab 226/29 April 841, and refused to step down when he grew old, causing some to dissociate from him.

Mujāhid b. Jabr (born 21/642, died between 100/718 and 104/722): a respected source of Qur'ānic interpretation.

Mūsā b. Mūsā b. 'Alī al-Izkawī (d. 278/891): Omani scholar and judge who became the real holder of power during the imāmate of al-Ṣalt b. Mālik, whom he eventually deposed, appointing Rāshid b. al-Naḍr in his place, and eventually deposing the latter as well and appointing 'Azzān b. Tamīm in his place. The removal of the imāms was highly contentious, leading ultimately to Mūsā's murder in a mosque in the town of al-Nizār, which sparked the outbreak of civil war.

Muslim b. al-Ḥajjāj (206–261/821–875): author of one of the two collections of Ḥadīth considered by Sunni Muslims to be *ṣaḥīḥ* (authentic).

al-Nasā'ī, Abū 'Abd al-Raḥmān Aḥmad b. 'Alī (215–303/830–915): author of one of the six canonical Sunni collections of Ḥadīth.

Nāṣir b. Abī Nabhān (1192–1263/1778–1847): the major Omani scholar of his generation, son of the famous Abū Nabhān Jā'id b. Khamīs al-Kharūṣī, he was a highly original thinker who composed a number of works exploring the ideas of non-Ibāḍī scholars and wrote a commentary on *Al-Tā'iyya 'l-kubrā,* a mystical poem by the famous Egyptian Sufi, Ibn al-Fāriḍ. Like his father, Nāṣir was known for his mystical and talismanic powers, purportedly instilling such fear in Sayyid Sa'īd b. Sulṭān, the ruler of Oman, that the latter kept Nāṣir with him wherever he went, even into battle. Nāṣir allegedly died with his head resting on Sayyid Sa'īd's lap.

al-Naẓẓām, Abū Isḥāq Ibrāhīm b. Sayyār (d. between 220/835 and 230/845): a Mu'tazilite theologian of the Basran school. He was a nephew and student of Abū 'l-Hudhayl, the first Mu'tazilite theologian.

Nūr al-Dīn al-Sālimī: see al-Sālimī, "Nūr al-Dīn."

Qābūs b. Sa'īd b. Taymūr (Qaboos bin Said bin Taimur) (b. 1359/1940): after studying in Great Britain, followed by six years of virtual house arrest, he overthrew his father, Sa'īd b. Taymūr, in a bloodless coup, and has reigned as sultan of Oman since 19 Jumāda 'l-ūlā 1390/23 July 1970. His reign has been a period of rapid modernization.

al-Qushayrī, Abū 'l-Qāsim 'Abd al-Karīm b. Hawāzin (376–465/986–1072): a Sufi and Ash'arite theologian of Khurāsān.

the Quṭb or *quṭb al-a'imma:* see Aṭfayyish, Muḥammad b. Yūsuf.

al-Rabī' b. Ḥabīb (d. 170/786): successor to the leadership of the Ibāḍīs in Basra after the death of Abū 'Ubayda b. Abī Karīma and purported author of the Ibāḍī Ḥadīth collection known as *Al-Jāmi' al-ṣaḥīḥ musnad al-Rabī' b. Ḥabīb.* In response to pressure on the Ibāḍīs following the death of the Caliph al-Manṣūr in 158/775, al-Rabī' migrated to Oman.

al-Rāghib al-Iṣfahānī, Abū 'l-Qāsim al-Ḥusayn b. Muḥammad b. Mufaḍḍal (d. early fifth/eleventh century): an influential religious and Arabic literary scholar, author of an alphabetical lexicon of Qur'ānic vocabulary, *Mufradāt alfāẓ al-Qur'ān.*

Rāshid b. al-Naḍr al-Fajḥī al-Yaḥmadī (d. 285/898): imām of Oman after he and Mūsā b. Mūsā deposed Imām al-Ṣalt b. Mālik in 273/851. His appointment as imām was highly divisive, leading to schism between the schools of Rustāq and Nizwā, a schism that lasted until the Ya'rubī imāmate in the seventeenth century. Many scholars were killed in the battle of al-Rawḍa in 275/888. Eventually, Imām Rāshid had a falling-out with Mūsā b. Mūsā, who removed Rāshid from power, imprisoned him, and appointed 'Azzān b. Tamīm al-Kharūṣī in his place. Rāshid was briefly made imām a second time after Imām 'Azzān died in battle, when the 'Abbāsids invaded the country in 280/893.

al-Rawāḥī, Nāṣir b. Sālim b. 'Udayyam al-Bahlānī, known as Abū Muslim (1273–1339/1860–1920): an Ibāḍī scholar, poet, mystic, and judge, who migrated from Oman to Zanzibar as a young man and made his career there.

al-Rāzī, Abū 'Abdallāh Muḥammad b. 'Umar b. Ḥusayn (543–606/1149–1209): known as Fakhr al-Dīn ("pride of the religion"), one of the most celebrated Ash'arite theologians, and author of an exegesis of the Qur'ān.

al-Rummānī, Abū 'l-Ḥasan 'Alī b. 'Īsā (296–384/909–994): an important linguist of Baghdad.

Sa'īd b. Aḥmad b. Sa'īd: the second ruler of the Bū Sa'īdī dynasty, he became imām in 1198/1783, but was unpopular and handed power over to his son Ḥāmid, in perhaps 1200/1786. Sa'īd was the last of the dynasty to use the title Imām; subsequent rulers of the nineteenth century were simply called *Sayyid*, while later rulers were called *Sulṭān*. Sa'īd died sometime in the decade after 1226/1811.

Sa'īd b. Khalfān b. Aḥmad al-Khalīlī (1231–1287/1816–1871): the greatest Ibāḍī scholar of Oman during his lifetime, a master in theology, law, rhetoric, and grammar, and a recognized poet and mystic, he is most famous outside Oman for leading a revolt in 1285/1868 that overthrew the sultan, Sālim b. Thuwaynī, and installing 'Azzān b. Qays as imām. After 'Azzān was killed in battle on 29 January 1871, Sa'īd surrendered to the British on 13 February, on condition that he be guaranteed safety. However, Col. Lewis Pelly handed him over to the new sultan, Turkī b. Sa'īd, who buried him and his teenage son alive.

Sa'īd b. Sulṭān b. Aḥmad b. Sa'īd: the greatest of the Bū Sa'īdī sultans, he ruled from 1220–1273/1806–1856, and was known simply as Sayyid Sa'īd. He definitively wrenched power from the Mazrū'ī family in Mombasa and established his rule along the Swahili coast from Mogadishu to Tunghi bay in northern Mozambique. In 1247/1832, he transferred the capital of the Omani empire from Muscat to Zanzibar. He invited both Ibāḍī and Sunni Muslim scholars to Zanzibar, making it a major center of Islamic scholarship. He was the last of the Omani sultans to rule both Oman and the Swahili coast, as the kingdom was divided between two of his sons after his death.

Sa'īd b. Taymūr b. Fayṣal: ruler of Oman from 1350/1932 until he was overthrown in a bloodless coup by his son, Qābūs (Qaboos), on 19 Jumāda 'l-ūlā 1390/23 July 1970, he ousted Ghālib b. 'Alī al-Hinā'ī, the last Ibāḍī imām of the interior, in 1955, thereby eliminating the separation of "Oman" from "Muscat." His reign is widely seen today as anti-modern and repressive.

Sālim b. Thuwaynī b. Sa'īd: ruler of Oman from 1282–1285/1866–1868. He seized power by murdering his father, and was in turn removed from power in a revolt led by the esteemed Ibāḍī scholar, Sa'īd b. Khalfān al-Khalīlī, who made 'Azzān b. Qays imām.

al-Sālimī, "Nūr al-Dīn" 'Abdallāh b. Ḥumayd (1286–1332/1869–1914): the most important Ibāḍī scholar of modern Oman, author of important works on theology and jurisprudence, and of the single most important source on the history of Oman, *Tuḥfat al-a'yān bi-sīrat ahl 'Umān*. His children's textbook on the basics of Islam, *Talqīn al-ṣubyān mā* *yalzimu 'l-insān,* continues to be used in Omani schools. In 1331/1913, he led a revolt that captured the al-Jabal al-Akhḍar (Green Mountain) region of the interior but failed to overthrow the sultanate, which retained control of the coast. The division of "Muscat" from "Oman" was formalized in the Treaty of Sīb in 1920, and remained until Sultan Sa'īd b. Taymūr conquered the interior and reunited Oman in December 1955.

al-Ṣalt b. Mālik: imām of the Ibāḍīs in Oman from Rabī' II 237/October 851 until 272/885. He was known for his asceticism and humility. His rule was a time when scholarship flourished. In his old age he became senile. Mūsā b. Mūsā and Rāshid b. al-Naḍr forcibly deposed him, but some continued to regard him as the rightful imām until he died in 275/888. His deposition led to schism between the scholars of Nizwā and Rustāq, and the civil war that ultimately destroyed the first imāmate of Oman.

al-Sanūsī, Abū 'Abdallāh Muḥammad b. Yūsuf (838 or 839–895/1435 or 1436–1490): an Ash'arite theologian and Sufi of Tlemcen, in present-day northwestern Algeria. He wrote several creeds, including one that became part of the religious curriculum for schoolchildren in the Ḥaḍramawt and on the Swahili coast.

al-Shāfi'ī, Muḥammad b. Idrīs (150–204/767–820): founder of the Shāfi'ī legal school of Sunni Islam and of the "roots of jurisprudence" as they are acknowledged by all Muslim schools.

al-Shahrastānī, Abū 'l-Fatḥ Muḥammad b. 'Abd al-Karīm (479–548/1086 or 1087–1153): a prolific scholar of Persia described as either Ash'arite or Ismā'īlī, most famous for his heresiography, *Al-Milal wa-'l-niḥal.*

Sībawayhi (second/eighth century): author of *Kitāb Sībawayhi,* the founding text of Arabic grammar.

al-Suddī, Ismā'īl b. 'Abd al-Raḥmān (d. 127/745): a *mawlā* (non-Arab Muslim) and preacher in Kufa, nicknamed "al-Suddī" because he sat by the threshold (*sudda*) of the mosque in Medina. The Qur'ān exegete al-Ṭabarī frequently used his interpretations, although some exegetes doubted his veracity.

Ṣuḥār b. al-'Abbās al-'Abdī, Abū 'l-'Abbās (50–100/670–718): one of the first Ibāḍī imāms. He was from the Banū 'Abd al-Qays tribe in Oman and was a student of Jābir b. Zayd and a teacher of Abū 'Ubayda Muslim b. Abī Karīma. Ibn al-Nadīm (1970, 194–95) described him as a Khārijite genealogist and preacher, author of a book called *Al-Amthāl* (Proverbs), a transmitter of a few ḥadīths, and knowledgeable about historical traditions.

al-Ṣuḥārī al-ʿAwtabī, Salama b. Muslim, known as Abū ʾl-Mundhir: Omani scholar of law, philology, and genealogy, who lived in the fifth/eleventh and sixth/twelfth centuries. He is best known for his encyclopedic work on law, *Al-Ḍiyāʾ*.

Tabghūrīn b. ʿĪsā b. Dāwūd al-Malshūṭī (sixth/twelfth century): Ibāḍī scholar of the Mzāb valley in Algeria, a student of Abū ʾl-Rabīʿ Sulaymān b. Yakhlaf (d. 471/1078). He is the author of *Kitāb Uṣūl al-dīn,* an important theological text commonly known as *ʿAqīdat Tabghūrīn,* on which Muḥammad b. Yūsuf Aṭfayyish wrote a commentary. *Kitāb al-Jahālāt,* a series of answers to questions on matters of theology, is also commonly attributed to him, though some have suggested that it is a compilation of answers from a number of scholars.

al-Taftāzānī, Saʿd al-Dīn Masʿūd b. ʿUmar (722–793/1322–1390): a renowned Shāfiʿite scholar and author on grammar, rhetoric, theology, logic, law, and Qurʾānic exegesis. His theological work, *Sharḥ al-maqāṣid,* reflects both Māturīdite and Ashʿarite positions.

Taymūr b. Fayṣal b. Turkī: ruler of Oman from 1331/1913 until he abdicated in favor of his son, Saʿīd, in 1350/1932.

al-Thamīnī, ʿAbd al-ʿAzīz b. Ibrāhīm, nicknamed Ḍiyāʾ al-Dīn (1130–1223/1718–1808): one of the greatest Ibāḍī scholars of the Mzab valley in Algeria, a student of the early reformer Abū Zakariyāʾ Yaḥyā b. Ṣāliḥ al-Afḍalī, he wrote a number of important works, including: *Al-Tāj ʿalā "al-Minhāj"*, a twenty-six-volume commentary on Khamīs al-Shaqṣī's *Minhāj al-ṭālibīn wa-balāgh al-rāghibīn; Kitāb al-Nīl wa-shifāʾ al-ʿalīl,* the main reference for Ibāḍī jurisprudence; *Maʿālim al-dīn,* on theology; *Al-Nūr,* a commentary on Abū Naṣr Fatḥ's theological poem, *Al-Nūniyya fī uṣūl al-dīn.*

Thumāma b. Ashras al-Numayrī, Abū Maʿn (d. 213/828): a student of Bishr al-Muʿtamir, founder of the Baghdad school of the Muʿtazila.

Thuwaynī b. Saʿīd b. Sulṭān: ruler of Oman from 1273–1282/1856–1866. He was murdered in his sleep by his son Sālim, who declared himself sultan.

al-Tirmidhī, Abū ʿĪsā Muḥammad b. ʿĪsā (210–279/825–892): author of one of the six canonical Sunni collections of Ḥadīth.

Turkī b. Saʿīd b. Sulṭān: sultan of Oman after the overthrow of Imām ʿAzzān b. Qays on 8 Dhū ʾl-Qaʿda 1287/29 January 1871, until 1305/1888.

ʿUmar b. ʿAbd al-ʿAzīz: an Umayyad caliph who reigned from 99/717 to 101/720; Muslims often regard him as the only pious caliph of the Umayyad dynasty. The quietist Khawārij, the ancestors of the Ibāḍīs, hoped that he would establish a righteous imāmate and accept them as the best of the *umma,* but they were disappointed.

ʿUmar b. al-Khaṭṭāb (d. 26 Dhū ʾl-Ḥijja 23/3 November 644): a forceful, close Companion of the Prophet, who was instrumental in securing the nomination of Abū Bakr as the first caliph, and who succeeded him when the latter died in 13/634. ʿUmar was a driving force behind the Muslim conquests of Palestine, Syria, Persia, and Egypt, and the creation of the Islamic empire.

ʿUrwa b. al-Zubayr (d. 93/711–712 or 94/712–713): son of one of the closest Companions of the Prophet, he was an eminent transmitter of Ḥadīth, especially from the Prophet's wife, ʿĀʾisha. Accounts of the Prophet's life and the great events of early Islam are often attributed to him. He was one of ten authorities on law appointed in Medina by the Umayyad caliph, ʿUmar b. ʿAbd al-ʿAzīz, in 87/706.

ʿUthmān b. ʿAffān (d. 18 Dhū ʾl-Ḥijja 35/17 June 656): an early convert to Islam from the powerful clan of Umayya in Mecca, he was selected to be the third caliph in 23/644 after the assassination of ʿUmar b. al-Khaṭṭāb. During his caliphate, the Muslim conquests of lands of the former Persian empire and North Africa continued, and an official canon of the Qurʾān was issued. Some of his policies were controversial, leading to widespread discontent in the Muslim army and his eventual assassination. Debates over the justice or injustice of this assassination led to the civil wars during the caliphate of his successor, ʿAlī b. Abī Ṭālib, and the eventual formation of the first Muslim sects.

Yaḥyā b. Ṣāliḥ b. Yaḥyā al-Afḍalī, Abū Zakariyāʾ (1126–1202/1714–1788): a major Ibāḍī scholar of the Mzab valley in Algeria, considered the first scholar of the modern Ibāḍī renaissance. He studied in Jirba for twelve years and several more years in Cairo, returning to his homeland in 1157/1744, where he began his career as teacher, preacher, and reformer.

Yazīd I b. Muʿāwiya b. Abī Sufyān: the second Umayyad caliph, who ruled from 60/680 to 64/683.

Yūnus b. ʿAbd al-Raḥmān (d. ca. 207–208/823): a Shīʿite jurist and prolific author who lived in Iraq and was a companion of Muḥammad b. Jaʿfar, son of the sixth Shīʿite Imām, Jaʿfar al-Ṣādiq.

al-Zamakhsharī, Abū ʾl-Qāsim Maḥmūd b. ʿUmar (467–538/1075–1144): an outstanding scholar of grammar, philology, and lexicography, best known for his Qurʾānic exegesis, *Al-Kashshāf ʿan ḥaqāʾiq ghawāmiḍ al-tanzīl wa-ʿuyūn al-aqāwīl fī wujūh al-taʾwīl,* which remains in great favor despite its author's adherence to the Muʿtazilite theological school.

REFERENCES

Dates when deceased authors lived are in brackets.

'Abd al-Kafi al-Tinawati al-Warjilani, Abu 'Ammar [d. before 570/1174]. 1978. *Ara' al-Khawarij al-kalamiyya [Al-Mujaz fi tahṣil al-su'al wa-talkhis al-maqal fi 'l-radd 'ala ahl al-khilaf]*, ed. 'Ammar al-Talibi, 2 vols. Algiers: al-Sharika 'l-Wataniyya li-'l-nashr wa-'l-tawzi'.

Abu 'Amr 'Uthman b. Khalifa al-Marghini al-Sufi [sixth/twelfth century]. n.d. *Al-Su'alat*, unpublished manuscripts in Mzab and Jirba.

Abu 'l-Barakat Hibat Allah b. Malka al-Baghdadi [l. ca. 470–560/1077–1164 or 1165]. 1938–39. *Kitab al-Mu'tabar fi 'l-hikma*, 3 vols. in 1. Heyderabad Deccan: Jam'iyyat Da'irat al-Ma'arif al-'Uthmaniyya.

Abu Dawud al-Sijistani, Sulayman b. al-Ash'ath [202–275/817–889]. 2000. *Sunan Abi Dawud [Kitab al-sunan]*, 2 vols. Vaduz, Liechtenstein: Thesaurus Islamicus Foundation.

Abu 'l-Hawari Muhammad b. al-Hawari [fourth/tenth century]. 1974. *Al-Diraya wa-kanz al-ghinaya fi muntaha 'l-ghaya wa-bulugh al-kifaya fi tafsir khamsa mi'at aya min tafsir al-Qur'an al-karim*. Damascus and Beirut: Dar al-Yaqza (photocopy of manuscript).

———. 1985. *Jami' al-Fadl ibn al-Hawari*, 5 vols. Muscat: Ministry of National Heritage and Culture.

Abu Ishaq Ibrahim b. Qays b. Sulayman al-Hadrami al-Hamadani [d. 470/1082–1083]. 1984. *Mukhtasar al-khisal*. Muscat: Ministry of National Heritage and Culture.

Abu Khazar Yaghla b. Zaltaf [d. 380/990]. 2008. *Al-Radd 'ala jami' al-mukhalifin*, ed. 'Amr Khalifa al-Nami (Ennami). Sib, Oman: Maktabat al-Damiri.

Abu Sa'id Muhammad b. Sa'id al-Kudami [third/ninth to fourth/tenth centuries]. 1405/1980a. *Kitab al-istiqama*, 3 vols. Muscat: Ministry of National Heritage and Culture.

———. 1980b. *Al-Mu'tabar*, 4 vols. Muscat: Ministry of National Heritage and Culture.

Abu Ya'qub Yusuf b. Ibrahim al-Warjilani [d. 570/1174]. 1984. *Al-'Adl wa-'l-insaf fi ma'rifat usul al-fiqh wa-'l-ikhtilaf*, 2 vols. Muscat: Ministry of National Heritage and Culture.

———. 1997. *Al-Dalil wa-'l-burhan li-ahl al-'uqul li-baghi 'l-sabil bi-nur al-dalil li-tahqiq al-madhhab al-haqq bi-'l-burhan al-sadiq*, 3 vols. Muscat: Ministry of National Heritage and Culture.

Ali, 'Abdallah Yusuf [1872–1953]. 1989. *The Meaning of the Holy Qur'an: New Edition with Revised Translation and Commentary.* Beltsville, Maryland: Amana Publications.

Ali, Maulana Muhammad [1874–1951]. 1991. *The Holy Qur'an: Arabic Text, English Translation and Commentary*, rev. ed. Lahore: Ahmadiyyah Anjuman Isha'at Islam.

al-Amawi, Abu Burhan 'Abd al-'Aziz b. 'Abd al-Ghani [1838–1896]. 1459. *'Iqd al-la'al.* From the library of His Highness Sayyid Muhammad b. Ahmad Al Bu Sa'idi, Sib, Oman.

———. *Taqrib "'Iqd al-la'al" ila fahm al-atfal. 667 ta'.* From the library of His Highness Sayyid Muhammad b. Ahmad Al Bu Sa'idi, Sib, Oman.

'Amrus b. Fath al-Masakini al-Nafusi, Abu Hafs [d. 283/896]. 1999. *Usul al-daynuna 'l-safiya*, ed. Ahmad b. Hamu Kurum. Muscat: Ministry of National Heritage and Culture.

An-Na'im, Abdullahi Ahmed. 1990. *Towards an Islamic Reformation: Civil Liberties, Human Rights, and International Law.* Syracuse: Syracuse University Press.

Arafat, Walid N. *Diwan of Hassan ibn Thabit.* 1974. 2 vols. Beirut: Dar Sadir.

al-Ash'ari, Abu 'l-Hasan 'Ali b. Isma'il [260–324/873 or 874–935]. 1963. *Kitab Maqalat al-islamiyyin wa-'khtilaf al-musallin*, ed. Helmut Ritter, 2nd ed. Wiesbaden: Franz Steiner.

Atfayyish, Muhammad b. Yusuf [1820–1914]. 1924–25. *Sharh al-Nil wa-shifa' al-'alil*, 17 vols. Cairo: Al-Matba'a 'l-Salafiyya, 1924–1925. Republished, 1985, Jiddah: Maktabat al-Irshad.

———. 1980a. *Al-Dhahab al-khalis al-munawwih bi 'l-'ilm al-qalis*, ed. Abu Ishaq Ibrahim Atfayyish. Algiers/Constantine: Dar al-Ba'th; Muscat: Dar al-`Alamiyya.

———. 1980b. *Tafsir al-Qur'an al-musamma "Hamayan al-zad ila dar al-ma'ad"*, 15 vols. Muscat: Ministry of National Heritage and Culture.

———. 1981. *Taysir tafsir al-Qur'an al-karim*, 2 vols. Cairo: Matabi' 'Isa al-Babi al-Halabi; published as *Taysir al-tafsir li-'l-Qur'an al-karim*, 15 vols. Muscat: Ministry of National Heritage and Culture.

———. 1986. *Al-Jami' al-saghir*, 3 vols. Muscat: Ministry of National Heritage and Culture.

———. n.d. *Sharh Usul Tabghurin*, unpublished manuscript.

al-'Awtabi al-Suhari, Salama b. Muslim [fourth/eleventh century]. 1990–93. *Kitab al-Diya'*, 23 vols. (18 published). Muscat: Ministry of National Heritage and Culture.

BBC News. 2005a. "Oman Jails 31 for Plotting Coup," May 2, http://news.bbc.co.uk/2/hi/middle_east/4505075.stm.

———. 2005b. "Oman Pardons 31 Coup Plotters," June 9, http://news.bbc.co.uk/2/hi/middle_east/4078138.stm.

Ba Ba 'Ammi, Muhammad b. Musa, et al. 1999. *Mu'jam a'lam al-Ibadiyya min al-qarn al-awwal al-hijri ila 'l-'asr al-hadir, qism al-maghrib al-islami,* 2 vols. Ghardaya, Algeria: Al-Matba'a 'l-'Arabiyya; Beirut: Dar al-Gharb al-Islami.

al-Baghawi, al-Husayn b. Mas'ud [d. 516/1122]. 1900. *Masabih al-sunna,* 2 vols. in 1. Cairo: Al-Matba'a 'l-Khayriyya.

al-Baqillani, Abu Bakr Muhammad b. al-Tayyib [d. 403/1013]. 1987. *Tamhid al-awa'il wa-talkhis al-dala'il,* ed. 'Imad al-Din Ahmad Haydar. Beirut: Mu'assasat al-Kutub al-Thaqafiyya.

Al Barwani, Ali Muhsin. 1997. *Conflicts and Harmony in Zanzibar (Memoirs).* Dubai: n.p.

al-Bayhaqi, Abu Bakr Ahmad b. al-Husayn b. 'Ali b. Musa [384–458/994–1066]. 1925–38. *Kitab al-sunan al-kubra,* 10 vols. Heyderabad al-Dakkan: Matba`at Majlis Dairat al-Ma`arif al-Nizamiyah.

———. 1995. *Al-Sunan al-sughra,* 4 vols., ed. Bahjat Yusuf Hamad Abu al-Tayyib. Beirut: Dar al-Jil.

Bencheneb, H. 1999. "Al-Sanusi, Abu 'Abdallah Muhammad b. Yusuf b. 'Umar b. Shu'ayb," *Encyclopaedia of Islam,* 2nd ed., CD-ROM version. Leiden: E.J. Brill.

Bosworth, Charles E. 2002. "Al-Karramiyya," *Encyclopaedia of Islam,* 2nd ed., CD-ROM version. Leiden: E. J. Brill.

al-Bukhari, Abu 'Abdallah Muhammad b. Isma'il [194–256/810–870]. n.d. *Al-Jami' al-musnad al-sahih al-mukhtasar min umur rasul Allah (Sahih al-Bukhari).* Beirut: Sharikat Dar al-Arqam b. Abi 'l-Arqam.

Chelhod, Joseph. 1999. "Kaffara," *Encyclopaedia of Islam,* 2nd ed., CD-ROM version. Leiden: E. J. Brill.

Cook, Michael. 1981. *Early Muslim Dogma: A Source-Critical Study.* Cambridge, London, New York, New Rochelle, Melbourne, Sydney: Cambridge University Press.

Cragg, Kenneth. 1988. *Readings in the Koran.* London: Collins Liturgical Publications.

Crone, Patricia, and Fritz Zimmerman. 2001. *The Epistle of Salim ibn Dhakwan.* Oxford, New York: Oxford University Press.

Cuperly, Pierre. 1991. *Introduction à l'étude de l'Ibadisme et de sa théologie.* Algiers: Office des Publications Universitaires

Custers, Martin H. 2004. "Ibadi Publishing Activities in Cairo, c. 1880–1960s," 109–63, in Frédéric Bauden (ed.), *Association pour la Promotion de l'Histoire et de l'Archéologie*

Orientales mémoires no. 3, Mélanges de langue arabe et d'islamologie offerts à Aubert Martin. Louvain, Paris, Dudley, MA: Peeters.

———. 2006. *Al-Ibadiyya: A Bibliography*, 3 vols. Maastricht: Universitaire Pers Maastricht.

Daiber, H. 1999. "Mu'ammar b. 'Abbad al-Sulami," *Encyclopaedia of Islam*, 2nd ed., CD-ROM version. Leiden: E. J. Brill.

al-Darjini, Abu 'l-'Abbas Ahmad b. Sa'id [d. 670/1271]. n.d. *Tabaqat al-mashayikh bi-'l-Maghrib*, ed. Ibrahim Tallay, 2 vols. Constantine, Algeria: Matba'at al-Ba'th.

al-Daylami, Shirawayh b. Shahradar [445–509/1053–1115]. n.d. *Al-Firdaws bi-ma'thur al-khitab al-mukharraj 'ala kitab al-shihab*, unpublished work.

Eickelman, Dale F. 1989. "National Identity and Religious Discourse in Contemporary Oman," *International Journal of Islamic and Arabic Studies* 6, 1–20.

Ennami, Amr Khlifa. 2008. *Studies in Ibadhism: Al-Ibadhiyah*, n.d. Republished Muscat: Ministry of Endowments and Religious Affairs.

Esack, Farid. 1997. *Qur'an, Liberation and Pluralism: An Islamic Perspective on Interreligious Solidarity against Oppression*. Oxford: Oneworld Publications.

Fahd, Toufic. 1999. "Sabi'a," *Encyclopaedia of Islam*, 2nd ed., CD-ROM version. Leiden: E. J. Brill.

Farsy, Abdullah Salih. 1989. *The Shafi'i ulama of East Africa, ca. 1830–1970*, trans. and ed. Randall L. Pouwels. Madison: University of Wisconsin African Studies Program.

Flanagan, J. 1999. "Al-Rummani," *Encyclopaedia of Islam*, 2nd ed., CD-ROM version. Leiden: E. J. Brill.

Fleisch, H. 1999. "Ism," *Encyclopaedia of Islam*, 2nd ed., CD-ROM version. Leiden: E. J. Brill.

Francesca, Ersilia. 1987. "L'elemosina rituale secondo gli Ibaditi," *Studi Magrebini* 19, 1–64.

———. 1998. "La fabbricazione degl *isnad* nella scuola ibadita: il *Musnad* di ar-Rabi' b. Habib," 39–59, in U. Vermeulen and J. M. F. van Reeth (eds.), *Law, Christianity, and Modernism in Islamic Society: Proceedings of the 18th Congress of the Union Européenne des Arabisants et Islamisants, held at the Katholieke Universiteit Leuven (Sept. 3–9, 1996)*. Leuven: Peters.

———. 1999. "From the Individualism to the Community's Power: The Economic Implications of the *Wilaya/ Bara'a* Dynamic among the Ibadis," *Annali dell'Istituto Universitario di Napoli* 59, 69–77.

———. 2002a. "Religious Observance and Market Law in Medieval Islam: The Controversial Application of the Prohibition of Usury according to Some Ibadi Sources," *Revue des Mondes Musulmans et de la Méditerranée* 99–100, 191–203.

———. 2002b. *Teoria e pratica del commercio nell'Islam medievale: I contratti di vendita e di commenda nel diritto ibadita*. Rome: Istituto per l'Oriente C. A. Nallino.

———. 2003. "The Formation and Early Development of the Ibadi *Madhhab*," *Jerusalem Studies in Arabic and Islam* 28, 260–77.

———. 2005. "Investigating Early Ibadi Jurisprudence: Sources and Case Law," *Jerusalem Studies in Arabic and Islam* 30.

Frank, Richard M. 1966. "The Structure of Created Causality According to Al-Aš'arî: An Analysis of the "Kitâb al-Luma', §§ 82–164." *Studia Islamica* 25, 13–75.

———. 1978. *Beings and Their Attributes: The Teaching of the Basran School of the Mu'tazila in the Classical Period*. Albany, NY: State University of New York Press.

———. 1992. "The Science of *Kalām*," *Arabic Sciences and Philosophy* 2, 7–37.

Gaiser, Adam R. 2010. *Muslims, Scholars, Soldiers: The Origin and Elaboration of the Ibadi Imamate Traditions*. Oxford and New York: Oxford University Press.

Gardet, Louis. 1953. "Al-Djubba'i," *Encyclopaedia of Islam*, 2nd ed. Leiden: E. J. Brill.

Gätje, Helmut. 1997. *The Qur'an and Its Exegesis*, trans. and ed. Alford T. Welch. London: Routledge, 1971; reprinted Oxford: Oneworld Publications.

Ghazal, Amal Nadim. 2005a. "The Other 'Andalus': The Omani Elite in Zanzibar and the Making of an Identity, 1880s-1930s," *MIT Electronic Journal of Middle East Studies* 5, 43–58.

———. 2005b. "Seeking Common Ground: Salafism and Islamic Reform in Modern Ibadi Thought," *Bulletin of the Royal Institute for Inter-Faith Studies* 7, 119–42.

———. 2010. *Islamic Reform and Arab Nationalism: Expanding the Crescent from the Mediterranean to the Indian Ocean (1880s-1930s)*. London: Routledge.

al-Ghazali, Abu Hamid Muhammad b. Muhammad al-Tusi [450–505/1058–1111]. 1980. *Tahafut al-falasifa*, 6th ed. Cairo: Dar al-Ma'arif.

Gilliot, Claude. 2007. "Attributes of God," *Encyclopaedia of Islam*, 3rd ed., 176–82. Leiden: E. J. Brill.

al-Harithi, Abu 'Abdallah Salim b. Hamad b. Sulayman b. Humayd [d. 2007]. 1974. *Al-'Uqud al-fiddiyya fi usul al-Ibadiyya*. Muscat: Ministry of National Heritage and Culture.

al-Haythami, Nur al-Din 'Ali b. Abi Bakr [734–807/1334–1405]. 2001. *Majma' al-zawa'id wa-manba' al-fawa'id*, 12 vols. Beirut: Dar al-Kutub al-'Ilmiyya.

Heffening, Willi. 1999. "Murtadd," *Encyclopaedia of Islam*, 2nd ed., CD-ROM version. Leiden: E. J. Brill.

Hinds, Martin. 1971. "Kufan Political Alignments and Their Background in the mid-Seventh Century A.D.," *International Journal of Middle East Studies* 2, 346–67.

Hoffman, Valerie J. 2004. "The Articulation of Ibadi Identity in Modern Oman and Zanzibar," *Muslim World* 14, 201–16.

———. 2005a. "Ibadi Muslim Scholars and the Confrontation with Sunni Islam in Nineteenth- and Early Twentieth-Century Zanzibar," *Bulletin of the Royal Institute of Inter-Faith Studies* 7, 91–118.

———. 2005b. "Muslim-Christian Encounters in Late Nineteenth-Century Zanzibar," *The MIT Electronic Journal of Middle East Studies* 5, 59–78.

———. 2006. "In His (Arab) Majesty's Service: A Somali Scholar and Diplomat in Nineteenth-Century Zanzibar," 251–272, in Roman Loimeier and Rüdiger Seesemann (eds.), *The East African Coast in Times of Globalization*. Münster, Hamburg, Berlin, Vienna, London: LIT Verlag.

———. 2009. "Historical Memory and Imagined Communities: Modern Ibadi Writings on Kharijism," 185–200, in James E. Lindsay and Jon Armajani (eds.), *Historical Dimensions of Islam: Essays in Honor of R. Stephen Humphreys*. Princeton: Darwin Press.

Hud b. Muhakkam al-Huwwari [third/ninth century]. 1990. *Tafsir kitab Allahi 'l-'aziz*, 4 vols. Beirut: Dar al-Gharb al-Islami.

Ibn Hajar al-'Asqalani, Ahmad b. 'Ali [773–852/1372–1449]. 1970. *Fath al-Bari bi-sharh al-Bukhari*, 28 vols. Cairo: Dar al-Kitab al-Jadid.

Ibn Hanbal, Ahmad [164–241/780–855]. 1998. *Musnad al-Imam al-Hafiz Abi 'Abdallah Ahmad b. Hanbal*. Riyadh: Bayt al-Afkar al-Duwaliyya li-'l-Nashr wa-'l-Tawzi'.

Ibn Ja'far al-Izkawi, Abu Jabir Muhammad [third/ninth century]. 1981. *Jami' Ibn Ja'far*, 6 vols. Muscat: Ministry of National Heritage and Culture.

Ibn Maja, Abu 'Abdallah Muhammad b. Yazid [209–273/824 or 825–887]. 2000. *Kitab al-sunan* (*Sunan Ibn Maja*), 2 vols. Vaduz, Liechtenstein: Thesaurus Islamicus Foundation.

Ibn al-Nadim, Abu 'l-Faraj Muhammad b. Ishaq. 1970. *The Fihrist: A Tenth-Century AD Survey of Islamic Culture* [completed 377/987–988], ed. and trans. Bayard Dodge. New York: Columbia University Press.

Ibn Rushd, Abu 'l-Walid Muhammad b. Ahmad b. Muhammad ["Averroës", 1126–1198]. 1954. *Averroës' Tahafut al-tahafut (The Incoherence of "The Incoherence")*, trans. Simon van den Bergh. E. J. W. Gibb memorial new series, 19. London: Luzac.

———. 1994. *Fasl al-maqal wa-taqrir ma bayna 'l-shari'a wa-'l-hikma min al-ittisal*, ed. Samih Dughaym. Beirut: Dar al-Fikr al-Lubnani.

Ibn Ruzayq, Humayd b. Muhammad [d. 1873]. 1992. *Al-Fath al-mubin fi sirat al-sada 'l-Bu Sa'idiyin* [completed 1274/1857–1858]. Muscat: Ministry of National Heritage and Culture.

Ingrams, W. H. 1931. *Zanzibar: its History and Its People*. London: H. F. G. Witherby.

al-Jaytali/al-Jitali, Abu Tahir Isma'il b. Musa [d. 750/1349]. 1995. *Qawa'id al-Islam*, 3 vols. in 2, ed. 'Abd al-Rahman b. 'Umar Bakalli. Muscat: Maktabat al-Istiqama.

Jeffery, Arthur, ed. 1958. *Islam: Muhammad and His Religion*. New York: The Bobbs-Merrill Co.

al-Jumahi, Muhammad b. Sallam. 1974. *Tabaqat fuhul al-shu'ara'*, ed. Mahmud Muhammad Shakir. Cairo: Matba'at al-Madani.

al-Juwayni, Abu 'l-Ma'ali 'Abd al-Malik [419–478/1028–1085]. 1950. *Kitab al-irshad ila qawati' al-adilla fi usul al-i'tiqad*. Cairo: Jama'at al-Azhar li-'l-nashr wa-'l-ta'lif.

———. 2000. *A Guide to Conclusive Proofs for the Principles of Belief: Kitab al-irshad ila qawati' al-adilla fi usul al-i'tiqad li-Imam al-Haramayn al-Juwayni*, trans. Paul E. Walker. Reading, U.K.: Garnet Publishing.

Kelly, J. B. 1968. *Britain and the Persian Gulf, 1795–1880*. Oxford: Oxford University Press.

Kenny, Joseph P. 1970. "Muslim Theology as Presented by Muhammad b. Yusuf as-Sanusi, Especially in his *Al-'Aqida 'l-Wusta*," Ph.D. dissertation, Edinburgh University.

Al-Khalili, Ahmad b. Hamad. 1984. *Jawahir al-tafsir: anwar min bayan al-tanzil*, 3 vols. Ruwi: Maktabat al-Istiqama.

———. 1993. "Al-'Umaniyyun wa atharuhum fi 'l-jawanib al-'ilmiyya wa-'l-ma'rifiyya bi-sharq Ifriqiya," 177–91, in Muhammad 'Ali al-Sulaybi (ed.), *Al-Muntada 'l-adabi: fa''aliyyat wa-manashit, husad anshittat al-muntada li-'am 1991–92*. Muscat: Ministry of National Heritage and Culture.

———. 2001. *Al-Haqq al-damigh*. Sib: Maktabat al-Damiri.

al-Khalili, Sa'id b. Khalfan b. Ahmad b. Salih [1226–1287/1811–1871]. 1986. *Tamhid qawa'id al-iman wa-taqyid masa'il al-ahkam*, 13 vols. Muscat: Ministry of National Heritage and Culture.

al-Khatib al-Tibrizi, Muhammad b. 'Abdallah [fl. 1337]. 1960–65. *Mishkat al-masabih*, 4 vols. in 5, ed. James Robson. Lahore: S. M. Ashraf.

al-Kindi, Muhammad b. Ibrahim [d. 508/1115]. 1984. *Bayan al-shar'*, 72 vols. Muscat: Ministry of National Heritage and Culture.

Lane, Edward William. 1863–93. *An Arabic-English Lexicon*, ed. Stanley Lane-Poole, 8 vols. London, Edinburgh: Williams and Norgate.

Lévi-Provençal, Evariste. 1999. "'Abd al-Rahman b. Habib b. Abi 'Ubayda (or 'Abda) al-Fihri," *Encyclopaedia of Islam*, 2nd ed., CD-ROM version. Leiden: E. J. Brill.

Lewicki, Tadeusz. 1953a. "Al-Ibadiyya," *Encyclopaedia of Islam*, 2nd ed. Leiden: E.J. Brill.

———. 1953b. "Al-Nukkar," *Encyclopaedia of Islam*, 2nd ed. Leiden: E. J. Brill.

———. 1955. *Etudes Ibadites Nord-Africaines*. Warsaw: Panstwowe Wydawnictwo Naukowe.

———. 1962. *Les historiens, biographes et traditionnistes ibadites-wahbites de l'Afrique du Nord du viiie au xvie siècles*, extrait des *Folia Orientalia* 3. Krakow: Polska Akademia Nauk, Oddzia Krakowie, Komisja Orientalistyczna.

Madelung, Wilferd. 1997. *The Succession to Muhammad: A Study of the Early Caliphate*. Cambridge: Cambridge University Press.

———. 1999a. "Hisham b. al-Hakam," *Encyclopaedia of Islam*, 2nd ed., CD-ROM version. Leiden: E. J. Brill.

———. 1999b. "Al-Maturidi," *Encyclopaedia of Islam*, 2nd ed., CD-ROM version. Leiden: E. J. Brill.

———. 2001. Madigan, Daniel A. *The Qur'an's Self-Image: Writing and Authority in Islam's Scripture*. Princeton and Oxford: Princeton University Press.

———. 2002. "Al-Taftazani, Sa'd al-Din Mas'ud b. 'Umar al-Taftazani," *Encyclopaedia of Islam*, 2nd ed., CD-ROM version. Leiden: E. J. Brill.

———. 2006. "'Abd Allah Ibn Ibad and the Origins of the Ibadiyya," 52–57, in Barbara Michalak-Pikulska and Andrzej Pikulski (eds.), *Authority, Privacy and Public Order in Islam: Proceedings of the 22nd Congress of L'Union Européenne des Arabisants et Islamisants*. Leuven/Dudley, MA: Peeters.

al-Mahruqi, Muhammad b. Nasir ibn Rashid. 1999–2000. *Al-Shi'r al-'umani al-hadith: Abu Muslim al-Bahlani ra'idan*. Beirut and Casablanca: Al-Markaz al-Thaqafi al-'Arabi.

al-Manhi, Abu 'Ali Salim b. Sa'id b. 'Ali al-Sayighi [attributed]. 1795–96. *Al-Jawhara 'l-farida*, unpublished manuscript in author's hand dated 1210 AH in the Ministry of National Heritage and Culture, Muscat.

Ma'ruf, Ahmad Sulayman. 1988. *Qira'a jadida fi mawaqif al-Khawarij wa-fikrihim wa-adabihim*. Damascus: Dar Talas.

al-Maturidi, Abu Mansur Muhammad b. Muhammad [d. 333/944]. 1953. *Islâm akaidine dair eski metinler: Ebu Mansur-i Matüridî'nin iki eseri, tevhid kitabi ve akaid risalesi*, abridged, ed. Yusuf Ziya Yörükân. Istanbul: Millî Egitim Basimevi.

Metzger, Bruce M., and Roland E. Murphy, eds. 1991. *The New Oxford Annotated Bible, with the Apocryphal/ Deutercanonical Books*. New York: Oxford University Press.

Morony, Michael. 1999. "Madjus," *Encyclopaedia of Islam*, 2nd ed., CD-ROM version. Leiden: E.J. Brill.

Mu'ammar, 'Ali Yahya. [1919–1980]. 1972. *Al-Ibadiyya bayn al-firaq al-Islamiyya*, 2 vols. Muscat: Ministry of National Heritage and Culture.

al-Munawi, 'Abd al-Ra'uf b. Taj al-'Arifin [952–1031/1545–1621]. 1994. *Fayd al-qadir, sharh "Al-Jami' al-saghir min ahadith al-bashir al-nadhir"*, 6 vols. Beirut: Dar al-Kutub al-'Ilmiyya.

al-Mundhiri, 'Ali b. Muhammad b. 'Ali b. Muhammad [1866–1925]. 1896. *Nahj al-haqa'iq* 2602, Omani Ministry of National Heritage and Culture, written in the author's hand and dated 2 Jumada I 1314 (9 Oct. 1896).

———. 1921. *Risalat ikhtisar al-adyan* 209. From the library of Nur al-Din al-Salimi, al-Mintirib, Bidiyya, Oman, dated 26 Rabi' al-Awwal 1340 (26 Nov. 1921).

———. 1980. *Kitab al-Sirat al-mustaqim* (written 1899). Ruwi, Oman: Maktabat al-Istiqama.

Musallam, Basim. 1983. *Sex and Society in Islam: Birth Control before the Nineteenth Century.* Cambridge and New York: Cambridge University Press.

Muslim b. al-Hajjaj al-Qushayri [206–261/821–875]. 1977. *Sahih Muslim,* 4 vols., trans. Abdul Hamid Siddiqi. New Delhi: Kitab Bhavan.

———. 2000. *Al-Jami' al-sahih (Sahih Muslim),* 2 vols. Vaduz, Liechtenstein: Thesaurus Islamicus Foundation.

al-Muttaqi, 'Ali b. 'Abd al-Malik [1480–1567]. 2001. *Kanz al-'ummal fi sunan al-aqwal wa-'l-af'al,* 2 vols. Riyadh: Bayt al-Afkar al-Duwaliyya li-'l-Nashr wa-'l-Tawzi'.

al-Nasa'i, Abu 'Abd al-Rahman Ahmad b. 'Ali al-Nasa'i [215–303/830–915]. 2000. *Kitab al-sunan (Sunan al-Nasa'i),* 2 vols. Vaduz, Liechtenstein: Thesaurus Islamicus Foundation.

Nasir b. Abi Nabhan Ja'id b. Khamis al-Kharusi [1778–1847]. 1848. *Tanwir al-'uqul fi 'ilm qawa'id al-usul* (vol. 3 of *Al-'Ilm al-mubin wa-'l-haqq al-yaqin*), unpublished manuscript copied by Salim b. 'Ali b. Su'ud b. Rashid b. 'Ali b. Muhammad al-Sa'di in Rajab 1264/June 1848, no. 1442, Ministry of National Heritage and Culture, Muscat.

al-Nawawi, Muhyi 'l-Din Abu Zakariya Yahya b. Sharaf [631–676/1233–1277]. 1994. *Sahih Muslim bi-sharh al-Nawawi,* 18 vols. Beirut: Dar al-Ma'rifa.

———. n.d. *Riyadh-us-Saleheen (Riyad al-salihin),* Arabic-English, 2 vols., trans. S. M. Madni Abbasi. Riyadh: Traditional Islamic Publishing House.

al-Qalhati, Muhammad b. Sa'id al-Azdi, Abu 'Abdallah (or Abu Sa'id) [eleventh/seventeenth century]. 1980. *Al-Kashf wa-'l-bayan,* ed. Sayyida Isma'il Kashif. Muscat: Ministry of National Heritage and Culture.

al-Qushayri, Abu 'l-Qasim 'Abd al-Karim b. Hawazin [376–465/986–1072]. n.d. *Risala fi 'ilm al-tasawwuf.* Cairo: Maktabat wa matba'at Muhammad 'Ali 'ubayh wa awladihi.

Peterson, John E. 1978. *Oman in the Twentieth Century.* London: Croom Helm, and New York: Barnes & Noble.

Pines, Shlomo. 1999. "Abu 'l-Barakat," *Encyclopaedia of Islam,* 2nd ed., CD-ROM version. Leiden: E. J. Brill.

al-Rabi' b. Habib [d. ca. 170/786]. n.d. *Al-Jami' al-sahih, Musnad al-Imam al-Rabi' ibn Habib,* ed. Abu Ishaq Ibrahim Atfayyish. Cairo: Maktabat al-Thaqafa 'l-Diniyya.

al-Raghib al-Isfahani, Abu 'l-Qasim al-Husayn b. Muhammad b. Mufaddal [d. early fifth/eleventh century]. 1970. *Mufradat alfaz al-Qur'an.* Cairo: Maktabat al-Anglo 'l-Misriyya.

Rahman, Fazlur. 1979. *Islam,* 2nd ed. Chicago and London: University of Chicago Press.

al-Rawahi, Nasir b. Salim b. 'Udayyam al-Bahlani [1860–1920]. 1980. *Diwan Abi Muslim al-Bahlani,* eds. 'Ali al-Najdi Nasif, vol. 1. Muscat: Ministry of National Heritage and Culture.

———. 1986. *Diwan Abi Muslim,* ed. 'Abd al-Rahman al-Khazindar. Muscat: Matabi' Dar al-Mukhtar.

———. 1987. *Diwan Abi Muslim.* Muscat: Ministry of National Heritage and Culture.

———. 2001. *Nithar al-jawhar fi 'ilm al-shar' al-azhar,* 5 vols. Muscat: Maktabat Musqat.

———. 2004. *Al-'Aqida 'l-wahbiyya,* ed. Salih b. Sa'id al-Qunubi and 'Abdallah b. Sa'id al-Qunubi. Muscat: Maktabat Musqat.

———. n.d. *Al-Manzumat al-arba',* photocopied manuscript in library of Oman Cultural Center, Sultan Qaboos University, al-Khawd, Oman.

al-Rawas, Isam. 2000. *Oman in Early Islamic History.* Reading, England: Ithaca Press.

Rosenthal, Franz. 1999. "Ash'ab," *Encyclopaedia of Islam,* 2nd ed., CD-ROM version. Leiden: E. J. Brill.

Rouvillois-Brigol, Madeleine, and Marcel Mercier. 1999. "Mzab," *Encyclopaedia of Islam,* 2nd ed., CD-ROM version. Leiden: E. J. Brill.

Rowson, Everett K. 1999. "al-Raghib al-Isfahani," *Encyclopaedia of Islam,* 2nd ed., CD-ROM version. Leiden: E. J. Brill.

al-Sabi'i, Nasir b. Sulayman b. Sa'id. 1999. *Al-Khawarij wa-'l-haqiqa 'l-gha'iba.* Muscat: Matabi' al-Nahda.

Sadgrove, Philip. 2004. "From Wadi Mizab to Unguja: Zanzibar's Scholarly Links," 184–210, in Scott S. Reese (ed.), *The Transmission of Learning in Islamic Africa.* Leiden, Boston: Brill.

al-Sa'di, Jumayyil b. Khamis b. Lafi [born 1206/1791–1792]. 1983–89. *Qamus al-shari'a al-hawi turuqaha 'l-wasi'a,* vols. 1–20. [Orig. 90 vols.] Muscat: Ministry of National Heritage and Culture.

al-Salimi, 'Abdallah ["Nur al-Din"] b. Humayd [1869–1914]. 1983a. *Ma'arij al-amal 'ala "Madarij al-kamal" bi-nazm "Mukhtasar al-khisal,"* 18 vols., ed. Muhammad Mahmud Isma'il. Muscat: Ministry of National Heritage and Culture.

———. 1983b. *Madarij al-kamal fi nazm "Mukhtasar al-khisal."* Muscat: Ministry of National Heritage and Culture.

———. 1995a. *Badhl al-majhud fi mukhalafat al-Nasara wa-'l-Yahud.* Sib: Maktabat al-Imam Nur al-Din al-Salimi.

———. 1995b. *Mashariq anwar al-'uqul.* Damascus: Al-Hikma.

———. 1996. *Al-Hujaj al-muqni'a fi ahkam salat al-jum'a.* Muscat: National Ministry of History and Culture.

———. 2000a. *Jawhar al-nizam fi 'ilmay al-adyan wa-'l-ahkam,* ed. Abu Ishaq Atfayyish and Ibrahim al-'Ibri, 13th ed. Sib: Maktabat al-Imam Nur al-Din al-Salimi.

———. 2000b. *Tuhfat al-a'yan bi-sirat ahl 'Uman.* Sib: Maktabat al-Imam Nur al-Din al-Salimi.

———. 2003. *Kashf al-haqiqa li-man jahala 'l-tariqa*. Sib: Maktabat al-Damiri.

al-Salimi, Muhammad b. 'Abdallah. n.d. *Nahdat al-a'yan bi-hurriyyat 'Uman*. Cairo: Matabi' Dar al-Kitab al-'Arabi.

Savage, Elizabeth. 1997. *A Gateway to Hell, A Gateway to Paradise: The North African Response to the Arab Conquest*. Princeton: Darwin Press.

al-Shahrastani, Abu 'l-Fath Muhammad b. 'Abd al-Karim [479–548/1086–1153]. 1923. *Kitab al-Milal wa-'l-nihal: Book of Religious and Philosophical Sects,* 2 vols. in 1 [written in 521/1127–1128], ed. William Cureton. Leipzig: Otto Harrassowitz.

al-Shammakhi, Badr al-Din Abu 'l-'Abbas Ahmad b. Sa'id [d. 928/1522]. 1989. *Muqaddimat al-tawhid wa-shuruhuhu,* ed. Abu Ishaq Ibrahim Atfayyish. Muscat: n.p.

al-Shaqsi al-Rustaqi, Khamis b. Sa'id b. 'Ali b. Mas'ud [eleventh/seventeenth century]. 1981–83. *Manhaj al-talibin wa bulugh al-raghibin,* 20 vols., ed. Salim b. Hamad b. Sulayman al-Harithi. Muscat: Ministry of National Heritage and Culture.

al-Shaybani, Sultan b. Mubarak and Muhammad Salih Nasir. 2006. *Mu'jam a'lam al-Ibadiyya min al-qarn al-awwal al-hijri ila 'l-'asr al-hadir: qism al-mashriq*. Beirut: Dar al-Gharb al-Islami.

Shehadi, Fadlou. 1995. *Philosophies of Music in Medieval Islam*. Leiden: E. J. Brill.

Shiloah, A. 1999. "Malahi," *Encyclopaedia of Islam,* 2nd ed., CD-ROM version. Leiden: E. J. Brill.

Smith, Jane Idleman, and Yvonne Yazbeck Haddad. 1981. *The Islamic Understanding of Death and Resurrection*. Albany: State University of New York Press.

al-Suyuti, Jalal al-Din [849–911/1445–1505]. 1981. *Al-Jami' al-saghir fi ahadith al-bashir al-nadhir,* 2 vols. Beirut: Dar al-Fikr.

al-Tabarani, Abu 'l-Qasim Sulayman b. Ayyub [260–360/873–971]. 1968. *Al-Mu'jam al-saghir,* 2 vols. Medina: Al-Maktaba 'l-Salafiyya.

al-Tabari, Abu Ja'far Muhammad b. Jarir b. Yazid 224 or 225–310/839–923]. 1954–68. *Jami' al-bayan 'an ta'wil ayy al-Qur'an,* 30 vols. in 12. Cairo: Mustafa al-Babi al-Halabi.

———. 1987. *The Commentary on the Qur'an,* trans. John Cooper, Wilferd Madelung and Alan Jones. New York, Oxford: Oxford University Press.

Tabghurin b. 'Isa b. Dawud al-Malshuti [sixth/twelfth century]. 2005. *Usul al-din aw al-usul al-'ashara 'inda 'l-Ibadiyya,* ed. Wanis al-Tahir 'Amir. Muscat: Maktabat al-Jil al-Wa'id.

al-Taftazani, Sa'd al-Din Mas'ud b. 'Umar [722–793/1322–1390]. 1957. *Sharh al-Talwih 'ala 'l-Tawdih li-matn al-Tanqih fi usul al-fiqh,* 2 vols. in 1. Beirut: Dar al-Kutub al-'Ilmiyya.

———. 1984. *Sharh al-maqasid,* 2 vols., ed. 'Abd al-Rahman 'Umayra. Cairo: Al-Kulliyya 'l-Azhariyya.

Talbi, Mohamed. 1998. "Religious Liberty," 161–68, in Charles Kurzman (ed.), *Liberal Islam: A Sourcebook*. New York, Oxford: Oxford University Press.

———. 1999. "Rustamids," *Encyclopaedia of Islam,* 2nd ed., CD-ROM version. Leiden: E. J. Brill.

al-Thamini, Diya' al-Din 'Abd al-'Aziz b. al-Hajj b. Ibrahim b. 'Abdallah b. 'Abd al-'Aziz [1130–1223/1718–1808]. 1967. *Kitab al-Nil wa-shifa' al-'alil,* 3 vols., ed. 'Abd al-Rahman Bakalli. Algiers: Al-Matba'a 'l-'Arabiyya.

———. 1981. *Al-Nur,* a commentary on Abu Nasr Fath al-Malshuti's theological poem, *Al-Nuniyya*. Cairo: Al-Matba'a 'l-Baruniyya, 1888–1889; reprinted Ghardaya, Algeria: Al-Matba'a 'l-'Arabiyya.

———. 1986. *Kitab Ma'alim al-din,* 2 vols. Muscat: Ministry of National Heritage and Culture.

———. 2000. *Al-Taj al-manzum min durar al-Manhaj al-ma'lum,* 7 vols, ed. Muhammad Ba Ba 'Ammi and Mustafa Sharifi. Muscat: Ministry of National Heritage and Culture.

al-Tirmidhi, Abu 'Isa Muhammad b. 'Isa [210–279/825–892]. 2000. *Al-Jami' al-sahih* (*Sunan al-Tirmidhi*), 2 vols. Vaduz, Liechtenstein: Thesaurus Islamicus Foundation.

Tritton, Arthur Stanley. 1999. "Al-Djurdani, 'Ali b. Muhammad," *Encyclopaedia of Islam,* 2nd ed., CD-ROM edition. Leiden: E.J. Brill.

van Ess, Josef. 1992. *Theologie und Gesellschaft im 2. und 3. Jahrhundert Hidschra: Eine Geschichte des religiösen Denkens im frühen Islam,* 3 vols. Berlin, New York: Walter de Gruyter.

———. 1999. "Al-Idji," *Encyclopaedia of Islam,* 2nd ed., CD-ROM version. Leiden: E.J. Brill, 1999.

———. 2002a. "Tashbih wa-Tanzih," *Encyclopaedia of Islam,* 2nd ed., CD-ROM version. Leiden: E.J. Brill.

———. 2002b. "Thumama b. Ashras," *Encyclopaedia of Islam,* 2nd ed., CD-ROM version. Leiden: E.J. Brill.

Vecca Vaglieri, Laura. 1999. "'Ali b. Abi Talib," *Encyclopaedia of Islam,* 2nd ed., CD-ROM version. Leiden: E.J. Brill.

Valeri, Marc. 2009. *Oman: Politics and Society in the Qaboos State*. London: Hurst & Co.

Versteegh, C. H. M., Oliver N. H. Leaman, and Jamel-Eddine Bencheikh. 1999. "Ma'na," *Encyclopaedia of Islam,* 2nd ed., CD-ROM version. Leiden: E.J. Brill.

Watt, William Montgomery. 1948.*Free-Will and Predestination in Early Islam*. London: Luzac.

———. 2002. *The Formative Period of Islamic Thought*. Edinburgh: Edinburgh University Press, 1973; reprinted Oxford: Oneworld Publications.

Wensinck, A. J. 1932. *The Muslim Creed: Its Genesis and Historical Development*. Cambridge: Cambridge University Press.

Wilkinson, John C. 1982. "The Early Development of the Ibadi Movement in Basra," 125–44, in G. H. A. Juynboll (ed.), *Studies in the First Century of Islamic Society*, 125–44. Carbondale and Edwardsville: Southern Illinois University Press.

———. 1985. "Ibadi Hadith: An Essay on Normalization," *Der Islam* 62: 231–59.

———. 1987. *The Imamate Tradition of Oman*. Cambridge: Cambridge University Press.

———. 1990. "Ibadi Theological Literature," 33–39, in M. J. L. Young, J. D. Latham, and R. B. Serjeant (eds.), *Religion, Learning, and Science in the Abbasid Period*. Cambridge and New York: Cambridge University Press.

———. 2010. *Ibâdism: Origins and Early Development in Oman*. Oxford and New York: Oxford University Press.

Williams, John Alden, ed. 1994. *The Word of Islam*. Austin: University of Texas Press.

Wolfson, Harry A. 1976. *The Philosophy of the Kalam*. Cambridge, MA: Harvard University Press.

al-Zamakhshari, Abu 'l-Qasim Mahmud b. 'Umar [467–538/1075–1144]. 1966–68. *Tafsir al-kashshaf 'an haqa'iq ghawamid al-tanzil wa-'uyun al-aqawil fi wujuh al-ta'wil*, 4 vols. Cairo: al-Babi al-Halabi.

INDEX

Note: "al-" and "'l-" are definite articles and are not considered in alphabetization.

'Abbad b. Sulayman al-Daymari/al-Saymari, 266–67, 291

al-'Abbas, uncle of the Prophet, 6, 226, 279, 291

'Abbasid caliphate, 6, 11, 279; decline of, 21; defeated first Omani imam, 13; end of *mawla* system, 44; Ibadi disputes in early 'Abbasid period, 18; recaptured Qayrawan, 14; support of Mu'tazilite doctrine on Qur'an, 38

'Abd al-Jabbar b. Qays al-Muradi, 197

'Abdallah b. 'Abd al-'Aziz, 19

'Abdallah b. Faysal b. Turki Al Su'ud, 16

'Abdallah b. Ibad/Abad, 11–12, 17, 177, 291

'Abdallah b. Wahb al-Rasibi, 10, 17, 19, 131, 291

'Abdallah b. Yahya al-Kindi ("Talib al-Haqq"), 13, 177, 291

'Abdallah b. Yazid al-Fazari, 19, 291

'Abd al-Malik b. Marwan, 11–12, 291

'Abd al-Malik b. al-Muhallab, 12, 291

'Abd al-Rahman b. Habib al-Fihri, 197, 292

'Abd al-Rahman b. Rustam, 14, 20, 177, 215, 292

'Abd al-Wahhab b. 'Abd al-Rahman b. Rustam, 19, 292

'Abduh, Muhammad, 46

Abode of Islam, 182, 279

Abode of War, 182, 279

Abraham, 23n24, 179, 212n2

Abrogation, 71

Abu 'l-'Abbas Ahmad, 21, 292

Abu 'Abdallah Muhammad b. Sa'id al-Azdi, 24

Abu 'Ammar 'Abd al-Kafi b. Abi Ya'qub, 22, 84, 292

Abu 'Amr 'Uthman b. Khalifa al-Sufi al-Marghini, 22, 162, 199, 293

Abu Bakr, 7–8, 131, 177, 181, 185, 293

Abu 'l-Baqa' 'Abdallah b. al-Husayn al-'Akbari, 86, 293

Abu 'l-Barakat al-Baghdadi, 140, 293

Abu Bilal Mirdas b. Udayya, 11, 293

Abu Dawud Sulayman al-Sijistani, 4n3, 293; citations of, 28, 31, 76, 157, 242, 256–57

Abu Dharr al-Ghifari, 110, 168, 209, 293

Abu Hafs. *See* 'Amrus b. Fath al-Masakini

Abu Hanifa, 27, 39, 293

Abu Hashim 'Abd al-Salam, 261–62, 265, 293

Abu 'l-Hawari Muhammad b. al-Hawari, 20, 293–94

Abu Ishaq Ibrahim b. Qays, 198, 294

Abu Ishaq al-Sha'bi, 119

Abu 'l-Khattab 'Abd al-A'la al-Ma'arifi, 13–14, 177, 294

Abu Khazar Yaghla b. Zaltaf, 21, 177, 215, 294

Abu Lahab, 169n17, 179

Abu Mas'ud Sabir b. 'Isa, 93
Abu Mu'ammar al-Sa'di, 119
Abu 'l-Mu'arrij, 19
Abu Nabhan Ja'id b. Khamis, 24–25, 294
Abu Nu'aym, 119
Abu Nuh Sa'id b. Zanghil, 21, 294
Abu 'l-Qasim Yunus b. Faysal Abi Zakariya', 93, 294–95
Abu 'l-Rabi' Sulayman b. Yakhlaf, 21, 295
Abu Sahl Yahya b. Sulayman b. Wijman, 84–85, 295
Abu Sa'id Muhammad b. Sa'id al-Kudami, 21, 47, 295
Abu Salih Badham, 119
Abu Salih Janun, 177, 295
Abu Sufra 'Abd al-Malik b. Sufra, 20, 295
Abu 'Ubayda Muslim b. Abi Karima, 12–13, 18–19, 295
Abu Ya'qub Yusuf b. Ibrahim al-Warjilani, 22, 184, 215, 295–96
Abu 'l-Yaqzan Muhammad b. Aflah, 20, 296
Abu Zakariyya' Yahya b. Abi 'l-Khayr al-Jannawuni. *See* al-Jannawuni, Abu Zakariya' Yahya b.Abi 'l-Khayr
Abu Zayd al-Ansari, 106, 296
Accident (*'arad*), 63, 246, 249
Accountability (*taklif*), 65–66
Acquisition, doctrine of. *See* Free will and predestination
Adam: created from clay, 59n3, 161; created in God's image, 138; father of humanity, 60; God commanded angels to prostrate before him, 188–89; God taught him the names, 149; necessity of affiliation with, 163
Adultery, 207, 272
al-Afdali, Abu Zakariya Yahya b. Salih. *See* Yahya b. Salih al-Afdali, Abu Zakariya'
Affiliation. *See walaya*
Aflah b. 'Abd al-Wahhab (Rustamid imam), 208–9, 296
Aflah b. Muhammad, 119
Age of Ignorance (*al-Jahiliyya*), 237
Ahl al-dhimma (people of protection), 221–22, 224–25, 279
Ahl al-istiqama (people of straightness), 10, 28, 55, 279
Ahmad b. Hamad al-Khalili, 5n6, 41, 296
Ahmad b. Hanbal, 33, 38–39, 137, 296; citations of, 109, 115, 118, 196, 257n8
Ahmad b. al-Husayn, 18, 20, 201, 296
Ahmad b. Sa'id Al Bu Sa'id, 14, 296
Ahmad b. Sumayt, 48n36
'A'isha bint Abi Bakr, 8–9, 119, 179n34, 296
Al-'Aqida 'l-Wahbiyya: manuscripts of, 51; publications of, 50–51; structure and topics of, 47–50; translation of, 55–237
Alexandria, Egypt, 227
Algeria, 10, 14, 21–22, 24, 26, 221n15
'Ali b. Abi Talib, 296–97; caliphate, 8–11; citations of, 83, 109, 119; embracing Islam, 171; in Ibadi doctrine, 7, 9–11, 176; in Kharijite doctrine, 9–10; killing Khawarij at Nahrawan, 10–11, 131n31; in Shi'ite doctrine, 6; in Sunni doctrine, 27
'Ali b. Mansur, 139
'Ali al-Rida b. Musa b. Ja'far, 108
Allah, as Arabic word and name of God, 81–86, 151–54
al-Amawi, 'Abd al-'Aziz, 48
'Ammar, 119
'Amr b. al-'As, 9, 131, 167, 178, 227, 297
'Amrus b. Fath al-Masakini ("Abu Hafs"), 20, 215, 297
Analogical reasoning, 42, 75–76
Angels, 60, 64–67; affiliating with, 159–60, 163, 179; God asked about the names, 149; and Iblis, 188–92; meaning of God's coming, 138; obligation to believe in, 68; obligation to know about, 231, 234; and

procreation, 189; prostrated before Adam, 188–92; Sabaeans worship of, 213
Animals, 65, 216–18, 220–21, 224–25, 248
An-Na'im, Abdullahi Ahmed, 181n37
Ansar, 8
Anthropomorphism. *See* God, anthropomorphic descriptions of
Apostasy/apostates, 140, 172, 180–84
'Aqil b. Abi Talib, 226
Arabic verbal forms, 81n8
Arabs, 226, 237
Arafat, Walid N., 113n9
Aristotle, 37n29, 50
Asbat b. Muhammad, 119
Ash'ab al-Tamma' b. Jubayr, 121
al-Ash'ari, Abu 'l-Hasan, 297; on anthropomorphic descriptions of God, 137; on free will vs. predestination, 34, 257; God not obligated to do what is best, 268; on God's attributes, 90n3; on God's names, 150–51; on God's speech, 39, 115; use of dialogue as literary form, 49
Ash'arite school, 279; on anthropomorphic descriptions of God, 136n37; compared to Maturidites, 90–92; on God's attributes vs. essence, 87–92, 100, 143; on God's speech, 39–40, 41n32; on human acts, 242–43, 264n22; Ibadis' embrace of doctrine on free will vs. predestination, 34, 48; on Moses hearing God's speech, 115; nonexistent is not a thing, 96; on origination of God's attributes of act, 91–92; predominated on Swahili coast, 35; on reason and revelation, 276; reject secondary causation, 104n15; on seeing God, 110–11, 115–16, 122, 132–33; use of Aristotelian proofs, 50; use of *bi-la kayf*, 122
Association. *See walaya*
'Ata' b. Yasar, 119
Atfayyish, Abu Ishaq Ibrahim b. Muhammad, 26, 214n8, 297
Atfayyish, Ibrahim b. Yusuf, 24, 297
Atfayyish, Muhammad b. Yusuf ("the *Qutb*"), 10, 19, 24, 26, 48, 51–52, 297. *See also* Atfayyish, Muhammad b. Yusuf, citations of
Atfayyish, Muhammad b. Yusuf, citations of: affiliation and dissociation, 163–211; Iblis not an angel, 190–92; ignorance of imams, 177n27; ignorance of theological opponents, 177–78; immunity from error, 160n3; knowledge and action, 231–37; looking toward God, 114; Name of Majesty (Allah), 81n7, 82n9; persisting in sin, 162; punishment of hypocrites, 69; treatment of people not in Muhammad's *umma,* 212–30
Atheism/atheists, 225
Attribute, meaning of, 98
Attributes of God: 37–38, 87–104, 130–31; adjectival (*al-sifat al-ma'nawiyya*), 144; attributist, 279; of essence vs. of act, 89–90; essential of (*al-sifa 'l-nafsiyya*), 142; Mu'tazilite doctrine, 32–33; necessity of knowing, 233; negative of (*al-sifat al-salbiyya*), 142–44; qualifying (*sifat al-ma'na*), 143–44. *See also* God
al-'Awtabi al-Suhari, Salama b. Muslim. *See* al-Suhari al-'Awtabi, Salama b. Muslim
Azariqa/Azraqites, 11, 17, 279–80
Azd tribe, 11–12, 280
'Azzaba councils, 21, 280
'Azzan b. Qays Al BuSa'idi, 15–16, 25, 45, 298

Ba Ba 'Ammi, 52, 72n12
Badr, 11, 113, 116, 131, 217, 280
al-Baghawi, al-Husayn b. Mas'ud, 116n14
Baghdad, 11, 34

al-Baghdadi, Abu 'l-Barakat. *See* Abu 'l-Barakat al-Baghdadi
al-Baqillani, 22, 90n3, 113n9, 243–45, 298
Bara'a (dissociation), 28–30, 178–206, 208–11, 216–17, 233, 280; affection for dissociates, 204; meaning of, 156, 161, 174–75, 178; necessity of knowing about, 60; obligation of, 156–62; politeness to dissociates, 203–5; status of those who deny its obligation, 169–70; suspended during *kitman*, 43; when obligatory, 161–62, 178–79, 185, 187, 193–94, 209–11
Barghash b. Sa'id Al Bu Sa'id, 15n18, 25, 48, 223n17, 298
al-Baruni, Abu Yahya Zakariyya b. Ibrahim, 18
al-Baruni, Sulayman b. 'Abdallah, 26, 298
Bashir b. Muhammad b. Mahbub b. al-Rahil ("Abu 'l-Mundhir"), 21, 299
Basra, 8, 11–13, 19–20, 80, 268n27, 280
al-Basri, al-Hasan. *See* al-Hasan al-Basri
bayda, 165–66, 195
al-Baydawi, 'Abdallah b. 'Umar, 299
Bayyud, Ibrahim b. 'Umar, 52
BBC, 17
Believer, defined, 28, 60–61, 107–8
Bencheneb, H., 47
Bible, 102n12
Bi-la kayf ("without how"), 36, 122, 126, 280
Bil'arab b. Sultan b. Sayf al-Ya'rubi, 23
Birth control, 42n34
Body (*jism*), defined, 64
Bombay, 15
Bosworth, Charles E., 137n39
al-Bukhari, Muhammad b. Ismail, 3, 4n3, 299. *See also* al-Bukhari, citations of
al-Bukhari, citations of: accusations of infidelity, 210; children of hypocrites and unbelievers, 170; dead cannot defend themselves, 209n63; God created Adam according to His image, 138; good deeds do not bring reward, 257n8; sinners will enter paradise, 27, 109–10; truthful person may speak, 211; virtues of Prophet's Companions, 176n26; vision of God in paradise, 35, 118n19; when a Muslim's blood may be shed, 181n37
Buraimi oasis, 15
Bu Sa'idi dynasty, 14–15, 25, 280. *See also* Ahmad b. Sa'id Al Bu Sa'id; Faysal b. Turki b. Sa'id Al Bu Sa'idi; Majid b. Sa'id b. Sultan Al Bu Sa'idi; Sa'id b. Sultan b. Ahmad Al Bu Sa'idi; Sa'id b. Taymur b. Faysal Al Bu Sa'idi; Salim b. Thuwayni b. Sa'id Al Bu Sa'idi; Sultan b. Ahmad Al Bu Sa'idi; Taymur b. Faysal b. Turki Al Bu Sa'idi; Thuwayni b. Sa'id b. Sultan Al Bu Sa'idi; Turki b. Sa'id Al Bu Sa'idi

Cairo, 26
Caliph, 280
Canning Award, 15
Carrion, 214
Cause and effect, 69, 77, 104, 259–60
Chelhod, Joseph, 183n41
Children, 59–60, 159, 170–74, 182, 187, 220, 225–27
Christians/Christianity: Abraham not a Christian, 23n24; choose pleasant parts of Gospel, 214; belief concerning Jesus, 39; belief in Mary's divinity, 164; ideas of God's perfection and immutability, 102n12; as infidels, hypocrites, or unbelievers, 215; and *jizya,* 106n2, 228–30; Muslim men may marry Christian women, 172n23; originally followed truth, 213; and parents, 170n20; permissible interactions with, 216–17, 220–26; al-Rawahi's discussion of treatment of,

50; refutation of, 22; Satan prescribed, 212; why called *al-Nasara,* 213
Companions of the Cave, 164
Companions of the Prophet, 280; affiliation with, 176; did not object to 'Umar's ruling on *jizya,* 227; did not say God would be seen with human eye, 118; disagreed on legal questions, 42; death of at Nahrawan, 10–11; using reports from as proof 164. *See also* Abu Bakr; Abu Dharr al-Ghifari; 'A'isha bint Abi Bakr; 'Ali b. Abi Talib; 'Amr b. al-'As; Hassan b. Thabit; Ibn 'Abbas/Ibn al-'Abbas, Mu'awiya b. Abi Sufyan; 'Umar b. al-Khattab; 'Uthman b. 'Affan
Compensation, 44
Consensus (*ijma'*), 75–76, 162–63, 183, 196, 253, 263
Cook, Michael, 5n5, 11
Corporealists, 137, 139
Cragg, Kenneth, 147n48
Crone, Patricia, 5n5
Cuperly, Pierre, 4–5, 19, 22
Curse/cursing, 178n30, 206, 223; Ibn 'Abbas's of Nafi' b. al-Azraq, 135n36; and parents, 76; people whom God, 102, 104, 157; and Satan, 188–90, 212
Custers, Martin H., 5n5, 26

al-Dahhak b. Muzahim, 118–19
Damascus, 11
al-Darjini, Abu 'l-'Abbas Ahmad b. Sa'id, 236n8
David, 212n2
al-Daymari, 'Abbad. *See* 'Abbad b. Sulayman al-Daymari/al-Saymari
Death, 59, 171, 223
Dhikr, 224, 281
Dinar, 227, 281
Dirham, 227, 281
Discourse, analysis of, 76–77
Disputation, 259
Dissociation. *See Bara'a*
Dogs, 163n7, 224
Dualists, 22

East Africa, 15, 47
Egypt, 7, 177, 227
Eickelman, Dale, 5n5, 26
Ennami, Amr Khlifa, 4–5, 18–19, 41n33, 42–43, 299
Esack, Farid, 105n1

Faith: meaning of, 106–9; profession of, 27, 59–60, 67, 184, 224; and works, 8, 27, 60, 232–37
al-Farabi, Abu Nasr Muhammad, 49, 101n11, 104n15, 299
al-Farisi, Sayf b. Muhammad b. Sulayman, 51
Farq, 12
Farsy, Abdullah Salih, 46
Fath b. Nuh al-Malusha'i ("Abu Nasr"), 22–24, 271n30, 299
Fatiha, 43, 281
Fatima, daughter of the Prophet, 6, 299
Fatimids, 14, 19, 281
Fatwa, 24, 184, 281
Faysal b. Turki b. Sa'id Al Bu Sa'idi, 299
al-Fazari, 'Abdallah b. Yazid. *See* 'Abdallah b. Yazid al-Fazari
Fighting, 206, 217–18, 224–26
al-Fihri, 'Abd al-Rahman. *See* 'Abd al-Rahman b. Habib al-Fihri
Fiqh. See Jurisprudence
Fiqh Akbar II, 39
Fleisch, H., 80n5
France, 221n15

Francesca, Ersilia, 5n5
Frank, Richard M., 36n28
Free will and predestination, 30–35, 201, 241–74; accountability for human acts, 248, 251–58, 268; acquisition of human acts, 34, 243, 246–48, 251, 254, 256–58, 279; acts defined, 246; capacity to act, 246; compulsion, 244–46, 248, 251–53, 257–58; creation of human acts, 241–48, 251, 256; divine determination, 257; divine guidance, 258; effects of human acts, 242–45, 248, 252–53, 259–67; human choice, 247–48; human power to act, 247–51, 256–59; intention in action, 247; secondary effects, 259–67; voluntary and involuntary acts, 243, 245, 248, 250, 257–58
al-Fudayl b. ʿIyad, 119

Gabriel, 163
Gaiser, Adam S., 5n5
Gätje, Helmut, 36n28, 106n2, 115n13, 118n18
Genesis, 180n36
Ghalib b. ʿAli al-Hinaʾi, 299–300
Ghassan tribe, 226
Ghazal, Amal Nadim, 5n5, 26
al-Ghazali, Abu Hamid Muhammad, 101n11, 104n15, 112, 115, 132, 268n27, 300
Gilliot, Claude, 90n3, 90n4
God: anthropomorphic descriptions of, 18–19, 22, 35–36, 99, 102, 114–15, 127, 134–47; changing His mind, 102; creative command of, 40–41, 140; creator of human acts, 241–48; difference from created things, 62, 95–96, 142; does no evil, 247; enmity for sinners, 201–3; essence and existence of, 142, 144–46; eternity of, 62, 142, 144; goodness of, 252n4, 268–72, 276; human knowledge of, 36–37, 61–62; invisibility of, 35, 110–34; justice of, 22, 219; knowledge of future, 32, 201, 255–56; knowledge of the nonexistent, 100–101, 201; nearness, 134–35; necessary attributes, 146–47; necessity of His existence, 96; no purpose to His acts, 269–70; not in a place/space, 121–22, 130, 134–36, 141; oneness of, 37–38, 62, 79–80, 96, 143; perfection of, 79; power of, 129, 143–45, 241–42; praised by all things, 97; proof of His creation of the world, 69–70; proof of His eternity, 78–79; proofs of His existence, 22, 62n5, 145–46; speech of, 38–41, 99–100, 115, 127, 143–44; Throne of, 36–37, 99, 139; uniqueness of, 78–79; will of, 22, 104, 143, 145, 241, 248, 252. *See also* Attributes of God; Free will and predestination; Names of God
Goliath, 179
Gospel, 100, 144, 212–14, 224, 229
Great Britain, 15–17, 30, 50, 221n15
Greek philosophy, translated into Arabic, 37n29
Greeting of peace, 59, 204–5, 224

Hadd (pl. *hudud*), 43, 175, 194, 200, 216, 281
Haddad, Yvonne Y., 202n56
Hadith, 3–4, 12n13, 20n21, 35, 180, 281–82; forgery of, 115, 118, 171, 176n26, 182; *hadith qudsi*, 282; Ibadi Hadith, 13, 20, 22; People of Hadith, 33–34, 39, 103n13, 139, 287. *See also* Hadith citations; *Isnad*
Hadith citations: Abu Bakr and ʿUmar, 181; angels dislike bad odors, 163n7; angel visits each unborn child, 31; believing sinners enter paradise through Muhammad, 27, 109–10; calling someone an infidel, 210; cheater is not believer, 157; children of hypocrites and unbelievers,

170–71; coitus interruptus, 42n34; community will never agree on an error, 75; courtesies due to a Muslim, 158, 167; dead cannot defend themselves, 209; determination is God's secret, 257; did you examine his heart? 175; dissociation, 157; do not form an opinion without knowledge, 206; do not leave us to ourselves, 256; every child is born a Muslim, 170n20; every word has two meanings, 114n12; first thing God created was the Pen, 31; forgetting the Qur'an is worst sin, 235; God cannot be seen, 120; God created Adam in His image, 138; God curses those who introduce a new thing into Islam, 157; God descends to lowest heaven, 138; God is surrounded by light, 116n14; God will place His foot in hellfire, 138; hearts are drawn to those who are kind, 204; knowledge must be paired with action, 219; loving and hating for God, 157; may God have mercy on Abu Dharr, 168; meaning of faith, 108–10; Muhammad's sayings cannot contradict the Qur'an, 118; Muhammad's vision of God through the heart, 116n14; no one enters paradise because of deeds, 257; Qadariyya oppose God, 272; search for knowledge is obligatory, 232; shaving the head and wailing in grief, 157; shedding a Muslim's blood, 181n37; think about God's commandments, not about God, 83; truthful may speak, 211; use of analogy, 76; vision of God in paradise, 35, 115, 117–18, 122. *See also* Ibadi Hadith, citations from

Hadramawt, 13, 15, 17, 47

Hafs al-Fard, 260, 300

Hajj, 183

al-Hajjaj b. Yusuf, 12, 300

Hamalat al-ʿilm (bearers of knowledge), 13

Hanafi school, 34, 43, 151, 193, 282

Hanbali school, 34, 102n13

Hanif, 23n24

al-Harawi, Salih Abu 'l-Salt, 109n4

al-Harith b. Talid al-Hadrami, 197

al-Harithi, Salim b. Hamad, 3–4, 10, 20, 300

al-Harithiyya, 18, 282

al-Hasan al-Basri, 118–19, 128n30, 300

Hashwiyya, 139, 282

Hassan b. Thabit, 45, 113n9, 300

Hatim b. Mansur, 19

Hawazin tribe, 226, 282

al-Haythami, Nur al-Din ʿAli b. Abi Bakr, 108, 157, 171

Heffening, Willi, 181n37

Hijra (emigration), 10, 282

Hinds, Martin, 6n8, 9n11

Hindus, 222n16

Hisham b. al-Hakam, 103n13, 139, 300–301

Hisham b. Salim al-Jawaliqi, 139, 301

Hoffman, Valerie J., 5n5, 47, 48

Hormuz, 24

Hud b. Muhakkam al-Huwwari, 20, 301

Hudud. See Hadd

Human acts, creation of. *See* Free will and predestination

Humud b. Muhammad Al Bu Saʿid, 48n36

Husayniyya, 18, 20, 42, 282

Hypocrisy/hypocrites, 68, 282; affiliate and dissociate without knowledge, 208; affiliate with sinning Muslims with reservations, 158–59; children of, 171; delay obligatory affiliation or dissociation, 169; dissociate from categories of people, 159; dissociate from jinn, 159; do not affiliate with Muslims, 162–63; do not call sinners to repent, 194; do not know that grave sins constitute infidelity, 234; do not prohibit contact with pigs, 220; greetings with, 205; marry impermissible

Hypocrisy/hypocrites (*cont.*)
women, 220; neglect religious obligations, 61, 169n18; obligatory to know sins that lead to it, 60; permit impermissible marriages, 225; punishment of, 68–69, 219; repentant, 183; who do acts of obedience, 202–3

Ibadi Hadith, citations from: community will never agree upon an error, 75; every word has two meanings, 114n12; God can never be seen, 118–20, 128n30; God is present everywhere, 135n36; God is unlike all things, 135n36; looking to God, 113n8; Muhammad's sayings do not contradict the Qur'an, 118; Muslim who calls his friend an infidel, 210; people cursed by God, 157; people who tell omens, 157; Qadariyya are Magians of *umma,* 242; saying good and bad about people, 167n12
Iblis/Satan, 64, 188–92, 194, 212
Ibn 'Abbas/Ibn al-'Abbas, 12, 84, 118–19, 135n36, 191, 228, 301
Ibn Abi Sitta, Abu Zayd b. Ahmad, 23, 301
Ibn al-Azraq, Nafi', 11, 119, 135n36, 301
Ibn al-Banna' al-Marrakushi, 258, 301
Ibn Baraka, Abu Muhammad, 21, 302
Ibn Hajar al-'Asqalani, Ahmad b. 'Ali, 171n21
Ibn Hanbal, Ahmad. *See* Ahmad b. Hanbal
Ibn al-Haysam, Muhammad. *See* Muhammad b. al-Haysam
Ibn Ibad/Abad, 'Abdallah. *See* 'Abdallah b. Ibad/Abad
Ibn Ja'far al-Izkawi, Abu Jabir Muhammad, 21, 302
Ibn Jumay', Abu Hafs 'Amr, 302
Ibn Karram, Abu 'Abdallah b. Muhammad, 137n39, 302
Ibn Kullab, 'Abdallah b. Sa'id, 39–40, 302
Ibn Maja, Muhammad b. Yazid, 4n3, 75, 109n4, 206n61, 232n4, 302
Ibn Rushd, 104n15, 303
Ibn Ruzayq, Humayd b. Muhammad, 14n16
Ibn Sina, Abu 'Ali al-Husayn, 49, 101n11, 104n15, 146, 303
Ibn Wahb, 'Abdallah. *See* 'Abdallah b. Wahb al-Rasibi
Ibn Zarqun, Abu 'l-Rabi' Sulayman, 215, 303
Ibrahim b. al-Ashtar al-Nakha'i, 119
Ibrahim b. Ibrahim, 236
al-Iji, 'Adud al-Din, 111n7, 218, 303
Ijtihad, 24, 42, 283
'Ikrima, 119
'Ilm al-kalam (theology), 57n1, 137
'Ilm al-sirr, 25
Imam/Imamate, 6n9, 13–17, 21, 23–25, 45, 283; affiliation with Ibadi, 177, 192; affiliation with subjects of a just, 165–66, 195; confirmed by trustworthy witnesses, 171–72; dissociation from unjust, 180, 192; first Ibadi, 12–13; Ibadi theory of, 17–19, 42; must call opponents to truth, 217; treatment of atheists and polytheists, 225–26; treatment of People of the Book, 220–24, 229
Immunity from sin (*'isma*), 66, 188–91
Impossibility, 74
Infidelity. *See Kufr*
Ingrams, W. H., 29
Inheritance, 59, 216
Injustice, 217
Insanity/insane people, 174, 187, 227, 255
Intellect, 71–73
Iraq, 7–8
'Isa b. Abi Yunus, 120
'Isa b. Ahmad, 162, 303
'Isa b. 'Aqlama, 19, 303
'Isa b. 'Umayr, 18
'Isa b. Yusuf, 72

al-Isfarayini, Abu Ishaq Ibrahim b. Muhammad, 243–45, 303
Islam, meaning of, 107
Islamic law: as basis of political legitimacy, 7. *See also* Jurisprudence
Isnad, 20, 109, 283; *marfu' isnad*, 285
Isra'il b. Yunus, 120
Isti'rad (religious assassination), 11, 283
al-Izkawi, Abu Jabir Muhammad b. Ja'far. *See* Ibn Ja'far al-Izkawi, Abu Jabir Muhammad

al-Jabal al-Akhdar, 17, 29, 283
Jabal Nafusa. *See* Nafusa Mountains
Jabir b. Zayd, 12, 17–18, 84, 135n36, 177, 184, 303–4
Jacob, 213
Jahm b. Safwan, 121, 304
Jalil b. 'Abd al-Majid al-Ta'i, 119
Jamil b. 'Abdallah b. Ma'mar, 116n15
al-Jannawuni, Abu Zakariya' Yahya b. Abi 'l-Khayr, 21, 304
Jarir b. 'Atiya, 113n9
al-Jawaliqi, Hisham b. Salim. *See* Hisham b. Salim al-Jawaliqi
Al-Jawhara 'l-farida, 82
al-Jaytali/al-Jitali, Abu Tahir Isma'il b. Musa, 22, 227, 304
Jesus, 212n2
Jews: Abraham was not a Jew, 23n24; are infidels, hypocrites, or unbelievers, 215; cannot be killed if pay *jizya*, 106n2; choose pleasant parts of Torah, 214; ideas of God's perfection and immutability, 102n12; mountain leveled as rebuke to, 129; Muslim men may marry Jewish women, 172n23; must pay *jizya*, 228–30; originally followed truth, 213; parents make their children, 170n20; permissible interactions with, 216–17, 220–26; refutation of, 22; Satan prescribed Judaism, 212; treatment of, 220–30; why called *Yahud*, 213
Jibrin, 24
Jihad, 10, 12, 21, 259
Jinn, 59, 64–65, 159, 179, 187–92, 270, 283
Jirba (Djerba), 14, 22, 23, 283
Jizya, 182, 215, 220–21, 224–29, 283
al-Jubba'i, Abu 'Ali Muhammad, 34, 261, 263, 268, 273, 304
Judah, 213
Judaism: *See* Jews
Judham tribe, 226
al-Julanda b. Mas'ud, 13, 177, 304
al-Jumahi, Muhammad b. Sallam, 113n9, 116n15
Jumayyil b. Khalfan b. Lafi al-Sa'di, 25, 34, 41, 44, 304
Jurisprudence (*fiqh*), 281; development of Ibadi, 20–21, 23; motives for laws, 270; al-Rawahi on, 46, 50; secondary effects in vs. theology, 267; summary of Ibadi, 41–45
al-Jurjani 'Ali b. Muhammad, 85, 304
al-Juwayni, Abu 'l-Ma'ali 'Abd al-Malik, 305; anthropomorphic descriptions of God, 136n37, 138n41; on eternal divine speech, 39–40; God's attributes not distinct from His essence, 88n1; on human acts, 242–45, 263–64; originated things do not inhere in God's essence, 140n45; on vision of God in afterlife, 110n6

al-Ka'bi, Abu 'l-Qasim al-Balkhi, 266, 305
Karramiyya, 137, 139–40, 284
Kaysaniyya, 284
Kelly, J. B., 16n19, 16n20
Kenny, Joseph P., 47, 133n33
al-Khadir/al-Khidr, 164
al-Khalil b. Ahmad, 82, 305

al-Khalil b. Shadhan, 14, 305
al-Khalili, Ahmad b. Hamad. *See* Ahmad b. Hamad al-Khalili
al-Khalili, Sa'id b. Khalfan. *See* Sa'id b. Khalfan b. Ahmad al-Khalili
Khamis b. Sa'id al-Shaqsi, 23, 24, 52, 305
Khardala, 18, 184, 305
Kharijites/Khawarij, 284; doctrines of, 27; historical development of, 8–13, 17; Ibadi relationship to, 3–4, 28, 30, 131n31, 170n20
al-Kharusi, Salim b. Rashid, 17, 45
Kharusi tribe, 24
Khurasan, 13
Killing, 59–60, 168, 181–82, 184–85, 216–19, 225–26
al-Kindi, 'Abdallah b. Yahya. *See* 'Abdallah b. Yahya al-Kindi
al-Kindi, Muhammad b. Ibrahim, 21, 305
Kitab Ma'alim al-din, 52–53
Kitman (concealment), 13, 17, 21, 42–43, 285
Knowledge: and action, 232–33, 236–37; as foundation of religious practice, 231; means of, 61–62, 75; obligation of, 61, 231–35. *See also* God, human knowledge of
Kufa, 8–9, 80, 227
Kufr (infidelity)/*Kafir*, pl. *kuffar* (infidel/s), 29, 284, 285; accusations, 27, 210; different Muslim perspectives on relationship of sin to, 27; grave sinners and, 22, 28, 232, 234; Naffathiyya and Husayniyya on those who hold incorrect opinion, 42; obligation to know its meaning, 60; People of the Book and, 215, 222; in relation to affiliation and dissociation, 158–59, 169, 179; Satan was, 189; saying originated things inhere in God's essence is, 140; should not be called believers or Muslims, 216; of those who permit prohibited things, 235; types of, 28, 67–68
Lakhm tribe, 226
al-Lamki, Nasir b. Sulayman, 46
Lane, Edward William, 265n23
al-Layth b. Sa'd, 120
Lewicki, Tadeusz, 5n5, 11–13
Libya, 14, 18, 197
Lot's wife, 180
Macdonald, Duncan Black, 35
Madelung, Wilferd, 5n5, 6–8, 9n11, 103n13
Madigan, Daniel A., 84n12
Maghrib/North Africa, Ibadis of, 13, 19–22, 91–92, 158, 186, 236. *See also* Algeria; Libya; Tunisia
Maharim, 214
Mahbub b. al-Rahil b. Sayf ("Abu Sufyan"), 305
Majid b. Sa'id b. Sultan Al Bu Sa'idi, 15, 305
Majus, 214
Makhul al-Dimashqi, 119
Malik b. Anas, 72, 119, 305
Maliki school, 34, 43, 193, 285
al-Ma'mun, 'Abbasid caliph, 38
Ma'na, 72n11, 99, 285
Mansur b. al-Mu'tamir b. Sulayman, 119
Markets, 223
Marriage, 171–73, 216, 220–21, 224–25
Marsuksun al-Sawini, 305
Ma'ruf, Ahmad Sulayman, 11
Mary, mother of Jesus, 164
al-Mas'udi, Abu 'l-Hasan 'Ali, 10, 305
Matthew, Gospel of, 214n8
al-Maturidi, Abu Mansur Muhammad, 34, 40, 110n6, 112, 306
Maturidite school, 40, 90–92, 285; on human acts, 243n1
al-Mawardi, Abu 'l-Hasan 'Ali, 6, 306
Mawla, 44
Mecca, 8, 10, 13
Medina, 7, 10, 13, 80n6
Mercier, Marcel, 52n37

Metzger, Bruce M., 180n36
Mihna, 38–39, 285
Mode(s) (*hal*, pl. *ahwal*), 243, 250, 285
Mongols, 11
Monotheism/monotheists, in Ibadi usage, 28, 59–60, 67, 285; accusations against, 209–10; affirming Muhammad's prophethood is part of, 234; compelling *ahl al-dhimma* to embrace, 224; greeting, 205; People of the Book attacking, 225; regulations pertaining to, 184, 216–18; to be treated as Muslims, 29, 167
Morony, Michael, 214n8
Moses: asked God to let him see Him, 116n14, 127–28; followed "servant of God" (al-Khidr), 101n10, 164n8; God spoke to directly, 127n27; heard God's essential, eternal speech according to Sunnis, 115; Pharaoh rejected exhortations of, 179n32; Pharaoh's wife found in a basket, 270n29; prophet in Islam, 212n2; raised in God's protection, 138
Movement, 63
Mu'adh b. Jabal, 206n61
Mu'ammar b. 'Abbad al-Sulami, 261, 306
Mu'ammar, 'Ali Yahya, 4, 306
Mu'awiya b. Abi Sufyan, 8–9, 11, 306
al-Muhakkima, 9, 285
Muhammad, Prophet of Islam: accused of composing poetry, 235n7; affiliation with, 163; ascension of, 116n14; ate meat slaughtered by Jews, 221; dissociation from people, 178; insults to, 184–85; intercession of, 22, 28, 30; kindness and courtesy of, 204; necessity of belief in, 59, 67, 212, 234; tried to alleviate suffering of sinner, 202; visions of, 134n35. *See also* Hadith; Hadith citations; Sunna
Muhammad b. 'Abdallah b. Sa'id al-Khalili, 306
Muhammad b. Ahmad Al Bu Sa'idi, 25n25, 51
Muhammad b. al-Haysam, 139–40, 306
Muhammad b. Ka'b, 119
Muhammad b. Mahbub, 198, 306–7
Muhammad b. al-Munkadir, 119
Muhammad b. Sa'id al-Azdi al-Qalhati, 307
al-Muhanna b. Jayfar al-Yahmadi al-Fajhi, 307
Mujahid b. Jabr al-Makki, 119–20, 307
Mujtahid, 24, 42, 166
Mukannaf al-Madani, 119
al-Munawi, 'Abd al-Ra'uf b. Taj al-'Arifin, 109n4, 181n38
al-Mundhiri, 'Ali b. Muhammad, 47, 178n30
Murji'a/Murji'ites, 27, 125, 137n39, 285
Murphy, Roland E., 180n36
Musa b. Musa b. 'Ali al-Izkawi, 307
Musallam, Basim, 42n34
Muscat, 15–16, 26
al-Musawi, Muhsin, 116n15
Music, 185–86
Muslim b. al-Hajjaj al-Qushayri, 3, 4n3, 109n4, 307; citations of, 31, 35, 118, 163n7, 257n8
Muslims, Ibadi definition of, 28, 202, 216, 234, 286
Mut'a marriage, 44
Mu'tazila/Mu'tazilites, 48, 286; anthropomorphic descriptions of God, 36, 103n13, 137; creation of Qur'an, 38; God cannot be seen, 125; God's acts, 268n27, 270–71; God's names, 80, 147–48; God's unity, 32–33, 37–38, 88–89, 140; human acts, 33–34, 241–45, 251, 253–55, 259–68; intermediate status of sinning Muslims, 28; reason and revelation, 36–37, 272–73, 275–76; refutation of, 21, 253–56, 261, 263–72
Mutrah, Oman, 16
al-Muttaqi, 'Ali b. 'Abd al-Malik, 115, 116n14, 138, 204, 235, 272

Mysticism, 25
Mzab valley, 14, 24, 26, 29, 52, 286

Nabhani dynasty of Oman, 14, 286
Naffathiyya, 42
Nafusa Mountains, 14, 20, 22, 29, 197, 286
Nahrawan, 11, 17, 131n31, 286
al-Nakitha/al-Nakkatha/al-Nukkath, 19, 147–48, 286
Nakkara/al-Nakkariyya. *See* Nukkar/Nakkara/al-Nakkariyya
Name (*ism*), meaning of, 80–81, 98
Names of God, 19, 22, 37, 83, 95, 123–24, 147–54
Naming (*tasmiya*), 98, 148–50, 155
al-Nasa'i, Ahmad b. 'Ali, 4n3, 307
Nasir b. Abi Nabhan, 25–26, 34, 40, 44–45, 101n10, 307
Nasir b. Murshid al-Ya'rubi, 23
Naturalists, 261
al-Nawawi, Muhyi 'l-Din Abu Zakariya Yahya, 163n7, 175
Nazareth, 213
al-Nazzam, Abu Ishaq Ibrahim b. Sayyar, 260, 308
Necessity, as a rational category, 74
Nishapur, 108, 109n4
Nizwa, 12, 14, 29n26, 166, 286
Noah, 171, 179
North Africa. *See* Maghrib/North Africa
Nukkar/Nakkara/al-Nakkariyya, 18–20, 80, 185, 201, 286
Nur al-Din al-Salimi. *See* al-Salimi, 'Abdallah b. Humayd

Obedience, necessity of, 232–33, 236–37
Oman: Ibadi scholarship in, 20–21, 23–26; Imams and sultans of, 13–17, 23, 25–26; Ministry of National Heritage and Culture, 51, 82n10; Oman and Omanis in early Ibadism, 11–13; Omani emigration to East Africa, 45
Ouargla. *See* Wargla

Pan-Islamism, 46
Peace, 225; greeting of, 59, 204–5, 224
Pelly, Col. Lewis, 16
People of the Book (Jews, Christians, and Sabaeans), 172–73, 215, 220–30, 237, 287. *See also* Christians/Christianity; Jews; Sabaeans/Sabaeanism
Persia, 214n8
Peterson, John E., 17
Pharaoh, 84n12, 164, 169n17, 179, 194
Philosophers, 89, 104n15, 146, 259–60. *See also* al-Farabi, Abu Nasr Muhammad; Ibn Sina, Abu 'Ali al-Husayn
Philosophy, Greek, translated into Arabic, 37n29
Pigs/pork, 220, 222, 230
Poetry, 234–35; quotations of, 113, 116, 125–32, 141
Polytheism/polytheists: dissociation from, 207, 211; in Ibadi doctrine, 28, 68, 194, 215; in Kharijite doctrine, 27; in Mu'tazilite doctrine, 38; in Nukkari doctrine, 19; testimony concerning, 207; treatment of, 225–26
Poor people, 228–29
Pork/pigs, 220, 222, 230
Possibility, as a rational category, 74–75
Prayer: for affiliates and nonaffiliates, 202–4; over the dead, 59; differences between Ibadis and Sunnis in, 43; on Fridays in Ibadi doctrine, 18, 43; knowing and forgetting during, 233–34; making up omitted, 183; *rak'a* (unit of

prayer), 287; status of one who neglects, 27, 169n18
Profession of faith. *See* Faith
Prophets: affiliation with, 160, 163; dissociation from is unbelief, 159; kept from grave sins, 66, 164; necessity of knowing about, 60, 165, 231, 234; rejection of is unbelief, 68, 215; see angels and jinn, 64; sent to people and jinn, 59n3
Psalms, 100, 144
Punishment in the grave, 202
Purity, ritual, 44, 183, 220, 233n5

Qa'ada (quietists), 11–12, 17
Qabus (Qaboos) b. Sa'id b. Taymur Al BuSa'idi, sultan of Oman, 15, 26, 222n16, 308
Qadariyya, 22, 32, 242, 255n7, 272, 287
al-Qa'ida (al-Qaeda), 17
Qalhat, Oman, 24
Qamus al-shari'a, 25, 34, 44
Qayrawan, Tunisia, 14
Qibla (direction of prayer), 28, 224, 230, 287
al-Qunubi, 'Abdallah b. Sa'id, 51
al-Qunubi, Salih b. Sa'id, 50–51
Qunut, 43, 287
Qur'an, 287; created or eternal, 18, 22, 38–41; metaphorical interpretation of, 114–15, 135, 137–38; miraculousness of, 235n7; obligation to remember, 234–35; recitation of, 224. *See also* Qur'an citations
Qur'an citations: Abraham (2:128, 2:258), 179, 212n2; Abu Lahab (Sura 111), 179; affiliation (3:28, 5:2, 4:144, 5:51, 9:71, 47:19, 48:29, 60:13), 157, 178; all things praise God (17:44), 83; ambiguous verses (3:7), 137n40; angels obey God (21:27, 66:6), 66, 188–89, 191; angels prostrated before Adam (2:34, 7:11, 17:61, 18:50, 20:116, 38:73–74), 188, 190; angels question God about creating humans (2:30), 66, 189n46; anthropomorphic descriptions of God (2:115, 2:210, 20:5, 20:39, 23:88, 28:88, 36:83, 38:75, 39:67, 40:7, 54:14, 67:1, 68:42, 89:22), 35, 98, 103n13, 130, 138; arrogance (57:23), 121; barrier between paradise and hellfire (7:46), 30; carrion (2:173), 214n9; Christians (5:69, 61:14), 213; Companions of the Cave (18:9–22), 164; compulsion in religion (2:256), 106, 229; creation (2:117, 3:47, 16:40, 18:51, 19:35, 40:68), 31, 40–41, 140; creation of people and jinn to worship God (51:56), 270; disobedience (18:50, 24:63), 232; dissociation (2:166–67, 3:28, 4:144, 5:51, 6:19, 6:78, 8:48, 9:1, 9:3, 9:114, 10:41, 11:35, 11:54, 26:216, 43:26, 54:43, 58:22, 59:16, 60:4, 60:13), 157, 161nn4–5, 178; eating wealth of orphans (4:2), 77; everything perishes except His face (28:88), 98; faith (2:143, 12:17), 106, 108; the faithful (2:9, 5:69, 9:71, 48:29, 57:19), 107, 157, 215; fighting (8:15–16, 9:36), 168, 217; *fitra* (30:30), 170n20; gloomy faces on Day of Judgment (75:24–25), 119; God called you Muslims (22:78), 94; God creates and chooses (28:68), 269; God creates through command "Be!" (2:117, 3:47, 16:40, 19:35, 40:68), 31, 40–41; God determines phases of moon (10:5), 31; God determines sustenance of mountains (41:10) and of people (89:16), 31; God determines time of death (6:2, 56:60, 74:19), 31; God is only creator (7:54, 13:16, 35:4), 78, 256; God's coming (2:210, 89:22), 138; God's decree (2:117, 3:47, 6:2, 17:23, 19:35, 40:68), 31; God's description (Sura 112), 79–80; God's difference from all else (42:11), 35, 115, 234;

Qur'an citations (*cont.*)
God's guidance and leading astray (6:125, 7:30), 31; God's knowledge (2:282), 255–56; God's name(s) (2:54, 7:180, 19:65, 55:78, 57:3, 59:23–24, 87:1), 83, 147, 149–50, 161n5; God's nearness (2:186, 50:16, 53:4–10, 58:7), 134nn34–35, 135; God's signs (41:53), 146; God's speech (4:164, 42:51), 127n27; God taught Adam the names (2:31), 149; Goliath (2:249–51), 179; good deeds take away bad deeds (11:114), 192; greetings (4:86), 205; hasten to forgiveness (3:133), 68; human ability to obey (2:286), 253; human will (10:99–100, 18:28–30, 76:29–30), 31; hypocrites (4:146), 69, 219; Iblis (2:34, 7:11–12, 15:36–38, 17:61, 18:50, 20:116, 38:73–74), 188–90; ignorance (7:33, 17:36), 206; interpreting verses of (3:7), 137; *islam*/ submission (2:131, 3:19, 3:85, 3:125, 4:125), 105–7; Jesus' disciples (3:51), 212n2; Jews (4:46, 5:69, 7:156), 213; jinn (18:50, 51:56, 72:1–2), 159n2, 188–89, 270; *jizya* (9:29), 228; the lie (24:11–20), 179; look toward ease (2:280), 114; Lot's wife (27:57), 180; marriage with unbelievers (2:221), 172n23, 225; measure for all things (65:3), 31; Moses and the servant of God (Sura 18), 101n10, 164, 179; Moses asked to see God (7:143), 116n14, 127n28; Moses rescued to be enemy and sorrow to Pharaoh (28:8), 270; Muhammad's authority (21:107, 53:3, 59:7), 75, 184; Muslims are median nation (2:143), 106; Noah's people (11:25–49, 25:37, 54:9–15, Sura 71), 171, 179n31, 180n35; obedience (68:10), 121; obligation (56:86), 106; offspring (18:50, 52:21, 71:27), 170–71, 189; people burned in the ditch (85:4), 164; people of remembrance (16:43), 232; People of the Book (3:83, 4:171, 5:69, 9:29), 105–6, 213, 228; perjury (24:4), 217; Pharaoh's family (40:28), 164; polytheism (7:127, 12:40, 21:43, 39:3), 84–85, 149, 237; prophets obey God (21:27), 191n48; punishment in hellfire (2:217, 4:146), 30, 219; pray for forgiveness (47:19), 157; reward in paradise (16:32), 257; Sabaeans (5:69), 213; Satan and his tribe watch you (7:27), 64; saying *uff* to parents (17:23), 76n2; seeing God/looking to God (2:55–56, 2:115, 6:103, 7:143, 75:22–23), 35, 83, 112, 116n14, 118–19, 123n24, 124, 127n28, 128nn29–30; sight on Last Day (50:22), 117n16; success given by God (11:88), 57; true religion (3:19, 9:29, 9:33), 106–7; two heavy burdens (55:31), 65; unbelievers (2:28, 4:165, 5:69, 25:37), 171, 215, 248, 254; wherever you turn, there is the face of God (2:115), 103n13; wife of Lot (15:60), 31

Quraysh, 6, 226, 287

Qurra' (Qur'an reciters), 9n11

al-Qushayri, Abu 'l-Qasim 'Abd al-Karim, 82, 308

al-Qushayri, Abu Nasr 'Abd al-Rahim, 114n10

Qutb: *See* Atfayyish, Muhammad b. Yusuf

al-Rabi' b. Habib, 13, 42, 114n12, 217, 308; Hadith collection ascribed to, 20, 22. *See also* Ibadi Hadith, citations from

al-Raghib al-Isfahani, Abu 'l-Qasim al-Husayn, 114, 308

Ramadan, 44, 183, 231, 272

Rashid b. al-Nadr al-Fajhi al-Yahmadi, 308

al-Rawahi, Nasir b. Salim ("Abu Muslim al-Bahlani"), 5, 10, 16n20, 26, 45–46, 308; citations from poetry of, 125–32, 141; perspective on *bara'a*, 29

al-Rawahi, Salim b. 'Udayyam, 45
al-Rawas, Isam, 42
al-Razi, Fakhr al-Din, 132, 255, 308
Reason and revelation: debates on, 18, 36–37; good and bad are not rational categories, 252, 272–76; in jurisprudence, 270, 272–76; knowledge of God through intellect, 61–62, 69–71, 75, 133; revelation confirms reason, 70–71, 79. *See also* God, proof of His creation of the world; proof of His eternity; proofs of His existence
Religion (*din*), meaning of, 105; roots of religion, 106, 231–32n3
Religious obligations, 231
Renaissance of Ibadi scholarship, modern, 24
Repentance, 166–67, 172, 174, 183–84, 192–200, 216–18
Rest, 63–64
Retaliation, 44
Revelation. *See* Reason and revelation
Reward and punishment in afterlife: of Abu Dharr, 209; of believers, 108–10; of children, 33–34; eternal punishment, 30; God not obligated to do what is best for people, 268–69; of hypocrites, 69, 219; linked to accountability and acquisition, 251–52, 254–58, 273; obligation to know about, 60; promise and threat of, 109, 232; in relation to affiliation and dissociation, 202; of sinners and non-Ibadi Muslims, 30; whoever counts God's names enters paradise, 148; would be best if humans were created in paradise, 268
Rightly-Guided caliphs, 6, 288
Riyad, Saudi Arabia, 15
Rosenthal, Franz, 121n22
Rouvillois-Brigol, Madeleine, 52n37
al-Rummani, Abu 'l-Hasan 'Ali b. 'Isa, 85, 309
Rustamid imams, 14, 19–21, 177, 288
Rustaq, 14, 23
Sabaeans/Sabaeanism, 107, 212–15, 220–30, 227, 288
al-Sabi'i, Nasir b. Sulayman, 4, 11
al-Sa'di, Jumayyil b. Khalfan. *See* Jumayyil b. Khalfan b. Lafi al-Sa'di
Sadgrove, Philip, 26
Sa'id b. Ahmad b. Sa'id Al Bu Sa'id, 15, 309
Sa'id b. Jubayr, 119
Sa'id b. Khalfan b. Ahmad al-Khalili, 15–16, 25–26, 49, 101n10, 309
Sa'id b. al-Musayyib, 119
Sa'id b. Sultan b. Ahmad Al Bu Sa'idi, 15, 25, 309
Sa'id b. Taymur b. Faysal Al Bu Sa'idi, 17, 309
Salaf (early Muslims), 242
Salafiyya Press, 26
Salim b. Rashid al-Kharusi, 17
Salim b. Thuwayni b. Sa'id Al Bu Sa'idi, 15, 25, 309
al-Salimi, 'Abdallah b. Humayd ("Nur al-Din"), 17, 25–26, 46, 48–49, 309–10; citations from, 14n16, 16, 23–25, 178n30
al-Salimi, Hamza b. Sulayman, 16
al-Salimi, Muhammad b. 'Abdallah, 16n20, 25–26
al-Salimi, Nur al-Din. *See* al-Salimi, 'Abdallah b. Humayd
Saljuqs, 34
al-Salt b. Malik, 14, 310
al-Samad, 80
San'a', 13
al-Sanusi, Muhammad b. Yusuf, 47, 133n33, 310
Satan: *See* Iblis/Satan
Saudi Arabia, 222n16
Savage, Elizabeth, 5n5, 12n14, 29n26
al-Sayighi al-Manhi, Abu 'Ali Salim b. Sa'id, 82n10
Sayyid, 15, 288
Shabibiyya, 32

al-Shafi'i, Muhammad b. Idris, 49, 72, 310
Shafi'i school, 34–35, 43, 47, 111n7, 155, 288
al-Shahrastani, Abu 'l-Fath Muhammad b. 'Abd al-Karim, 103n13, 310
al-Shaybani, Sultan b. Mubarak, 50
Shehadi, Fadlou, 185n43
Shi'i Islam/Shi'ite Muslims, 288; doctrine on leadership, 6–7; early anthropomorphism, 102n12, 103n13, 137; Fatimids, 14; jurisprudence of, 41, 43–44; al-Mas'udi's sympathies, 10n12; on neglecting duties, 169n18; theology, 38, 125; Twelver imams, 109n4; in Zanzibar, 16n20;
Shiloah, A., 185n43
Shirk (unbelief)/*Mushrik* (unbeliever): accusations of, 209–10; fighting, 217; greetings with, 205; Ibadi definitions of, 28, 59–61, 67–68, 208, 212, 215–16, 233–34, 286, 288; marriage with, 172, 225; obligation to dissociate from, 158–59; repenting from, 194
Shura (consultation), 8
Shurat (those whose loves were "purchased" for Islam), 17, 288
Sib, Treaty of, 17
Sibawayhi, 82n9, 310
Siffin, 8–9, 289
Sinning Muslims, status of, 7–8, 18, 22, 27–28, 173, 216, 235
Sins, grave and minor, 185–86, 215–17, 234
Sira, 19, 289
al-Siyabi, Ahmad b. Su'ud, 46
Smith, Jane I., 202n56
Slavery/slaves, 59, 172–73, 175, 182, 217, 220, 223, 225–27
Sodom and Gomorrah, 180n36
Speaking ill of the Muslims, 218–19
Statement of faith. *See* Faith
Stetkevych, Suzanne 113n9
Substance (*jawhar*), 64
al-Suddi, Isma'il b. 'Abd al-Rahman, 123, 310
Suffering, 202
Sufis, 103n14, 164n8
Sufriyya, 17, 289
Sufyan al-Thawri, 119
Suhar al-'Abdi, 255, 310
al-Suhari al-'Awtabi, Salama b. Muslim ("Abu 'l-Mundhir"), 21, 193, 195, 311
Sultan b. Ahmad Al Bu Sa'idi, 25
Sunna, 10, 75–76, 110, 178, 181, 253, 289
Sunni Islam/Sunni Muslims, 289; creed of al-Sanusi, 47; doctrine on anthropomorphic descriptions of God, 35–36, 136n37; doctrine on free will vs. predestination, 33–34; doctrine on God's names, 150–51, 155; doctrine on grave sinners, 27–28; doctrine on neglecting duties, 169n18; doctrine on Qur'an, 38–40; doctrine on reason and revelation, 37; doctrine on reward and punishment in afterlife, 30; doctrine on seeing God in afterlife, 110–12, 115–17, 120, 132–33; Hadith of, 12n13, 20n21, 27–28, 33, 35, 115; Ibadi conversions to, 47; jurisprudence of, 41–44; meaning of "people of the *sunna*," 10; meaning of *sayyid* among, 15n17; political theory of, 6; predominance in Zanzibar, 35; profession of faith of, 184n42. *See also* 'Abduh, Muhammad; Abu Hanifa; Ahmad b. Hanbal; al-Ash'ari, Abu 'l-Hasan; Ash'arite school; al-Ghazali, Abu Hamid Muhammad; Hanafi school; Maliki school; al-Maturidi, Abu Mansur Muhammad; Maturidite school; al-Razi, Fakhr al-Din; al-Shafi'I, Muhammad B. Idris; Shafi'i school; al-Tabari, Muhammad b. Jarir; al-Taftazani, Sa'd al-Din
Sur, Oman, 16
Suspending judgment. *See Wuquf*
al-Suyuti, Jalal al-Din, citations of: faith, 108, 157; follow Abu Bakr and 'Umar, 181n38;

forgetting Qur'an, 235; hearts are drawn to those who are kind to, 204; knowing and not acting, 219; think about God's commands, not about God, 83; those who have no awareness, 170; whoever counts God's names enters paradise, 148
Syria, 8, 227
Syriac, 85, 100, 144

al-Tabari, Muhammad b. Jarir, 36n28, 115n13
Tabghurin b. ʻIsa al-Malshuti, 22, 219, 311
Tafsir (commentary on the Qur'an), 20
al-Taftazani, Saʻd al-Din ("al-Saʻd"), 85, 118, 133–34, 311
Tahart, Algeria, 14, 20
Talbi, Mohamed, 181n37
Talib al-Haqq. *See* al-Kindi, ʻAbdallah b. Yahya
Talisman, 25
Taqiyya, 21, 203, 289
Taqlid, 36, 41, 61–62, 289
Tawhid, 57–61; definition of, 58n2, 289
Taymur b. Faysal b. Turki Al Bu Saʻidi, 311
Testimony, 175–76, 187, 198–200, 207, 209, 216–17
Testimony of faith. *See* Faith
al-Thamini, ʻAbd al-ʻAziz, 24, 35, 52, 125, 311; citations of, 193, 204n58
al-thaqalayn, 65
Theology: defined, 58; nobility of, 57; usefulness of, 58
Thumama b. Ashras al-Numayri, 261, 311
Thuwayni b. Saʻid b. Sultan Al Bu Saʻidi, 15, 311
al-Tirmidhi, Muhammad b. ʻIsa, 4n3, 33, 158, 167, 181n38, 257n8, 311
Tobacco, 230
Torah, 100, 144, 212–14, 224, 229
Tripoli, Libya, 14, 18, 197
Tunisia, 14, 21–23, 26
Turki b. Saʻid Al Bu Saʻidi, 15–16, 311
Tyrants, 30, 218

Uhud, 131, 289
ʻUmar b. ʻAbd al-ʻAziz, 10, 12, 311–12
ʻUmar b. al-Khattab, 7–8, 312; citations of, 167, 178, 196, 220; covenant with *ahl al-dhimma*, 221n15; as exemplar, 131, 181; setting the *jizya*, 227
ʻUmar b. Saʻid b. Muhammad b. Zakariyya, 23
ʻUmayriyya, 18, 290
Umayyad caliphate, 6, 8, 10–13, 44, 290
Umma, 28, 147, 157, 290
Unbelief. *See Shirk*
ʻUrwa b. al-Zubayr, 197–98, 312
ʻUthman b. ʻAffan, 5–9, 27, 176, 312

Valeri, Marc, 17, 26
van Ess, Josef, 3n1, 5n5, 139n44
Vecca Vaglieri, Laura, 10
Versteegh, C. H. M., 72n11
Vision of God. *See* God, invisibility of

Wahb b. Munabbih, 110n5
Wahbi, 10, 19, 290
Wahhabis, 15–16, 290
Wakiʻ b. al-Jarrah, 119
Walaya (affiliation/association), 29, 156–79, 198, 200–202, 208–11, 290; duty toward affiliates, 195; God's with people, 200–201; with *imams*, 192; meaning of, 156, 160, 174–75; obligation to know about, 60; people's with God, 201; person receiving *zakat* must be a *wali*, 44; rights of affiliates, 201–2; suspended during *kitman*, 43; with whom it is obligatory, 163–65, 174–77; works on, 21

Walker, Paul E., 40n31, 96n8
Warfare: *See* Fighting
Wargla (Ouargla), 22, 52, 290
Wasiyat Abi Hanifa, 39
Watt, W. Montgomery, 30n27, 32, 268n27
Way, Major A. Cotton, 16n20
Weighing of deeds on Day of Judgment, 36–37
Wensinck, A. J., 27, 35, 39
Wilkinson, John C., 5n5; on Abdallah b. Ibad, 17–18; on *bara'a* as excommunication, 29n26; challenges Ibadi historical narrative, 6n8, 18; on date of Ya'rubi dynasty, 23n23; on development of Ibadi literature, 21; on Ibadi Hadith, 13n15, 20; on Jabir b. Zayd, 12, 18; on Nabhani dynasty, 14; on al-Thamini's *Kitab al-Nil,* 24
Williams, John Alden, 40
Wine, 220–22, 230
Wolfson, Harry A., 37, 39
Women, 226–27; testimony of, 175–76, 187. *See also* Marriage
World, origination of, 22
Wuquf (suspension of judgment), 178, 205–6; concerning children, 170–71, 173–74; concerning converts to Islam, 166; concerning grave sinner, 196; concerning Prophet's Companions, 176

Yahya b. Abi Zakariya b. Abi Ziyad, 120
Yahya b. Salih al-Afdali, Abu Zakariya', 24, 52, 257, 312
Ya'rubi dynasty, 14, 23, 290
al-Ya'rubi, Sayf b. Sultan II, 14n16
Yazid I, 11, 312
Yemen, 13, 15n17, 47, 206n61
Yunus b. 'Abd al-Rahman, 139, 312

Zakat, 15, 19, 44, 227, 290
al-Zamakhshari, Abu 'l-Qasim Mahmud, 36n28, 106n2, 312
Zanzibar: under British, 50, 221n15; Christian cathedrals in, 223n17; Omani emigration to, 45; part of Omani empire, 15; printing press in, 25–26; al-Rawahi in, 46; ruler of Zanzibar assisted in ending Imamate, 15–16; sultans of, 172n22; Sunni-Ibadi relations in, 178n30
Zimmerman, Fritz, 5n5
Zoroastrians/Zoroastrianism, 170n20, 212, 214–15, 225, 227
al-Zuhri, Abu Bakr Muhammad b. Shihab, 119
Zunnar, 221–22

Valerie J. Hoffman is professor of religion and Director of the Center for South Asian and Middle Eastern Studies at the University of Illinois at Urbana-Champaign, specializing in Islamic thought and practice. She is the author of *Sufism, Mystics and Saints in Modern Egypt* and numerous articles on Sufism, Islamic gender ideology, Ibadism, Islam and human rights, and contemporary Islamic movements.